BUDDHIST PHILOSOPHY IN INDIA AND CEYLON

BUDDHIST PHILOSOPHY IN INDIA AND CEYLON

A. BERRIEDALE KEITH

GYAN

Published by

Gyan Publishing House
5, Ansari Road
Daryaganj, New Delhi-110002
Phone: 011-47034999, 9811692060
E-mail: books@gyanbooks.com

Distribution Network
gyanbooks.com
India, USA, Canada, UK, Australia, France

ISBN : 978-81-212-4502-9 (HB)
First Published, 1923

2nd Impression 2020

Printed at: Gyan Press, Delhi.

Buddhist Philosophy in India and Ceylon
Author: A. Berriedale Keith

BUDDHIST PHILOSOPHY

IN INDIA AND CEYLON

BY

A. BERRIEDALE KEITH, D.C.L., D.Litt.

OF THE INNER TEMPLE, BARRISTER-AT-LAW, AND OF THE SCOTTISH BAR
REGIUS PROFESSOR OF SANSKRIT AND COMPARATIVE PHILOLOGY
AT THE UNIVERSITY OF EDINBURGH; AUTHOR OF 'INDIAN
LOGIC AND ATOMISM', ETC.

OXFORD
AT THE CLARENDON PRESS
1923

PREFACE

To attempt a short account of Buddhist Philosophy in its historical development in India and Ceylon is a task beset with difficulties. The literature of the subject is vast in extent, and much of it buried in Tibetan and Chinese translations, which are not likely to be effectively and completely exploited for many years to come. The preliminary studies, on which any comprehensive summary should be based, have only in a few cases yet been carried out, and Buddhist enthusiasts in England have concentrated their attention on the Pali Canon to the neglect of other schools of the Hīnayāna and of the Mahāyāna.

To these inevitable difficulties there has been gratuitously added a further obstacle to the possibility of an intelligible view of the progress of Buddhist thought. Buddhism as a revealed religion demands faith from its votaries, and for sympathetic interpretation in some degree even from its students. But it is an excess of this quality to believe, on the faith of a Ceylonese tradition which cannot be proved older than A.D. 400, that the Buddhist Canon took final shape, even in its record of controversies which had arisen among the schools, at a Council held under the Emperor Asoka probably in the latter part of the third century B.C., a Council of which we have no other record, although the pious Emperor has recorded with infinite complacency matters of comparative unimportance. To credulity of this kind it is of negligible importance that the Canon is written in an artificial literary language which is patently later than Asoka, or that the absurdity of the position has been repeatedly demonstrated.

Yet another, and perhaps more serious, defect in the most popular of current expositions of Buddhism is the determination to modernize, to show that early in Buddhist thought we find fully appreciated ideas which have only slowly and laboriously been elaborated in Europe, and are normally regarded as the particular achievement of modern philosophy. Now there is nothing more interesting or legitimate than, on the basis of a careful investigation of any ancient philosophy, to mark in what measure it attains conceptions familiar in modern thought; but it is a very different thing to distort early ideas in order to bring them up to date, and the futility of the process may be realized when it is remembered that every generation which yields to the temptation will succeed in finding its own conceptions foreshadowed. Truth compels us to admit that the adherents of Buddhism were intent, like their master, on salvation, and that their philosophical conceptions lacked both system and maturity, a fact historically reflected in the Negativism of the Mahāyāna. But instead of a frank recognition of these facts—of which Buddhism has no cause to be ashamed, for man seeks salvation rather than philosophical insight—we have interpretations offered to us as representing the true views of Buddhism, which import into it wholesale the conceptions of rationalism, of psychology without a soul, of Kant, of Schopenhauer, von Hartmann, Bertrand Russell, Bergson, *et hoc genus omne.* We are assured that Buddhism was from the first a system of subjective idealism, although history plainly shows that such a conception slowly came into being and took shape in the Vijñānavāda school which assails the realism of the more orthodox; we are equally assured that space was an ideal construction in the Buddhist view, though even in mediaeval Ceylon and Burma there is not a trace of the view, and it frankly contradicts the Canon and all the texts based upon it.

It is easy to understand this attitude as a reaction against the still practically complete failure of western philosophers to realize that, if they claim to be students of the history of thought—as *a priori* they should be—they have omitted a substantial part of their duty, if they do not make themselves reasonably familiar with the main outlines of Indian philosophy. But it is unphilosophical to exaggerate or distort, even in a just cause. Indian philosophy has merits of its own far from negligible, which are merely obscured by attempts to parallel the Dialogues of the Buddha with those of Plato, and the undeserved neglect which it has suffered in the west is largely excusable by the unattractive form in which Indian ideas are too often clothed.

My chief obligations, which I most gratefully acknowledge, are to the writings of the late Professor Hermann Oldenberg and of Professor de la Vallée Poussin; of others mention is due to Professor and Mrs. Rhys Davids for the admirable translations which more than redeem the defects of the texts issued by the Pali Text Society, and to Professors Beckh, Franke, Geiger, Kern, Oltramare, Stcherbatskoi, and Walleser. To my wife I am indebted for both criticism and assistance.

A. BERRIEDALE KEITH.

EDINBURGH,
July, 1922.

CONTENTS

PART I. BUDDHISM IN THE PALI CANON

PART II. DEVELOPMENTS IN THE HĪNAYĀNA

PART III. THE PHILOSOPHY OF THE MAHĀYĀNA

PART IV. BUDDHIST LOGIC

ABBREVIATIONS

ADS. Abhidhammatthasaṁgaha of Anuruddha, ed. JPTS., 1884; trs. PTS 1910.
AK. Abhidharmakoça. Book iii, ed. Poussin, London, 1918: other citations from Paris (Asiatic Society) or Burnouf MSS.
AKB. Abhidharmakoçabhāṣya of Vasubandhu.
AKV. Abhidharmakoçavyākhyā of Yaçomitra.
AN. Aṅguttara Nikāya, ed. PTS. 1885-1900.
APP. Aṣṭasāhasrikā Prajñāpāramitā, ed. BI. 1888.
Asl. Atthasālinī of Buddhaghosa, ed. PTS. 1897.
BB. Bibliotheca Buddhica, Petrograd.
BC. Buddhacarita, ed. Cowell, Oxford, 1893.
BCA. Bodhicaryāvatāra of Çāntideva, ed. BI. 1901 ff.: trs. Poussin, Paris, 1907.
BCAP. Bodhicaryāvatārapañjikā of Prajñākaramati, ed. BI.; ix also in Poussin, *Bouddhisme, Études et Matériaux*, London, 1898.
BI. Bibliotheca Indica, Calcutta.
BS. Brahma Sūtra of Bādarāyaṇa, ed. BI. 1854-63.
BSB. Bodhisattvabhūmi, summary in *Le Muséon*, vi and vii.
CHI. Cambridge History of India.
Compendium. Trs. of Abhidhammatthasaṁgaha, PTS. 1910.
DK. Dhātukathā, ed. PTS. 1892.
DN. Dīgha Nikāya, ed. PTS. 1890-1911; trs. SBB. ii-iv, 1899-1921; by Franke, Göttingen, 1913.
DS. Dhammasaṅgaṇi, ed. PTS. 1885; trs. PTS. 1901.
EI. Epigraphia Indica.
ERE. Encyclopædia of Religion and Ethics.
Geiger, M. and W. PD. Pāli Dhamma, Munich, 1921.
GGA. Göttingische gelehrte Anzeigen.
GN. Nachrichten der königl. Gesellschaft der Wissenschaften zu Göttingen.
GSAI. Giornale della Società Asiatica Italiana.
IA. Indian Antiquary.
ILA. Indian Logic and Atomism, by A. B. Keith, Oxford, 1921.
J. Jātaka, ed. Fausboll, London, 1877-97.
JA. Journal Asiatique.
JAOS. Journal of the American Oriental Society.
JASB. Journal of the Asiatic Society of Bengal.
JBRAS. Journal of the Bombay Branch of the Royal Asiatic Society.
JPTS. Journal of the Pali Text Society.
JRAS. Journal of the Royal Asiatic Society.

KF. Aufsätze zur Kultur- und Sprachgeschichte Ernst Kuhn gewidmet, Breslau, 1916.
KM. The Karma-Mīmāṁsā, by A. B. Keith, London, 1921.
KV. Kathāvatthu, ed. PTS. 1894-7 ; trs. as *Points of Controversy*, PTS. 1915 ; comm. ed. JPTS., 1889.
MA. Madhyamakāvatāra, trs. Poussin, *Le Muséon*, viii and xi.
MASI. Memoirs of the Archaeological Survey of India.
MB. Outlines of Mahāyāna Buddhism, by D. T. Suzuki, London, 1907.
MBh. Mahābhārata.
Mhv. Mahāvastu, ed. Senart, Paris, 1882-97.
MK. Mūlamadhyamakakārikās, ed. Poussin, BB. 1913.
MKV. Prasannapadā of Candrakīrti on above, ed. Poussin, u. s.
MN. Majjhima Nikāya, ed. PTS. 1888-1902.
MSA. Mahāyānasūtrālaṁkāra, ed. and trs. S. Lévi, Paris, 1907-11.
MSIL. History of the Mediaeval School of Indian Logic, by S. C. Vidyābhūṣaṇa, Calcutta, 1909.
MV. Mahāvagga, ed. Oldenberg, Vinaya Piṭaka I, London, 1879.
Mvy. Mahāvyutpatti, ed. Petrograd, 1887.
NB. Nyāyabindu of Dharmakīrti, ed. BI. 1890.
NBL. The Sanskrit Buddhist Literature of Nepal, by Rājendralāla Mitra, Calcutta, 1882.
NBT. Nyāyabinduṭīkā of Dharmottara, ed. BI. 1890.
NBTT. Nyāyabinduṭīkāṭippaṇī, ed. BB. 1909.
NK. Nyāyakandalī of Çrīdhara, ed. Benares, 1895.
NM. Nyāyamañjarī of Jayanta, ed. Benares, 1895.
NP. Nettipakaraṇa, ed. PTS. 1883.
NV. Nyāyavārttika of Uddyotakara, ed. BI. 1887-1904.
NVT. Nyāyavārttikatātparyaṭīkā of Vācaspati Miçra, ed. Benares, 1898.
Oldenberg, LUAB. *Die Lehre der Upanishaden und die Anfänge des Buddhismus*, Göttingen, 1915.
—— VWW. *Vorwissenschaftliche Wissenschaft. Die Weltanschauung der Brāhmaṇa-Texte*, Göttingen, 1919.
Oltramare, P. FBDC. *La formule bouddhique des douze causes*, Geneva, 1909.
Poussin, L. de la Vallée. *Bouddhisme. Bouddhisme, Opinions sur l'Histoire de la Dogmatique*, Paris, 1909.
—— —— TDC. *Bouddhisme, Études et Matériaux. Théorie des douze causes*, Ghent, 1913.
PP. Puggalapaññati, ed. PTS. 1883.
PTS. Pali Text Society publications.
RHR. Revue de l'histoire des religions.
Ç. Çikṣāsamuccaya of Çāntideva, ed. C. Bendall, BB. I, 1902.
SBA. Sitzungsberichte der königl. Akademie der Wissenschaften zu Berlin.
SBB. Sacred Books of the Buddhists, Oxford.
SBE. Sacred Books of the East, Oxford.
SBNT. Six Buddhist Nyāya Tracts in Sanskrit, ed. Haraprasād Shāstrī, BI. 1910.

SDS. Sarvadarçanasaṁgraha of Mādhava, ed. Ānandāçrama Sanskrit Series, no. 51, 1906.
SN. Saṁyutta Nikāya, ed. PTS. 1884-1904.
SS. Sāṁkhya Sūtra, ed. BI. 1888.
SSS. Sarvasiddhāntasaṁgraha, attributed wrongly to Çaṅkara, Madras, 1909.
Sumaṅg. Sumaṅgalavilāsinī, I. ed. PTS. 1886.
TRD. Tarkarahasyadīpikā of Guṇaratna, ed. BI. (with Ṣaḍdarçanasamuccaya), 1905.
Ui, H. VP. Vaiśeṣika Philosophy according to the Daśapadārtha-śāstra, London, 1917.
VOJ. Vienna Oriental Journal.
VP. Vinaya Piṭaka, ed. Oldenberg, London, 1879.
YS. Yoga Sūtra of Patañjali, ed. Bombay Sanskrit Series, xlvi, 1892.
ZDMG. Zeitschrift der Deutschen Morgenländischen Gesellschaft.

PART I

BUDDHISM IN THE PALI CANON

CHAPTER I

THE PERSONALITY AND DOCTRINES OF THE BUDDHA

1. *The Problem and the Sources*

THE most attractive and influential expositions of Buddhism in England and Germany present us with a simple and effective picture of an Indian sage, who spent a blameless life in the years 563 to 483 B.C. engaged in the development of a remarkably sane and modern ethical doctrine. This sage turned aside from idle metaphysical speculations; if he held views on such topics, he deemed them valueless for the purpose of salvation, which was his goal as it was that of his contemporaries, and declined to discuss these issues generally. But he had emancipated himself from the theory of the existence of any permanent entity in the nature of a soul, such as it was understood by his contemporaries; he had abandoned an ego-centric position, and found greater truth in the conception of constant change under a law of causality, thereby effecting a Copernican revolution in the tendency of philosophical thought. This realization of the unreality of the self led him to a wise and reasonable ethical system; the end of man, Nirvāṇa, consists not in strivings, inevitably painful, for the sake of a self which has no real existence, but in the eradication of passion of every kind, which brings man to supreme bliss, attainable and attained only on this earth, a view free from the delusion of a life of perpetual happiness after death.

This portrait of an early rationalist, introducing the blessings of common sense into a world which knew nothing better than the mysticism of the Upaniṣads, or something still more crude, is unquestionably fascinating. 'Surely a notable milestone in the history of human ideas,' an enthusiast[1] has said, 'that a man reckoned for ages by thousands as the Light not of Asia only but of the World,[2] and the saviour from sin and misery, should call this little formula [the doctrine of the chain of causation] his Norm or Gospel, or at least one aspect of that Gospel.' The exponents of this view are far too well informed to ignore the difficulties in their theory, above all the perplexing fact that a rationalist should have assumed as self-evident the reality of a process of transmigration not less real because it is not the transmigration of an ordinary soul; but their faith can remove mountains, and there are diverse ways of escape. The Buddha could not disregard the ordinary terminology of his time[3]; his teaching had to be expressed in the terms of his day, and accommodated for practical purposes to ordinary intelligences; the new wine had to be poured into old bottles. Or again, when the crudities of the Buddha's views become painful to modern rationalism, recourse may be had to the subtle irony[4] which distinguishes Buddhist utterances and presents a key which, skilfully turned, is fitted to open any locked door of Buddhist doctrine. Or, more frankly, we may accept the view that the Buddha himself was a true rationalist, and absolutely declined to accept the dogma of transmigration, conscious that to do so would be to stultify, as in fact it does, his teaching and reduce his followers to painful intellectual straits. Further, we must admit, however reluctantly, that the masses of Asia, who have seen in the Buddha the Light of the World, have not done so because of his rationalist doctrines, his chain of causation, which they have understood as little as do we, or even his wise advice to still passion. They have adored him, because they have regarded

[1] Mrs. Rhys Davids, *Buddhism*, p. 89. A true Buddhist (Aung, *Compendium*, pp. 283–5) follows authority, not reason.

[2] But see Poussin, *Nirvāṇa*, p. 168.

[3] Cf. Mrs. Rhys Davids, *Budd. Psych.*, p. 21; JRAS. 1903, p. 590; *Compendium*, p. 278.

[4] Rhys Davids, SBB. ii. 33, 160, 163; cf. Poussin, JA. 1902, ii. 250.

him as the God of Gods, and believed that by devotion to him they shall attain eternal salvation, consisting of perpetual bliss. It is necessary, then, for believers in a primitive rationalism to admit that in some manner the simple humanity of the wise teacher has been overlaid by a divinity not his own, one moreover which on his own theory he would have treated as wholly absurd. This is a remarkable fate for a rationalist, and it is idle to claim to render it plausible by quoting the case of Kṛṣṇa. There is not the slightest ground beyond conjecture for the belief that the character of Kṛṣṇa developed from a devout teacher mentioned once in the Upaniṣads to the interesting and popular divinity familiar to India. Supporters of this view rely on the parallel of the Buddha, and in both cases the contention is one which must be established, if at all, on its own merits without the insecure support of the other. In Kṛṣṇa's case every consideration of probability points to the view that he was a tribal god who gradually attained the rank of a universal deity[1]; but the modes of attaining divinity are diverse, and the case of the Buddha should be discussed in the light of the evidence of the relevant texts and not on the basis of dubious and uncertain analogies.

Now it is admitted that the evidence for the rationalistic theory of the Buddha depends on the texts of the Pali Canon of the school of the Vibhajyavādins, undoubtedly the most precious record of Buddhism preserved to us. The pious respect attributed to the antiquity and authority of these texts by devout Buddhists is as natural as it is laudable. But it is strange to find that western criticism, ruthless in probing the claims of its own sacred scriptures, has treated the Pali Canon with a respect so profound as to regard with open hostility[2] any attempt to apply to these sources of information the same dispassionate scrutiny which is demanded from the researcher into the history of Christianity. The problem, it must be realized, is not whether, given the texts and the orthodox tradition regarding their origin and authenticity, it is possible, by a liberal use of constructive imagination, to

[1] See Keith, *Indian Mythology*, pp. 123 ff., 187 ff.

[2] Winternitz, *Ind. Litt.* ii. 357 ff. Walleser's views (PGAB., pp. 15 ff.) are gravely affected by his erroneous identification of the Pali and Northern Abhidharma texts.

make the tradition harmonize more or less tolerably with the obvious facts revealed in the texts themselves. The issue is whether the texts, fairly interpreted, yield a result compatible with the traditional account of their origin and date. Nor is it legitimate in such an examination to adopt the view that what can be shown to be possible really happened. Nothing is more fallacious than the belief which transforms what is conceivable into what is actual. We must accept the limitations which the state of our sources often imposes upon us, and be content, when we have attained a position in which decision is impossible, to recognize that this and nothing else is the legitimate and scientific conclusion to be recorded.

Faith, it would seem clear on normal principles of interpretation, is decisively out of place in Buddhist traditions of the origin of their scriptures, when it is realized that the primary source, the *Cullavagga*, XI and XII, a chapter appended to the *Vinaya Piṭaka*, gives an account which is frankly incredible.[1] We are asked to believe that the Vinaya and the Dhamma were rehearsed in a Council held immediately after the death of the Buddha, when in the Dhamma, i. e. the *Sutta Piṭaka*, itself appear references to a date posterior to the Buddha's death, and the Vinaya can be analysed into sets of rules, an ancient commentary upon them, and a further careful elaboration based on the rules and the comment. If our faith in tradition is thus shattered at the outset, it becomes hard to ask us to accept as valid the legend of a second Council held a hundred years later at Vaiçālī, which condemned ten errors of discipline of the Vajjian monks and at which, the *Cullavagga* tells us, the Vinaya was once again recited. The Sinhalese sources, beginning with the *Dīpavaṅsa* (c. A. D. 400),[2] show their inferior value by further embroidering the story; the excommunicated Vajjiputtakas hold another great concourse of their own, while at the Council of the orthodox both the Dhamma and the Vinaya are recited. When the northern sources are

[1] See Minayeff, *Recherches sur le Bouddhisme*, chs. ii. and iii; Kern, *Ind. Buddh.*, pp. 101 ff.; Franke, JPTS. 1908, pp. 1 ff.; Poussin, IA. xxxvii. 2 ff.; *contra* Oldenberg, VP., pp. xxv ff.; ZDMG. lii. 613 ff.; cf. Smith, JRAS. 1901, pp. 843 ff.; Barth, RHR. xlii. 74 ff. See also Franke, DN., pp. xlii. ff.

[2] Cf. Franke, VOJ. xxi. 203 ff.; Smith, IA. xxxii. 265 ff.

compared, the confusion and obscurity deepen, and it is impossible, with any regard to the value of evidence, to come to any conclusion whatever regarding it, which can claim to be more than a mere hypothesis. Yet upon belief both in the fact of the Council and of its date—say not later than 377 B.C.—is based the leading argument for the date of the *Vinaya Piṭaka*. That text, it is urged, must have been completed before the condemnation of the ten points at the Council, or these points would have been disposed of, directly or indirectly in the text, and not left to the *Cullavagga*. The argument, however, breaks down hopelessly in view of the facts; the tenth of the breaches of discipline, the acceptance of gold and silver, is clearly condemned in the Vinaya, and the majority, if not all, of the other matters can be shown to be condemned more or less clearly in that text. It may, indeed, as legitimately be concluded that the compilers of the Vinaya, as we have it, were aware of the errors in question and took trouble to secure that they were not left unprovided against. At any rate a purely negative conclusion is alone possible.

The evidence for an early date of the *Sutta Piṭaka* is still less satisfactory. Reliance is specially placed by supporters of an early date on the Bhābrū edict of Asoka, in which he recommends seven passages or topics of the law for the study of his co-religionists. Ingenuity has identified all seven with certain passages of the *Sutta Piṭaka*, but there is a lamentable lack of unity in these identifications, as was only to be expected when terms so vague as all but one of the names are concerned.[1] Even in that case, the instruction of Rāhula on falsehood, it is absurd to claim that Asoka knew the text as we have it in the *Majjhima Nikāya*. All that we do know from this passage of Asoka's records, as from their general tone and expression, is that Buddhist texts were already in existence, probably of the type preserved in the *Sutta Piṭaka*, and proof of such a fact is hardly necessary. Yet these conflicting identifications are still apparently taken as serious evidence that the *Sutta Piṭaka* had come into existence, such as we have it, before Asoka's date.

[1] Winternitz, *Ind. Litt.* ii. 13; D. Kosambi, IA. xli. 37 ff.; Smith, *Asoka*[3] p. 157; JRAS. 1915, p. 805; IA. xlviii. 8 ff.

This conclusion is strengthened, in the opinion of those who hold it, by the tradition, not recorded until the fifth century A.D. in the commentators Dhammapāla and Buddhaghosa, that the *Kathāvatthu* in the *Abhidhamma Piṭaka* was composed by Tissa, son of Moggalī, at the court of Asoka at Pāṭaliputra in the middle of the third century B.C.[1] As such a tradition contradicts the view, asserted then to be current, that all the Canon was held to be the work of the Buddha, it is urged that the tradition must have been of overwhelming weight so as to overcome the scruples of the commentators. But the commentators escape the difficulty by accepting the authorship of the Buddha and ascribing a subordinate rôle to Tissa, and it is a delusion to imagine that their mention of that sage must have been based on tradition. For he is part and parcel of the Third Buddhist Council held, according to the Ceylonese tradition, under Asoka, approximately in 247 B.C., and of that Council, at which the *Abhidhamma Piṭaka* took final shape according to the same authorities, we have no other information. It is incredible that it ever took place without receiving some mention in the numerous records of Asoka; the efforts of those[2] who try to find a place in Asoka's reign for the Council at such a time as to explain his silence are mistaken attempts to justify a tradition, the antiquity of which is wholly uncertain, but which is first recorded six centuries after the event whose happening it asserts. The desire to save the credibility of the Council has indeed led Mr. Vincent Smith to a paradox; he admits candidly that the Ceylonese date, sixteen or eighteen years after the consecration of Asoka, must be erroneous, since, if it had then met, it must have been recorded in the seventh Pillar Edict which reviews all the internal measures taken up to that date by the sovereign for the promotion of the law of piety. He admits further that any attempt to reconstruct a narrative of the actual proceedings of the Council is hopeless, in view of the conflict of traditions, and he recognizes[3] that the Council of Vaiçālī is a

[1] Mrs. Rhys Davids, *Points of Controversy*, pp. xxx ff. Contrast Poussin, *Bouddhisme* (1898), p. 56, n. 4.

[2] Smith, op. cit., pp. 55, 217; but see Fleet, JRAS. 1910, p. 426.

[3] JRAS. 1901, pp. 843 ff. Geiger's defence of the Ceylonese records (ZDMG. lxiii. 540 ff.) is ineffective; see Franke, DN., pp. xliv. ff. There is

figment. Yet, in face of these facts, he throws over the Ceylonese date in an effort to preserve the Council. Unless Asoka's Council is formally revealed to us by an inscription yet to be discovered, the only verdict of scientific history must be that the Council was a figment of the pious or fraudulent imaginings of a sect, which desired to secure for its texts, and especially for the new Abhidhamma, a connexion with the greatest of Buddhist sovereigns, and that the northern tradition does well to ignore the Council entirely. Tissa himself, son of Moggalī, bears a suspicious aspect [1]; his name seems to be reminiscent of Upatissa, alias Sāriputta, and Moggallāna, the dearly beloved disciples of the Buddha, and independent authority for his existence there is absolutely none. His legend may be founded on the existence of some teacher of eminence in Asoka's time; a Moggaliputta is mentioned on a Stūpa at Sānchi,[2] a fact which absurdly has been hailed as evidence of the historical existence and activity of Tissa. Equally absurd is his identification [3] with the Upagupta of the northern tradition, for we have copious information regarding that sage and not a word of the alleged Council, so that we are asked to assume that the northern legends preserved faithfully his reputation, but omitted the most important happening of his life.

Nothing more definite can be learned from the *Milindapañha*, on which, however, much stress has been laid in support of the antiquity of the Tripiṭaka, on the score that practically the whole of the Piṭakas were known and regarded as a final authority when the work was produced, that is in the north-west of India about the time of the Christian era. The fatal defect of this argument,[4] which its author has unhappily still overlooked, is that the quotations from the Piṭakas which establish his thesis are confined to Books IV to VII and to passages in the earlier books which are

not the slightest evidence that they ever rested on any ancient tradition and they abound in admitted absurdities.

[1] Kern, *Buddh.*, ii. 352: Walleser, PGAB., pp. 23 f. To Sāriputta, be it noted, tradition ascribes nos. 33 and 34 of the *Dīgha*, which are in effect Abhidhamma texts; see SBB. iv. 198 ff.

[2] Marshall, *Guide to Sānchi*, p. 137.

[3] Waddell, Proc. ASB. 1899, p. 70. See Barth, RHR. xlii. 73.

[4] SBB. II. ix, x.; still maintained in SBB. IV. vii. ff., despite the new facts.

patent additions[1] much later than the main body of the text; the date even of the latter is uncertain, and may be considerably later than the Christian era.

We come to firmer ground when we find in the inscriptions at Sānchi[2] the terms *dhammakathika*, 'preacher of the Law', *sutātikinī*, 'one who knows a Suttanta', *peṭakī*, 'one who knows a Piṭaka', and, most important of all, *pacanekāyika*, 'one who knows the five Nikāyas'. The term *peṭakī* is dubious in sense; it might mean 'one who knows the Piṭakas', whether two or more, but it is more probable that only one Piṭaka is meant, and that in this period that name, unknown to the Canon, was applied to the five Nikāyas, as indeed it is certainly applied in the work *Peṭakopadesa*, while Suttanta was specifically applicable to the dialogues. The date of these records, therefore, becomes of real importance; it may conceivably be the second century B.C., but it is quite possible that it should be placed a century later.[3] We have, therefore, moderately secure ground for thinking that in the two centuries after Asoka the *Sutta Piṭaka* of the Pali Canon was coming into being, and in the same period we may place the redaction of the *Vinaya Piṭaka*, in the composite form in which we have it, thus avoiding the absurdity of supposing that Asoka knew these great collections and yet managed to avoid ever mentioning them. It is needless to say that there is nothing in Indian history to make us doubt this result; if Asoka's empire was brief in duration, Buddhism went on developing and flourishing, receiving, it is clear, patronage from the Greek and Çaka invaders until it received once more imperial patronage from the Kuṣāṇa Kaniṣka, probably at the close of the first century A. D. The date suggested is rather strengthened by the fact that under Kaniṣka there is evidence of literary activity in dealing with the scriptures of the Sarvāstivādin school, which may, therefore, have been coming into form much in the same period as the texts which we have in the Pali Canon.[4]

[1] Winternitz, *Ind. Litt.* ii. 140, 146.

[2] EI. ii. 93 f.; ZDMG. xl. 58 f.; IA. xxi. 225 ff.; SBB. II. xii. f.

[3] The early dating of Waddell (JRAS. 1914, pp. 138 ff.) is incorrect; cf. MASI. i. 14 f.

[4] Lévi, *T'Oung Pao*, 1907, pp. 114 ff.; JRAS. 1910, pp. 1017 ff.; JA. 1914, ii. 495.

The evidence of the Chinese translations[1] as well as of the fragments in Sanskrit and various languages used in Central Asia,[2] which have been recently discovered, shows the existence of a series of texts, the *Dīrghāgama*, the *Madhyamāgama*, the *Saṁyuktāgama*, the *Ekottarāgama*, parallel with the four Pali Nikāyas, and of several texts, *Sthaviragāthā*, *Udāna*, *Dharmapada*, *Sūtranipāta*, *Vimānavastu*, *Buddhavaṅça*, which are found in the fifth Pali Nikāya. There is also conclusive evidence of strong similarity in the Prātimokṣa rules of the Vinaya, and we are justified in seeing the growth of a common tradition in India in the period immediately succeeding Asoka, which is preserved in varying purity in our texts.[3]

Within the Nikāyas themselves it is impossible to establish any very definite chronological strata. The division is artificial: into long texts, called Suttas in a terminology which differs from the use of Brahmanical texts; middle sized texts; texts united by subject matter—understood very vaguely; and texts grounded on a numerical basis in accordance with the regrettable practice of Buddhism, late and early, to form groups of ideas on the basis of number. There is some ground for treating this last Nikāya as younger than the other three[4] but while the *Saṁyutta Nikāya* may be suspected of being late, it is impossible to assert[5] that the *Dīgha* is as a whole the oldest source of our knowledge of Buddhism. What is clear from the enormous amount of common material, both verse and prose, is that the Nikāyas, as we have them, are redactions of floating material, in which old and new are commingled; it is unnecessary to go further and postulate one master mind for the redaction of each Nikāya[6]; the theory is open to the objection that it requires too much subjective judgement to discover

[1] See Anesaki, *Trans. As. Soc. Japan*, xxxv. (1908.)

[2] See references in Winternitz, *Ind. Litt.* ii. 186 f., 374; A. F. R. Hoernle, *Manuscript Remains of Buddhist Literature* (1916.)

[3] Cf. Lévi, *Les Saintes Écritures du Bouddhisme* (1909); JA. 1912, ii. 495 ff. Oldenberg, GN. 1912, pp. 197 ff. The relative priority of *Vinaya* and *Sutta Piṭakas* is uncertain; cf. Kern, *Ind. Buddh.*, p. 2; Winternitz, *Ind. Litt.* ii. 17; Franke, JPTS. 1908, pp. 8 ff., 68 ff.; SBB. iii. 75 f.

[4] Winternitz, *Ind. Litt.* ii. 50, 365.

[5] Franke, ZDMG. lxix. 455.

[6] Franke, ZDMG. lxviii. 473 ff.; VOJ. xxix. 134 ff. for the *Majjhima*; *Festschrift Windisch*, pp. 196 ff. on the *Suttanipāta*; DN, pp. iv. ff.

the master mind, even measuring its mastery on the Buddhist standard of relevancy. The texts of the *Khuddaka Nikāya* still less admit of reference to any one period; they contain old matter and new, even within the limits of one and the same text. That we have in the *Udāna* or *Itivuttaka* the actual words of the Buddha is wholly implausible, and old as the *Suttanipāta* is reckoned, we find already the Buddha surrounded with an elaborate mythology. The *Jātaka* book is a strange conglomerate of old and new verses with new prose; some of its tales, as we know from Buddhist sculpture and a stray citation or two, go back to the Asokan epoch or shortly after; as folk-lore its contents are often of undeniable age, but as Buddhist fables their antiquity is uncertain.

The case of the *Abhidhamma Piṭaka* is far worse than that of the *Sutta* and *Vinaya Piṭakas*. These two texts know nothing of such a Piṭaka; the division recognized is that of Dhamma, i. e. Sutta, and Vinaya with Mātikā, 'lists' as the third, the germ, doubtless, of the actual Abhidhamma.[1] None the less the most grandiose claims have been advanced for the Abhidhamma books. Mrs. Rhys Davids[2] claims that the *Dhammasaṅgaṇi* is to be dated about 385 B. C., basing the assertion on the internal evidence of form and content as compared with the *Kathāvatthu* (247 B. C.). Professor Walleser[3] denies the validity of the argument, but resorts to the view that the *Dhammasaṅgaṇi* is the *Dharmasaṁgraha* of Çāriputra among the northern Abhidhamma texts, and is referred to by Asoka as the Upatisa-pasine, Upatissa being the other name of Sāriputta; the suggestion is impossible of credit, and it is certain that the *Dharmasaṁgraha* is wholly different from the *Dhammasaṅgaṇi*. A useful antidote to these extravagant estimates is afforded by Professor Rhys Davids[4] who places the four Nikāyas at the period assigned to the *Dhammasaṅgaṇi* and brings that text down later than the late texts of the *Khuddaka Nikāya*. He himself,[5] however, asserts that in the subjects of which it treats and its style the *Kathāvatthu*, the latest text of the Piṭaka, accords perfectly with all we know or expect of Asokan India, but the assertion is idle and is unsupported by any evidence. On the

[1] Geiger, PD., pp. 118 f. [2] *Psych. Ethics*, pp. xviii. f.
[3] PGAB., pp. 20 ff. [4] CHI. i. 197. [5] SBB. II. xi.; CHI. i. 194.

contrary the work shows the clearest signs, as Mrs. Rhys Davids[1] candidly allows, of much addition, which has deprived it of coherence or order. The admission is necessary in view of the obvious confusion of the work, and it deprives of all point the only serious attack made on Minayeff's criticism of the traditional origin of the *Kathāvatthu*; the inclusion in the text of a heresy known to have been held by the Vetulyakas in the second century A. D. in Ceylon and later does not prove that the work was only begun then, but it indicates that in all probability it was still open to additions in the second century A. D. and later. Moreover the theory that it is the latest of the Abhidhamma books is without foundation; it ignores three of them, *Dhātukathā*, *Puggalapaññatti*, and *Yamaka*. The scholastic character of these works suggests that they are divided by no small space from the other Piṭakas, and are very possibly younger than the older portion of the *Milindapañha*,[2] which refers to the Abhidhamma only in passages certainly late. The lateness of the Abhidhamma is confirmed also by the Ceylonese tradition itself. When it tells of the Great Council held by the heretical Vajjiputtakas, it says that they rejected the Abhidhamma books, along with the *Paṭisambhidā* and the *Niddesa* and portions of the *Jātaka* from the fifth Nikāya, and the *Parivāra* appendix of the Vinaya. Now it is not disputed that the *Paṭisambhidā* and *Niddesa*, which are really commentaries or Abhidhamma, are late, that the *Jātaka* is full of late matter, and that the *Parivāra* is not original; we are confirmed, therefore, in the view that the Abhidhamma has no claim to the antiquity asserted for it. This is supported by the undeniable fact that, while the *Sutta* and *Vinaya Piṭakas* have parallels in other schools, based on a common tradition, the Abhidharma of the Sarvāstivādins, of which we now have information,[3] utterly disagrees with the Pali Abhidhamma. As this Abhidhamma existed at the time of the Council of Kaniṣka, it is doubtless to it and not to the Pali Abhidhamma that we have to refer the term Trepiṭaka,[4] which

[1] *Points of Controversy*, p. xxxi; cf. Poussin, ERE. iv. 184.
[2] Barth, RHR. xlii. 73.
[3] Takakusu, JPTS. 1904–5, pp. 67 ff. A Dharmagupta Abhidharma also existed. JA. 1916, ii. 20, 38.
[4] EI. viii. 176. It is important to note that DN. no. 33, Saṅgīti Suttanta, is

appears in an inscription of this time, and we are left to conjecture a date for the Pali Abhidhamma. All that can be said is that in the third century A. D. the *Abhidhamma Piṭaka* seems to have been studied in Ceylon,[1] and that in the commentators of the fifth century we find the *Abhidhamma Piṭaka* treated as authoritative, as also in the late additions to the *Milindapañha*. But we are without means of judging precisely at what date the old Mātikās were formed into our present texts, possibly after the Christian era.

The place of the production of the Pali Canon is uncertain; it comes to us as that of the Vibhajjavādin school of the Mahāvihāra of Ceylon; and its connexion with Ceylon is recognized in Sanskrit texts. But that is not to say that the Pali Canon was redacted in Ceylon; we need credit the Ceylonese tradition of the early conversion of the people to Buddhism as little as we do any other part of its legends. We may, therefore, treat the Canon as the work of an Indian school, and note the Ceylonese tradition recording its reduction to writing[2] under Abhaya Vaṭṭagāmani, perhaps at the close of the first century B. C., as perhaps applicable to the two older Piṭakas, though not necessarily in their present form in detail; certainly not in the case of the Jātaka book. It is a different question whether the *Abhidhamma Piṭaka* was a product of Ceylon; there is nothing to prove its northern origin, and accordingly the matter must remain open, in view of our almost total ignorance of the facts on which a conclusion of value could be framed.

Part of this ignorance arises from the uncertainty of the origin of Pali, the language of the Canon. One fatal objection to the orthodox theory, and to the attempts of recent authorities to defend it, is the fact that the language of the Canon is plainly and undeniably a post Asokan literary dialect, assuming much communication between the learned monks of different parts of India.[3] Even if we

parallel with the *Saṁgītiparyāya* of the Sarvāstivādins; this suggests that it was the Sarvāstivādin example which induced the Vibhajjavādins to develop a separate Abhidharma. For other Abhidhamma matter in the *Sutta Piṭaka* see MN. i. 299 ff.

[1] Hardy, *Eastern Monachism*, p. 156.

[2] This record is not favourable to the theory that Piṭaka means box for MSS. (Bühler, *Ind. Alph.*, pp. 86 ff.) Cf. SBE. xxxv. 28, n. 1.

[3] See Lévi, JA. 1912, ii. 495 ff. (Geiger's reply (*Pāli*, pp. 1 ff.) is ineffective.)

assumed that the Canon was established by Asoka, we would have to admit that it has been radically altered in form, and it would be absurd to claim that the alteration in form had taken place without change of substance. The complexity and artificiality of the language as it stands are shown by the extraordinary diversity of the suggestions as to the vernacular which must lie at the basis of Pali. Oldenberg[1] found it in the region south of the Deccan; Rhys Davids,[2] on historical grounds, in Avantī; Franke,[3] on linguistic considerations, in the tract whose centre was Ujjayinī; while Grierson,[4] accepting Windisch's contention in favour of the Indian tradition which makes Māgadhī the basis of Pali, finds that Pali is the literary form of the Māgadhī language, the then Koine of India, as it was spoken and as it was used as a medium of literary instruction in the Takṣaçilā University, the vernacular of Takṣaçilā being Paiçācī Prakrit, whose home he places in the north-west though Konow[5] locates it about the Vindhya region; or again it is held that Ardha-Māgadhī underlies our Pali texts. The obvious deduction is that Pali came into being, such as we have it, by a slow and complex process occupying some centuries, and variations of place.

2. *The Conclusions attainable*

If we adopt, as we must if not precluded by obligations of faith, the conclusion that the Pali Canon came into its present shape long after the death of the Buddha, the question presents itself whether any effective result can be achieved in selecting parts of the Canon as earlier and more authentic than others. The results attainable[6] in this regard are from our point of view of negligible importance; the fifth Nikāya contains miscellaneous

Cf. Grammont, *Mél. Lévi*, pp. 65 ff. Rhys Davids (SBE. xxxvi. 269) suggests a Ceylonese origin of the *Parivāra*.

[1] VP., p. liv. [2] CHI. i. 187; cf. *Buddhist India*, pp. 140 ff.

[3] *Pāli und Sanskrit*, p. 138.

[4] *Bhandarkar Commem. Essays*, pp. 117 ff.; Windisch, *Actes du XIV*e *Congrès International des Orientalistes*, i. 277. But see SBA. 1913, pp. 1003 ff.

[5] ZDMG. lxiv. 114 ff. Paiçācī is attributed to the Sthaviras by Wassilieff, *Bouddhisme*, p. 268; cf. Lacôte, *Bṛhatkathā* p. 44.

[6] See references in Winternitz, *Ind. Litt.* ii. 51, 53, 365; Rhys Davids, *Buddh. Ind.*, pp. 165 ff.

matter, some old in part at least, like the *Suttanipāta*, *Udāna*, *Thera-* and *Therī-gāthās*, *Dhammapada*, and *Itivuttaka*, some new like the *Peta* and *Vimāna-vatthu*, the *Buddhavaṅsa*, *Apadāna*, and *Cariyāpiṭaka*; the Abhidhamma is clearly a late and deliberate working over of the Dhamma in its technical aspect. But the bulk of the *Sutta Piṭaka* and the *Vinaya Piṭaka* represents the same stage of ideas; they may have been redacted contemporaneously, and any attempt to trace strata of diverse ages involves a determination on other grounds of what elements should be early and what should be late. On the theory of Buddhist rationalism, we can decide that all the supernatural element is secondary, but we are faced with the insistent question whether we have any right thus to proceed. Granted that a preacher of a gospel of pure reason may be deified by some accident, it is at least certain that it is much more easy to deify an inspired seer who deems himself to be an embodiment of the divine, and that India in particular has been specially prone to accept as real such embodiments. If we reason *a priori*, and lay aside our natural desire to modernize and to find reason prevailing in a barbarous age, we should rather expect to find that the Buddha was one who was indeed human, but who at the same time felt himself to be, and was regarded by his followers as, something far superior to humanity, a great divinity in the eyes of his followers, a deity even to those who were not of the chosen circle. The conclusion is doubtless embarrassing to rationalism, but, if we are content to seek historical truth, we must be prepared to shed our personal predilections and to accept the conclusion which evidence indicates. The case for this view is greatly strengthened by the nature of the texts of the Pali Canon. The Vibhajyavādins were plainly prepared to rationalize as far as practicable;[1] as opposed to other schools they minimize the supernatural element in Buddhism, and the salient fact is that even in the records of these would-be rationalists we find abundant proof that the orthodox and prevalent view of the Buddha made him far removed from ordinary humanity.

[1] Cf. Barth, RHR. xlii. 57; Poussin, *Bouddhisme, Études et Matériaux* (1898), p. 42; *Bouddhisme*, pp. 216 ff; cf. ERE. i. 95.

In the Mahāpadāna Suttanta [1] of the *Dīgha Nikāya* we have in the fullest and most categorical form the declaration of the transcendental character of the Buddha. He is no mere mortal reformer, but a sage whose divine insight enables him to pierce back to the ninety-first Aeon ago when the Buddha Vipassin came to earth to be followed in the thirty-first Aeon by Sikhin and Vessabhu, and in this Aeon by Kakusandha, Koṇāgamana,[2] and Kassapa, and finally by Gotama himself. Theirs is no mortal birth; they descend in full consciousness amid surpassing radiance throughout the universe into their mother's womb, in which they abide in happiness, completely visible to their mothers for ten months before birth. At birth gods receive them, streams of water fall to bathe them, they stride seven paces proclaiming their pre-eminence, the worlds are illuminated; their mothers bear them standing and without defilement, but die on the seventh day. The infants bear already the marvellous marks, thirty-two in number, which mark them out as Great Males, destined either to become Emperors of the World or Buddhas, the flat feet, the dustless skin, the long tongue, the mole between the eyebrows, and the turban-like protuberance on the head. Each passes through the same stages of worldly life, of enlightenment, of teaching and attainment of Nirvāṇa. No two Buddhas can coexist, and it is the privilege of the Buddha to extend his life to the full length of an Aeon; shame on Ānanda who in heedlessness failed to accept the hint repeatedly pressed upon him by Gotama, and to beg his master to exercise this power, instead of passing away at the age of eighty, like a mere man.[3] Gotama's adversaries are much more than human; the legend of the varied temptations by Māra,[4] the god of death or the desire which leads to death, is not to be explained away as metaphorical or the fruit of a poetic fancy; to the Buddha himself as to his followers we may easily believe the experience was as real as anything else in the world; does not our own age

[1] Waddell's reading, Mahāpadhāna, i. e. Buddha as supreme being (JRAS. 1914, p. 674), is implausible.

[2] His human reality is not proved by Asoka's reference. Smith, *Asoka*, p. 224.

[3] DN. ii. 115 ff.

[4] Windisch, *Māra und Buddha*; Burlingame, HOS. xxviii. 11 ff.

suffer from the puerilities of spiritualistic phenomena of far inferior order? The divine nature reveals itself again in the transfiguration of the Buddha's colour on the night in which he attains supreme insight and on that on which he passes away, and in the earthquakes which mark the various stages in a Buddha's career.[1] His powers include that of assuming diverse forms at pleasure; he can discourse to assemblies of nobles, Brahmins, householders, and wanderers and to the hosts of the Guardian Gods, the Thirty-Three Gods, of the Māras, and the Brahmās, and none of these can say who indeed he was.[2] The Buddha is the first of beings, lord and controller of the whole world and those that are within it, Māra, Brahmā, men and gods, ascetics and Brahmins.[3] At his mere word the demon of the eclipse, Rāhu, slinks away, releasing the moon which had appealed to the Buddha for safety.[4] The great voice of the Buddha penetrates countless universes, and he rebukes the graceless Udāyin when he mocks Ānanda for the awe which this peculiarity in the master inspired.[5] The *Milindapañha*[6] frankly styles him the sovereign god of gods (*devātideva*), and the Canon makes a simple Arhant above the gods (*atidevapatta*). Significant is the Buddha's reply to the Brahmin Doṇa, who had viewed with amazement the thousand-spoked wheels which adorn the feet of the Blessed One. Questioned as to his identity he denies that he is god, or Gandharva or Yakṣa[7] or man; like a lotus born in the water which rears its head above the water and is no longer defiled by the water, he has left the world and its defilements, and is a Buddha.[8] Gotama in fact neither has the appearance of a man, nor will he admit that he is a man. If he dies, he does so voluntarily, laying aside the possibility of prolonging his life; miracles mark his death and his funeral, and his relics form forthwith the object of eager veneration.

The evidence might be accumulated, but it is sufficient to remark that there is nothing to set against it; the Pali Canon contains no hint that even the greatest of Buddhist rationalists

[1] DN. ii. 134 (cf. SBB. iii. 223, n. 1); 109. [2] DN. ii. 109.
[3] AN. ii. 23; SN. i. 67. [4] SN. i. 50. [5] AN. i. 227 f.
[6] p. 381; SBE. xxxvi. 305, n. 1. [7] He is so styled; MN. i. 386.
[8] AN. ii. 37; Kern, *Ind. Buddh.*, p. 64.

questioned the supernatural character of the Buddha. The intellectual standard of the *milieu* in which the *Dīgha Nikāya* was compiled is sufficiently proved by the admission into the Canon of the Pāṭika Suttanta, in which the Buddha appears as a magician of a trivial and vulgar kind.[1] The Mahāsudassana and Cakkavattisīhanāda Suttantas among others indicate how full the minds of the Buddhists were with the legend of the sun god, and the solar disk is the obvious source of the later doctrine of the wheel of the law or norm; the concept of the Great Male reminds us of Nārāyaṇa, who is identical, or identified, with Viṣṇu, [2] and, more distantly, of the primeval male by whose dismemberment in sacrifice the gods created the world.[3] It is significant that the Jaṭilas, or fire-worshippers, were among those early converted, by the aid of a series of miracles of moderate interest;[4] they had, it is clear, no fundamental difficulty in transferring their adoration to another form of divinity, but it is idle to suppose that they would have abandoned their faith for a cold rationalism. It was the age of the growth of the great gods, Çiva and Viṣṇu in their various forms, [5] and the Buddha's success was due to the fact that he either had claims to divinity, or his followers attributed it to him and won general acceptance for the view. It is conceivable that divinity was thrust upon him against his will, but every ground of probability supports the plain evidence of the texts that he himself had claims which necessarily conferred upon him a place as high as the rank of the greatest of gods. The Buddha treats Brahmā, regarded as the highest of the gods, and all the hosts of heaven, with a cool superciliousness which is explicable more easily on the ground of his conscious divinity than as an outcome of a rationalism, which certainly his disciples did not understand. Given the psychological conditions of the times, it would have been a miracle had the Buddha been capable of the rationalism imputed to him, and it is unhistorical to neglect the clear testimony of the Canon of the least supernaturalist of all the schools.

[1] SBB. iv. 1 ff. [2] Hopkins, *Epic Mythology*, pp. 206, 208. [3] RV. x. 90.

[4] MV. i. 15 ff. The Ājīvakas, once counted as adorers of Nārāyaṇa, cannot so be reckoned; Bhandarkar, IA. xli. 286 ff.

[5] The scant mention of either (Veṇhu in DN. ii. 259; SN. i. 52; Siva, i. 55) is no proof to the contrary.

How far is it possible to ascribe to the Buddha the philosophical views which we find in the *Sutta Piṭaka*? The elaborations of the Abhidhamma are obviously not his, but the Suttas themselves are far from presenting a single coherent doctrine. They exhibit many streams of thought, here and there welded into a fairly effective whole, but sometimes merely put together roughly without serious attempt at harmonization. We realize that the Buddhist doctrine as we have it has passed through a long period of development,[1] and the Canon represents a compromise of contending views; the eight Jhānas, for instance, are compounded of two sets, diverse in origin and in moral tone.[2] Yet there are certain features of Buddhism which are so emphatically presented in the *Sutta Piṭaka* and later as to impress upon us the view that they represent the views of the great sage himself.[3] He believed, we cannot doubt, in the reality of what the vulgar called metempsychosis, but which he transformed to suit another belief, the non-existence of a substantial permanent soul such as that accepted by the teachers of the Upaniṣads. He held, as did the thinkers of the Upaniṣads, a faith in the mysterious power of the act which automatically determined man's life from moment to moment, without divine intervention. He believed, much more decidedly than did the thinkers of the Upaniṣads, that life in whatever form was a striving which inevitably involved pain, but release from it he found, not in the realization of the unity of the self and the absolute, the doctrine of the Upaniṣads, but in the appreciation of the truth of pain, its causation, its cessation, and the means of attaining freedom from it. The path to this freedom lay neither in asceticism or in worldly striving, but in a middle way, involving self culture, the restraint of the passions, and the practice of intense meditation. On the positive content, if any, of the state attained by these means the master must have been silent, whatever his personal view; for the texts present us with abundant evidence to this effect and his reticence harmonizes well with the other assured fact that he declined himself to engage in, or permit

[1] Cf. Franke, ZDMG. lxiii. 1 ff.; lxix. 455 ff.; DN., pp. ix. ff.; VOJ. xxix. 134 ff.

[2] See below, ch. vi, § 2.

[3] Poussin, *Bouddhisme*, ch. i; Beckh, *Buddhismus*, i. 100 ff.

to others, speculations on metaphysical questions, which did not tend directly to the welfare of the individual seeking truth. He was, we may be assured, dogmatic in his utterances; his insight enabled him, with the aid of his power to recollect the past, to explain the structure of reality to his disciples in such measure as was profitable for their salvation. Doubtless it was this consciousness of insight and memory which impressed on the Buddha himself and on his disciples the conception that he was far above humanity; this is the simple psychological explanation of a claim which seems more bizarre and unreal to the western world than it ever has seemed in India. The popular appeal of his teaching lay doubtless largely in this fact; the disciples were not compelled to change their mentality, but only to accept a new object of reverence, and to follow in some measure the dictates of a new creed, on the whole sane and free from the excess of asceticism which has always had attractions for Indian opinion. Hence we may explain the permanence of the fraternity which he founded, in comparison with the evanescence of most of the other groups, formed by teachers who, to judge from the Buddhist texts, made no claim whatever to more than normal humanity. It is characteristic of the Indian thought of the period that the other contemporary movement which succeeded in maintaining itself was Jainism, whose founder likewise had claims to supernatural nature.

But, while we may accept these broad outlines as representing with approximate truth, on the strength of the available evidence, the teachings of the Buddha, it is clearly impossible with the materials at our disposal to develop in detail his position, or to consider how he strove to combine views, far from according, at least when closely probed. We can follow in many points the disputes of the schools, but it is impossible to say how far in each aspect they represent the opinions of the master. The point is important, when we recognize how late our texts really are, as contrasted with the view that they are authoritative for the century after Buddhism,[1] when they would probably represent the teachings of the Buddha himself.

[1] So still Rhys Davids, CHI. i. 192 ff. On the illiteracy of early Buddhism, see Windisch, KF. pp. 2 ff.; Oldenberg, GGA. 1917, pp. 143 ff.

Moreover, it must be added, that a certain doubt still exists, not indeed as to the historical existence of the Buddha,[1] but as to his date. The normally accepted date, placing his death in the decade 487–77 B. C., depends on a correction of the Sinhalese tradition, which strictly interpreted would give rather the date 544–3 B. C. for the Parinirvāṇa of the Blessed One.[2] A singularly unhappy attempt has, indeed, recently been made to resuscitate the traditional date, based on the absurd suggestion that there exist actual portrait statues of the Çaiçunāga dynasty and an implausible interpretation of an inscription of Khāravela of Kaliṅga.[3] But a more serious difficulty inevitably suggests itself; to what extent can we trust the tradition of the Pali Canon which makes the Buddha contemporaneous with Ajātasattu, apart from the question of the true date of that monarch? Is it not possible that the synchronism is fictitious, a view which would rid us of the unpleasant spectacle of the Buddha conversing amicably with a parricide? We have, of course in the Upaniṣads the name of Yājñavalkya associated with that of Janaka of Videha, and no one probably would care to insist on the contemporaneity. We have, moreover, some positive evidence of confusion in the records, for the history of Jainism renders it probable that Mahāvīra died in 468 B. C.,[4] that is, after the death of the Buddha, while the Canon[5] is absolutely clear in asserting that Mahāvīra died in the Buddha's lifetime. This is one of many inconsistencies and errors in the canonical statements,[6] and there is thus justification for the doubt expressed by inquirers so different as Franke and de la Vallée Poussin as to the date of the Buddha, though the case against the traditional date is insufficient to justify its rejection out and out.[7]

[1] Cf. Franke, ZDMG. lxix. 456; Poussin, *Bouddhisme*, p. 47, n. 2.

[2] See e.g. Fleet, JRAS. 1912, pp. 239 ff. Rhys Davids (CHI. p. 172) shows prudent reserve.

[3] Jayaswal, JBORS. iv. 364 ff.; v. 88 ff.; see R. Chanda, IA. xlviii. 25 ff.; 214 ff.; R. C. Majumdar, ibid., 29 ff.; 187 ff.; K. S. Śankara Aiyar, IA. xlix. 43 ff.

[4] See Charpentier, IA. xli. 118 f., 125 f., 167 f.; CHI. i. 156; Jacobi, SBE. XLV. xiii. ff.

[5] DN. iii. 117, 209 f.; MN. ii. 243 f.

[6] Admitted even by so convinced a believer as Winternitz, *Ind. Litt.* ii. 360. Cf. Barth, RHR. xlii. 77; Franke, VOJ. xxiv. 1 ff.; ZDMG. lxiii. 8 ff.

[7] The alleged relics of the Buddha in the Piprāhvā Stūpa and in a casket of Kaniṣka (see ref. in Franke, DN. p. 254, n. 2; JRAS. 1909, pp. 1056 ff.) do not help to establish either his date or reality, for the invention of relics is world-wide.

CHAPTER II

THE SOURCES AND LIMITS OF KNOWLEDGE

1. *Authority, Intuition, and Reason*

WHEN we are asked to treat Buddhism as a rationalism, it is well to remember that in the words of Kern,[1] 'Buddhism is professedly no rationalistic system, it being a superhuman (*uttarimanussa*) Law, founded upon the decrees of an omniscient and infallible Master.' It is characteristic that in the Bhābrū edict Asoka commits himself to the assertion that whatever has been said by the Blessed Buddha is well said; the same sentiment is preserved in a passage of the *Aṅguttara Nikāya*[2] where the Buddha appears as the granary whence men bring every good word. The Kevaddha Sutta neatly emphasizes the supreme authority of the Buddha; the searcher after the truth appeals successively to the various ranks of gods to learn the answer to his inquiry where the four great elements cease; the Great Brahmā himself censures his folly in seeking him, ignoring the Buddha, and the Buddha himself gently rebukes the penitent inquirer. Yet again the Buddha contrasts himself in his embracing wisdom with other teachers, who are likened to the blind men whom a king bade describe an elephant, and who gave accounts of the monster based on the partial knowledge attained by contact with a portion only of the quadruped.[3] The Blessed One can never lie, though the sky fall and the earth mount to the heaven.[4]

The Buddha is the ultimate source of all true knowledge and of salvation, for his doctrine, we must remember, is not delivered for the sake of imparting knowledge on its own account, but as a remedy against the pain of life, which is inevitably miserable.

[1] *Ind. Buddh.*, p. 50. See Poussin, *Bouddhisme*, pp. 130 ff.; JRAS. 1902, pp. 363 ff.; JA. 1902, ii. 252 f.

[2] iv. 163 f.; Smith, *Asoka*, p. 154.

[3] *Udāna*, p. 68; SBB. ii 187.

[4] *Divyāvadāna*, p. 272; Ç., p. 174.

Hence the importance attached in the Canon to the decision of the Buddha, tardily arrived at, on the direct intercession of Brahmā himself, to make known his doctrine to the world instead of passing into Nirvāṇa, and leaving the world without a saviour. From the Buddha and his succession of disciples the essential knowledge comes;[1] the doctors of the school carry weight, not on their own merits, but because they expound the words of the Buddha; even in the later school of the Mahāyāna the doctrine persists: their greatest teacher Nāgārjuna[2] claims our respect because the Buddha, five centuries before, prophesied his advent and his ability to teach, and all that is true in our age can be traced to the utterances of the Buddha, as in other ages to the words of other Buddhas. It is in harmony with this that the later texts[3] at any rate recognize that the individual Buddhas, who appear at the time when the law of the Buddha is not preached and the community is dissolved, obtain their knowledge, not by their own unaided intuition, but through recollection of the teaching of a Buddha heard by them in a previous birth when a Buddha was in existence.

A disciple, therefore, who seeks to become a Buddhist cannot attain his end, unless he has the necessary faith as an indispensable preliminary. He must believe that the Buddha is indeed fully enlightened, the teacher of gods and men, the exalted and awakened one; that the truth has been proclaimed by the Buddha, of advantage in this world, passing not away, welcoming all, and to be attained by the wise each for himself; and that the Order of the Buddha is worthy of honour, gifts, and reverence, is the sowing ground of merit for the world, and is possessed of the virtues praised by the wise, untarnished by desire of future life or by belief in the efficacy of outward acts and conducive to concentration of the heart.[4] Faith is the root of correct knowledge; man does not think out the doctrines of the Buddha by the independent light of reason; he must hear them taught and explained. Faith is the means by which a man may cross the

[1] BCAP., p. 431; MKV., p. 268.
[2] MA., p. 76; Watters *On Yuan Chwang*, ii. 204; Ui, VP., p. 48, n. 3.
[3] MA. in Poussin, p. 135, n. 1.
[4] DN. ii. 93.

depths of the river of existence to the safety of Nirvāṇa;[1] the teaching of the Buddha saves him who has faith, but destroys the faithless,[2] a reflection which may have strengthened the Buddha in his hesitation to preach the truth to a world which would probably be unable to comprehend it.

There is indeed some place for the operations of reason; Kumārila[3] asserts with perfect truth that the teaching of the Buddha is supported by reasoning. The Buddha's miracles are rather an adornment of his discourses than an essential method of proselytism; the logicians found or invented a Sūtra bidding men test the law as gold by fire. In point of fact the Suttas are not couched in the form of an apocalypse; the Buddha is represented often as reasoning in a more or less Socratic manner, and in inducing his interlocutor insensibly to adopt a view essentially different from the starting-point of ordinary belief, yet attained without any violent breach of continuity;[4] indeed the Buddha seems at times perilously complacent to vulgar error in his teaching. He insists that his disciples should acknowledge that they have not accepted views from respect for him, but have by themselves attained full understanding of the topic;[5] the Buddha's teaching, therefore, appears as the occasion, but not as the cause of the knowledge, which develops within each hearer, brought into efficacy by the suggestion of the master's discourse. Thus, happily enough, is a bridge built between the final authority of the Buddha and the demand of the individual for respect to his intellectual independence. The individual again has another mode of testing the value of the Buddha's teaching; its end is freedom from desire; the Buddha himself in the night when he gained enlightenment experienced, with his development of insight into the truths of pain, its cause, its end, and the means to its cessation, the realization of freedom from the bonds of desire. He is omniscient and he himself claims to be completely free from fault, one in whom no blemish can be found.[6] The disciple has the

[1] Mil., p. 36; it ranks in AN. iii. 21 with intuition (contra SBE. xxxv. 56, n. 1); Beckh, *Buddhismus*, ii. 22 ff.

[2] Cited in Sumaṅg., p. 31.

[3] TV., p. 117.

[4] Cf. SBB. iv. 168; Beckh, *Buddhismus*, i. 103 ff.

[5] MN. i. 265.

[6] AN. iv. 82.

same means of testing the value of the Buddha's teaching;[1] he realizes, as he appreciates and accepts it, assimilating it as part of his own stock of ideas, that he is attaining the freedom from desire which is the means to the final cessation of pain.

It must, however, be admitted that the possibility of human knowledge by no means equals that of the knowledge of the Buddha. 'If there are depths which his wit cannot sound', the *Ratnakūṭa*[2] tells us, 'he does not in this case deny; for he feels, "Here the Tathāgata alone is my witness, the Tathāgata knows, I do not know; boundless is the enlightenment of the Buddhas."' It is no disgrace to say that one admits something by faith;[3] if it is one's duty to understand and appreciate the intelligible parts of the doctrine taught, it is equally incumbent to accept the other portions, recognizing that they fall within the domain of the Buddha and not of the individual.[4] There are, it must be added, vast tracts on which investigation is forbidden by the Buddha, on the score that it does not lead to salvation, including no less a question than the nature of the action of Karman itself.[5] Nor is it permissible for any one to interpret at pleasure the sacred texts; their interpretation is handed down in the authoritative tradition of the teachers of the school.

Strictly speaking, therefore, the way seems closed to independence of thought, and authority dominates the field. Needless to say, the Buddhists were as little willing as other Churchmen to permit their thought to remain in effective bondage, and diverse methods of circumvention were available. Granted that, strictly speaking, the word of the Buddha must be found in the Sūtra and the Vinaya and be in accord with the law or norm, it is possible to extend its comprehension. A good word may be defined as possessing four characteristics;[6] it is well said, conforms to salvation, pleasant and true as opposed to the opposites of these, and such a word by its intrinsic merit may be assumed to be spoken by the Buddha, despite the fact that no text contain-

[1] MN. ii. 173. [2] Ç., p. 55. [3] AN. iv. 82.
[4] BSB. I. xviii; MSA. i. 12.
[5] Cf. AN. ii. 80; DN. iii. 138; Mil., p. 189; MA. vi. 42.
[6] *Suttanipāta*, p. 78.

ing it is available. Hence we read[1] that anything that is well said is a word of the Buddha, and its characteristics are given as four; it refers to truth, not to untruth; to the law, not to the non-law; it lessens sin, not increases it; it shows the advantages of Nirvāṇa, and does not indicate those of continued rebirth. The change of view is characteristic; originally the word of the Buddha was the norm, and hell the fate of him who, when the lion voice uttered its decrees, had the temerity to disbelieve the Buddha's superhuman knowledge, and to think that his norm was founded on dialectic, accompanied by reasoning or experience, made of individual intuition.[2] The new attitude does not contradict the old; the word of the Buddha remains authoritative, but we are entitled to treat as the word of the Buddha every teaching which conforms to the essential characteristics of his teaching. The logic is sound enough; granted that the Buddha's word has the extraordinary virtue of leading to salvation, and that this is a unique quality, it does follow that, if we can ascertain the characteristics of his utterances, such other sayings as possess these characteristics must be his, though not contained in the canonical records. Obviously these records neither are, nor pretend to be, complete accounts of all the declarations of a generation of active instruction to very diverse audiences. Again, we must allow for the fact that the Buddha even in the Suttas shows a clear willingness to accommodate his views to the opinions of his interlocutors; he is the physician, whose aim is to heal, and who, accordingly, is most anxious to find the best means of effecting this result, and does not concentrate his attention on the precise and absolute value of the means in themselves, a conception which later in the Mahāyāna appears in full development in the doctrine of the two forms of truth.[3]

The texts themselves clearly demand the exercise of reason; it is necessary doubtless to regard the letter, nor must a teacher be hastily accused of subordinating the sense to the literal meaning.[4] But mere reading of the text is far from sufficient; the law is a doctrine which must be understood, just as a serpent must be

[1] Ç., p. 15; BCAP. ix. 43. [2] MN. i. 71; cf. SN. iii. 103.
[3] Cf. Çañkara, BS. ii. 2, 18; SDS. ch. ii; below, ch. ix. § 1. [4] Ç., p. 96.

handled with skill lest it slay the holder. To dispute on words is an error and a waste of energy, and it is essential to distinguish between those pronouncements which are complete and explicit, and those which are made for a special occasion, and cannot be taken as adequate unless understood in regard to the special subject matter involved.[1] The context of passages must be considered as well as the mere words. Even then doubt may arise, and there is scriptural authority to make it clear, as is asserted in the Mahāyāna in categoric terms, that there is no binding value in the interpretation of any teacher; the Buddha in his own time had to complain that there were those who cherished texts composed by poets and other men of letters to the neglect of the profound doctrines of the Buddha, superhuman, and consecrated to the doctrine of the void.[2] But, if no teacher is authoritative, there must still be some final authority, and that authority must lie in the law or norm itself, or, regarded from another point of view, in reason which alone under these circumstances can decide what the law is. There are of course narrow limits to the autonomy of the reason; the Buddha tolerates no heresy; 'can a man, dominated by passion, go beyond the teaching of the master?' is his crushing rebuke to the monk who sought to penetrate a veil which he had declined to lift.[3] The reasoner must, therefore, see that his views conform to the law, or he will be guilty of the crime of the arch-traitor Devadatta. But this does not exclude expert interpretation of the law, nor even the assertion that such and such texts, which are inconvenient, are lacking in authenticity,[4] though such a contention is rare, doubtless because of the rule governing Buddhist controversy, which aims at achieving results on the ground of arguments based on beliefs accepted by both parties to the controversy.

But the place available for the exercise of discursive reasoning is also limited by a further consideration. The Buddha in the Suttas reasons indeed, and instructs by analogy and parable and simple inductive argument, but it is not claimed that he attained

[1] MN. ii. 240; MKV., pp. 41, n. 1; 44, 276, 597: *nītārtha* and *neyārtha*.
[2] BSB. I. xvii; SN. ii. 267. [3] SN. iii. 103.
[4] Cf. Minayeff, *Recherches*, pp. 221 f.; Poussin, JA. 1902, ii. 251.

his saving insight by this means, and still less that the insight itself consists of any such reasoning. The Buddha attains enlightenment in a complete intuition, the fruit of a long process in which he has overcome all form of empiric knowledge, and the way of intuition lies open for the disciple, and indeed must[1] be followed if the end is to be attained. Hence it is essential and proper to develop the capacity for winning such visions, and this is and must be a matter for individual experience, and in it the autonomy of the individual successfully emerges from the constraint of authority in an experience which is essentially ineffable, however real it may be to him who experiences it.

2. *Agnosticism*

Of the individual traits of the teaching of the Buddha none is really more assured than his definite insistence on the limits to the investigation of reality which are imposed on his disciples. The one aim which he sets himself is to make an end of pain or ill for the individual who is willing to accept his teaching, and he reserves to himself the absolute right to decide what matters are profitable to the attaining of this end. He makes no promise to a disciple to teach him anything save what tends to the final end; he is a physician to heal a wound, who has no need and no time to answer such foolish questions as those affecting the personality of him who inflicted the injury or the kind of missile with which he worked his evil will.[2] The Brahmajāla Sutta[3] gives, under the fallacious guise of an enumeration of existing doctrines which the Buddha rejects as of final authority, a list of sixty-two views which are laid aside as matters beyond the limits of legitimate research.

The first groups of these consist of eternalists,[4] teachers who believe in the eternity of the soul and of the world, induced to this conviction in the first three cases by memories of former births, extending for periods reaching in the last case forty Aeons, and

[1] We hear of persons delivered by faith alone (AN. i. 118; PP. iii. 3), but this is abnormal. Intuition is possible in early Buddhism without trance; below, ch. vii., § 3.

[2] MN. i. 426.

[3] DN. i. 17 ff.; cf. below, ch. vii.

[4] Cf. DN. i. 56; *Sūtrakṛtāṅga*, i. 1. 1. 15, 16; ii. 1. 21 f.; Ui, VP., p. 20.

in the fourth case by reasoning and sophistry. The next four groups are represented by those who maintain that the soul and the world are partly eternal and partly not; the first of these groups arises through the delusion of memory of one who has come to life again after a world period in the retinue of Brahmā; like Brahmā himself he thinks that Brahmā is absolutely the first of beings, and he thinks that he is created by Brahmā, and, when he is reborn in the fullness of time as a teacher on earth, he deems that Brahmā is eternal, while others are impermanent. The second and third groups have their origin in the memories of those teachers who were once gods in heaven, but by moral defects, love of pleasure or envy towards one another, fall from their high estate, and erroneously compare themselves as impermanent with the permanent deities who shared not their defects. The fourth group rely on reasoning; the body and the organs pass away, but the soul as heart, or mind, or consciousness, is abiding amid the impermanence. A third set of four groups includes those who by application of intuitive thought convince themselves that the world is finite, or infinite, or finite vertically and infinite horizontally, or by reasoning conclude that it is neither finite nor infinite.

Other four groups are formed by equivocators, who are agnostics of the most pronounced sort, and not merely, like the Buddha, unwilling to speculate on certain topics. Their motives differ; some fear error, and the remorse arising from thus hindering their development; others fear to create the grasping spirit which causes rebirth and produces remorse; others feel conscious that they know neither good nor evil and that they could not explain them, so that they might be rebuked, if they tried, by others, and feel remorse; while yet others are simply too stupid. All agree in such answers to any question as these: 'I don't take it thus. I don't take it the other way. But I advance no different opinion. And I don't deny your position. And I don't say it is neither the one nor the other.' These fascinating views they are represented as applying impartiality to the propositions: There is another world. There is not another world. There both is and is not another world. There neither is nor is not another world. Similarly they reason on the interesting question of the existence, &c., of chance beings, those that come into existence through former merit without the tedious intervention of human parents; of the fruit of good deeds and, last not least, of the continued existence of the Tathāgata, the perfect saint, after death. Amusing as the position is, it has the merit of every appearance of historical reality; Sañjaya of the Belaṭṭha clan, appears in Sāmaññaphala Sutta[1] as expounding these precise views, and the love of the fourfold exposition of possible views is prominent in Buddhism itself.

Then come two groups who believe in the fortuitous origin of the world and the soul. Memory again accounts for the first; these teachers were once gods in the form of unconscious beings, who fell from that state in the course of time, when an idea occurred to them. The second consists of teachers who reason, and on the ground of their reasonings conclude that the soul and the world came without cause into being.

These eighteen views concern the past; the remaining deal with the future. The first sixteen maintain that the soul, after death, does not suffer decay but is conscious, and their divergence of view depends on the point of the actual condition of the soul; thus some hold that it has form, is formless, is both, is neither; some maintain it is finite, is infinite, both, or neither; some that it has one mode of consciousness, or various modes, or limited consciousness, or unlimited consciousness; some that it is altogether happy, altogether miserable, both or neither; a curious opportunity of further enumeration is lost in the failure to specify the results attained by combining these sixteen different views. Eight groups approve an unconscious existence after death for the soul, their divisions resting on the four possibilities regarding form, and finite character. Eight more groups accept the doctrine that the soul is neither conscious nor unconscious after death, with the same grounds of subdivision. The scholastic character of these divisions is apparent enough, but we are assured by Buddhaghosa that the Ājīvakas accepted the conscious survival of

[1] DN. i. 59; Franke, DN., p. 50, n. 6.

a soul possessing form, while the Nigaṇṭhas held that the soul was formless.

Then follow seven doctrines preaching the annihilation out-and-out of the soul, the divergences depending on the state of the soul when it is annihilated. The simplest view is that the soul perishes with the body, the opinion of the Cārvākas who were probably represented by the Lokāyatas [1] in early Buddhist times.[2] In the next view the soul is more than human, but possesses form, belongs to the sensuous sphere and feeds on solid food, though it is not perceptible; this soul also dies with the body though it is different from it. The next is a divine soul, having form, made of mind, complete in all parts; the next one that has passed beyond all ideas of form into the realm of the infinity of space; the next one that has advanced still further to the infinity of consciousness; the next one that has attained the realm of no resistance or nothingness; and the last one that is in the realm where there is neither consciousness nor yet unconsciousness. The division here is again scholastic; the last four states are clearly taken from the four Jhānas or conditions of meditation which are a valuable aid on the path of Nirvāṇa;[3] the first three remind us faintly of the first of the five divisions of the soul in the *Taittirīya Upaniṣad*,[4] the material, the breath, and the mind souls, which in the Upaniṣad are followed by the soul whose essence is intelligence and the inmost soul, which is pure joy.

The same scholasticism and desire to work in other parts of the Buddhist doctrine are seen in the next five views, which hold that in this present world the living being can attain complete salvation. The first of these views is the Cārvāka opinion that in the pleasures of the five senses is the highest and only good that man can claim; the remaining four place it in the four Jhānas which, with the four already mentioned, make up the eight perfections or attainments (*samāpatti*), which, if we may believe the Jātaka com-

[1] Rhys Davids' view to the contrary (SBB. ii. 166 f.) is clearly untenable; cf. below, ch. vii., § 1; *Sūtrakṛtāṅga*, ii. 1. 15; Hillebrandt, KF., p. 15.

[2] Supported by experiments on criminals by Pāyāsi; DN. ii. 332 ff.

[3] Below, ch. vi., § 2; cf. the three in DN. i. 195: material (*oḷārika*), made of mind, immaterial; Beckh, *Buddhismus*, ii. 71 f.

[4] ii. 1 ff.

mentary, were constantly practised by pre-Buddhist recluses. In the first of these there is investigation and reflection accompanied by zest and pleasure; in the second zest and pleasure; in the third pleasure; and in the fourth complete indifference, a state which suggests the Nirvāṇa, but is deliberately distinguished from it, however evanescent such a distinction may seem to us to be.

Such are the views in which these speculators are hopelessly enmeshed; but the Tathāgata knows that these views thus insisted upon will have such and such an effect on the future condition of those that trust in them. But he knows far better things than these; he understands the rising and passing away of the sensations which create the craving whence arises the basis of becoming, the harbinger of rebirth with its attendant results of death and grief, lamentation, pain, sorrow, and despair. It is in the knowledge of the origin and end, the attraction, the danger, and the way of escape from the six realms of the senses that liberation is attained. These are the things, profound, difficult to realize, hard to understand, tranquillizing, sweet, not to be grasped by mere logic, subtle, comprehensible only by the wise, which the Tathāgata, having himself realized and seen face to face, has set forth, and it is concerning these that they who would rightly praise the Tathāgata in accordance with the truth should speak. The Tathāgata, we are bidden to understand, has complete intuitive knowledge, and he is aware that speculation on these other matters is definitely hostile to the attainment of liberation.

In the Poṭṭhapāda Sutta [1] again we have a list of ten important questions which are left undetermined by the Buddha. They raise the eternity or the reverse of the world; its finiteness or infinity; the identity or difference between the body and the soul; and the questions whether the enlightened man lives after bodily death, does not live, both lives and does not live, and neither lives nor does not live. These questions are included in those of the Brahmajāla save those concerning the identity of the soul and the body. Knowledge of these things, it is insisted,

[1] DN. i. 187 f. The scholastic takes the world as the self, clearly wrongly. Soul here is Jīva, vital principle.

does not tend to tranquillization of heart or purification from lusts or to Nirvāṇa. Such an attitude, it is obvious, must raise controversy and provoke ridicule, and in the Pāsādika Suttanta[1] the Tathāgata expounds, with special emphasis and fervour, his own position in response to such attacks, which are treated as taking in part the form of astonishment that the Tathāgata, omniscient as to the past, is less well informed as to the future. On the contrary, the Tathāgata, while able to remember all the past, has enlightenment as to the future to the effect: 'This is the last birth; there is no more coming to be.' Nor does the Tathāgata reveal all that is past; what is not true, what is not fact, what does not redound to the good of mankind, he leaves alone; nor does he reveal what is true, what is fact, but what does not redound to good; but he reveals what redounds to the benefit of man desirous of salvation, both as regards the past, the present, and the future. He knows whatever throughout the world is discerned, striven for, accomplished, or devised, by gods or men; all that he spoke between his enlightenment and his passing away was true; as he does according to his word, and his word is according to his going, he is styled Tathāgata.[2] We must accept, therefore, from him the decision that no explanation is to be given to a long series of issues: Is the enlightened one existent after death, non-existent, both or neither? Are the soul and the world eternal, not eternal, both, neither? Are they self-made, made by another, both, or neither, having come into existence fortuitously? Do these descriptions apply to pleasure and pain? Does the soul possess after death visible form, or is it invisible, both, or neither? Is it conscious, unconscious, both, or neither? An important new reason is given for the reticence of the Buddha on these issues. He is silent,[3] not merely because knowledge of these matters does not tend to Nirvāṇa, but because men hold various opinions regarding them. What perhaps is more important is that we find that the Buddha admits that he does not reveal the past even when true and in accordance with fact, when

[1] DN. iii 134 ff.

[2] Cf. JRAS. 1898, pp. 103 ff.; 865 ff.; AJP. xxxii. 205 ff.; Franke, DN. p. 287; Eliot, *Hinduism and Buddhism*, i. 133, n. 2.

[3] *Udāna*, p. 11; SN. v. 437; DN. i. 179.

it does not tend to edification, and we are driven to admit that these doctrines may, in his view, actually represent the truth without being worthy of exposition. This leads clearly to the conclusion that agnosticism in these matters is not based on any reasoned conviction of the limits of knowledge; it rests on the two-fold ground that the Buddha has not himself a clear conclusion on the truth on these issues, but is convinced that disputation on them will not lead to the frame of mind which is essential for the attainment of Nirvāṇa.

The originality of such a position is obvious; it is artificial in a high degree at the same time as it is ingenious, and it is legitimate to accept this fact as evidence of the reference of the doctrine to the Buddha himself. On any logical basis, of course, his position was easily assailable; he accepted the impermanence of all reality which results in the negation of self, and later in the utter negativism of the Madhyamaka; on the other hand, he believed in the doctrine of the act with its abiding power potent to bring about transmigration, without, it is true, the apparatus of a soul, and this doctrine, by insistence on the mental aspect of action as alone real, leads us directly to the idealism of the Vijñānavāda. Both his doctrines are emphatically metaphysical, involving as difficult and fundamental issues as any of those which he laid aside as not tending to edification, and it was inevitable that the free play of reason which he had not effectively discouraged would result in the building up of metaphysical speculation of the very kind he had deprecated. But his own doctrine is clear, and we have not the slightest ground to seek to determine what were his views on any of the issues which he declined to explain. If indeed he had formed any conclusions on them at all, and we have no reason to suppose this to be the case and have his dying assurance to the contrary,[1] it is certain that he deliberately withdrew them from publicity. This fact alone explains how early in the history of Buddhism conflicting views of great divergence could arise on

[1] DN. ii. 100; cf. Mil., p. 144; J. ii. 221, 250. Schrader's opinion (JPTS. 1904-5, p. 158) to the contrary seems unreasonable; cf. Jacobi, GN. 1896, pp. 43 ff.; contra, Oldenberg, *Buddha*[5], p. 240; Beckh, *Buddhismus*, i. 115, 120 who compares rather too seriously the Kantian antinomies. See Oltramare, *Muséon*, 1916, p. 10.

points which he had left untouched; the authority of the master forbade effective speculation on many issues, but it left the indeterminates (*avyākata*) open, and it was too much to expect that the self-denying ordinance of the master would be respected by monks whose mental activity and independence he had restricted seriously in other regards.

CHAPTER III

THE FUNDAMENTAL CHARACTER OF BEING

Idealism, Negativism, or Realism

It is a natural tendency to read the past in the light of later developments, and to seek to find in the later stages of a doctrine nothing that was not, at least implicitly, contained in it from the first. To this temptation, often fatal to historical accuracy, Professor Franke has fallen a victim in his able and fascinating attempt[1] to prove that the early Buddhist view was, like that of the Mahāyāna, negativist, though his argument rather establishes, even taken on its own claims, that the view was idealistic, with a tendency, not wholly conscious or articulate, to negativism. But the issue is vital, and there is the authority also of Kern[2] for the view that from the outset Buddhism was an idealistic nihilism; there is nothing internal nor external for him with true discernment, and a realization of non-existence is the means to secure a safe crossing of the tumult of life.

All the world of appearance, and this is the only world recognized by the Buddha, the argument runs, is summed up by him in the phrase the five groups of assumption (*upādāna-kkhandha*), that is, our coming into relation with the apparent things of this world; this very phrase shows conclusively that only psychical value was attributed to the world, and this conclusion is confirmed by the use of the world of the term Saṁkhāras, denoting ideas or presentations. Had the Buddha believed that there was anything real behind the presentations, he could never have committed himself to the doctrine of the Kevaddha Sutta[3] that all the great elements and name and form

[1] KF., pp. 336 ff.; cf. ZDMG. lxix. 467 ff.; DN., pp. 307 ff.
[2] *Ind. Buddh.*, p. 50, following Waddell, *Buddh. of Tib.*, p. 384; cf. JRAS. 1908, p. 886, n. 1; *Suttanipāta*, pp. 203, 194.
[3] DN. i. 222 f.

are comprehended in the intellect of the Arahant, dying out when it does. Name and form again, denoting the whole of the apparent world, are made in the formula of causation[1] to be dependent on intellect, from which they are produced, and the same formula asserts that existence depends on assumption, while the body elsewhere is expressly declared to be nothing but the groups of assumption.[2] But the case is even stronger; if anything is to exist, it must exist for a subject, and the Buddha, by denying the existence of any self, deprives the appearance of any possibility of reality; the self is a mere idle name, and one of the modes of furthering liberation is the consciousness that no self exists (*an-atta-saññā*); nay more, we have the assertion that even in pain, the most real of all things for the Buddha, there is no self, and more generally all objects of our perception are declared to be without a self (*sabbe dhammā anattā*).[3] The belief, 'I am', is a delusion which must be laid aside, and he who has entered on the path to salvation is already freed from the false belief in the existence of a real body (*sakkāya-diṭṭhi*). Form is nothing but bounded space. The Buddhist is bidden to be guarded as to the doors of sense; when he sees a colour with the eye, hears a sound with the ear, smells an odour with the nose, he is not to assume an object corresponding to the sensation (*na nimittaggāhī hoti*).[4] The changing, painful character of existence is correctly held by the Buddhists to be inconsistent with true reality, and it is significant that the Buddha declines to discuss the question, from the nihilistic point of view absurd, of the continued existence after death of the soul, or the eternity of the world. An essential part of the discipline to attain Nirvāṇa consists in the overcoming of the delusion of the existence of forms; in the Jhānas the expert attains the conviction of utter non-existence (*ākiñcañña*).

Even more clearly the idea of negativism is claimed to exist in the *Majjhima Nikāya*; the every day man, we are told, who knows nothing of the law, takes earth for earth (*saṁjānāti*) and believes in it as earth (*maññati*), and so on with a wide range of terms, including the four Buddhist Jhānas, unity, plurality, and,

[1] Below, ch. v. [2] MN. i. 299.
[3] DN. iii. 243; MN. i. 228, 435. [4] DN. i. 70.

last but not least, Nirvāṇa itself. But the man with true enlightenment thinks very differently; he accepts (*abhijānāti*) earth as earth, Nirvāṇa as Nirvāṇa, but in them and in all else he does not believe (*sa nibbānaṁ na maññati*).[1] Or again, the Buddha declares that though he first appreciated the earth as earth, yet when he recognized that it was without the essence of earth it ceased to exist for him; and the essential condition of release is freedom from the delusion 'I am', 'I shall be', or 'I shall not be' and ideas regarding the eternity of the world. Belief in the existence of ideas is merely a raft to enable men to cross the ocean of existence; this accomplished, it should be cast away for the useless thing it is.[2] It is significant that the desires are called empty, hinting at the non-existence of the objects of desire, and the *Majjhima* freely contains the idea of voidness;[3] more important still, the Saṅgīti Suttanta of the *Dīgha* recognizes concentration described by three epithets, recognized in the Mahāyāna, which may be rendered as concentration which interprets things as void (*suññato*), which recognizes no objects of perception (*animitto*), and which is without desire for such objects (*appaṇihito*); the suggestion that these three significant termini have been interpolated from the Mahāyāna in the *Dīgha* may safely be dismissed as wholly implausible.[4]

The negativism of the Buddha, therefore, appears in effect as the belief that all that exists is unabiding presentation, deprived of any true reality through the absence of any self, so that the Buddha decidedly casts Berkeley in the shade by the fervour of his scepticism. We cannot deny *a priori* the possibility of so advanced a view, but we are equally not compelled to accept it because it is that of the Mahāyāna; the evidence must be scrutinized impartially and without prejudice for or against.

Here at once we meet with difficulties in the way of the suggested interpretation; the five Upādānakkhandha may more easily be rendered as referring to the five physical and mental

[1] MN. i. 4 f.; cf. APP., p. 9; KV. ix. 2; trs., p. 233, n. 1.
[2] MN. i. 329; iii. 246; i. 134 (*Vajracchedikā*, 6).
[3] ii. 261; i. 297: *suññam idaṁ attena*.
[4] DN. iii. 219; cf. Walleser, PP., p. 12; *Dhammapada*, 92 has *suññato animitto ca*.

constituents, which make up the individual such as Buddhism recognizes it, and which arise from grasping, from desire of life; nothing is thus determined as to the nature of the objects grasped; or in a slightly different sense it may be rendered as groups (of objects) after which there is grasping, equally in conflict with the suggested rendering; grasping, in fact, is not the subjective creation of ideas, but the effort of the individual to seize what he foolishly desires. This is the precise sense of the doctrine that becoming depends on grasping; there is nothing here to suggest that becoming is a mere fiction of the mind.[1]

As little can we accept the doctrine that Saṁkhāras denote ideas or perceptions, which is supported by the remarkable doctrine that in the first member of the formula of causation we have an assertion that our ideas all rest upon ignorance, interpreted as ignorance of the illusory nature of the world; the last view is wholly without authority in the Canon; ignorance which produces the Saṁkhāras is ignorance of the four noble truths of pain or misery, its origin, its destruction, and the path for that end.[2] Saṁkhāra, like the Sanskrit Saṁskāra, is a term of varying, but consistent and intelligible meaning; it denotes the making ready or complete something for an end—an idea emphasized in the compound Abhisaṁkhāra, and also the result of the activity when achieved. Hence it has no exclusive application to the psychical sphere; the movement given to a potter's wheel is styled an Abhisaṁkhāra;[3] the wheel rolls on so long as the impression thus communicated lasts. Hence Saṁkhāras may be divided, as often, between those of the body, speech, or thought; expiration and inspiration are Saṁkhāras;[4] when the Buddha decides to enter Nirvāṇa he lets go his Āyusaṁkhāra,[5] his disposition to live, the motive force which but for his decision would have continued to keep alive his mortal frame; it is inconceivable that nothing more is meant than that the Buddha laid aside

[1] Cf. Rhys Davids, SBB. iii. 24; Oldenberg, *Buddha*[6], p. 271 n.; GGA. 1917, p. 153; below, ch. v., § 3.

[2] SN. ii. 4; MN. iii. 17 in no wise support Franke. Nor is ignorance cosmic as Beckh (*Buddhismus*, ii. 105) contends.

[3] AN. i. 112; cf. ch. iv., § 3.

[4] MN. i. 301; SN. iv. 293; Vibh. 135.

[5] DN. ii. 106; cf. MN. i. 295 f.; SN. ii. 266; J. iv. 215; SBB. iii. 113; Beckh, *Buddhismus*, i. 70, n. 2.

merely a subjective process. The same point arises regarding the Saṁkhāras which affect the form of rebirth of the dead; a monk who forms a resolve to be reborn in a noble family achieves this result from the Saṁkhāra thus framed;[1] here again we cannot believe that the rebirth is a pure figment of the creative imagination, just as little as it is credible that a man who has the disposition to pay a visit (*gamikābhisaṁkhāro*) has merely the idea of himself as on a journey.[2] Such a conception is clearly far from the texts, which frankly tell us that a man forms the Saṁkhāra of the body when a body exists, and it is incredible that the body, which is described as the ancient deed made ready (*abhisaṁkhatam*) and made real by mental activity (*abhisaṁcetayitam*), is really to be understood as merely the ancient act conceived or presented to consciousness as existing.[3] The difficulty of Franke's view appears still more clearly when it is remembered that the Saṁkhāras are one of the five Khandas which constitute the individual of Buddhism; they rank alongside of material form (*rūpa*) or body, feeling (*vedanā*), perception (*saññā*), and intellect or consciousness *viññāna*), and there is clearly no room here for the concept of ideas; rather they are the dispositions which lead to rebirth, precisely parallel to the Saṁskāras, which in the Sāṁkhya system represent the predispositions of the individual resulting from the impressions left by former thoughts and deeds. In the chain of causation the Saṁkhāras play the same rôle; they are not the creation of ignorance of the illusory character of the world; something much simpler is meant; by reason of his ignorance of the doctrine of misery as taught by the Buddha, the unfortunate man commits actions and so produces dispositions which lead on to fresh birth.

Nor is there any possibility of giving an idealistic interpretation to the derivation in the chain of causality of name and form from intellect or consciousness. Here again we are confronted with the excessive desire to read idealist tendencies into our sources. Taken in themselves, the words might be interpreted as an objective idealism; the intellect as absolute might create the whole universe; such an interpretation is impossible for

[1] MN. iii. 100; DN., p. 310. [2] MV. vi. 31. 2. [3] SN. ii. 64 f.

Buddhism, but a subjective idealism is equally and ludicrously out of place; the Mahānidāna Sutta gives us the simple sense: 'Were cognition not to descend into the mother's womb, would name and form become constituted therein?' Moreover it is the continuance of this element in the womb which leads to the growth of the embryo, and its final birth. We have here a crude enough idea, but it is perfectly plain in sense, and the idealistic interpretation of Franke is wholly impossible.[1]

There is no more substance in his other contentions; to watch over the senses conveys the reality and danger of sense impressions, not their non-existence. The man who perceives forms does not pay attention to their specific peculiarities (*nimitta*);[2] that is a very different thing from not recognizing the existence of objects of sense, regarded as the cause of our sensations, a meaning unknown to *nimitta* in the Canon.[3] The enlightened man is not so unwise as to disbelieve in Nirvāṇa, the final truth; but he is not to engage in idle thought regarding it, and, if one learns to disregard the earth, it is only because one realizes how little of a permanent all embracing entity it is, not that it is void of earth character. It is perfectly in keeping with Buddhist views to deny that the predicate self can apply to pain or misery, which is the true sense of the phrase *dukkhe anattasaññā.* The third Jhāna gives no aid to the theory; it is not an expression of the truth of reality, but merely a phase of meditation in which the spirit attains a condition of nothingness, preparatory to entering into a further state which is neither consciousness nor unconsciousness. Nothing can contradict more effectively the idea of the mention of meditation on the void, as meaning the unreality of existence, than the Cūlasuññata Sutta of the *Majjhima*;[4] the process consists of meditation, first on the conceptions man and village, thence to the more abstract idea of the wild, then to the more abstract earth as such, then to the boundlessness of space,

[1] DN. ii. 63; Walleser (PGAB., pp. 53 ff.) converts this into metaphysics with the aid of Schopenhauer.

[2] Cf. KV. x. 3, p. 388.

[3] As cause even it is rare (Therag. 1100, MN. iii. 137 may be cases); Aung, CP., pp. 67, 211; Oldenberg, GGA. 1917, p. 161. On the transl. of MN. i. 329, see Oldenberg, *Altind. Prosa*, p. 44, n. 1.

[4] No. 121; cf. also DN. ii. 156.

then to the infinity of consciousness, thence to the sphere of nothingness, then to that of neither consciousness nor unconsciousness, then to a concentration which is without specific characteristic (*animitto*), and thence to liberation; in this state there is voidness of the defilements (*āsava*) of desire, becoming and ignorance, but non-voidness regarding the corporeal body, whose reality thus stands out in the clearest way.

The same frank realism meets us once more in the doctrine of perception. Already in the Canon [1] the process of sensation is compared with the rubbing of two sticks to produce fire, the simile clearly applying to the contact of the organ of sense and the object. Nor was this view abandoned even in the late *Milindapañha*, where the contact of the eye and the object is likened to the butting of two rams or the clashing against each other of cymbals. Naïve realism no doubt, but unmistakable, and the genuineness of the feeling is shown by the effect it has on the doctrine of the act. The Canon [2] no less than the *Milindapañha* admits that accidental happenings are possible; disease and the forces of nature may overwhelm with misfortune a man who has deserved no such ills, a dogma which is frankly destructive of the full efficacy of the doctrine, and whose acceptance shows how little early Buddhism was able to rise above the simple and natural realism of early thought throughout the world.[3]

It is, further, a misunderstanding of early Buddhism to treat it as regarding everything as phenomenal, whatever its real reference, on the score of the use of the term Dhamma to cover all objects. The contention appears to be that, because Dhamma is sometimes used to denote the objects of mind as opposed to the objects of the senses, therefore, when it appears used to cover all objects or things, the meaning is that all things are primarily at any rate mental data, states, or phenomena. The conclusion is wholly impossible; it is true that Dhamma is used of the data with which the mind, as opposed to the senses, works, but it is emphatically not used of the material on which the senses work,

[1] MN. iii. 242; Mil., p. 60; ch. x. § 3.

[2] Cf. KV. xvii. 3; xvi. 8; Mil., pp. 135 ff., 180. KV. xvi. 8 is indeed perhaps a direct denial of an idealism of the Andhakas and Sammitiyas.

[3] For other arguments for negativism, see below, § 3, *ad fin.*

and its general application is not to be explained by any theory of phenomenalism; as will be seen, it may be either the result of the natural extension of a term in meaning, mental conditions obviously having a special importance in the eyes of teachers whose aim was mental training, or the use may be inherited by Buddhism from Brahmanism, in which the way for it was certainly paved in the Upaniṣads, but more probably it is simply due to the fact that it is mind that really knows and discriminates sense objects. The generality of the use is sufficiently indicated by the synonimity with Saṁkhāra, a term which includes all sides of existence, material and spiritual.[1] It is significant that in the first work, where the term Dhamma appears used systematically, the Dhammas as objects are distinguished as material (*rūpino*) and immaterial (*arūpino*). There is not a trace of a suggestion that the different kinds of matter are merely ideal, or that 'we only know of the elements and their derivatives as reflected in, constructed by, human intelligence.'[2]

Curiously enough Professor Walleser,[3] who recognizes that the subjective character claimed for Dhamma is erroneous, himself believes that early Buddhism accepted the doctrine that the whole world, whatever its transcendental character, as known by our senses is a product of consciousness. This doctrine is derived from a very ingenious, but extremely improbable, explanation of the doctrine in the chain of causation that name and form depend on consciousness (*vijñāna*). Name and form, it is claimed, denote the phenomenal being in its entirety, as possessed of qualitative discriminations which are appreciated by consciousness through resistance contact (*paṭigha-samphassa*), and of different descriptions which are gathered by designative contact (*adhivacana-samphassa*).[4] The converse doctrine, also canonical, that consciousness depends on name and form[5] is explained as the other side of the relation; the empirical consciousness is impossible save in relation to an

[1] DP. 277 ff.; AN. iii. 134; vi. 102 ff.; Oldenberg, ZDMG. lii. 687, n. 2; MN. i. 228, 230; SN. iii. 132; PD., p. 86.

[2] *Psych. Ethics*, pp. xxxii. ff.; *Buddhism*, pp. 51 ff. give Mrs. Rhys Davids' view; cf. JRAS. 1914, p. 465.

[3] PGAB., pp. 33 ff., 51 ff., 97 ff. His deduction of idealism from DS., §§ 1044 f. ignores the realism of § 1050.

[4] DN. ii. 62.

[5] SN. iii. 114.

object. The explanation is highly ingenious; but it is clearly contrary to the obvious meaning of the terms, and the rôle regularly played by consciousness and name and form in the chain of causation. The distinction of the two kinds of contact mentioned in the passage of the *Dīgha* relied on is explained for us by the *Vibhanga*, and Buddhaghosa, whose evidence on the sense of technical terms such as these may be safely regarded as valid. In that text perception (*saññā*) is distinguished as perception of resistance (*paṭigha*), which is the case of ordinary sense impressions of external objects, and mental as perception by name as when one asks a question and learns the thought of another by speech. These two kinds of contact, says our passage in the *Dīgha*, can be explained only if both name, i.e. the spiritual aspect of the individual, and form, the material aspect, exist. Were there matter alone, there could be no designative cognition; if spiritual elements alone, no resistance cognition. There is, therefore, nothing whatever here to suggest that early Buddhism accepted the doctrine that 'die Welt ist meine Vorstellung', a doctrine which it is probable they would have found it far from easy to comprehend.[1]

A similar misunderstanding of a passage in the *Añguttara* and *Saṁyutta Nikāyas* has led Professor Rhys Davids[2] to give credit to the doctrine that 'the world, as we know it, is within each of us', being attributed to early Buddhism. The Buddha is represented as saying: 'Verily, I declare to you, my friend, that within this very body, mortal as it is and only a fathom high, but conscious and endowed with mind, is the world and the waxing thereof, and the waning thereof, and the way that leads to the passing away thereof.' We are asked to accept as parallel with this Schopenhauer's[3] saying: 'One can also say that Kant's teaching leads to the view that the beginning and end of the world are not

[1] A different version, based on AKB. 50, is suggested by Poussin, TDC., pp. 19, n. 2. 22. Denominative contact simply refers to mind activity in assigning names. But the canonical tradition may be correct; SBB. iii. 59, n. 1; DS., § 4; trs., p. 7, n. 2.

[2] SBB. ii. 274. Beckh (*Buddhismus*, ii. 99, 102, 110, 119) also denies the recognition of any material reality by Buddhism; cf. Hardy, JRAS. 1901, p. 133; Aung, *Compendium*, pp. 223, 255 admits an underlying reality.

[3] WWV. i. 538.

to be sought without but within us.' Professor Walleser[1] is content to accept this assertion as another statement of the doctrine of the fact that the world can exist for a man merely in his presentation of it, while he justly denies that it is intended to be a statement regarding transcendental reality. But we must go further; the statement, in fact, is not intended to be a deliverance on metaphysics; it is merely an assertion of the simple truth, from the Buddhist point of view, that the essential fact of existence is the misery which affects the individual and from which it is the individual, who by his own effort in following the true path of salvation, must work out his own destiny.

2. *The Impermanence and Misery of Existence*

Such measure of validity as may seem to belong to Professor Franke's theory lies precisely in the fact that the value ascribed by the Buddha to the things of the world of experience was extremely low. It is perhaps a natural and easy step to be led hence to the belief in the unreality of existence, but it is a step which the Buddha, it is clear, never took. For him the reality of existence was unquestioned; it was the deplorable fact of the misery prevailing, which led to his elaboration of the doctrine of salvation; and to have adopted the view of the unreality of the misery which he sought to teach men to escape would have been to destroy the basis of his teaching, and to deprive men of every incentive for adopting the course of self discipline which he inculcated with a fervour which leaves no doubt, even through the formality of the Canon, of his sincerity in his belief in his mission of healing the wounds of humanity.

We may, indeed, for once believe that we have reached a doctrine which goes back in form to the Buddha himself, in the fact that his central teaching is always represented as the exposition of the four noble truths of misery, its origin, its cessation, and the path leading thereto. The parallelism with the Sāṁkhya and Yoga division of topics regarding liberation is striking, but more interesting is the comparison with the division of medical topics into

[1] PGAB., pp. 63 ff.; cf. *Psych. Ethics*, p. xcv.

disease, origin of disease, health and healing, though we are still without proof that the medical is the older application.[1] Birth, old age, disease, death, union with what is disliked, separation from what is dear, unsatisfied desire, and all the elements that make up the individual are misery. The ground of this judgement is plainly expressed in the great sermon at Benares[2] when he expounded to his first disciples the doctrine of the distinguishing marks of the non-self. The five constituents of the empirical individual, material form, perception, feeling, dispositions, and intellect are each declared not to be the self; they are admitted to be unenduring, and therefore misery is predicated of them. Whatever is impermanent is misery; whatever is misery is not the self; whatever is not the self is not mine, I am not that, that is not myself. The essence of impermanence is misery, and the doctrine is held so strongly that it is impossible to ignore its intellectual antecedent in the doctrine of the Upaniṣads, which finds in the immutable one absolute the completeness of bliss, and contrasts with it, and therefore casts a pessimistic atmosphere over, the changing manifold of the world of experience. But the doctrine is not a conclusion on metaphysical grounds; it is supported as an observation of fact[3] made by the omniscient. The waters of the four great oceans are less than the tears shed by man in the interminable course of existence for the loss of father, mother, brother, sister, children, relatives, and goods. The mother who at the burning place calls in sorrow to her daughter Jīvā, is answered that eighty-four thousand maidens of this name have been burned at the spot. The pains of birth, of old age, of death, of disease, and decay are omnipresent; the merchant strives hard amid difficulties of climate to win wealth, which he then must anxiously guard against the greed of the sovereign and the danger of fire and water. To gain their desires men commit theft and murder; they pay penalties of cruel torture on earth, and even more horrible is their fate in hells to come. The gods share in the common lack of

[1] YS. comm. ii. 15; cf. Oldenberg, LUAB., p. 329.

[2] MV. i. 6. 38 ff.; cf. MN. no. 35; LUAB., pp. 115 ff., 238 ff.; Keith, SS., pp. 13, 15 f.

[3] See e.g. SN. ii. 179; iii. 151; i. 133; MN. i. 85 ff.; AN. v. 144; Oldenberg, *Buddha*, Pt. II, ch. i.

permanence; doubtless they possess length of life, like the gods of Empedokles, but they like men must bow to the law of the act; the merit which has won them their places will be exhausted and a new existence will begin for them. It is difficult to resist the impression created by the endless repetition of the idea of misery as dominant, expressed, frequently in beautiful form, in the stanzas of the *Dhammapada* and the *Thera-* and *Therīgāthā*, that the belief in the misery of existence was no product of dialectic, but was founded on the physical and social conditions of the time, acting on minds of special intellectual acumen and sensibility. Another factor, however, must be allowed for; the opposite side of the picture is the happiness which is the lot even in this earth of the disciples who follow the path laid down by the Buddha, and it is but natural that the dark side of life without this consolation and assurance should be depicted in vivid colours; it was natural for those who had abandoned the lusts of the senses to regard the world without them as blazing with fire and enveloped in the smoke of the burning. But it would nonetheless be contrary to all probability to minimize the reality of the empirical basis of the pessimism, which is an undeniable and essential feature of the world view of the Canon, although its darkness is mitigated by the fact that the teaching of the Buddha offers release from it. In the ultimate issue, it is true, the view of existence as a whole[1] cannot be deemed to be pessimistic, but all empirical existence falls under this ban.

It will be seen that the whole discussion of the issue of misery is based either on the preconception regarding the possibility of happiness for the absolute only, or on empiric observation of the actual misery of existence. There is nothing in the Canon to show a full appreciation of the fundamental issue whether in itself desire is pleasurable or painful; the idea that the normal exercise of activity is actually pleasurable, so that in any individual case the ordinary life of man is made up in the main of pleasure, not pain, is one which seems not to have occurred, doubtless because the

[1] See DP. 94, 197 ff., 373; DN. i. 69 ff.; *Udāna*, ii. 1; SN. iv. 126. So in the Yoga; cf. Beckh, *Buddhismus*, ii. 90 f., who justly contrasts the views of Schopenhauer or Hartmann. The doctrine of pessimism is unorthodox; KV. ii. 8.

psychological analysis of the Buddhists contented itself in the general run with verbal investigations. We have no guarantee from the Buddhist attitude that the normal judgement of the average Indian of the time, in the region where Buddhism arose, found life on the whole unpleasant, and the empirical basis of the Buddhist view may well be denied serious validity. The philosophical preconception, however, would as often be sufficient to meet any questions which might have been raised on this score, and doubtless to him who was predisposed on logical grounds to take a pessimistic view of the world, there was much to justify the conclusion that the life and aims of the ordinary unenlightened man were rather a pitiful thing.

The impermanence of the world, which causes its misery, is asserted with as much emphasis as by Herakleitos, and, as we have seen, with as little sense of its unreality, despite the constant process of change which never ceases. There is no attempt to prove the impermanence of the universe, and the Canon does not attempt to define carefully what the term means; we are here in the realm of ordinary common sense; the things of the world are obviously evanescent, though they abide more or less constant for various periods; the body is far longer enduring than the actions of the mind, and hence is to that extent more like the true conception of a self than any mental functions.[1] Here again it is probable that the point of view of the Buddha was strongly influenced by considerations of a philosophical character; the doctrine of the Upaniṣads had found the true reality in an absolute without change of any sort, which all the empirical world was relegated at the best to a secondary and quasi-unreal form of existence, and its very being by some bold spirits held to be doubtful. The Buddhist view is again a middle way, a mediation between the extremes of 'All is' and 'All is not'. The world is rather a constant stream of change, an oscillation between existence and non-existence, according as regards the matter of the spirit to a causal law, but in other matters largely accidental. We cannot hold that the essence of the world process was the law of causality,[2] not merely because,

[1] SN. ii. 94; cf. KV. xxii. 8. See below, ch. ix, § 2.

[2] Walleser, PGAB., p. 60, n. 1. Rhys Davids, (SBB. ii. 1) makes the chain of causation pre-Buddhist.

as Professor Oldenberg has recognized, such a concept is not in accord with Buddhist tendencies of thought, but because the Canon does not extend the rule of the formula of causation beyond the sphere of psychic events. What is asserted [1] as a universal law is that all forms of existence are impermanent; the Saṁkhāras or the Dhammas,—the terms come to be used practically as identical—covering the material no less than the psychical world, are without self, perishing, and full of misery.

The process of impermanence is eternal, one might expect the Canon to say, but on this point we are confronted with the doctrine that it is not a matter for us to inquire into whether there is any beginning in time of the world or again any end, just as we may not know whether there are limits in space to the extension of the universe. We are reminded once more of the narrow and severely practical basis of the Buddhist outlook on existence; all that we know or are to be allowed to know is that we live in an existence of constant change which essentially brings with it misery, and the one path of liberation is to obtain freedom from any part or share in this existence of unrestful change. If 'ultimate reality and "our supreme and vital need" is no fixed basis, nor moveless central stand, but throbbing energies whirling in ordered rhythm, whether of solar systems or of our own hearts and intelligencies, the consciousness of a dynamical order replacing that of a statical order; a Way of life which like the spinning globe, bears us forward on its bosom, more swiftly than we can journey on it; so that beyond our best there ever rises a better hope', then surely there is no greater travesty of facts than to say [2] that such seems to be the end and outcome of Buddhist philosophy.

[1] AN. i. 286; SN. ii. 25; DN. ii. 198. A philosophy must be judged by what it asserts, not by what it implies to modern thought. That Buddhism accepts uniformity of nature even in the psychic sphere is absolutely denied in KV. xxi. 7, 8, against Andhakas and Uttarāpathakas. Magic potency is allowed to thwart natural law; xi. 5; xxi. 4.

[2] Mrs. Rhys Davids, *Buddhism*, pp. 246, 247. The relevancy of the comparison of Buddhist views of cause with those of Demokritos (pp. 46 f., 99, 101) appears wholly lacking; the latter believed in material, not psychic causes, the former deals with the latter. Buddhism has no interest in science or the world of nature; it aims at effacing natural desire by a narrow mental culture, which stigmatizes the essential bond of family life as a base hindrance (*Udāna*, i. 8).

3. *The Absolute and Nirvāṇa*

The emphasis laid by Buddhism on the impermanence and non-substantiality of the world is plainly in harmony with the depreciation of all empirical existence by the thinkers of the Upaniṣads who exalted the permanence of the one absolute. The question, therefore, inevitably presents itself whether the Buddhist condemnation of the world of experience stands on the same basis or whether, as at first sight appears the case, the condemnation survived, and was even emphasized from the period of earlier thought,[1] but the ground of that depreciation was abandoned, presumably as a matter incapable of proof, and therefore a mere idle speculation of constructive imagination.

It is noteworthy on examination to find that in the great sermon at Benares on the characteristics of that which is not the self, the doctrine extends emphatically to deny the permanence as existent of all empirical things; it does not, in point of fact, deny in express terms that there may exist another realm of existence which is exempt from empirical determination, and which therefore might be regarded as absolutely real. Whether such a realm does exist arises in a concrete form for Buddhism in the shape of the issue as to the fate of the enlightened man on the passing away of his physical life. Nirvāṇa, there is no doubt, can be attained and normally is attained before the bodily death of the sage; it brings with it happiness of the highest order,[2] and inspires the poetry of many of the stanzas of the *Thera-* and *Therīgāthās*. But, when the bodily apparatus ceases to operate, what is the condition of the enlightened one? Are we to believe that at this stage the existence of the enlightened one ceases, as is the view which appeals to modern rationalism? Or does the Parinirvāṇa mean the final severance of connexion with the world of experience, and the enjoyment of another sphere of existence which is true reality, and accordingly exempt from possibility of explanation by empirical descriptions? The problem of the continued existence of the

1 Cf. below, ch. vii., § 2.

2 It is accompanied by consciousness of the destruction of existence and rebirth; DN. i. 84; Beckh, *Buddhismus*, ii. 112 ff.

Tathāgata after death is in the ultimate issue the same as the problem of the existence of a true self; if such exists, then the enlightened one must necessarily, as the highest product of the world, be the possessor of such a self.

The answer given by the Buddha in the Canon is clear enough; it is a definite relegation of the issue to the sphere of the indeterminates, marking the issue as one on which the master has not thought right to declare any doctrine. When Vacchagotta[1] asks the Buddha if the self exists, the latter remains silent and, questioned by Ānanda as to the cause of this reticence, explains his reasons convincingly enough. To assert the existence of the self would be understood as acceptance of the adherents of the permanent self of the Upaniṣad type; to deny the self would be to approve the doctrine of those who believe that the self, without purification to ensure liberation, does not on death transmigrate but is utterly destroyed. Again, to assert the existence of the self would certainly not have lead Vacchagotta to accept the essential doctrine that all the empirical world is essentially not-self, while to deny it would have thrown him into confusion: 'My self, did it not previously exist? Now it exists no more.' The reasons are essentially pragmatic, but, even if we may feel that in such a passage the idea is hinted at that the true answer implies the negation of an absolute, it is perfectly obvious that we have no right to go beyond the plain assertion of the text as to the doctrine of the Buddha. We have the same doctrine expressed with much force in the Māluṅkyāputta dialogue of the *Majjhima Nikāya*,[2] where the disciple very energetically presses the Buddha to answer the puzzles of the limits of the world in space and time and the continued existence of the enlightened man after death. The Buddha's refusal is perfectly categoric; he insists that he made no undertaking to instruct his disciples in these matters. He is instead a physician who gives such instruction as leads to the freeing of man from bondage, and information on the points in question tends in no way to the desired end, and therefore is not imparted by the master.

To deny that the teaching of the Buddha himself stopped at

[1] SN. iv. 400. [2] i. 426; cf. AN. iv. 67 ff.

this attitude of agnosticism appears contrary to every sound principle of criticism. It is true that it has been suggested that it is impossible to conceive that the master would be contented with offering nothing more positive in the way of a hope for the future, but this is obviously to beg the question. By leaving the matter unexplained the Buddha allowed men to frame their own conceptions of the future of the enlightened man after death; those who entertained strong desires for some permanent form of life, even after liberation, were as entitled to cherish the hope, as were others to accept utter annihilation as the due result, and we really have no means of saying to what proportion of the disciples either prospect would appeal; western analogies show sufficiently that there are many earnest thinkers who believe in the reality and purpose of the universe—which the Buddha did not—and yet accept the destruction of the individual on death with satisfaction or resignation. It has, however, been urged[1] that we cannot suppose that so able a thinker as the Buddha was without personal convictions on such a vital issue, even though he may have deemed on good grounds that it was neither advantageous nor necessary to explain his opinions to his disciples. Here again we are confronted with bare possibilities; it is quite legitimate to hold that the Buddha was a genuine agnostic, that he had studied the various systems of ideas prevalent in his day without deriving any greater satisfaction from them than any of us to-day do from the study of modern systems, and that he had no reasoned or other conviction on the matter. From the general poverty of philosophical constructive power exhibited by such parts of the system as appear essentially Buddha's, one is inclined to prefer this explanation.

The case[2] for a positive answer to the existence of an absolute reality, as entertained by a section at any rate of the early disciples, is a totally different question and admits of serious support. Some

[1] Schrader, JPTS. 1904-5, p. 158. The etymology of Nirvāṇa ('without craving (*vāna*)' according to ADS. vi. 14), 'blowing out,' does not help (cf. JPTS. 1919, pp. 53 ff.; ZDMG. lxix. 477).

[2] Schrader, JPTS. 1904-5, pp. 160 ff., whose views greatly exaggerate the philosophical insight of the Buddha. Equally dubious is Walleser's counter-argument (PP., pp. 8 f.) that denial of a self inevitably carried with it the denial of an absolute.

of the contentions in favour of this view will certainly not bear scrutiny; neither the Buddha nor his disciples strike one as necessarily possessed of sufficient philosophical capacity to be incapable of entertaining a negative view on this topic, even if it be granted as true that philosophy is forced to accept the metaphysical conception of the absolute one, although, if this idea be realized in perfect sharpness, we are as unable to think as to deny that the absolute one is either identical with, or different from, the world. But it may be possible that the fair interpretation of some passages in the Canon supports the belief that the teachers of these doctrines did accept an absolute reality as the basis of their depreciation of the world.

The doctrine of non-self (*anattā*) clearly asserts that there are no eternal substances in the world nor yet substances which perish utterly, but that the whole world is a process of becoming; anything in time could not be the true reality. Again the universe in time includes and is equivalent to the five constituents of nature (*khandhas*), namely the four or including ether (*ākāsa*) five material elements and whatever consists of them, and every kind of consciousness or spiritual existence, extending to that of sensual beings like ourselves (*kāmaloka*), of the Great Brahmās and other gods (*rūpabrahmaloka*), and even of the most etherial unlimited consciousness existing in the very highest spheres of nature (*arūpabrahmaloka*). But it does not embrace a being which cannot be called corporeal or spiritual or both (*nāmarūpa*) in any sense, which would be a true absolute. Now in the Alagaddūpama Sutta of the *Majjhima*[1] there is a striking denial by the Buddha, following on an exposition of the doctrine of the not-self and a declaration of the nature of the enlightened one as beyond nature and inconceivable already in this life. The accusation is made that the Buddha holds the destruction of a real entity (*sato satassa*). This he denies absolutely; what he bids men throw off is the non-ego consisting of the five constituents, bodily form, perception, feeling, the dispositions, and intellect; as the owner of a wood, the argument seems to run, is not injured by the taking away of the grass, boughs &c. so the real entity is not destroyed by the

[1] i. 140 ff.

laying aside of the constituents. This view may be strengthened by the observation that the Buddhist formula applied to everything in nature: 'This is not mine; I am not this; this is not myself (*n' etaṁ mama; n' eso 'ham asmi; na m' eso attā*)' is applied by the Sāṁkhya [1] school in almost exactly the same form (*nāsmi; na me; nāham*) to exactly the same object, the whole of material and spiritual nature, but with the single aim of expressing the absolute otherness of the self (*puruṣa*) from nature. Nor is it inconsistent with this view that the same Sutta contains a very emphatic denial of the reality of a permanent self identical with the world, a view which we must understand in the sense of the self of the Upaniṣads: 'World and the self are one; that shall I be after death; eternal, firm, everlasting, not subject to change, like the everlasting one; thus shall I stay:' is not that, O monks, a mere complete doctrine of fools? This doctrine may quite legitimately be interpreted as an emphatic denial of the pantheistic view which appears in certain of the Upaniṣads and which would certainly be wholly repugnant to the Buddha. We may, therefore, see in this passsage a clear recognition that the absolute must be regarded as standing wholly aside from empirical determinations, as being without even the attribute of consciousness (*vijñāna*) admitted in the Upaniṣads.

A further argument can be derived from the simile of the flame applied early and frequently to the passing away of the enlightened one. 'As the flame', the *Suttanipāta* [2] tells us, 'blown down by the vehemence of the wind goes out, and can be named no more, even so the sage, liberated from individuality, goes out and can be named no more.' In the Aggi-Vacchagotta Sutta of the *Majjhima Nikāya* [3] we have a complete working out of the idea; the flame ceases to appear when the fuel is consumed; similarly, when the different constituents of the enlightened one disappear, the fuel of the Tathāgata's fire is consumed. But the Tathāgata, liberated from these constituents of spirit and material form, is deep, unmeasurable, difficult to fathom, like the great ocean. The comparison is indeed significant, for there is no doubt that the Indian idea of the extinction of fire was not that which occurs to

[1] *Sāṁkhyakārikā*, 64; Poussin, JA. 1902, ii. 289, n. 1. [2] 1074. [3] i. 487.

us of utter annihilation, but rather that the flame returns to the primitive, pure, invisible state of fire in which it existed prior to its manifestation in the form of visible fire. This view is expressly attested in the *Çvetāçvatara Upaniṣad*,[1] which can reasonably be regarded as good evidence for the period of the coming into existence of the Canon. The same Upaniṣad contains, also, the comparison of the supreme self with a fire, the fuel of which has been consumed, showing emphatically that the extinction of the fuel has nothing to do with the destruction of the fire, though it ceases to be visible, and the *Maitreyī Upaniṣad*,[2] a text of the Yoga philosophy, with which Buddhism has much in common, applies the simile to the action of the thinking principle: 'As fire for want of fuel comes to rest in its own place of birth, so, through the cessation of its motions, the thinking principle comes to rest in its own birthplace.'

In an interesting conversation[3] between King Pasenadi of Kosala and the nun Khemā we find again the refusal to answer the question as to the continued existence of the Tathāgata after death, and an emphatic assertion of the deep nature of the Tathāgata, illustrated by the impossibility of reckoning the sands of the Ganges or the water drops in the ocean. Is this not to argue that the Tathāgata apart from the mortal constituents is something real but ineffable? True, it is possible to explain the doctrine in the light of the negativism of the Madhyamaka; if all be void (*çūnya*), the nature of the Tathāgata is a specially deep void, and especially ineffable. But it is unwise to insist on seeing negativism in passages where another explanation is not merely possible, but probably more in accordance with the ideas of the teachers of the early Canon.

A similar difficulty arises in the case of the discussion of the view of an heretical monk, Yamaka,[4] who formed the not unnatural conception that the master taught that the enlightened one, who had purified himself from all sin, when his body ceased to harbour

[1] i. 13 (cf. Mil., p. 327); vi. 19. [2] Older than Maitr. Up.

[3] SN. iv. 374 ff.; cf. Poussin, JA. 1902, ii. 246; *Bouddhisme*, pp. 172, 415; Oldenberg, *Buddha*[9], p. 324.

[4] SN. iii. 109 ff. Cf. *Paṭisambhidāmagga*, i. 143-5.

life, was utterly annihilated. Sāriputta confronts Yamaka with the question whether the true self of the Tathāgata is his material form, and receives a negative reply. Similar replies are given to the questions whether he is in the material form, or it in him, or different from it, and so on with the four other constituents which make up the apparent individual. Yamaka also admits that the five constituents all taken together do not make up the Tathāgata, nor again is he without the five constituents taken together. Sāriputta then confronts Yamaka with the conclusion that even in life he cannot comprehend in truth and essence the Tathāgata, and that *a fortiori* it is absurd to make assertions of him after his death. Does this mean that even in life Yamaka cannot show the Tathāgata really to exist, and still less of course in death can his nature be stated? The interpretation is possible, and in entire harmony with the Madhyamaka view, but it certainly does not suggest itself here as natural. We have far better reason to assume that we have once more an agnosticism coupled with an indication that there is much more than the mere constituents in the composition of the Tathāgata. Insufficient weight perhaps has been given in the discussion to this aspect of the question; if in life the Tathāgata is ineffable, and not to be regarded as merely made up of the constituents, there is every reason to realize that he is still more ineffable in death.

We have, however, more positive assurances of the reality of something over and above the empirical world. The end of misery is conceived as a place where there is neither earth nor water, light nor air, neither the infinity of space, nor the infinity of intellect, nor the absence of everything, nor the laying aside both of consciousness and unconsciousness, neither this world nor yonder world, where there is neither movement nor rest, neither birth nor death.[1] Moreover, there is something not born, not having become, not made, not formed; were there not such a thing, there would be no escape for that which is born, has become, been made, been formed. The same text[2] alludes to the fate of the enlightened who have attained Nirvāṇa; as the path of the fire when extinguished cannot be traced, so we cannot trace

[1] *Udāna*, viii. 1; cf ii. 10. [2] Ibid., viii. 3, 10.

the path of those who have been completely set free, who have escaped the fetters of desire, and have attained unchanging happiness (*sukha*). But it is not unimportant to remember that these utterances are from the *Udāna* and that we must not press unduly isolated assertions. Moreover, we must remember that in all likelihood the term Nirvāṇa as indicating the final end was taken over by the Buddhists from existing speculation, for the term is freely found in the philosophic parts of the *Mahābhārata*, which, though late in their present form, represent earlier doctrine, and the Jains also accept it as an apt description of it as the safe, happy, and quiet place which the great sages reach, putting an end to the stream of existence.[1] Associations strictly speaking not characteristic of Buddhism might easily cluster around such a term, and we have in fact proof of this in the term Nirvāṇa, element free from determinations (*anupādi-* or *anupadhi-sesā nibbāna-dhātu*).[2] Such terminology may be traced back to the distinction between Brahman as the absolute without determinations (*upādhi*), through which the absolute appears as the universe, but on the faith of such an argument to claim that, to the Buddhist, Nirvāṇa is essentially the absolute parallel with the Brahman would be to ignore the fact that Buddhism, like every new belief, was largely compelled to put its wine into old bottles.

4. *The Conception of Dhamma or the Norm*

It is now possible to appreciate the precise significance to be attached to the view of Normalism, conceived as the reign of impersonal law, as the essential doctrine of Buddhism.[3] Dhamma enters Buddhist thought with an interesting history: the Vedic period shows us in the Brāhmaṇas the development, to the detriment of the older term Dharman, of Dharma conceived not so much as relating to physical order, but as the moral order of the world, including in that term all matters pertaining to

[1] *Āyārañga Sutta*, i. 5. 6; ii. 15. 25; for Yoga influence cf. ch. vii, § 3. That Nirvāṇa is positive may be argued from its distinction from the inferior state of nothingness (*ākiñcañña*) attained in meditation; Beckh, *Buddhismus*, ii. 122.

[2] Dahlmann, *Nirvāṇa*, pp. 23 f., 114 f.; Oldenberg, *Buddha*[1], pp. 438 f.; ch. vii, § 3.

[3] Mrs. Rhys Davids, *Buddhism*, pp. 235 ff.; Rhys Davids, SBB. iv. 54 ff.

spheres later discriminated as law, custom, and etiquette. The conception is admirably illustrated by a passage in the *Bṛhadāraṇyaka Upaniṣad*[1] which tells of the absolute, Brahman, creating the lordly class, the commonalty, and the servile class. But still the creation was imperfect: 'he created further a better class, the law. This is the power of the lordly class, the law. There is nothing higher than the law. So a weak man controls a strong man by the law, just as if by a king. Verily, that which is the law is truth. Therefore they say of a man who speaks the truth, "He speaks the law," or of a man who speaks the law, "He speaks the truth." Verily, both these are the same thing.' Or again[2]: 'the waters are the law; hence, whenever the waters come down to the world, everything here is in accord with the law. But whenever there is drought, then the stronger seizes upon the weaker, for the waters are the law.' The conception of regularity in the physical and the moral sphere is thus as effectively brought out as the parallelism between the two aspects of order. The conception is as old as the *Rigveda*, for it is embodied in the conception of Ṛta as moral and physical order, and the parallelism of the Avestan counterpart of Ṛta even suggests that the idea is Indo-Iranian. Nor in the *Rigveda* is the moral order the creation of a god, even of Varuṇa; Ṛta itself is divine and independent of the gods even if Varuṇa and the Ādityas are its guardians *par excellence*.[3] Normalism is, therefore, present in the earliest Indian thought known to us, just as the gods of Homer are faced with Anagke; the Tao of Chinese thought presents another obvious parallel.[4]

Buddhism, therefore, in laying stress on the presence of law in the nature of things, was merely developing a doctrine which was fully realized in the Brahmanic circles, though in the new belief much greater stress was directed to this conception, as a result of the lack of concentration on the absolute as real. Dhamma is freely and widely applied; it denotes the laws of nature: man's body falls under the rule of decay; it equally

[1] i. 4. 14. See Oldenberg, VWW., pp. 188 ff. [2] ÇB. xi. i 6. 24.

[3] Oldenberg, *Religion des Veda*, pp. 194 ff.; Keith, *Indian Mythology*, pp. 23 ff.

[4] Grube, *Die Religion und Kultur der Chinesen*, pp. 86 ff.

applies to the law of impermanence enunciated by the Buddha; whatever comes into being is subject to the law of destruction. It applies with special appropriateness to the chain of causation; he who sees the chain sees the law, and *vice versa*. The various members of the chain stand in a relation of accordance with law (*dhamma-ṭhiti*), and the knowledge of this relationship is itself subject to the law of evanescence (*khaya-dhamma*). The progress to enlightenment on the part of the individual is regulated by law; the aspirant who has entered on the path to salvation is subject to the rule that he cannot fall away from the fulfilment of his purpose; the non-returner (*anāgāmin*) to the rule that he cannot be born again in this world. Dhamma applies equally to law in the sphere presided over by the king and his judges. It covers again the norm for the castes, and the duties which that norm exacts from them, and all action in accord with duty, in contrast with Adhamma, disobedience to, or discord from, the norm. It denotes whatever is righteous or good, with the same contrast; indeed in the *Milindapañha*[1] we find a curious quasi-personification of the idea, just as in the *Çatapatha Brāhmaṇa*[2] a god, Dharma, the embodiment of righteousness, appears formally. In a less pregnant sense Dhamma denotes any usage or practice, without regard to its moral quality; it expresses the characteristic of any person or thing. Still more vaguely it comes occasionally to be used almost as a synonym of cause or ground (*hetu*), with which the commentators identify it.[3]

By a natural development of meaning Dhamma comes to be selected as the description of the Buddha's doctrine, but equally it can be applied to the views of other teachers; in the first use it is often qualified as the good law, or the noble (*ariya*) law, a term in which it is unwise to see any ethnical consciousness, or the law of the good man. In the compound Dhamma-vinaya we have an expression for dogma and disciplinary regulation, or, as one idea, the teaching in its complete form, for the order is as essential an element of Buddhism or most of the rival faiths as the doctrine itself. The essence of the Buddha's Dhamma is variously given,

[1] p. 207; SBE. xxxv. 295, n. 2; Poussin, JA. 1903, ii. 406, n. 2.
[2] xiii. 4. 3. 14.
[3] Geiger, PD., pp. 32 f.

though the result is the same; it embraces the four noble truths, or their equivalent, the knowledge of the true character of the empiric world (*sakkāya*); the chain of causation; the nature of the aggregates (*khandha*) which constitute the individual as impermanent, of the six senses, and of the six elements including consciousness.

In keeping with the Brahmanic tradition is the frequent use of Dhamma in the sense of truth or reality, though Dhamma actually appears alongside of truth (*sacca*), in which case it denotes something superior to ordinary accuracy. In this sense we may best take the common phrase 'he sees the Dhamma' and the term 'insight into Dhamma' (*dhamma-vipassanā*), and 'the eye of the Dhamma (*dhamma-cakkhu*)'. But of course such passages admit of the interpretation of Dhamma as denoting more than mere truth, as signifying the essence of things. That Dhamma has this sense appears clearly enough from its obvious substitution for the idea of Brahman, or its use alongside of the older expression; thus the way of the Dhamma replaces the path of the Brahman, though that also occurs;[1] he who thinks of the Tathāgata dwells with the Brahman or Brahmā;[2] the eightfold path which leads to Nirvāṇa is styled indifferently either the Brahmayāna or the Dhammayāna; the followers of the Buddha are sons and heirs of the Dhamma, even as the Brahmins claim to be born of and heirs of the Brahman; the Tathāgata is said to have the Dhamma as his body, the Brahman as his body, to be one with the Dhamma, one with the Brahman.[3] Very rarely the Dhamma seems to be regarded as replacing the Ātman in the Brahmanic use as a synonym of the absolute.[4]

How far can we hold that the norm is regarded as more than an abstraction, as something truly real lying at the bottom of, and determining, the world? It is clear that the norm is sometimes regarded as almost, or completely, equivalent to the highest reality or force. We find the expression 'pay homage to the norm'; the wise show reverence to it; Upāli instructs the elders

[1] SN. i. 141; Therag., 689; Chānd. Up., iv. 15. 5.
[2] AN. i. 207. [3] DN. iii. 84, 81.
[4] Cf. SN. v. 6; DN. ii. 100; attadīpā, dhammadīpā; J. v. 66.

in discipline, standing out of regard for their seniority, while they stand also out of regard for the norm (*dhammagāravena*).[1] Especially interesting is the tale of the difficulties of the Buddha after he had attained full enlightenment; he felt the need to study under a teacher to pay him honour and respect, but could see none in the world of gods, Māras, Brahmās, ascetics, or recluses; 'this norm then, wherein I am supremely enlightened, what if I were to live under it, paying it honour and respect?'[2] The norm is incorporated in the Tathāgata; hence the *Milinda-pañha*[3] explains there cannot be two Buddhas simultaneously, for the earth could not bear the weight of so much Dharma. The norm as a motive force appears also prominently in the Aggañña Suttanta,[4] where the claims of the Brahmins to pre-eminence on the ground of birth are dismissed; in every class there are cases of virtuous dispositions and of evil ones, and an Arahant may arise in any, possessing pre-eminence by reason of the norm, not without its co-operation. It is because of recognition of the norm that Pasenadi, the Kosala king, holds the Buddha in honour, though the Buddha's people, the Sākiyas, are inferior to him and pay him homage as mere vassals. So, too, the followers of the norm are superior to Brahmins. The theme is further elucidated by a tale of the origin from time to time of the world, after it has been dissolved into the lowest form of being; at this time most spirits have been reborn in the world of radiance, but, as there is evolution of the earth, there is decadence among the spirits, whose radiance declines; in the course of evolution the lordly class of Khattiyas arises to preserve order, Brahmins further morality, Vessas perform various trade tasks, and Suddas live by hunting and low occupations, all in accord with the norm, which marks out the Arahant as the highest in the world.

The conception, it is plain, is vague, and does not really advance further than the old Vedic idea of Ṛta or the later Brahmanic Dharma; it recognizes, however, that there is more than mere change based on causation in the world; there is immanent in reality the norm which makes the Arahant the

[1] VP. ii. 168.
[2] SN. ii. 138 f.; AN. ii. 20 f.
[3] pp. 237 f.
[4] DN. iii. 80 ff.

highest of beings, and which in its special application to the classes of mankind secures them appropriate occupations. What is specially significant is that this norm has no vision of the progressive improvement of the world; the whole is pictured perfectly steadily as a process of evolution and involution, which persistently proceeds developing the same results; there is here no room for visions of a golden age to be attained on earth, nor material on which a reforming spirit could arise. The Arahant seeks and attains under the norm an enlightenment for himself, and thus subtracts himself for ever from the otherwise endless series of births and rebirths.

It is less easy to trace in the early Brahmanic literature the conception of Dharmas as objects or things, a sense which unquestionably is common in the extreme in Buddhism. We have, however, the idea clearly in two passages of the *Kaṭha Upaniṣad*;[1] the man who regards objects (*dharmān*) separately, who sees no unity, pursues after them, and the wise man is urged to lay aside what is material (*dharmya*) and seek what is subtle (*aṇu*). It is quite impossible to accept the view[2] that the primary sense of Dhamma is idea, for there is no conceivable ground, etymological or otherwise, whence this meaning could emerge, and it is obviously not found in the Upaniṣadic use of the term. Equally impossible is the suggestion[3] that the term denotes the regularities which are the relations for the mind of the super-sensuous reality of change, which is the absolute truth for Buddhism. More tenable is the suggestion[4] that the plural use of the term, which is presumably the older, as it is by far the most frequent, arises from things being regarded as manifestations of the natural and spiritual law which underlies reality. Yet this is perhaps too deliberately metaphysical a conception, and it is more plausible that the origin should be looked for in Dharma, considered as the fundamental or regular nature of a thing; in Buddhism[5] we have the conception of the Dhammatā, or essential

[1] iv. 14; ii. 13; cf. i. 21; *aṇur eṣa dharmaḥ*.
[2] Franke, DN., p. 275, n. 3. [3] Beckh, *Buddhismus*, ii. 119.
[4] Geiger, PD., p. 9; Oldenberg, LUAB., p. 300.
[5] Mil., p. 234; MN. i. 320; SN. i. 140; DN. iii. 147; MN. i. 325; Mil., p. 179.

characteristic of a Buddha, e. g. that he decides to preach on the invitation of the god Brahmā, of a Bodhisattva, or of a disciple; the same conception appears in the case of a stone. Dharma then would mean simply object or thing,[1] without any metaphysical implication of a far-reaching nature. With this accords perfectly the fact that in Buddhism we find an express distinction made between Dhammas as internal (*ajjhattika*) and external (*bāhira*);[2] the former term applies to the mental presentation, the latter to the object which is conceived as the source of the mental presentation. It can hardly be supposed that Buddhism first appreciated things as mental, and then assigned them to an external cause; the obvious interpretation of usage is that the external thing (*dhamma*) was later analysed into the thing proper, and the mental image, an obvious and common step in the history of psychological analysis. The existence of external reality is, history testifies, a primitive view, which was widely spread in the Buddha's time as the activity of materialists[3] testifies, and psychological investigation is a later stage in which existing terms are reconsidered and given new significations.

There is a similar error in interpreting idealistically the signification of Saṁkhāra[4] when used as a synonym of Dhamma of things in general. We should not regard the Saṁkhāras as things in relation to mind (*saṁkhata*); rather the term has the more general signification of product, as well as of producing, and it is therefore naturally and directly applied to the whole world of external reality as well as to mental products. The Vijñānavādins would have us believe that Buddhism was always idealist, but the Madhyamakas deny it energetically, and the early texts bear witness in their favour. It is a heresy to hold that material things endure but for the moment of the thought which apprehends them;[5] the body by reason of its duration is in a sense a truer self than consciousness with its constant change.[6]

[1] For its wide use in this sense see PD., pp. 88 ff. [2] MN. i. 191.

[3] Cf. H. Jacobi, KF., pp. 38 f. with Oldenberg, GN. 1917, pp. 248 ff.; below, ch. vii, § 1.

[4] Geiger, PD., pp. 85 f.; Franke, DN., pp. 307 f.; Beckh, *Buddhismus*, ii. 104 ff.

[5] KV. xxii. 8. [6] SN. ii. 94.

CHAPTER IV

THE PHILOSOPHY OF SPIRIT AND NATURE

1. *The Negation of the Self*

The strong divergence of views between the Buddhist schools on the doctrine of the self suggests inevitably the conclusion that the teaching of the master was deficient in clearness of expression, and that the way was left open for the development of divergence of opinion. We may readily believe that the Buddha's chief aim was to teach men to end their misery, and that he laid stress on the negation of the self in the sense that he recognized that for man to aim directly at the welfare of his self is the surest means of defeating the end of attaining that absence of desire which means, in the Buddhist view, happiness. The most effective therapeutic against the folly of seeking to gratify longings was the realization that there was no truth in the doctrine of a permanent self.

However this may be, the Pali Canon treats the doctrine earnestly and seriously, making no concession, voluntarily at least, to the doctrine of the self, for we may, of course, dismiss mere popular expressions, which it would have been impossible to eradicate from the language. It is impossible to understand the arguments to prove this result without realizing that the conception of a self accepted from older speculation by the Buddhists treated it as permanent, possessed of bliss, and autonomous; the Buddhist contention is that nothing empirical can possibly be endowed with these characteristics, and that, therefore, nothing empirical is the self. In another form the argument takes the shape of a contention that, whatever is permanent, cannot be subject to modification, and stress is laid also on the moral argument; all misery arises from the delusion of self which causes man to strive to profit himself and to injure others.

The doctrine of the characteristics of the non-ego are effectively set out in the sermon at Benares;[1] matter cannot be the self, for if it were, then the body would not be subject to disease and one would be able to control one's body at pleasure, the self being assumed as autonomous. The same argument is applied to the other four aggregates constituting the spiritual nature of man, the feelings, perceptions, dispositions, and intellect; in each case they cannot be equated with the self. Then it is pointed out that the body is shifting and ever in change, and that it therefore is ever accompanied by misery; accordingly it cannot be the self, and the same argument is then repeated of the other aggregates. Then, it is added, when a man realizes that all these things are not the self he turns away from them and by the extinction of desire he attains release. An interesting form of the argument is given in the Mahānidāna Sutta of the *Dīgha Nikāya*,[2] where three hypotheses are selected for investigation. The first is that the soul is feeling; to this it is replied that feelings are threefold pleasant, painful, and neutral; that they are impermanent, succeeding one another; and that they are products and certain to pass away. If then, when a pleasant feeling is experienced, the conclusion is arrived at: 'This is my soul;' then when a painful feeling supersedes it one must conclude: 'My soul has passed away'. To call, therefore, feeling the self is to make out as self a thing which is impermanent, blended of happiness and pain, and liable to begin and end. Secondly, the hypothesis is made that the soul is neither feeling nor is insentient—that is, doubtless, the soul and the body are identical. But this contention is defeated by the simple consideration that where there is no feeling it is impossible to say: 'I am'; that is, a soul without self-reference has no meaning. Thirdly, the soul is regarded as not identical with feeling but as possessing feeling; but this doctrine is also rejected, on the ground that, were feeling of every kind to cease absolutely, then, there being, owing to the cessation, no feeling whatever, no one could say: 'I myself am.' Therefore, the conclusion is drawn, one should lay aside these false views of the self, and thus save oneself from desire and attain complete rest. The same doctrine appears in a tedious

[1] MV. i. 6. 38 ff. [2] ii. 66 ff.

scholastic form in the other Nikāyas,[1] where, by the use of permutations and combinations, twenty theories of the possible identification of the soul with one or more or all the five aggregates are enunciated and disapproved. A dialogue between Sāriputta and Yamaka in the *Saṁyutta Nikāya* develops the same theme; the self is not to be found in any of the aggregates or in their combination, and the realization of this has the usual practical effect of leading a man to final peace. The doctrine is consistently carried out; when the Buddha is asked who has feeling or other sensation, his answer is to point out that he does not assert that any one feels, but that there is feeling, which is a totally different proposition. Similarly it is not correct to ask who undergoes old age and rebirth.[2] Indeed, if one is to assert that anything is the self, it is really more correct to give the name to the body, for that may endure for as much as a hundred years, while consciousness in all its forms is impermanent, in constant flux, comparable to the ape in the forest which seizes one branch, only to let it go and grasp another.[3] The constant change is illustrated by the metaphors of the fire or the movement of water.[4]

Interesting and drastic form is given to the idea in a saying of the nun Vajirā, who was approached by the tempter Māra and asked: 'By whom is the person (*satta*) produced? Who is the creator of the person? Where is the person who comes into being? Where is the person who disappears?' The nun is too wise to be misled by the tempter; she points out firmly that there is no such thing as a person, but merely a collection of changing aggregates, and she illustrates her meaning by the simile of the chariot, which is merely the name for a collection of various parts. The doctrine forms the subject of deliberate elaboration in the *Milindapañha*, where the king is instructed by Nāgasena by means of the parallel of the chariot, and shows that the name Nāgasena denotes no soul, but is merely an appellation of the five aggregates which constitute the empirical individual.[5]

[1] MN. i. 138, 300; SN. iii. 66; iv. 34; Vin. i. 13.

[2] SN. ii. 13; 62. [3] SN. ii. 94 f.

[4] Cf. MV. i. 21; SN. i. 133; iv. 392 f.; and iv. 157. So in Herakleitos.

[5] SN. i. 135; Mil., pp. 25 ff., where Walleser's re-arrangement of rôles (PGAB., p. 120) is clearly wrong.

There is, indeed, no doubt that for the Canon the position is essential and fundamental, though we cannot say that it was really so for the Buddha himself. But it was obviously difficult even for the early teachers of the orthodox doctrine to make the tenet which denies any soul fit effectively the doctrine that there is recompense of deeds; such recompense no empirical observer could dream of placing normally in this world, but the reward or punishment must come later. The early Buddhists accepted this idea of the continuance of existence in some sense or another; they denied energetically the doctrine of utter destruction, which was evidently current in their day, and the chain of causation is a theoretical explanation of the mode in which the continuance of existence is carried on. But, granting the truth of the doctrine of the act (*karman*), are we to reconcile it with the absence of a self? Naturally it was not left to western scholarship 'to attempt to find a loop-hole through which at least a covert or esoteric belief in the soul and in future life (that is, of course, of a soul) can be recognized, in some sort of way, as part of so widely accepted a religious system'.[1] Honest disciples were evidently perplexed, and no wonder, at the discrepancy of the two teachings; if there were no self, was this not equivalent to destroying effectively the whole basis of the doctrine of action?

It cannot be said that the attitude adopted in reply by the Buddha of the Canon is precisely satisfying. He is asked: 'If the body is not the self; if feeling, perception, dispositions, and intellect are not the self, then who is affected by the works which the not-self has performed?' The Buddha reproves the questioner: 'Shall one who is under the dominion of desire think to go beyond the mind of the master?'[2] A little more definite is the result achieved in the case of the monk Sāti, who[3] though an adherent of the faith, 'went so far as to tell the Buddha that he must, as he admitted transmigration, have meant that the Viññāna did not really depend upon, was not really bound up with, the body, but that it formed the link in transmigration. In perhaps the most earnest and emphatic of

[1] Rhys Davids, SBB. ii. 189. [2] SN. iii. 103.
[3] MN. i. 256 ff.; SBB. ii. 87, n. 3.; Mrs. Rhys Davids, *Buddh. Psych.*, pp. 15 f.

all the Dialogues, the Buddha meets and refutes at length this erroneous representation of his view.' But there are defects in the refutation, which is certainly earnest enough. Sāti maintains that consciousness or intellect (*viññāna*) transmigrates without alteration (*anañña*), while the Buddha argues that consciousness comes, e.g., from the eye and coloured matter in the case of visual cognition (*cakkhu-viññāna*), and similarly in other cases. Now, if we are to understand, as does Professor Rhys Davids, this argument as disposing of the idea of some permanent or continuing element in transmigration, we are compelled to assume that the Buddha adopts the doctrine that from the eye and coloured matter there is produced consciousness without any previous consciousness existing. Such a doctrine, it is clear, if pressed, inevitably leads us to the conclusion of Ajita Kesakambalin which asserts the destruction of the self at death, or to the heresy of Makkhali Gosāla, which denies the existence of the act.[1]

It will not do to rescue the Buddha at such a cost, and the true solution appears to lie in recognizing that the error of Sāti was not in asserting that consciousness transmigrated, but in asserting that it transmigrated unchanged (*anañña*). This accords in fact excellently with certain other passages which are evidently orthodox. In the *Saṁyutta Nikāya*[2] the Buddha denies equally the doctrines: 'He who feels is identical with the feeling' or the reverse; 'The soul is identical with the body' or the reverse; 'All exists' or the reverse; 'He who acts reaps the result' and 'One acts; another reaps', declaring that his doctrine is a mean, and enunciating as the solution the well-worn chain of causation. Now the chain of causation explains clearly enough the possibility of change in the consciousness, for it does not contemplate an autonomous consciousness persisting unchanged, but allows the determination of its content by extraneous objects of consciousness, which, of course, adequately show that there is alteration. To what extent, of course, this argument was realized fully in the Canon is uncertain; but, if this view be accepted, it has the great merit of explaining

[1] For these schools see ch. vii, § 1; for the doctrine of consciousness, ch. x, § 3. Cf. Poussin, JA. 1902, ii. 262, 281, n. 2.

[2] ii. 75 f.; 17, 20, 23, 60; iii. 135; TDC., p. 60. Cf. also AN. iv. no. 77; MA. i. 6; MKV., p. 269.

the assertion in the Mahānidāna Sutta[1] that there is descent of the consciousness into the womb of the mother preparatory to rebirth. 'The animistic implication adhering to this term (i. e. descent: *okkamissatha*) would, of course, have no significance for Buddhist doctrine,' we are assured, but the assurance appears to beg the question, and is certainly not effectively supported by the fact that Buddhaghosa adds the qualification 'so to speak'. There are in fact two different points involved, and, even accepting Buddhaghosa's addition, only one of them is affected. The phrase 'descent of the consciousness' certainly implies a continuity of consciousness between the old and the new lives, and it may imply that this consciousness was accompanied by some form of body, if we take the word 'descent' literally; in fact the schools differed on this point,[2] and Buddhaghosa is consistent with his own view in negating the question of a corporeal accompaniment of the consciousness. But this has nothing to do with the far more important animistic implication, namely, that there is a continuity of consciousness, which the Buddha seems frankly to admit. The conclusion gathers strength from the amusing tale of the worthy Godhika,[3] whose suicide is approved in the Canon because disease prevented his successful maintenance of trance. The evil Māra is represented in the form of smoke as searching for the rebirth consciousness of the sage, but as failing to find it, since it has utterly disappeared with his attainment of Nirvāṇa. Here again, if we press the idea, we have a visible consciousness that is—one with some sort of material body—but, letting this point pass as fanciful, we still have absolutely clearly the assertion of some measure of continuity, and nothing but an absolute disinclination to depart from a cherished theory can explain the attempts to get rid of the incident as a form of Buddhist humour, a device which has been seriously overworked. The truth is that there is a consistent body of evidence proving that even in the early school there was a recognition of the necessity of finding some

[1] DN. ii. 63; SBB. iii. 60, n. 1; cf. SN. ii. 13, 91, 101.
[2] See below, ch. xi, § 2.
[3] SN. i. 120 ff.; cf. ii. 66; iii. 124; Mrs. Rhys Davids, *Buddh. Psych.*, p. 21; JRAS. 1903, p. 590. Cf. DN. iii. 332 ff. On former births, cf. DN. i. 81; *Itivuttaka*, p. 99.

means of continuity if the doctrine of the act were not to fall into disrepute, and if remembrance of former births were to be possible.

There is, indeed, strong proof of this in the *Milindapañha*,[1] a text of unblemished orthodoxy, in which the question of continuity and moral responsibility is energetically put. The text asserts with extreme precision the doctrine that the only individual is the collection of changing aggregates, but it recognizes the necessity of continuity, and for this it provides by the doctrine of the continuity of consciousness in change throughout life and on to the next life, the death and the new life being made simultaneous. The idea is helped out by a wealth of illustration; the milk turns to curds, butter, ghee; the being transmigrates neither as the same nor as another. It is hardly necessary to emphasize the point; the most orthodox of texts finds it necessary to supply a real link of connexion and does so with fair effect, a result later more completely achieved in the Sautrāntika school.[2]

2. *Personalist Doctrines*

Although the doctrine which denied a self was certainly orthodox, from the point of view of the Pali Canon, it is certain that other Buddhists were perfectly contented with the conception of a true person (*pudgala*) which for all practical purposes may be regarded as an effective self. We need not accept from them, any more than we do from the advocates of the not-self, the view that their opinion was precisely that of the Buddha; it is sufficient to accept the obvious fact that they represent one branch of the early Buddhist belief, although not the branch which finally prevailed in the philosophical schools. It is important to note that the comment on the *Kathāvatthu*, where the heresy of the belief in a person occupies the first place, ascribes the doctrine to the Sammitiyas and the Vajjiputtakas within the schools and to many teachers outside the Buddhist community; the Vajjiputtakas are reckoned in the orthodox tradition as the first of the seceders, a valuable hint of the antiquity of their doctrine.

[1] pp. 40 ff. [2] See below, ch. ix. § 3.

The hint is confirmed by the occurrence in the *Saṁyutta Nikāya*[1] of the Sūtra of the burden-bearer. We learn there of the bearer of the burden, the burden, the taking up of the burden, and the laying down of the burden; the burden is the five aggregates viewed as modes of clinging to existence (*upādāna*); the taking up is desire which leads to rebirth; the depositing is the laying aside of desire; the bearer is the individual the person (*pudgala*) of such and such a family. He, it is, who on enlightenment, having laid aside his heavy burden, does not take up another, but attains Nirvāṇa. Now it is possible to explain away the Sūtra, as do Buddhaghoṣa, Vasubandhu, Candrakīrti, and Yaçomitra; but it is equally obvious that it is mere explaining away, and that the author of the Sūtra did not entertain the view that the person is nothing save the five aggregates as these authorities insist, and all those who maintain that the Sūtra accepts a person are justified, including Uddyotakara who argues from it that the Buddhists in accepting the doctrine of the non-ego were contradicting their own master. To say that the aggregates are the bearer is to contradict the text, and the preservation of the doctrine of the person in the Canon is the most striking proof of its authenticity.

There are other passages which permit of a similar rendering; the Buddha declares there are four kinds of persons, he who applies himself to the good of another not of the self, &c.;[2] the self is declared to be the lord of the self, the witness of its good and evil, in the *Dhammapada*,[3] and it is clearly no adequate answer to argue that the self is nothing but the thought (*citta*), for that is merely a question of phraseology. What we recognize in such expressions is the fact that there is a dominant element in the individual, the object of taming, and we find in the *Milinda-pañha*[4] the analogous conception in the intellectual sphere; the intelligence (*viññāna*) is compared with the guardian of a city, who,

[1] iii. 25; cf. AKV. 474 b5 (Burnouf, *Intr.*, p. 507); Minayeff, *Recherches*, p. 225, n. 2; BCAP. ix. 73; NV., p. 342; Poussin, JRAS. 1901, p. 308; JA. 1902, ii. 266 ff.; Hardy, JRAS. 1901, p. 573.

[2] AN. ii. 95; PP., p. 54; KV. comm., p. 8.

[3] 160 compared in AKV. and BCAP. with 35: *cittassa damanaṁ sādhu*; MKV., p. 354.

[4] p. 62.

seated at the cross roads, watches the coming of men from diverse directions.

The contention of the personalists is supported by arguments of a dialectical character; they appeal, of course, to the obvious difficulty of any real action of Karman if it is held that the individual who suffers is not he who sinned; but they use also the contention[1] that the Buddha would not have condemned the proposition that the Tathāgata does not exist in Nirvāṇa, unless the Nirvāṇa were existence, and they contend, of course, that Nirvāṇa is real, which doubtless accords with the general tone of the Canon itself. Another scholastic contention is based on the refusal of the Buddha to answer the questions: 'Is the Jīva the same as the body? Is the Jīva different from the body?' In its original sense the questions may have referred to the issue of the identity of the vital principle (*jīvitendriya*) and the body; but the argument of the personalists treats it as applying to the person (*pudgala*) and the five aggregates, and they contend that, if the person were really no more than an insecure method of describing the five aggregates, the Buddha must have accepted as correct the identification of the Jīva and the body. They can appeal also to such declarations as the doctrine that the doer of the deed is neither the same as, nor different from the sufferer of the penalty; the person who has a sensation is neither the same as nor different from the sensation.[2] Similarly the person is neither identical with the aggregates, nor yet is he distinct from them; the relationship is properly described as ineffable (*avācya*), a position which forms the subject of attack by the Madhyamaka as well as by Vasubandhu.[3] Its merits, however, are obvious; it mediates, in the best Buddhist manner, between phenomena with a basis and the permanent unchanging self of the Brahmanic tradition. It accords also, though the point seems not to have been noted,

[1] Poussin, *Bouddhisme*, p. 162 citing Nāgārjuna on MK. xxii. 13, but Walleser's trs. does not give this.

[2] SN. ii. 20, 23, 61, 76.

[3] MKV., p. 283 (cf. p. 64, n. 3); BCAP. ix. 60; Wassilieff, *Bouddhisme*, pp. 252, 270; the Saṁkrāntivādins appear (p. 258) as antiphenomenalists; MA. vi. 146; AKV. in Poussin, p. 163, n. 2 (theory of Vātsīputrīyas Sāmmitīyas).

with the position asserted by Sāriputta in his discussions with Sāti,[1] for there we find that the Tathāgata is declared neither to be the five aggregates nor to be different from them. In truth the doctrine of the purely phenomenal self was one which presented interminable difficulties, and it is characteristic of the lack of serious attempt to deal with these difficulties in the orthodox school that the Canon makes no effort on its own doctrine to explain the phenomena of memory, leaving the problem for later definition.

3. *The Empirical Self and the Process of Consciousness*

The account of the empirical self given in the Canon is in the highest degree naïve, and, if it is an advance on earlier thought, that is merely because in the Upaniṣads mysticism pervades the ideas, and observation is at a discount. The possibility of precise and effective observation in Buddhism was in large measure annulled by the ethical aspect given to all psychical states; throughout Buddhist philosophy states of mind are looked at as essentially good or bad, a point of view which is fatal to precise psychology.

As we have seen it is difficult to form any precise picture of the nature of consciousness as it appeared to early Buddhism; that it was an 'intermittent series of psychic throbs associated with a living organism beating out their coming to know through one brief span of life' is a conjecture[2] based on the instruction of Sāti alone, and doubtless misrepresents that text. No other passage in the Canon even suggests that thought is to be treated as an intermittent series of thought-flashes or of mental electrification of the organism. We are, in fact, in the presence of primitive ideas, and to interpret them in the terms of modern psychology is fundamentally to misrepresent, though doubtless largely to improve, the doctrine of the Canon.

Intellect (*viññāna*) is undoubtedly the chief term which comprehensively covers mental phenomena in the Canon, as might be

[1] MN. i. 256 ff.

[2] Mrs. Rhys Davids, *Buddh. Psych.*, p. 16, whose collection of matter is as valuable as her theories, dominated by an obsolescent psychology, are unsubstantial; cf. Barth, RHR. xlii. 72.

expected from the earlier Brahmanical tendency to use the word in this generic way. It represents such unity as there is in the self of experience. Synonymous with Viññāna, according to Buddhaghosa and to usage, are Citta and Manas, but there are obvious preferences in use; Viññāna often occurs in special connexion with sense cognition; Manas again is, in accordance with Brahmanical usage, preminently the intellectual function of consciousness, and Citta the introspective aspect of self-examination, but these are only nuances. From Brahmanical tradition the compound Nāma-rūpa serves to denote spirit and matter, specialized normally to denote the concrete individual, in which both are united, while the old term self (*attā*) constantly occurs in those phrases which are the source of its reflexive use in grammar, when the person is divided mentally into a dominant part and its object.

By a division,[1] which seems to have no precedent in Brahmanical texts, and which has certainly no merit, logical or psychological, the individual is divided into five aggregates or groups (*khandha*), the Sanskrit equivalent of which means 'body' in the phrase Dharmaskandha in the *Chāndogya Upaniṣad.* The first is Rūpa, which denotes simply matter, or material quality, and covers the elements and their compounds; the term aggregate has obviously considerable appropriateness as applied to the complex admixture which makes up the human body, and it is clearly absurd to infer from it any conception of constant dynamic conditions in the body, which, indeed, is treated by the Canon as relatively stable and long-lived.

Of the four psychical aggregates the first in the stereotyped order is feeling (*vedana*), a term wide enough to cover sensation but predominantly indicative of pleasure or pain. But, in addition to these two aspects of feeling, there is recognized a third which is neutral; pleasure has stationariness as pleasant, change as unpleasant, the opposite applies to pain, while neutral feeling has knowledge as pleasant, ignorance as unpleasant, a statement which is not enlightening. The psychological heresy of neutral feeling is prompted doubtless by ethical considerations, for it is

[1] Beckh (*Buddhismus*, ii. 81 f.) compares the three imperfect conceptions of self as body, made of mind, and made of ideas (*saññā*) in DN. i. 195 ff.

the aim of man in his process of attaining perfection to rid himself of all positive feeling of any kind. The term aggregate applied to feeling is obviously intended to indicate that the individual is constantly experiencing one feeling after another.

Perception (*saññā*), covers both sense-perception and the wider form of perception which takes place, not through the sense, but by the agency of mind; the former in the technical terminology of the *Vibhaṅga* is resistance-perception (*paṭigha-saññā*), the latter designative perception (*adhivacana-saññā*), denoting, for instance, the understanding through speech of the mental state of another, although an alternative interpretation assigning to this form of perception the giving of names to objects cognized by sense is suggested by Vasubandhu.[1] The term aggregate here is presumably collective, but the mention of Saññā along with Viññāna is otiose and decisive proof of the lack of psychological interest or acumen of the observers.

Fourth in the complex is the aggregate of dispositions (*saṁkhāra*), a term which is explained as denoting that which compounds what is composed, whether matter or psychic, a definition peculiarly without value. The vagueness of the term is illustrated in the Abhidhamma,[2] where some fifty mental constituents are subsumed under it, and generally any other causally induced incorporeal phenomena exclusive of the other three psychic aggregates. The root conception is doubtless the impressions resulting in dispositions,[3] predispositions or latent tendencies, which will bear fruition in action in due course, but in the Abhidhamma at any rate it covers will, attention, application, concentration, zest, faith, energy,

[1] AKB., pp. 50 f.; above ch. iii. § 1. This simple sense is found e.g. MN. i. 293; Mil., p. 61; Asl., p. 110; the term, however, also denotes higher mental activity; its ambiguity is due to the complex function of mind in sense-perception and higher ideation; cf. Oldenberg VWW., pp. 69 ff. In SN. v. 315 resistance-perception is asserted of internal and external things (*dhammas*).

[2] Below, ch. x. § 4.

[3] The denial of this in *Kindred Sayings*, i. 158, n. 4 is clearly invalid, Cf. Aung, *Compendium*, pp. 273 ff. where they are treated as concomitants performing their respective functions in combination. When applied to matter (*rūpa*) physical causes are, of course, meant: the interpolation of 'mental' in the trans. of the comm. in *Buddh. Psych.*, p. 51 makes nonsense of the comment, and is wholly illegitimate, agreeing as it does with Franke's (DN., pp. 307 ff.) view of Saṁkhāras as ideas only.

mindfulness, insight, rectitude, modesty, discretion, disinterestedness, no covetousness, no malice, grasp and balance and various other groups. The explanation is simple enough; the category, having a vague sense, served effectively to cover all those mental activities for which the division had no obvious and convenient place; but it hardly needs remark that such a procedure is at once proof of the paralysing effect of tradition, and proof of lack of psychological interest. Dispositions, however, it must be remembered may be physical as well as mental, and the term Saṁkhāra in the sense of product of disposition is used, like Dhamma, to apply to the empirical world as consisting of compounded things. In psychic application the term aggregate is obviously wholly appropriate.

The last aggregate is Viññāna, and, as it is credited with appreciation of feeling as well as perceptive power, it is clear that, even in this collection of terms, it practically is wide enough to include both perception and feeling. This is admitted in a dialogue in the *Majjhima*,[1] and no defence of the failure to revise the fivefold division seems possible, unless we accept the hint of Buddhaghosa which suggests that the breaking of intellect into four aggregates was intended to emphasize the doctrine of non-ego. But in their account of Viññāna the early teachers do develop a more elaborate psychology of perception than is found in the Upaniṣads, which were concentrated on fundamental philosophical issues and not on empirical psychology. But we must not exaggerate their defects as compared with the Canon.[2] The senses had already been distinguished and enumerated as five, although those of smell, taste, and touch are subordinated in consequence to that of sight, and touch in particular is not accorded its due importance. But the idea of a central unity, with its abode in the heart, by which sense-impressions are co-ordinated and comprehended, is enunciated, and it is possible that the question of the comparative activity of sense or sense-object had raised interest. In Buddhism, if we find more interest in the object than in the subject, the value of

[1] i. 292 f.

[2] Mrs. Rhys Davids, *Buddh. Psych.*, pp. 57 ff.; Oldenberg, VWW., pp. 69 ff., 83 f.

psychological investigation was marred by the love of symmetry which involves the determination to fit each sense into the same mould, in place of allowing each its appropriate distinctions.

The canonical[1] doctrine of perception runs: 'Depending on eye, in consequence of visible matter (*rūpa*) arises eye-consciousness; the concourse of the three is contact; on account of contact arises feeling', and then the remaining psychical aggregates are enumerated or some equivalent of mental development, as for instance in the *Milindapañha* the series after contact is given as feeling, perception or idea, thought or will (*cetanā*), abstraction or concentration (*ekaggatā*), sense of vitality (*jīvitindriya*) and attention (*manasikāra*).[2] Occasionally the matter is simplified by making the contact of two factors only, the eye and visible matter in the case of sight.[3] The third factor involved is clearly, as later discussion suggests, the consciousness, which is always an essential part of the individual, in the form of attention directed towards the eye,[4] and, when this aspect is omitted, we may assume that it is done merely for the sake of simplicity, not as deliberate modification of the theory, or that it was believed that the physical contact of matter could create intelligence. The theory is plainly one of naïve realism; two physical contacts presided over by consciousness operating in the appropriate sphere produce the mental results of feeling; perception; disposition, in the shape doubtless, if we may supplement the texts, of an impression of the precept, its feeling aspect and volitional reaction; and consciousness. In

[1] SN. ii. 72; iv. 68, 86; MN. iii. 281 ff.; Sumañg. i. 183. Later analysis adds light and space (*Çālistamba* in MKV., p. 567) or (KV. i. 6. 23 f.) light (cf. NP., p. 80). Cf. SDS., p. 16; Poussin TDC., pp. 20 f.; Oldenberg, *Buddha*[5], p. 271; MV. i. 21; AK. iii. 2. In the case of mental perception, mind serves as sense and act of attention.

[2] Mil., p. 56; at p. 60 the series after *cetanā* has initial and applied attention (*vitakka, vicāra*) to which p. 63 adds consciousness (*viññāna*). See also DS. 62 (i–vi); ch. x. § 4; SN. ii. 244 f.; iii. 225 ff. has desire; DN. ii. 308 ff. also both forms of attention.

[3] MN. i. 111 f.; 256 f. (ch. iv. § 1); SN. ii. 97; that this is not seriously meant is shown in SN. iv. 67, for at 68 the three appear, and Mil., p. 60 has two, but p. 56 the three. Curiously enough the point is ignored in *Buddh. Psych.*, pp. 63 f.; *Psych. Ethics*, p. 5, n. 2. The estimate of the value of Buddhist psychology in *Buddh. Psych.*, p. 61 is not to be taken seriously.

[4] MN. i. 190 has *samanvāhāra*, act of attention; so MK. xxvi. 4, 5; KV. i. 6. 23 f. has attention and a physical medium, e.g. light; in the case of mind it is *vatthu* which Geiger (PD., p. 81) would render 'matter' in general.

the process of consciousness falls the essential aspect of the work of mind; the five senses, of which in the Canon sight and hearing preserve their old pre-eminence, touch being still ignored as of primary value, have separate spheres and do not interfere one with another; mind, however, is their resort and shapes their field and range;[1] in more modern terminology it succeeds immediately to simple visual cognition and produces an apparent unity and simultaneity in the perceptions which we have. Mind also is the active element in the perception or comprehension of ideas as opposed to sense-precepts. But, though central and special in function, it often ranks simply as if it were a sixth sense, and it has a physical basis, undefined in the Canon, just like a sense.

Detailed effective analysis of the sense apparatus is lacking; the idea of doors of sense appears only metaphorically, and is suggested by the 'openings (*suṣayaḥ*)' of the Upaniṣads, and the question of the knowledge of like by like is not touched upon expressly until Buddhaghosa, and does not appear to be known to the early schools. The lack of curiosity is explained effectively by their pre-occupation with ethical considerations, and secondarily by the lack of positive science in the contemporary intellectual sphere. Amid the many allusions to human activities in the Canon we hear of practically nothing scientific, save the pseudo-science of astrology and the practical art of medicine, which unquestionably deeply coloured the outlook and method of the Buddha as the great healer of human evils. It is this preoccupation with ethical needs which explains the psychological laxity which uses the term Dukkha to denote psychological feeling as painful, and the misery of the world which is implicit in pleasure, if that is the pleasure of the senses leading on to rebirth. But importance certainly attaches to the recognition of the fact that feeling is inseparably bound up with perception.

Of the process of ideation the Canon has nothing systematic to tell. Initial consideration (*vitakka*) is distinguished from further

[1] MN. i. 295; SN. v. 218; cf. MKV., p. 33; VM. in Warren, p. 297; Asl., p. 400; KV. xviii. 9; Wassilieff, *Bouddhisme*, p. 280. See also Therag. 804 ff.; DN. ii. 338; MN. iii. 300; SN. v. 74; AN. v. 30; Mil., pp. 54, 86; KV. ii. 7. 5; PD., p. 81.

reflective investigation (*vicāra*); attention (*manasikāra*) and reflection are insisted upon, while ethical considerations emphasize the importance of mindfulness (*sati*) which is also associated with memory as the condition of it, but there is no attempt to explain memory. Self awareness, deliberate intellectual activity leading to self possession (*sampajañña*) is also important in an ethical aspect, while in other terms regarding investigation stress rests on the element of volitional effort in inquiry (*vicaya, vīmaṁsā, cintā*). Ethical again is the motive which discourages such deliberate speculation (*cintā*) on the range of Buddhaship, the intuitive powers of one sunk in meditative ecstacy, the working of the act, and the nature of the world.[1] For higher intellectual activity we find the terms gnosis (*jñāna*) and insight (*paṇṇā*), the latter fated to be deified in the later conception, but either term may be used of inferior knowledge. In Jhāna and Samādhi we have forms of that deep concentration in meditation which are essential elements in the latter stages of the path of salvation. Their importance is great, and like the other terms for the higher knowledge they indicate the essential nature of such knowledge, an intuition of the whole quite distinct from a discursive process of reasoning.

The view of intuition as the source of true knowledge, and at the same time a decisive cause of emancipation from rebirth is characteristic of Buddhism as of the Upaniṣads, and explains why in neither do we find any serious contribution to epistemology. The Buddha, like the sage of the Upaniṣad, sees things as they truly are (*yathābhūtaṁ*) by a mystic potency, which is quite other than reasoning of the discursive type. The truth of his insight is assured by it alone, for it is obviously incapable of verification in any empirical manner. But the Canon does not treat intuition (*paññā*) as being wholly distinct from, and unconnected with, discursive knowledge; not only does the term continue to be used for the lower forms of knowledge, but stress[2] is laid on the fact that intuition is intimately connected with intelligence (*viññāna*), perception (*saññā*), and feeling, or, as it is elsewhere put, it is allied to deliberate and searching mental appreciation (*yoniso*

[1] *Buddh. Psych.*, pp. 92 f.; AN. iv. no. 77.
[2] MN. i. 292 ff.; *Buddh. Psych.*, p. 133.

manasikāra). But from intelligence intuition differs by reason that the former is to be understood, the latter to be cultivated and developed; in other words, by means of exercises of concentration, which form an essential part of the way of salvation, a high degree of intuitive power is to be attained, surpassing any mere understanding, a condition styled also complete knowledge (*pariññā*) and elimination (*pahāna*), the latter characteristic emphasizing the elimination of empirical factors of any kind. It may then be regarded as 'that effort of intellectual sympathy by which the mind can place itself within the mobile reality of things' in Bergsonian phraseology.

Of the psychology of will and the emotions the Canon has almost nothing systematic. The dependence of volition on desire and of desire on feeling is elaborated in the chain of causation but without psychological insight or purpose. The connexion of thought and action is close (*cetanā, saṁcetanā*); thinking, one acts by deed, word, or thought,[1] a distinction of modes emphasizing the element of purpose as essential to characterize the moral quality of action. The planning out of a course of action or deliberate resolve is denoted by Saṁkappa, a fashioning or moulding. The union of intellectual activity with attention and pleasure, the product seems to be denoted by the term Pīti, for which zest is perhaps the best rendering available.

Of emotions we have merely popular classifications especially the threefold divisions into appetite (*lobha*), with its congeners, greed, lust, passion, &c.; aversion (*dosa*) with its congeners, anger, hate, malevolence, &c.; and delusion (*moha*), which is regarded as ignorance or confused consciousness. In the usual schematic fashion there are opposed to these disinterestedness (*alobha*), amity (*adosa*), and intelligence (*amoha*),[2] the last being sometimes treated as equivalent to intuition (*paññā*). But more importance attaches as part of the exercises of the path of salvation to the generation of feelings of friendship or love (*mettā*), of sympathy with suffering (*karuṇā*), and of sympathy with happiness (*muditā*).[3] But these again are treated of as ethical elements, not psychologically.

[1] AN. iii. 415. [2] AN. i. 134 f. [3] AN. i. 183.

4. *Matter and Spirit in the Universe*

On the nature of matter the Canon is practically silent; it accepts from Brahmanical tradition the four elements, earth, fire, air, water; on the vexed question of ether (*ākāsa*) it now counts it with the elements, now omits it from the list, while in the Abhidhamma it is severed from the four elements, which are treated as underived matter, and made a derivate.[1] From the nature of the meditation of the infinity of ether or space, we see that its conception is what remains when all material things are eliminated from the field of experience. In what manner the elements were conceived in early Buddhism there is nothing to show, nor have we any reason to treat as primitive the later atomic view. What is clear is that every material thing is a compound (*saṁkhāra*), which may, as in the case of the body, endure for a long time, but will nevertheless ultimately pass away. Things are impermanent (*anicca*); in early Buddhism they are not literally momentary, a refinement of later thought.

Matter exists not merely externally to us, but also as an aggregate (*khanda*) in the empiric individual; the connexion of body and spirit is clear to the insight of the saint, but it is not explained to us, and doubtless was accepted as an obvious datum, connexion and interaction raising no difficulty. There is no suggestion that matter always forms an aggregate of some spirit; the *Milindapañha*[2] with perfect orthodoxy emphasizes that matter exists as independent of spirit.

The universe consists of innumerable world systems, each equipped with earth, heavens and hells, and each system or sphere is divided into three regions (*avacaras*), worlds (*loka*) or layers (*dhātu*), the first the realm of desire (*kāma*), the next of matter or material form (*rūpa*), the third that without form (*arūpa*).[3] In the first are hells or purgatories eight or more in number, while others exist between the spheres (*lokantarika*; the

[1] DS., §§ 638, 722; *Psych. Eth.*, pp. lviii, lix; MN. i. 423; ii. 17.

[2] pp. 136 f., 271. Cf. KV. xvi. 8; ix. 3; vii. 7, 8; xii. 3, 4, all passages showing matter as independent.

[3] Cf. Kern, *Ind. Buddh.*, pp. 57 ff.; DN. no. 14; i. 195; 34 ff.; 215 ff.; MN. nos. 49, 129; *Suttanipāta*, iii. 10; on Asuras, SN. i. 216 ff.

animal world; the abode of ghosts (*pretas*); the abode of Asuras or demons; which make up the places of punishment (*apāya*); then comes the abode of men and then six abodes of gods (*devalokas*). In the second we have the Brahma-lokas, sixteen in number of sections according to the number of the gods free from desire who abide there; entrance to these is assured to those who practice the four Meditations, and to those who are non-returners among the disciples, and who will therefore attain Nirvāna in heaven in lieu of rebirth on earth.[1] In the world without matter we find the place of those who carry out the Formless Meditations; thus he who frees his mind from any thought save that of infinite space is reborn in such a world, abiding there in that mental condition; he that has attained to infinity of consciousness or intelligence (*viññāna*) abides in such a world; and so with the world of nothingness, and of neither ideation nor non-ideation.

These conceptions are, of course, partly popular, borrowed from the contemporary Brahmanic view of heavens and hells, and partly philosophical in character. The Upaniṣads know a world of Brahmā of celestial delights which is the reward of the soul not yet fitted for emancipation by union with the absolute Brahman; the Buddhists improve upon this idea, and adapt it to the schemes of meditations which they take over from Brahmanism. That these views were accepted as true by disciples as well as the laity we can hardly doubt; the Canon represents the Buddha as visiting the Brahma-loka; he represents himself as having received a visit from Brahmā Sahampati; the gods, Brahmā and Indra especially, play a great part in the tradition, in subordination to the Buddha.[2] Was this irony? Did the Buddha himself, did the disciples know that there were no gods such as the Brahmins feigned? Or did they really believe in these gods, as superior beings, though not immortal, and not differing in essence from men, to whose place all men may strive? The answer must be in favour of their

[1] Matter here is subtle; smell, taste, and touch do not exist, only sight, hearing, and mental co-ordination, KV. viii. 7. The abode of Asuras is denied as separate by KV. viii. 1 against Andhakas and Uttarāpathakas on the strength of MN. i. 73. For the gods as long-lived see AN. ii. 33.

[2] MN. i. 326; 458; AN. ii. 20; iv. 302 ff.; Kern, *Ind. Buddh.*, p. 59; Beckh, *Buddhismus*, ii. 55 ff.

belief, in the absence of a single hint to the contrary in the texts of early Buddhism, and in face of the belief of pious Buddhists throughout the ages. If the master really laughed at these fancies, we must admit that it has been left to us to discover the fact. The course of Buddhist philosophy and religion has advanced under the conviction of the existence of all these beings, and it is not for an age which tolerates spiritualism to attribute greater reason to early India in the centuries before Christianity.

Speculative questions on the infinity and duration of the world are among those to which the Buddha declined any answer; if he faced the problem whether there would still persist matter if all the spirits won liberation, he did not answer it; in all probability the idea never occurred to him.[1] He did believe, we are assured by the whole evidence of the Canon, in the doctrine of the periodic dissolution and re-evolution of the universe or the world systems; there are Aeons of evolution, of dissolution, and of both, an idea developed by Jainism at tedious length. Fanciful pictures of the process of evolution as one of decadence, possibly intended as such, are found in the Canon in the Buddha's mouth, but they contain nothing of interest or value.[2]

Of more interest is the possibility that Buddhism began its philosophical career with a doctrine of six elements, all real, whose interaction explained the existence of the world, to which it added the Nirvāṇa element, the state of release.[3] There was a precedent for this in earlier thought,[4] Pakudha Kaccāyana recognized the ordinary four, the soul, pleasure, and pain, but denied interaction, while Ajita, who asserted four elements only, admitted also tacitly the existence of space, into which the senses, creations of the elements, pass on death. To add the conception of consciousness to the four material elements, to subsume under

[1] Above, ch. ii. § 2; Oldenberg, *Buddha*,[5] p. 387; *lokacintā* is deprecated; AN. iv. no. 77.

[2] DN. i. 17 f.; iii. 85 f.; Mhv. i. 338 ff.; Kuhn, *Festschrift Vilhelm Thomsen*, pp. 214 ff.

[3] *Itivuttaka*, 44, 51, 73; immortal element (*amatā dhātu*), AN. iv. 423 f.; SN. v. 139, 232; AN. iii. 356; Beckh, *Buddhismus*, ii. 54, 124 f. It is, of course, absurd to treat these elements as anything but absolutely real; cf. Aung, *Compendium*, pp. 255 f.

[4] See below, ch. vii. § 1.

it pleasure and pain, and to accept space would be a natural and logical construction. We have direct evidence of it both in the *Aṅguttara* and the *Majjhima Nikāyas*; it accords precisely with the conception of the nature of rebirth described in the *Dīgha Nikāya*, and, with the omission of space, is adopted in the later Pali scholasticism. In any case it is essential to note that early Buddhism in its admission of the four material elements was realistic, and also admitted that physical changes were based on such elemental permanent existences.

The distinction between the elements, in the world and as part of the complex which makes the individual, is well brought out in the *Majjhima*, where the latter are styled as appropriated, taken up, assimilated (*upādinna*); they are the matter which the consciousness assumes as the mode of continuing the existence to which it is bound by its earlier actions.[1]

[1] AN. i. 176; MN. iii. 239 f.; DN. ii. 63; Ç., p. 244; NP., p. 75; Poussin, TDC., pp. 43 f.

CHAPTER V

THE DOCTRINE OF CAUSATION AND THE ACT

1. *Causation*

In striking conflict with the modern suggestion that the real emphasis of the Buddha's teaching lay in the doctrine of causality as pervading all the things of experience, and that his normalism was a new and Copernican revolution of thought, is the meagre and inadequate examination accorded to causation in the Canon. The idea is repeatedly expressed, regularly in the form: 'That being, this becomes; from the appearance of that, this appears; that is to say, by reason of ignorance &c. (*imasmiṁ sati idaṁ hoti; imass' uppādā idaṁ uppajjati; yadidaṁ avijjāpaccayā*).[1] The duplicate character of the formula is explained variously by later scholasticism; it serves at any rate to make clear that the intervention of a substrate in the form of a self is negated. But in any event the extraordinarily imperfect character of the definition is obvious; the first member expresses the idea of an essential condition; the next a coefficient; and the last, the cause of a generation. If, as we are assured, the Buddhist chain of causation was inculcated at least as much for the sake of the idea as for the sake of the conclusion, the explanation of misery, it is incredible that no further analysis should have been attempted. In truth the case is clear; the origin of evil evoked the chain, and interest in causation was wholly subordinate, and this explains the variations and omissions found in the chain. The lover of causation would have insisted on each link; for the practical Buddhist all that was necessary was to show that evil was caused, and the minor details could be left vague.

The vagueness of the conception is reflected in the language

[1] *Udāna*, i. 1; MN. i. 1. 2; SN. ii. 28, 65; MN. i. 262; ii. 32; iii. 63; MKV. p. 9.

which uses without attempt at differentiation a whole series of terms[1] (*hetu, paccaya, nidāna, samudaya, jātika, pabhava, kāraṇa, nimitta, liṅga*). The point is essential, for it explains how in the chain of causation the idea of cause is applied in varying aspects without consciousness of inappropriateness.

2. *The Development of the Chain of Causation*

The insistence on the doctrine of the causation of misery was doubtless in Buddhism inspired by opposition to the pessimism of the Ājīvakas under Makkhali Gosāla, who insisted that purity and depravity arose without cause or condition, that the fate of men depended neither on their own nor others' action or effort; that no human power was efficient, and that all things with life were without inherent force. Ajita also held that there was no fruit of good or evil deeds nor result of the deeds of others or previous lives. Such doctrines[2] were, it is plain, destructive of any orderly conception of existence, and the Buddha's message of deliverance is based on the conviction that misery exists because it is produced and will continue to exist until its process of production can be stopped.

The essence of the doctrine of the causation of misery is expressed in the second noble truth; the cause of the origin of misery is thirst—that is, desire—leading to rebirth, accompanied by pleasure in the object and attachment, taking pleasure here and there, the thirst of lust, the thirst of becoming, the thirst of non-becoming. This brings misery, for it produces, whether directly aimed at rebirth or not, the fact of such rebirth, and, as the first truth assures us, birth, age, death, all the incidents of life, are misery.

This in effect is the kernel of the doctrine, and we may doubt the emphatic assurance of the texts that the Buddha's attainment of enlightenment was closely involved with the gaining of knowledge of this further elaboration in the chain of causation in its stereotyped set of twelve links.[3] The doubt is strengthened

[1] DN. ii. 57; SN. ii. 37, 81; MN. i. 261; *upanisā*, SN. ii. 30; cf. TCD., p. 51, n. 1; it may be for *Upaniṣad*; cf. AKV. (MS. Burn. f. 133^{b}) in MKV., p. 76, n. 7.

[2] Below, ch. vii. § 1.

[3] MV. i. 1; SN. ii. 10.

when we find the germs of the twelve contained in a text of the *Suttanipāta*[1] in which other ancient doctrines are preserved. There we find a set of eleven couples which illustrate the principle of causation: 'That being, this becomes.' In each case misery is the second element; the first are, in order, action which, based on ignorance, leads man to constant rebirth; ignorance; dispositions (*saṁkhāra*), allied to perception (*saññā*); consciousness; contact; feeling; thirst, which leads to grasping (*upādāna*); grasping which leads to becoming (*bhava*), rebirth, death, and misery; efforts; aliments (*āhāra*); and movements. There is here no attempt to erect an elaborate series, but the chain is already largely present in germ. Another text[2] of the same collection traces discord back to desire (*chanda*), based on feeling, based on contact, based on name and form, the empiric individual.

These suggest a simple enough idea; misery as rebirth might have been explained by the individual consciousness under the influence of ignorance and impressions or dispositions, the result of past deeds, entering into contact with the world, receiving thence feelings of pleasure or pain, conceiving thirst or desire leading to action or grasping producing a new becoming. But the classical formula is less simple; it runs in twelve members:[3] 'By reason of ignorance dispositions; by reason of dispositions consciousness (*viññāna*); by reason of consciousness name and form; by reason of name and form contact; by reason of contact feeling; by reason of feeling thirst; by reason of thirst grasping; by reason of grasping becoming; by reason of becoming birth; by reason of birth old age, death, grief, mourning, pain, sorrow, and despair.' The reverse order also applies; the destruction of ignorance serves to set about a chain of destruction as effective as the creation. This is the formula of dependent (literally going-towards) production (*paṭicca-samuppāda*), a term which moves

[1] 724 ff.; SBE. x. 129. The work exists in Sanskrit, JRAS. 1916, pp. 709 ff.
[2] 862 ff.; SBE. x. 159.
[3] DN. ii. 55 ff.; 32 ff. (the first two links are omitted in DN.); MN. i. 49 ff., 261; AN. i. 177; Nidāna S., esp. v. 388; Poussin, TDC.: Oltramare, FBDC.; Beckh, *Buddhismus*, ii. 94 ff.

scholasticism[1] to ask whether the effect goes towards the cause, or the cause to the effect. Frequently as the formula occurs, there are variants from the normal twelve; sometimes the first two elements disappear; in one case the third, fourth, second, and the last two appear in that order, and there are minor variants. The psychological reasons which prompted its development as it stands are uncertain, but there must be taken into account the chain of derivation which is given from the absolute in the *Kaṭha Upaniṣad*, and of which a later development presents itself in the Sāṁkhya system, or the possibility of Yoga influence.[2]

3. *The Links of the Chain*

Ignorance in the chain has, it is certain, a purely limited sense, and no cosmic significance, similar to that of ignorance in the Vedānta, through which the absolute passes into the empirical. It is repeatedly defined, and is always the individual's ignorance of the four noble truths, or an equivalent: the origin and disappearance of the aggregates making up individuality, or the delusion which recognizes a self. Ignorance is traced in the Canon[3] to diverse causes, the five hindrances (*nīvaraṇas*), hankering after the world, the desire to injure, torpor, flurry and worry, and wavering; these are nourished by sins of body, speech and thought; failure to subdue the senses, to note precisely disagreeable impressions, imperfect attention, failure to listen to the law and to frequent the saints. More briefly, it is desire or thirst which produces ignorance, and thirst in turn arises because the feelings which evoke it are permeated by ignorance.[4] Thus we have as long as the one lasts the other; there can be no question of finding a beginning for ignorance, just as in the Sāṁkhya the failure to discriminate between soul and nature leaves an impression on the internal organs which produces in the next birth the same fatal ignorance. Yet, though the cycle is normally unending, ignorance has a right to the title of 'root' given in the

[1] MKV., pp. 5 f.; TDC., pp. 48 f.

[2] Below, ch. vii. § 3.

[3] AN. v. 113 f.

[4] Cf MN. i. 54 f.; ignorance and the defilements (*āsava*) as reciprocal causes; AN. v. 116; NP., pp. 86, 109; VM. in HOS., iii. 171; FBDC., p. 34.

Milindapañha, for it is the link which can be destroyed by the gaining of intuition.

The dispositions which ignorance produces can hardly be misunderstood; they must be interpreted in the same sense as the Saṁskāras of the Sāṁkhya system, in which ignorance creates impressions on the inner organ, which in a future life result in continued ignorance, while the attainment of the saving knowledge prevents the further growth of the seeds of future misery sown in the Saṁskāras or impressions of acts done in ignorance. This leads inevitably to the conclusion that ignorance generates acts which leave impressions on the individual, which result in determining his future existence. This accords well with the position of the dispositions as one of the aggregates of the individual, and with the doctrine that thought takes its stand on the dispositions to last and develop itself, and in so doing it renews them and brings them to fruition in act, word, or deed. Yet it is certain that, although the dispositions are classed as good, bad, or neutral, or in six classes according to the object which evokes them, the regular explanation of their occurrence in the chain is that they are the dispositions of the body, expiration and inspiration; of speech, initial and continued application, as the preliminary conditions of speech; and of thought, ideation or perception (*saññā*),[1] and feeling. To accept this view as valid is impossible; the creation of two such curious bodily complexes alone by ignorance is as amazing as the selection of two elements of thought which in the individual form aggregates side by side with the dispositions, while feeling appears in a position of its own in the chain. Nonetheless, the confusion is significant of the lack of skill of the interpreters of the Canon; the Tibetan translators of the chain have anticipated modern investigators in equating dispositions with action (*karman*), and the Sanskrit scholasticism agrees in this view.

The relation of consciousness to name and form is expressly made out in the *Dīgha Nikāya*;[2] if consciousness did not enter

[1] MN. i. 301; SN. iv. 293; *Vibhaṅga*, p. 135; JPTS. 1886, p. 29; MKV., p. 543; Warren, HOS. iii. 84.

[2] ii. 63; MKV., p. 552.

the womb, there would be no living embryo; if it did not continue there, the embryo would die. The evidence is clear; the action is real; consciousness is even classed with the four elements and ether as an element (*dhātu*);[1] it passes from death to life whether we regard it as quasi-corporeal in itself—for it is visible—or as accompanied by a subtle body, a question which vexed the schools.[2] But it does in no sense create the matter of the body, and it is essentially dependent for its development, rebirth, death, &c., on matter, as it is only in the compound of name and form that it exists. Hence the doctrine that the two stand to each other in the position of two bundles of reeds;[3] consciousness cannot exist save with name and form, and name and form cannot exist without consciousness, the third and fourth links in the chain thus being mutually dependent, a serious enough logical objection to such a chain. Name and form must here, it is clear, represent the individual in whom consciousness is involved with matter; the term is old, taken over from a more primitive thought when the name was treated as if it were a possession and part of the individual. The logical interpretation of the term must be that of later scholasticism;[4] the form is matter, the name is the other four aggregates, feeling, perception or ideation, dispositions, and consciousness itself, but, doubtless to make the causal series more logical, an early text takes name as feeling, ideation, will, contact, and attention, and later authorities equate it with the three aggregates other than consciousness itself. The vital fact remains that it essentially represents the union of consciousness with matter to form the individual; whence, if one causes the other, it nonetheless is dependent upon it; but the causal relation is expressed as it is because matter cannot be said to evoke consciousness; there is matter without connexion with consciousness and when they coexist the initiative lies with consciousness. The chain, it must be added, must not be understood as asserting here an

[1] AN. i. 176; MN. iii. 239; cf. ch. vii. § 1.

[2] Below, ch. xi. § 2. Cf. SN. ii. 66, 90, 101 as to name and form in transmigration; iii. 46, 56, the senses.

[3] SN. ii. 104; DN. ii. 63.

[4] AK. iii. 30; Ç., p. 222; DS. § 1309; *Vibhaṅga*, p. 136. See SN. ii. 3; MN. i. 33.

invariable relation, for at a high stage of development consciousness is reborn in the formless or immaterial sphere where matter is not.

The power which drives the consciousness to its new birth and determines its form is that of action; on this topic the Canon is emphatic and as clear as the nature of the subject permits; the force of action cannot be evaded by any device; excuses are vain; punishment is certain and inevitable, save only if the necessary intuition is found to break the chain of existence; then, though the law of action is broken for the future, the deeds of the past must be worked out in a form in which their seriousness is lost; the man guilty of many murders is repaid by a few blows. This suggests that between consciousness and dispositions there is a transition from the old to a new life.

The six sense organs are viewed in a double light; the first five, eye, ear, smell, taste, touch, are material but invisible, thus being distinguished from the fleshy organ in which they reside; they function by resistance contact (*paṭigha*); the same term (*āyatana*) is used for the objects as spheres or fields of sense in another aspect of the word; these objects are material and external.[1] The mind is immaterial, invisible, not affected by resistance contact; it is composed of a mind element of obscure character and has a physical basis of some sort; its objects are both exterior objects mediated by the other senses and ideas.[2] The relation of the six senses to name and form is simple; they really represent them in another formulation, as the texts[3] show which omit from the list either the six senses or both consciousness and name and form.

Contact is the mediation between the senses and their objects, and is of high importance in the theory of cognition; the fairest rendering is that it denotes the collision or co-operation of the attention aspect of consciousness directed to the organ in connexion with an object; the scholastics interpret it as denoting

[1] MKV., p. 126, n. 1; Ç., p. 250, n. 3; *Psych. Eth.*, p. 173; TDC., pp. 18 f.; SN. iv. 175.

[2] The mind element seems indistinguishable from the consciousness element, mind being essentially consciousness; cf. *Buddh. Psych.*, p. 19. Cf. SN. iv. 1 ff.; *Yamaka*, i. 52 ff.; PD., pp. 80 ff.

[3] *Suttanipāta*, 870; DN. ii. 62; SN. ii. 13; iii. 46, 94.

the consciousness resulting from the contact, and not the contact itself.

Feeling, as pleasant, painful, or neutral, is the outcome of contact, simultaneous to it in the canonical view, though later thought distinguishes the moments of contact, sensation production, and feeling. Though distinguished from cognition it must have a cognitive aspect, for contact is the application of consciousness to the knowledge of an object, and in harmony with this the *Milindapañha* makes contemporaneous with feeling perception, conceived intention, initial and sustained application and consciousness, while their intermixture is asserted in the Canon itself.

Thirst is born of feeling, but only in the case of the unenlightened man whose ignorance renders his feeling a danger; the saint has feelings but not thirst. Thirst in its turn nourishes ignorance, for it produces the delusive conception of being. It is of six kinds, according to the sense organs and objects; triple as thirst for union with pleasant feeling, for severance from painful feeling, and as desire not to be parted from that neutral feeling which marks states of meditation in which there is no pleasure or pain but which tend to Nirvāṇa. In the formula of the second noble truth it is thirst for the things of sense, for existence, or even for non-existence, also a mistaken craving, since it implies the reality of existence. Thirst is characterized by attachment, and thus forms the starting-point for grasping, though according to the scholastic it arises simultaneously with it.

Grasping is thus an aspect of rather than distinct from thirst;[1] it is hyper-thirst, demanding never to leave the pleasure possessed and asking more. It is also thirst for existence; thirst generates the false idea of a self, and hence we have a fourfold division of grasping into the contaminations (*kleça*) of attachment to the pleasures of sense, to heretical views, to moral and ascetic practices regarded as adequate to salvation, and to the belief in the self; the first is pure thirst, the others ignorance. But the term denotes also the object of attachment or grasping; thus thirst is the Upādāna when consciousness passes to a new

[1] SN. iii. 14, 101, 167; iv. 89, 400; MKV., p. 565.

existence, and in this sense we have the doctrine that the five aggregates constituting the individual are the objects grasped. Akin is the idea that the Upādāna serves as support in the sense of aliment, in the shape of the assimilation of food for the body and of psychic matter for the spirit; thus grasping is treated as taking upon oneself the five aggregates, material and psychic, and making them one's own by assimilation. Some such idea seems to explain the term aggregates of grasping (*upādāna-kkhandha*) which often replaces the aggregates in the Canon.[1]

Becoming or existence (*bhava*) is in the scholastic definitely treated as the act which produces future birth, the term then indicating the effect in lieu of the causes. In the Canon it normally denotes rebirth, passing from one existence to another, or three sorts of existence are distinguished, in the sphere of desire, in that of matter, in that of non-matter. In the Sanskrit scholasticism we have originating existence (*upapatti-bhava*), the continuation of the preceding death existence in the constant flow of consciousness, each part of which is conditioned by all the past and conditions the future. But the term is also applied to the condition of a being in a state intermediate between death and rebirth.[2]

Birth denotes strictly the union of consciousness and matter in the womb, which is the commencement of the new life, not the ejection of the foetus.

The last member of the chain is obviously popular rather than scientifically conceived; old age and death are not in the Canon causes of the rest of the series, which possibly was omitted in some forms of the chain. Old age was doubtless meant literally, though the Canon[3] already has the doctrine that even in youth age, that is change, is setting in, the prototype of the doctrine of death at every moment, which is made clear in the later scholastic. That scholastic makes it also clear that at death the subliminal consciousness (*bhavaṅga*), the foundation of life,

[1] MN. i. 511; iii. 240; SN. iii. 94; MKV. xvi. 3; xxvii. 6.

[2] *Vibhaṅga*, p. 137; VM. in Warren, p. 201; MKV., p. 556; DN. ii. 57; AK. iii. 37.

[3] SN. v. 217; gods die without ageing, NP., p. 23. See comm. SN. i. 122.

disappears in a thought of departure (*cyuti-citta*) or of death, to reappear after the thought which heralds the new existence (*pratisaṁdhi-citta*).

4. *The Interpretation of the Chain*

Pali scholasticism[1] presents us with a perfectly definite picture of the significance as a whole of the chain whose links we have examined. Misery arises from action and it from passion or infection; the chain must be distributed among these three aspects. Infection is either ignorance or passion or thirst, which mutually act as cause without beginning or end; this section includes ignorance, thirst, and grasping. Action again is not *eo nomine* in the list, but it must cover the dispositions, as they have moral qualifications, and, more artificially, becoming or existence treated as the act producing this result. All the other members fall to the realm of misery. The chain also must be divided in point of time; the first two members belong to the past, the next eight to the present, the last two to the future life.

The construction is ingenious, but the objection that the three lives are so diversely presented is serious; even in the present life we must imply ignorance and the dispositions, for they explain why feeling creates thirst in the normal man but not in the saint; the third life must be regarded merely as set out to illustrate the nature of misery, and the first must be supplemented by adding thirst, grasping, and existence taken as volition. Orthodox, therefore, as it is, the doctrine, though accepted in some degree by Oldenberg and de la Vallée Poussin, does not impose itself as necessarily representing the intention of its creators. But the conception presents us with the possibility of pictorial representation, for it gives a wheel of existence with three spokes, and it may have attracted general acceptance in that it recalled memories of the rolling of the wheel of the law by the Blessed One as well as more philosophic conceptions such as the renewal of death, the inter-relation of thirst and ignorance.

No other traditional interpretation has any chance of being original, and among European interpreters divergence is great.

[1] Aung, *Compendium*, pp. 259 ff.; cf. AK. iii. 18 ff.; MKV., p. 522.

Childers[1] would solve the riddle by denying any real chain: each item explains existence in some aspect; the order then is indifferent. Burnouf[2] regarded it as the evolution of a concrete entity from non-existence. Kern[3] holds it to be based on a cosmogonic myth, describing the creation and destruction of the world, showing the phases observed in the phenomena of life and nature; man awakes from sleep; his vague impressions become clear knowledge; sense produces feeling, desire, action; a transition period is followed by birth and death. Kirste[4] treats it as an evolution of successive phases which are not changes which appear in an organism, but independent temporary existences which disappear to make room for others. Thus vague tendencies, clarified by intelligence, yield to the idea which by contact with the external world leads to desire for self-realization, effected in conception; ignorance is prefixed as a concession to popular Indian thought; it denotes the dreamless sleep between death and life.

Other interpretations insist more on the incoherence and derivative character of the chain. Jacobi,[5] and in further detail Pischel,[6] derive it from the Sāṁkhya; the parallel is close; ignorance in both is not cosmic; it produces dispositions which determine the next life; the intellect (*buddhi*) is akin to consciousness; the former produces individuality (*ahaṁkāra*), which is much the same as name and form; the six organs are the same in each; thirst is a Yoga term though its emphasis is Buddhist; grasping is the good and evil (*dharmādharmau*) of the Sāṁkhya, and existence is the cycle of being (*saṁsṛṣṭi*). There is too much insistence in this suggestion on completeness; the fact of Sāṁkhya influence in itself is patent. Senart[7] claims that the first two terms are borrowed from the Sāṁkhya, for, if ignorance is, as in Buddhism, empiric, it has no claim to head the list of terms. The construction is late, an amalgamation, without strict order, of independent categories, in which we must not seek 'une theorie autonome sortant tout armée d'une speculation maîtresse

[1] Colebrooke, *Essays*², ii. 454.
[2] *Introduction*, pp. 486 f.
[3] *Ind. Buddh.*, pp. 47 f.
[4] *Album Kern*, pp. 75 ff.
[5] GN. 1896, pp. 1 ff.; ZDMG. lii. 1 ff.
[6] *Buddha*², pp. 65 ff.
[7] *Mélanges de Harlez*, pp. 281 ff.

d'elle-même.' The aggregates are twice present, in terms two-eight and again in the ninth. Warren[1] also holds that there is contamination, and that to make any sense we must admit that the connexion is not always causal, but may take the form of the relation of general and particular. There are two new births between the second and third and the tenth and eleventh terms, and the Buddha probably himself added the first two members, ignorance being the evil he aimed to destroy by his science of knowledge, while the rest was older material, originally not combined into one chain. Franke[2] also uses the method of denying causality in the same sense between the links; all is really timeless misery, and the chain must be made entirely ideal. The complex is arbitrary; while most of the links are to be treated as giving results, this is strained as between ignorance and presentations, as he takes Saṁkhāra; name and form are the content, not the product, of consciousness; existence is the logical consequence of grasping in its nature as mental assumption, there being no real birth whatever.

Oltramare[3] offers a divergent explanation, based on the view that the Buddha aimed at explaining misery, not the origin of life, and at doing so without a self, as if misery were evolving *in abstracto* by the sole force of ignorance. He wishes his disciples to say: 'I live a life of misery, because I am born; I am born because I belong to the world of becoming; I become because I incessantly nourish existence in myself; I do so because I have thirst, appetites; I have thirst because I have feelings; I feel because I enter into contact with the external world; I enter into contact because I have senses; my senses act because I oppose myself as individual to the not-self; I am an individual because my consciousness is imbued with the idea of personality; this consciousness has been so made by my previous experiences; these have infected my consciousness by reason of my ignorance.' The suggestion is ingenious, but too coherent and logical to be primitive.

[1] HOS. iii. 115. [2] ZDMG. lxix. 470 ff.

[3] FBDC., pp. 28 f. Deussen (*Gesch. d. Phil.* I. iii. 133 ff.) exaggerates the confusion by asserting a contamination of a doctrine of desire as the root of being with the Vedānta doctrine of ignorance and the Skandha theory.

Beckh[1] suggests a theory, based on his conception of Buddhism as denying the existence of matter in any form, and as holding that all that is real is becoming, which is purely ideal in character, and on the view that the theory of early Buddhism was strongly affected by the doctrines of the Sāṁkhya and Yoga. Moreover, he rejects absolutely the idea that the chain can be spread over three lives; it was discovered by the Buddha as a solution of the question how physical existence comes into being and with it, inevitably, misery. The senses, contact, feeling, thirst, do not apply to an existing individual; they are inherent in the mysterious being, Gandhabba of the Canon, which is necessary along with the union of the parents to bring into being the individual, and becoming (*bhava*) has the definite sense of conception. The idea is parallel to that of the subtle body of the Sāṁkhya, but, unlike the Sāṁkhya, the Buddhist view denies matter; the process in the Sāṁkhya is one of the gradual development of gross matter from subtle super-sensible matter; in Buddhism we begin with a process of psychic becoming, in lieu of subtle matter, and end with misery, which is the reality in what we call physical matter. With this accords the fact that to the Sāṁkhya also the senses are super-sensible. Name and form as the *prius* of the senses correspond with the egoism (*ahaṁkāra*) of the Sāṁkhya, which is a mere illusion, the principle by which we erroneously believe ourselves to act and suffer, while the true self (*puruṣa*) is exempt from action or passion. In Buddhism name and form cover this imaginary personality, which is really nothing save a process of becoming. The earlier members of the chain are wholly prior to personality; the relation of consciousness to the dispositions is parallel with the Yoga doctrine[2] of the working of unconscious tendencies which reveal themselves ultimately in consciousness, while ignorance, though psychic, and therefore different from the material Prakṛti of the Sāṁkhya, is cosmic, since it arises before personality and gives rise to the false belief in personality. Thus through ignorance of the truth of suffering in a spiritual essence arises the whole process, which results in the misery of the apparent individual. In addition to this psychological chain of

[1] *Buddhismus*, ii. 94 ff. [2] YS. ii. 4, 12.

causation we have the cosmological side in the Aggañña Suttanta with its tale of the decline of beings from happiness to a life of misery on earth essentially through the evil effects of desire, which led them to taste the earth, and thus gradually to acquire material qualities and sex distinctions. This is the Buddhist parallel to the doctrine of the Fall, not into sin, but into misery. The suggestion is ingenious, but it assumes erroneously the disbelief of early Buddhism in matter, it exaggerates its conception of becoming, and it reduces the chain too largely into pre-personal, super-sensible personal, and sensible personal elements, rendering it more complicated than the traditional version of the scholiasts and much less easily intelligible.

5. *The Significance of the Chain*

We can see now the limited character of the chain of causation ; it is intended to explain the coming into being of misery, but the coherence of the whole is not effective, and we can hardly suppose that even to its compilers the construction had much demonstrative force. Certainly they cannot have believed that they were announcing a programme for universal causation, an idea wholly foreign to the Canon. Moreover, it must be remembered that the chain does not explain fully the working of action (*karman*) ; that is essentially one of those reserved issues on which the Buddha gives no enlightenment.[1] The reason is simple enough ; to assert the operation of action was one thing, to show its actual working something very different, and nothing was farther from the Buddhist mind than to envisage the whole world and every happening in it as the result of action.[2] The question is attacked effectively in the *Milindapañha*[3] in connexion with the objection to the sinlessness of the Buddha that he suffered pain from disease and when a splinter of rock struck him when Devadatta hurled a rock against him. But it is emphatically laid down that the fruit of action is much less than the pain arising from other causes

[1] Cf. AN. ii. 80; DN. iii. 138.
[2] Cf. KV. xii. 2–4 ; xvii. 3 ; xxi. 8 and xi. 7, 8 repudiate determinism of action and generally. See also Mil., p. 271.
[3] pp. 134 ff. ; cf. p. 271.

and that none but a Buddha can discern the extent of the working of action. The sufferings of the Buddha were as little due to his past deeds as the impact of a clod of earth upon its surface is the outcome of such an act by the earth.

On the other hand, as Buddhaghosa[1] puts it, the chain of causation serves to negative the existence of any permanent self, the passive recipient of pleasure and of pain; the process is possible without the idea of a self, even if it does not absolutely exclude such an underlying reality. It excludes also the idea that rebirth is due to the intervention of a personal deity, such as Brahmā, who from the exoteric point of view appears in the Vedānta as allotting fresh lives to souls according to their merit, for the process works mechanically. The fact of the essential dependence of misery also opens the possibility at least of its destruction, which would be inconceivable if there were a thing in itself. On the other hand, to make misery dependent on the chain of causes avoids the danger of asserting that it is caused by another, which would import the doctrine of annihilation (*ucchedavāda*) of the destruction of action without the fruit being realized.

The system is incoherent enough even so, but it was meant, it is plain, for practical edification, and it would be foolish to criticize it too closely, remembering always that the issue whether pleasure and pain are self-caused or caused by another is one of the indeterminates. But the doctrine is placed in a very difficult position by a passage in the *Saṁyutta Nikāya*, where the chain is opposed not merely to fortuitous origin (*adhicca*), but also to production by self, by another, by both combined. This is precisely the doctrine of Buddhapālita in his disproof of the possibility of any production at all and the resulting proof of vacuity; but we need not assume that any such idea was present to the *Saṁyutta*; we have only one of these characteristic exaggerations of the importance of the chain, parallel to the declaration of the *Aṅguttara* that the retribution of action is incomprehensible.[2]

[1] Warren, HOS. iii. 169. Cf. SN. ii. 20; FBDC., p. 31.
[2] ii. 113; cf. Ç., p. 225; MKV., p. 76.

6. *The Breaking of the Chain*

As the chain itself represents, and sometimes replaces or is woven into, the second noble truth, so the chain in reverse action is occasionally substituted for the third noble truth, the suppression of misery by complete detachment. It differs from it in that, while the noble truth concentrates on the removal of desire, the chain begins with the suppression of ignorance, a distinction of form rather than of essence. But we have, of course, the simpler view of the direct action of the destruction of ignorance on thirst; even after feeling has arisen, the tendency to create grasping can be destroyed by the suppression of the nascent thirst.[1] But the ordinary course of suppression rests on the effect of misery, which, by the terror it inspires, destroys thirst; the process is: from birth comes suffering; thence faith, that is in the Buddha, the law, and the order; thence lightheartedness, thence zest, thence confidence, thence pleasure or contentment, thence concentration. thence the intuition of the truth.[2] Again, we are told that it is possible to abandon thirst by thirst, the delusion or pride of self by pride; there is a good thirst, a good pride, the desire to be delivered from passions as are the saints.[3]

The serious difficulty of conceiving the cessation of the chain is faced in the Poṭṭhapāda Sutta of the *Dīgha Nikāya*[4] where in connexion with trance the doctrine of the suppression of consciousness is discussed; the views alleged include the act of magicians in infusing consciousness into a man and withdrawing it; the presence and absence of the soul; and the suggestion that ideas come to a man without cause or reason and pass away likewise, consciousness existing or disappearing accordingly. This last assertion is categorically denied by the Buddha, who insists, that it is for a reason and a cause that ideas arise, namely, by training (*sikkhā*), by which he means the whole scheme of salvation beginning with faith in the Buddha as a teacher. But it is clear that the fundamental difficulty remains; how is the training possible? How can ignorance existing from all time be brought to a cessation?

[1] SN. iv. 87. [2] SN. ii. 31; cf. NP., p. 66.
[3] AN. i. 145; cf. NP., p. 87. [4] i. 280.

The Canon cuts the knot by ignoring it; denying any intervention of a deity, it could not adopt the system of divine grace which is found in the *Kaṭha Upaniṣad*, and it was too honestly convinced of the phenomenality of the individual to ascribe to that transient aggregate of factors a power of directing itself to the desired goal. In the Abhidhamma[1] we find a negation of the doctrine of predetermination, ascribed to the Andhakas, on the score that thus Nirvāṇa would become impossible of attainment by the exclusion of the possibility of breaking the chain of existence. The later doctrine[2] is equally unable to solve the problem, save by the hint, which cannot be made consistent with the doctrine of impermanency and not-self, that there is an inherent tendency in the individual to attain release.

7. *Causation in Nature*

The chain of causation is essentially an explanation of misery; it tells us nothing regarding physical causes, and, as we have seen, the Abhidhamma expressly denies as heretical the idea of action as determining events in the physical world. How far was the conception attained that there was causation active in the world of nature? The idea of absolute regularity of causation was excluded for the world of human action by the necessity of recognizing free will and the possibility of release, and in these circumstances it would have been impossible to develop the idea of a natural causality prevailing in the physical sphere. We obtain, therefore, nothing more than the vague general assertion[3] that things as compound come into being under the effect of causes, but we have to put beside this the doctrine that we do not know anything definite as to their operation; we must not inquire whether the world is self-made, made by another, both, or neither, that is, fortuitous, since all these issues belong to the realm of the indeterminates.[4] Indeed, if we were so unkind as to press this doctrine strictly, it would be fatal even to the idea of any material causation at all, as the Madhyamaka readily shows.

[1] KV. xi. 7, 8.

[2] See cit. in *Bhāmatī* (1891), p. 25; Pathak, JBRAS. xviii. 343.

[3] SN. ii. 25; AN. i. 286: so of all Dhammas, *Dhammapada*, 279.

[4] Above, ch. ii. § 2.

The vagueness of the canonical view is confirmed by the *Milindapañha*,[1] where we find the threefold divisions of beings born of action as conscious; of fire and other things growing out of seed, as cause-born, the result, that is, of a previously existing material cause; and the earth, hills, water, wind, as season-born, depending for existence on reasons connected with the weather, while space and Nirvāṇa exist independently of all three forms of cause. In the face of this to assign to Buddhism faith in the uniformity of the causal process or of nature is absurd.

8. *The Doctrine of the Act*

The insistence of the Buddha on the doctrine of the act (*karman*) can clearly be explained as an outcome of his revolt against the pure materialism of teachers like Ajita or the negation of any true human activity as insisted upon by Pūraṇa Kassapa, Pakudha Kaccāyana, and Makkhali Gosāla, despite their divergent views on other points. It is more difficult to ascertain the degree of originality in this assertion of the doctrine of the rewards and penalties of action, for the references to the doctrine in the Upaniṣads are scanty, enlightenment being the main object of these treatises.[2] But we know that the Jaṭilas were authorized to be admitted to the Buddhist order without the normal novitiate of three months because of their belief in the doctrine, and the success of the teaching of the Buddha in this regard is infinitely more probable if it were already a widely accepted doctrine of the ascetics and nobles than if the conception were wholly new. Nor is the presentation of the doctrine in our texts favourable to the view that it was new; the stress laid on the chain of causation rather than on the mere fact of Karman hints at the originality, such as it is, of the chain, not of the fact of Karman.

But if we may judge from the case of the Jain doctrine of Karman, which is frankly materialistic and imagines that bodily or verbal action creates a subtle matter to envelop the soul and produce retribution, it was possible for the Buddha to make an important step in advance, and to sever the idea from connexion

[1] p. 271.   [2] Cf. Oldenberg, LUAB., pp. 108 ff.

with the old Vedic conception of sin as a sort of physical contamination which might be removed by fire or water, to whose influence the Jains succumbed. Action for the Buddha seems to have been volition (*cetanā*), and what is done after volition whether in the form of action or of speech. To resolve to kill is one thing, to act another, to approve the act after it has been performed a third, and all three elements must coincide to make an act complete. A gift should be accompanied by intention, and to regret the generosity is to ruin its effect; a sin, on the other hand, is in part counteracted by confession, which is also the accomplishment of the duty of truthfulness, and this fact explains the importance laid by the community on the formal confession of sins.[1]

A further and important result is derived from this rationalizing of the conception of action. The morality of action predominates in the Buddhist view, and ritual practices such as sacrifice[2] and purification, nay even offerings to the dead, become merely surplusage, superstitious usages (*sīlabbata*), which have no value. But it must be admitted that there is no attempt to demonstrate the principles which render an act moral or immoral; it is not until late that we have the suggestion that an act is good or bad according as it benefits one's neighbour or injures him, and even then there is no more far-reaching criterion than the mere idea of goodness as pleasure and evil as pain. Moreover, the true Buddhist essentially seeks release, and that has nothing in itself to do with either goodness or badness. The monk, indeed, is compelled to attain his end to concentrate his interest on himself alone;[3] his actions like those of the sage of the Upaniṣads are essentially for the sake of the self; and the path of salvation requires that he should lay aside, as did the Buddha, all the human class of duty towards wife or children, since family life is a barrier to the attainment of release.

[1] SN. ii. 99; cf. MKV., p. 306; Poussin, *Nirvāṇa*, ch. iii.

[2] Yet it is allowed, DN. ii. 88; MV. vi. 28. 11; on ritual bathing see *Therīgāthā*, 239, and later Āryadeva's *Cittaviçuddhiprakaraṇa* (JASB. lxvii. 2); Vasubandhu, *Gāthāsaṁgraha* (Mél. asiat. viii. 559 ff.); on offerings to the dead *Petavatthu*, (PTS. 1888).

[3] Cf. *Bṛhadāraṇyaka Up.*, i. 4. 8; ii. 4; iv. 5.

CHAPTER VI

THE PATH OF SALVATION, THE SAINT, AND THE BUDDHA

1. *The Path of Salvation*

THE end of man is to free himself, if possible, in this life from the intoxicants, the lust of being born again in this world, or in the world of subtle matter, or the world without matter, and the ignorance of the four noble truths. His aim is to break the chain of causation, to destroy any one of its members and thus end the whole; to free himself from desire or appetite, aversion and dullness. There are, it is clear, two sides involved; there is the extinction of desire, and the extinction of ignorance; true the two are intimately related; there can be no extinction of desire if ignorance prevails, and therefore the extinction of ignorance is fundamental. But it is not surprising that a purely intellectual solution for the removal of ignorance is not accepted by Buddhism; the training of conduct may be, and indeed is, a lower plane of endeavour, but it is essential, and, unlike the sage of the Upaniṣads, the seeker for liberation must accept the duty of a strict morality. Hence the doctrine that conduct (*sīla*) concentration (*samādhi*) and wisdom or intuition (*paññā*) are all essential; that concentration pervaded by conduct is fruitful; that intuition pervaded by concentration is fruitful; and that the self, pervaded by intuition, is freed from the corruption of desire, becoming, false views and ignorance. But concentration is rather a stage in the attainment of intuition than an independent entity, and a Sutta of the *Dīgha Nikāya* mentions conduct and intuition as the essential pair, both inseparably united, since neither without the other performs its part.[1]

[1] DN. i. 124.

Conduct, it follows, from the end of man,[1] must be such as to aid him in his end; it must secure for him either progress to Nirvāṇa or rebirth at least in a superior form of life. The action of Karman may not be unbroken or absolutely regular, but it is assumed for practical purposes to have these qualities, and man will profit or suffer according to his own deeds and deserts. Moreover, man has the power to act; strange as it may seem when one ground of the denial of a self is remembered, and the apparent determinism of the chain of causation, the Buddha has no doubt whatever that the determinism of Makkhali Gosāla is the most detestable of all heresies. The position is the more remarkable, because one of the arguments in the Canon and later against the existence of a self is that such a thing must be autonomous, while all in the world is conditional and causally determined. But the issue is solved by the simple process of ignoring it, and Buddhism rejoices in being freed from any error of determinism to menace moral responsibility.

There is no attempt to create a reasoned moral system based on a calculus of goods. The main tenets are adopted from Brahmanical tradition; they are, however, extended and deepened; the prohibition to kill is applied to all living things to the inconvenience of the monks in daily life; all forms of illegitimate appropriation are forbidden, and restrictions placed on those allowed; the order not to commit adultery becomes one of celibacy for the monks; the injunction to avoid falsehood is expanded into a eulogy of friendly speech and the bringing about of concord. But monastic orders are nothing if not fond of regulations, and the simple lists are expanded by forbidding all sorts of luxuries harmless and otherwise, as well as the practice of many useful modes of livelihood, a rule which resulted in the monks living a life almost without possibility of useful work other than the duties arising from the necessities of daily life in a simple community, whose members supplied food and clothing and, later, vied in providing monasteries.

[1] Including women, admitted reluctantly to the order at the cost of halving the duration of the faith; CV. x. 1 ff. Women played some part in the early history of Buddhist discussion, as also in Brahmanism, but later disappear as serious factors; cf. JRAS. 1893, pp. 517 ff., 763 ff.; and Mrs. Rhys Davids, trs. of the *Therīgāthā*, PTS. 1909.

Nothing illustrates better the true character of Buddhist ethics than the conception of friendship or love (*mettā*) which Pischel[1] has compared with the love inculcated, however vainly, by Christianity. The Buddhist will endure injuries and insults; he will seek no revenge and offer no resistance; but he does so because selfmastery is greater to him than anything else. As part of his meditations to secure the saving grace of indifference to the world, he will in a lonely place practise the generation of a feeling of friendship for all things, hostile or not; the practise has potent magic powers; by it the Buddha stayed the onslaught of the elephant instigated against him by the traitor Devadatta, and the mere ordinary man can guard himself against snake-bite by it. The element of calculating prudence is ever present; the prince who spares his enemy in lieu of revenging his murdered parents wins a kingdom. Moreover, the power deprives others of the ability effectively to injure us; the wise man can build round himself a protection which the enemy cannot pierce. But, of course, in practice, we may well believe, the love of the Buddhist was as truly emotional as that of the Christian, and was neither limited nor motived by formal rules; there are traces of the affection of the monks and nuns in their Gāthās, and the spirit of affection for the wild beasts of the woods is as attractive as it is an undeniable feature of the life of the Buddhist wanderer.

Much more disappointing is the lavish praise given to liberality, provided that its object was the monk; the wild exaggerations of Brahmanical admiration of asceticism, which the Buddha traditionally reproved, are here reproduced, and the inclusion of the *Vimānavatthu* in the Pali Canon is sufficient proof that nothing of this kind was too exaggerated to excite distaste among the redactors of the Canon. Prince Vessantara, driven from his Kingdom hands over all his goods to beggars, and goes to the wild

[1] *Buddha*,[2] p. 80. See Oldenberg *Aus Indien und Iran*, p. 121; *Aus dem alten Indien*, pp. 1 ff.; Beckh (*Buddhismus*, ii. 132 ff.) exaggerates its rôle in the legend of the future Buddha, Metteyya. The essential value of love is that it frees the heart (*cittavimutti*) from desire; as universal feeling—not action—it counteracts particular passion (DN. ii. 251; MN. i. 297, 351; ii. 207; AN. ii. 129). Sympathy in joy and sorrow, and indifference do the same, but love is extolled in *Itivuttaka*, p. 19 f. as pre-eminent, but this is isolated.

with his wife and children; the god Sakka comes to try his faith in the shape of a Brahmin, and receives his two children, and then on a second errand his wife as a free gift. Sakka's rôle is reminiscent of the actions of the gods in sending nymphs to seduce ascetics when the fervour of their asceticism menaces the gods themselves, and it is Sakka again who accepts the wise hare's gift of his body as alms in the lack of anything else worthy of presentation to a guest. But, be it noted, self-sacrifice like this is demanded only of one who will not in the present life attain enlightenment, and the Buddha performs none of these deeds in his last earthly life.[1]

The due observance of the rules of conduct brings with it the assurance of the power of self-restraint and corresponding satisfaction. But there are still further matters to be observed by the disciple, which cannot be formulated, like the rules of conduct, in precise directions but must be carried out at his own discretion.[2] He must be watchful over the sense intimations which come to him whether direct or as ideas; he must practise to disinterest himself in them, and to prevent any evil states of mind arising which would foster desire. Secondly, he must be mindful and self-possessed; in all his deeds the monk must keep ever before him the nature of the act; its ethical significance; whether or not it conduces to the end at which he aims; and the real facts underlying the mere phenomenon of the outward act; the rule is the Buddhist analogue to the Christian order: 'Whether therefore ye eat, or drink, or whatsoever ye do, do all to the glory of God.' Thirdly, the monk must study contentment and be satisfied with the bare minimum of robes and food wherewith he may travel like a bird with its wings. In diverse fashions these principles are inculcated; the habit of self-observation is ever insisted upon as the most effective way to root out those evil cravings which lead to rebirth and its miseries.

By these means the monk is qualified to lay aside hankering

[1] Ch. i. 9, 10; DP. 428; on Sakka cf. Rhys Davids, SBB. iii. 294 ff.; on prohibited occupations, DN. i. 58 f; on gifts, ii. 356 ff.; SBB. ii. 347 f.; AN. iv. 236, 246; KV. vii. 4.

[2] DN. i. 62 ff.; and parallels, SBB. ii. 59 f.

for the things of the world; the desire to injure; torpor of heart and mind, or mind and body; flurry and worry; and perplexity, the five hinderances (*nīvaraṇa*); he is as one freed from debt, disease, prison, slavery, or wandering on a desert road; he is filled with great joy and peace, and is ready to enter on the First Meditation (*jhāna*), and thereafter to advance to the final intuition and enlightenment.

But this scheme of pr edure which is laid down in the Sāmaññaphala Sutta is not the only possibility; indeed, it is clear that the ethical and other prescriptions are the result of much co-operative work and redaction. The oldest form of the plan of emancipation may be the noble eightfold way, which is the fourth of the noble truths, and possibly, therefore, to be attributed to the Buddha himself. It demands right views, knowledge of the four noble truths; right aspiration towards renunciation, benevolence, and kindness; right speech, abstaining from lying, slander, abuse and idle talk; right action, abstaining from taking life, or what is not given, or from carnal indulgence; right livelihood, abstaining from any of the forbidden modes of living; right effort, to suppress the rising of evil states, to eradicate those which have arisen, to stimulate good states, and to perfect those which have come into being; right-mindfulness, the looking on the body and the spirit in such a way as to remain ardent, self-possessed and mindful, having overcome both hankering and dejection; and right concentration, in the shape of the Four Meditations. The lack of system and clearness of the path is probable enough evidence of its age; the scheme seems to have been remodelled upon it.[1]

Without the meditations, to which either system leads up as the normal climax, the whole makes a natural system of moderately rigorous ethics intended for monks. For laymen the Buddha has much the same creed without the elaborate paraphernalia of minor regulations, and he has five good reasons for righteousness on the part of householders; the wicked man becomes poor through sloth; of evil repute; loses his place in society; dies in anxiety; and is rewarded by an evil rebirth, while the reverse of these woes

[1] Cf. Franke, ZDMG. lxix. 482 ff.

is secured for the good man. The Sigālovāda Sutta[1] has a charming little picture of lay ethics; the Buddha reinterprets the worship of the quarters, and instead inculcates the duties of parents to guide and protect their children; of children to honour their parents and maintain the family traditions; of teachers to instruct their pupils and to receive due honour in return; of husbands to be courteous, faithful, and respectful to their wives, to give them authority in the home, and provide them ornaments in return for fidelity, and due performance of their duties; of friends to show courtesy, generosity, and benevolence to one another, to observe the golden rule, and to keep faith; of masters to give just labour tasks to their servants, to feed and pay them, tend them in illness, and afford them luxuries, if possible, and recreation, and of servants to rise before and retire after their masters, to be content, work well and praise their employers; of laymen to show affection by act, word, and thought to monks, and to supply their temporal needs, and of monks to teach laymen and restrain them from evil.

On political issues there was no room for a Buddhist creed; the Buddha, however, on the occasion of Ajātasattu's determination to attack the Vajjians predicted their successful resistance so long as they observed their old constitution; met regularly for counsel; acted in concord; made no innovations in institutions; hearkened to the advice of the elders; permitted no detention of women or girls among the clans; honoured the village shrines and kept up religious rites; and paid due reverence to Arahants; a doctrine of pure conservatism, but probably of practical good sense, and evidently containing a pointed warning against the practice of marriage by capture.[2]

Precisely the same attitude of conservatism is to be found in the attitude of the Buddha towards the issue of caste distinctions. The clear opposition of the Buddhists to the claims of the Brahmins naturally suggested earlier in the study of Buddhism the conception of the master as striving against the privileges of the Brahmin caste. This theory was, however, so obviously incompatible with the facts that it evoked instead the suggestion

[1] DN. iii. 180 ff.; *Suttanipāta*, ii. 4. 14. [2] DN. ii. 73 ff.

that the Buddha failed as a social reformer, since he was content to recruit his order from the upper classes, the Brāhmaṇas or Kṣatriyas, neglecting the claims of the downtrodden multitude, eaten by their greedy kings. To this again exception has been taken, and we are asked instead to believe that caste, as we understand it, did not exist in the Buddha's time, and that, if his views on it had been followed, social divisions would have developed on western lines and the iniquities of caste would never have been perpetrated.[1]

It is, however, impossible to accept this last opinion; caste, it is true, was by no means as rigid in the Buddha's period as it has come to be, for the institution is essentially one in constant growth and modification. But there is the clearest proof that the great classes of Brāhmaṇas, Kṣatriyas, Vaiçyas or Çūdras existed, and that the priestly and ruling classes were selfish oppressors in union of the people and the serfs or slaves, while each class was hardening into caste divisions. The Buddha's formal treatment of the origin of the castes destroys any possibility of treating him as a reformer; on the contrary, in keeping with the doctrine of action, he traces all to their deeds in the beginning of the present world system, and thus enunciates a dangerous conservatism. His own practice was in harmony with his theory; the ascetic communities of his day recognized in theory, and to some extent in practice, the right of any person to be associated with them; the Buddhist excluded slaves unless emancipated, and the majority of their adherents seem to have belonged to the upper classes. The Buddha, we may assume in point of fact, was not a social reformer; he had a message of healing for misery which consisted in denial of anything in the world of enduring value, and such a message was not such as to induce its promulgator or his disciples to strive against the established social order, apart from the dangers which such an effort would have involved to the new faith. The Buddha sought, indeed, it would seem, to establish his followers as Brāhmaṇas, by the adoption of the principle that birth

[1] Rhys Davids, SBB. ii. 99 ff. But see Oldenberg, *Buddha*,[9] Pt. I, ch. iv.; Keith, CHI. i. 92 ff. The contract theory (DN. iii. 93) of the origin of Kingship appears also later in the *Mahāvastu* and *Jātaka*; see Law, *Ancient Indian Polity*, pp. 94 ff. No protest is made against barbarous punishments, e. g. DN. ii. 332 ff.

cannot make a man a Brāhmaṇa but only virtue, but this attempt, if seriously intended, failed utterly of success.[1] He did, however, it is clear, hold forth the temporal advantages in the shape of respect and consideration which fell to the lot of a member of the Order, and we know that there were many mixed motives, as was inevitable, among its members, fear of royal tyranny, or of robbers, or worry from debt, while others had no higher motive than that of finding a comfortable means of livelihood.[2]

Though stress is normally laid on conduct and intuition, it must be remembered that the whole edifice of salvation is built up on the fact of faith in the Buddha. It is when a Buddha appears and teaches the holy truth, that it becomes possible for the householder or other person to listen to the teaching, to attain faith in the teacher, and to realize that worldly life is a hindrance to purity, and therefore to abandon it for the existence of a yellow-robed monk.[3] Faith thus lies at the root of knowledge, and it is only inferior to knowledge[4] in the sense that intuition is a higher stage; a monk begins with faith and ends with intuition, as a normal rule at any rate, although saints saved by faith[5] seem to have been admitted. Faith, however, is not to be regarded as an inferior mode of salvation or as unessential; there can, it is clear, be no intuition unless there has first been faith, save in the case of the Buddha alone.

2. *The Forms of Meditation*

The Canon is singularly rich in diverse devices intended to secure the production of a state of mind in which there shall be no presence of empirical reality. The Yoga practices of which India has ever been so fond were doubtless the object of eager study, and forms of self-hypnosis were the objects of research. We have in all likelihood echoes of these experiments in the records of the power to see heavenly visions and hear heavenly

[1] Rhys Davids, SBB. ii. 104 f., 138 f., 141. Cf. *Bṛhadāraṇyaka Up.*, iv. 4. 23.

[2] Mil., p. 32. Corruption in the order is attested in Therag. 920 ff., 949 ff.; Therīg. 400 ff.; hence regarded as late by Winternitz, *Ind. Litt.* ii. 87 f.

[3] DN. i. 62; Mil., p. 36; AN. iii. 21; MN. i. 176; Sumaṅg. i. 231. See also SN. ii. 31; *Udāna*, i. 8.

[4] MV. v. 1. 21; SBE. xxxv. 56, n. 1.

[5] AN. i. 118; PP. iii. 3.

sounds, in the imagination of wrestlings in controversy with the evil Māra,[1] in whom the power of desire and the temptations of the life of the world are personified. The life of the monks and nuns, with their scanty nutriment and eager desire to secure experiences of rapture, must have tended to the abnormal development of psychic powers and the induction of hallucinations and self-hypnosis. All the methods seem to have aimed at one end; despite occasional combination in the texts they may fairly be held to have been originally independent modes of gaining a common end.

Simplest and least unattractive is the formal practice of regulated breathing accompanied by a simple assertion of the act, a device loved according to tradition by the Buddha himself as occupation for the rainy season when his wandering life of preaching ceased.[2] Repellent in the extreme is the meditation of impurity, demanding the presence of the monk at a cemetery, and the careful meditation on all the hateful aspects of a corpse in decay, a drastic measure of convincing even the greatest lover of human beauty of the vanity of the love of the flesh, but perhaps necessary for Indian monks, since even the highest ascetics are regarded by Brahmanical tradition as singularly apt to fall victims to female blandishments.[3] Of much more attractive kind are the forms of meditation which lead with certainty to rebirth in the world of Brahmā, the Brahma-vihāras. In the wild one first practices the feeling of friendliness to all creatures; then develops sympathy as compassion in its place; then sympathy in their joy; and thence passes to the true end of the meditation, the attainment of absolute indifference of feeling (*upekkhā*), a striking warning against any conception of love as the end of man.[4]

More abstruse are the Positions of Mastery (*abhibhāyatanāni*)[5] which are essentially modes of contemplating external forms finite or boundless, and coloured blue, yellow, red, white, and appreciating their true impermanence, and thus presumably render-

[1] Windisch, *Māra und Buddha*; Oldenberg, *Aus Indien und Iran*, pp. 101 f.; SN. i. 103 ff.

[2] VP. iii. 70 f.; SN. v. 326; Poussin, *Bouddhisme* (1898), p. 92.

[3] DN. ii. 292 f., 298 f.

[4] AN. i. 183; iii. 225; DN. iii. 224.

[5] DN. ii. 110; iii. 260; DS. § 204.

ing vacant the mind. Akin to these exercises are the first three of the Stages of Deliverance (*vimokkha*)[1] which seem to be, first the contemplation by a man of his own material form, then of external form, and then the attainment of intentness. Then by passing beyond any conception of matter or idea of sensation, and suppressing the idea of multiformity, he attains the state of mind in which the only idea present is the infinity of space (*ākāsānañca*). On this follows a stage in which the infinity or unboundness of intellect (*viññānānañca*) is alone present. The next stage is reached when there is nothing at all present to the mind (*ākiñcaññāyatana*). Then is achieved the stage when neither the presence of ideas nor the absence of ideas is specifically present (*nevasaññānāsaññāyatana*). Finally is attained the state where there is suppression of both sensation and idea (*saññāvedayitanirodha*). The same idea reappears in a different form in the doctrine of the seven Resting Places for Consciousness (*viññānaṭhitiyo*) and the two Spheres.[2] The first of the resting places or stages is that of men, some gods and dwellers in hell; the second of the gods, differing in body but uniform in intelligence, of the Brahma-loka; the third of the gods uniform in body but not in intelligence; the fourth of the All lustrous gods uniform in both; the last three and the two Spheres cover the four stages beginning with the infinity of space, the two Spheres being the realms without idea and where is neither ideation nor yet non-ideation. The four or five rank as the Āruppajhānas, for their essence is that they assume that the adept has left all conception of matter far behind, and advances step by step in the sphere of pure consciousness, and finally the disappearance of any content whatever. We have here an interesting historical record, which explains to us the presence of the fifth form in the shape of the suppression of both idea and feeling; Āḷāra Kālāma and Uddaka Rāmaputta, two teachers of the Buddha, had carried their power of meditation to the extent of attaining the meditation of nothingness, and neither the presence nor the absence of ideas; it followed therefore that the Buddha

[1] DN. ii. 112 ff.; 70 f.; iii. 262 f; AN. iv. 306, 349; DS. §§ 248 ff.; Franke, DN., pp. 210, n. 4, 212, n. 6.
[2] DN. ii. 68 ff.; AN. iv. 39 f.

must go further and invent a fifth meditation, in which everything disappears save the life and the warmth of the body; that is, in effect, a cataleptic condition in the fullest sense.[1] We must assume, therefore, that the Buddha approved this form of meditation. But the addition of four of the forms to the ordinary Four Meditations in order to make up eight Perfections or Accomplishments is clearly artificial, for the two forms of meditation differ in essence and cannot be made rationally complementary. They must have been favoured for different purposes and occasions, though with one end.

This other set of four[2] occurs with great frequency in set phraseology, and without the variations in enumeration of the other set. They seem often even in the early school to have been preceded by a form of concentration intended to aid entry into them, the Kasiṇas,[3] the essential feature of which is the contemplation, say of earth, water, fire, wind, dark blue, yellow, blood-red, white, light or a narrow aperture. By intense concentrated gazing on the object chosen he obtains a mental reflex, which is devoid of the specific character of a simple mental image. The process is to be carried on to the accompaniment of thoughts on the wretchedness of sensual pleasure, which produce indifference to such pleasures; with reflections on the merits of the Buddha, the doctrine, and the community of monks, which produce joy and gladness; and with the deliberate effort thus to become a partaker of the blessings of isolation. The attainment of this mental reflex opens the way to the first Meditation or Trance.

This condition, is one in which, freed from all desire and evil dispositions, the adept enjoys, as a result of isolation and concentration, a condition of zest and pleasure (*pīti-sukha*), while engaged in initial and sustained application, doubtless to the truths of the system. By the suppression of either form of application, he obtains inner peace, the concentration (*ekodibhava*)[4] of thought

[1] MN. i. 164 f. It is clear there is no disapproval of these states; Oldenberg, GGA. 1917, p. 170. Cf. BC. xii. 45 ff.

[2] DN. i. 73 ff.; Heiler, KF., pp. 357 ff.

[3] MN. ii. 14; AN. i. 41; v. 46 f., 60; VM. in Warren, HOS. iii. 293 ff.; DS. §§ 160 ff; Poussin, *Bouddhisme* (1898), pp. 94 ff.

[4] On this cf. Franke, DN., p. 39, n. 6; Kern, SBE. XXI. xvii; Lévi, MSA. xiv. 14; Oldenberg, GGA. 1917, p. 170, n. 1.

(*cetas*) produced by deep reflection (*samādhi*), and characterized by zest and pleasure. The third stage is one in which zest with the activity which it implies disappears; the adept remains mindful and intent (*satimān*), but indifferent (*upekkhaka*), enjoying, however, pleasure; the interpretation of indifference here is not evidently hedonistic; the state is not one of neutral feeling, but intellectual; the adept looks with impartial tolerance on all mental states. Then, by the putting away of all pleasure and pain, by the destruction of elation or dejection, he attains the fourth state which is one of pure or complete self-possession and indifference (*upekkhāsatiparisuddhi*) without pleasure or pain. This last state is not altogether easy of interpretation, for the term, which may indicate the purity or completeness of self-possession and indifference, has also been interpreted as denoting the removal [1] of these qualities from the adept, which would result, therefore, in a condition somewhat akin to that produced by the last of the other type of Meditations. In favour of this interpretation can be cited the fact that otherwise the fourth Meditation appears to leave us with a condition which seems indistinguishable from the final intuition of the saint, which it is certainly not to be identified with,[2] as that is represented as following on the last Meditation; but this objection is not fatal, for intuition is more than self-possession and indifference, which may well be treated as leading up to it. If so, then this series of Meditations clearly leads to a different result spiritually than the first, as it starts with a different procedure, for, although artificial aids to mental concentration are used, the adept engages in mental reflection on Buddhist truths, and not in a mere effort to isolate thought.[3] Perhaps this fact was regarded as making it inferior, for the other Meditations appear later to have been preferred to it. Like the former set, it is not doubtful that the Meditations are taken over from Brahmanic

[1] Senart, RHL. xlii. 349 f. On *sati* cf. Rhys Davids, SBB. iii. 322 ff. Cf. Franke, DN. p. 76, n. 5.

[2] DN. ii. 156; i. 38. Intuition includes definite recognition of non-rebirth; DN. i. 84. Cf. Beckh, *Buddhismus*, ii. 48 f.

[3] Meditation (Jhāna) is a narrower idea than Samādhi, concentration, which includes it and is generic; Buddhism has not the YS. iii. 1 ff. distinction of Dhāraṇā, Dhyāna, Samādhi.

practice ; there are traces of them in the Yoga and the *Mahābhārata*, and they are not claimed as original or as inventions in Buddhism.

Both sets of meditations are deemed to be distinguished by happiness, a view which seems in obvious contradiction with the absence of pleasure from the last stages in the latter set, and the catalepsy of the last stage of the former set, but the difficulty may be resolved by accepting the distinction between the actual pleasure of the state, and the value of it as tending to the final end ; this double use of happiness is another proof of the logical weakness of the Canon.[1]

It is, however, essential to note that there is nothing necessary in regard to these trances, though their use was constant among the monks, and directions are given in the Vinaya to secure that monks adept in meditation should be located together so as not to interfere with one another in trance.[2] A similar form of meditation is contained in the threefold concentration (*samādhi*), with initial and continued application ; with the latter only ; without both, and another set of three views things as void, probably of lusts and evil dispositions ; without taking note of any special peculiarity, that is indifferently ; and without predilection.[3] Ānanda, who carried out the former kind of concentration, seems to have had the vision of an aura and of forms. There is much similar matter recorded in the mysticism of the west,[4] but Christian mystics show distinct characteristics which have been traced to the double origin of their views in Neo-platonic philosophical conceptions and the prophetic tradition ; their aim is union with God ; they recognize the grace of God in the course of the progress of their meditations, as does the *Kaṭha Upaniṣad* ; they show a personal element which distinguishes the state of each mystic from that of another.

[1] Ledi Sadaw, *Yamaka*, ii. App., p. 248 ; *Buddh. Psych.*, pp. 83 ff.

[2] *Theragāthā*, 522 f., 537 f. ; MN. i. 276 ; MV. v. 6 ; CV. iv. 4. 4 ; Oldenberg, LUAB., p. 322.

[3] MN. iii. 157 ff. ; DN. iii. 219 ; DS. § 344 ; *Yogāvacara's Manual*, p. xxvii. f.

[4] Besides Heiler, see *Buddh. Psych.*, p. 107 ff. The set of four is later alternatively made five by dividing the first into two, initial attention being eliminated in the second ; DS. §§ 168 ff.

3. *Intuition and Nirvāṇa*

The end of the meditations of the disciple is to lead to the final intuition of the four noble truths which brings with it the recognition that there is no chance of rebirth. This is the essential fact of Nirvāṇa; the monk is freed from the intoxicants or defilements (*āsava*)[1] of desire, of becoming, of false views, of ignorance; all appetite, all aversion, all dullness and confusion are departed; the outward form remains, it is true, while life lasts, but the essential result is achieved, and what happens to the monk when physical death sets in cannot alter this fact; we can understand how the Buddha was willing to rule such questionings out as inadmissible, because he had formed a conception of the *summum bonum* as Nirvāṇa, which provided for its being attained in this life. The conception is entirely parallel to the man released in life (*jīvanmukta*) of the Vedānta and of the Upaniṣads, and was doubtless adopted from earlier speculation. Should then, since the monk knows that he has attained release, he remain longer alive in the world? The answer is that, as the world is indifferent to him, so he craves neither for life nor death, but awaits like a servant his wages—a strange confusion of ideas but characteristic; yet suicide is permissible now and then as Godhika's case shows.[2] On death there is now no continuity of consciousness; the Viññāna transmigrates no longer, for the chain of causation is broken for ever. Man has attained the Nirvāṇa element (*nibbāna-dhātu*) without any remainder of empirical existence; the *Milindapañha* co-ordinates Nirvāṇa with the ether which is uncreate and endless, and the Abhidhamma classifies Nirvāṇa as the uncompound element, distinguishing it radically from all the passing world.[3]

Positively of the state there is asserted happiness or holiness of release or enlightenment (*vimutti—*, *sambodha—*, *sukha*); the terms

[1] That of false views (*diṭṭhi*) is omitted in DN. i. 83; MN. i. 23, 155; AN. i. 167; SN. iv. 256. For the four, DN. ii. 98: DS. § 1096; 'intoxicant' (*ā -su*) is possible, SBB. ii. 92, n. 3; iii. 28, n. 2; *āsrava* is probably a mere Sanskritization; *āçraya* is possible, TDC., p. 8; *āsnava*, IF. xxiii. 267.

[2] Mil., p. 45; cf. *Theragāthā*, 1002 f. On suicide, see SN. i. 120 f.; DPC., p. 255; (Vakkali), SN. iii. 123 f.

[3] Mil., p. 271; *Psych. Eth.*, p. 367 f.

seem at first sight contradictory since pleasure (*sukha*) is empirical, and therefore out of place; 'Nirvāṇa is happiness', Sāriputta asserts, and, when asked how that can be when feeling does not exist, he asserts that it is happiness because there is no feeling.[1] Feeling, as we have seen, is transitory and therefore in the wide sense misery; happiness therefore must be distinct from feeling, but beyond that we cannot go. All empirical qualifications are unfitted to describe the ineffable. What we are assured by the overwhelming evidence of the Canon is that Nirvāṇa is the blissful end for which every one must strive and which, when attained, is worth the pains to win it.

This is the general aspect of Nirvāṇa, but there are indications also of a more prosaic kind of the nature of the intuitive consciousness, which is the final product of the Meditations and other exercises, and from the elaboration with which details of this state are set out in the Canon and later we would err gravely if we treated Nirvāṇa in any abstract way. It was, while life lasted, a state of extremely marked psychic powers, conferring on the saint powers of a varied, and to western ideas, incongruous kind.[2] The first is the power of perceiving the interrelation of consciousness and the body,[3] and this leads to the second, higher fruit of the power to create a body made by,[4] or of, mind, a conception to which we owe, it may be feared, the astral body of Spiritualism and other follies. Then he enjoys magic power (*iddhi*); he can multiply himself and become one again; be visible or invisible; penetrate a wall as if air, or the ground as if water; walk on water; fly like a bird in the sky; touch sun and moon, and reach in body the heaven of Brahmā. The next power is less remarkable; he can hear sounds celestial and human, far and near. Then he knows the minds of others, in all their manifold natures and conditions. Then he can remember his former births, through many an Aeon in all details and modes. Then with the heavenly

[1] AN. v. 414; cf. VP. i. 2, 3; Nirvāṇa as happiness, Mil., p. 313.
[2] DN. i. 76 ff.
[3] The terminology and idea here are decidedly not Sāṁkhya-Yoga. The relation is real.
[4] Sumaṅg. i. 222, not followed by Franke; 'of mind', SBB. ii. 88; *Buddh. Psych.*, p. 127. This is borne out by DN. i. 195; below, p. 209, n. 5.

eye he discerns the destinies of all persons dying and being reborn according to their deserts. Then he directs his mind to the destruction of the intoxicants of desire, becoming, ignorance, by the knowledge first of the four noble truths, and then by like knowledge of the intoxicants, their origin, their cessation, and the path. In him then is accomplished liberation from the intoxicants; there arises the knowledge of his emancipation; 'Rebirth has been destroyed; the higher life has been fulfilled; what had to be done has been done; after this present life there will be no beyond.' This is the highest fruit of the life of the recluse, to see as clearly as one can in a clear pool the shells and the pebbles, and the swimming shoals of fish.

We need not suppose that all these powers were either claimed or enjoyed by all saints; the last is obviously the essential intuition, but the whole body of the potencies beginning with the celestial ear is given the style of super knowledge (*abhiññā*), and, with the prior members, of aggregate of intuition (*paññā-khandha*) or simply intuition or knowledge (*vijjā*).[1] Or, again, the wisdom of the saint is described as the eye of intuition (*paññā-cakkhu*) which ranks not merely above the heavenly eye—Ānanda had it but not the latter—but also above the eye of the law (*dhamma-cakkhu*), the technical term for entering on the path which leads to liberation.[2] We need not doubt that the possession of such powers was duly believed in by adepts, nor need we ascribe them to anything more wonderful than the hallucinations[3] which the meditations were certain to produce; that in the east men claim to-day to remember previous births aids in explaining the origin of such ideas; it confers no validity upon them.[4]

4. *The Saint and the Buddha*

The narrative of the Buddha's work of conversion shows the simple form of a disciple realizing forthwith the impermanence

[1] The technical sense of *abhiññā* is found in VP. iii. 87, but is late; SBB. ii. 62, n. 1, but see DN. iii. 281. On *iddhi* see DN. i. 211 f.; SBB. ii. 88 f., 372 f.

[2] *Itivuttaka*, § 61; SBB. ii. 95, n. 1.

[3] See e. g. James, *The Varieties of Religious Experience*, pp. 219, 251 f., &c.

[4] Contrast Eliot, *Hinduism and Buddhism*, I, lvii.; Rhys Davids, *Buddh. Psych.*, p. 129.

and misery of existence, whence, if he persist in this assurance and strive hard, he will attain by the destruction of desire Nirvāṇa even in this life.[1] So simple a conception was certain to be elaborated, especially if the faith were to meet the views of those who, doubtless many in number, were not altogether enamoured of Nirvāṇa and could be better won to the cause if they could be offered the chance of happier rebirth, an idea which appealed with irresistible force to many lay adherents. Hence we find a classification by four stages. The first is he who has entered on the stream (*sotāpanna*); he is rid of the first three bonds (*saṁyojana*) of the false belief in individuality, doubt, and belief in the efficacy of ceremonial; he is assured that he cannot be reborn in the worlds of hell, or animals, or ghosts. The once-returner (*sakadāgāmin*) has further reduced to a minimum affection (*rāga*), aversion, and dullness; he will once more only return to be born on earth. The non-returner (*anāgāmin*) has destroyed the fourth and fifth bonds, attachment to things of sense, and antipathy; he will be reborn only in a Brahma-loka, and there will he find liberation. The last is the saint, Arahant, who has freed himself from all the bonds, in whom no defilements remain, who will never suffer rebirth.[2]

There is no early evidence that these stages must be strictly observed, but from the first the rule was clear that Nirvāṇa must normally be confined to the monk. The exception, however, was allowed that a layman, who adhered to the faith, might attain the extinction of rebirth, if his last thought were directed to this end, and later the general doctrine is laid down that a layman may attain liberation, but only either by dying on the day he does so, or by entering the order at the moment when he attains it; he who has gained Nirvāṇa cannot remain in secular life. Later also is the idea that in the barber's shop at the time of the tonsure on admission to the order the highly gifted novice attains Nirvāṇa.[3]

The qualities of the saint are elaborated in the texts; he has four Paṭisambhidās, powers of comprehension and exegesis;

[1] MV. i. *passim*. [2] DN. ii. 92 f., 200.
[3] SN. v. 410; Mil., p. 265; KV. iv. 1.

intuition (*paññā*, *abhiññā*), true insight (*vipassanā*), quietude (*samatha*); he works miracles by fourfold exertion (*padhāna*); he is *par excellence* noble (*ariya*); as a hearer of the doctrine (*sāvaka*) he can be so designated, though the term applies to any disciple. But he is inferior to the individual, Pacceka, Buddha,[1] the solitary, who in an age when no universal Buddha exists and the order is dissolved, attains enlightenment but cannot preach it, and who is inferior in omniscience to the Buddha proper; the later view is clear that he cannot coexist with a true Buddha, but this is unknown earlier. In any case the idea is of little consequence.

The universal Buddha ranks high over all saints or Pacceka Buddhas. The Canon, we have seen, contains traces of the abnormal character of the Buddha of history, but a strong tendency to treat emphatically the human side is apparent; the Buddha compares himself in his destruction of the enveloping covering of ignorance to the first chicken which breaks its shell;[2] he is the eldest but not in essence different from others; they must free themselves, though they follow his teaching. But even in the most orthodox view the Buddha possesses characteristics tediously scholasticized which assign to him the perfection of power, of wisdom, of peace, of mercy. He claims himself to be omniscient, all overcoming; he who has taught himself without a master; peerless in the worlds; the perfectly enlightened one, the highest teacher; who has attained Nirvāṇa. He is a hero born for the joy of the world to bring gladness to gods and men. The disciple follows his teaching; he does not aspire to become a Buddha, for from the mere fact that he is a disciple he can make no claim to attain such a result. Whether he could become a Pacceka Buddha is left obscure in the texts.

Beside the historic Buddha, however, there are others through the ages, all born in eastern India, with varying length of life, but in essence of one type; each preaches the doctrine, and it abides for a period, only to pass away again; that of the Buddha is to abide five hundred years only, for the admission of nuns

[1] DN. ii. 142; *Apadāna*; PP. ix. 1. He appears later as a hermit philosopher, Mhv. i. 301; Kern, *Ind. Budd.*, p. 61.

[2] *Suttavibhaṅga*, *Pārājika*, i. 1. 4; MN. i. 265. Contrast MV. i. 6. 8; AN. i. 22. See ch. ii. § 2.

has shortened the thousand years it else might have claimed.[1] No two universal Buddhas can coexist at least in one world system, though possibly even the Canon recognizes that there may be other Buddhas in other such systems.

But, if these Buddhas exist and from the teaching of each men attain knowledge and liberation, will the time come when every individual shall be set free? The Mahāparinibbāna Sutta suggests an affirmative reply, with the implication that the necessity of Buddhas themselves would cease, but the *Milindapañha* suggests a negative reply and this prevails in the later doctrine.[2]

The relation of the disciple to the Buddha is one of peculiar character. To the layman[3] was permitted and inculcated the merit of the worship of the relics of the dead master by his special command, and they did not fail to enshrine them in Stūpas, and to adore them at festivals with offerings of flowers, lights, and ceremonial ablutions. We need not deny the religious quality of such reverence; whether the Buddha himself claimed divine power and origin or not, the laity made him divine. But to the monks and nuns no less than the laity was it enjoined by the master himself to make pilgrimage, with assurance of reward if dying in the task, to one or other of the four holy places, of his birth, enlightenment, setting in motion the wheel of the law, and death. Moreover, every monk and nun can attain liberation only by taking refuge in the Buddha, the law, and the order. The Buddha doubtless is dead; he can extend no grace to the disciple; but he is the finder of the way, who taught the saving texts, and founded the order within whose bosom alone is sainthood to be won. The reverence he inspires can hardly, then, be denied the name of religion; there are races who recognize high gods, though they have ceased or never begun to make them offerings or to pray to them, and gratitude for the ineffable boon of liberation is surely cause enough for true religious emotion.

It is in accord with a primitive spirit of devotion and reverence that we find no idea in early Buddhism of seeking to become

[1] DN. ii. 2 f.; CV. xii. 2. 3; x. 1. 6. As to coexistence see AN. i. 27; Mhv. i. 123 ff.; Mil., pp. 236 ff.

[2] DN. ii. 157; Mil., p. 69; Mhv. i. 126.

[3] The Arahant is assumed to pay adoration at relic shrines; KV. xvii. 1.

a Buddha; the Buddhas are few and far between; the advent of one Buddha to be, namely Metteyya, is recognized in the Canon,[1] but the full conception of Bodhisattvas[2] makes its appearance only in late texts. Metteyya appears as the Buddha of age to come, to supervene on a period of exaggerated evil and sin. At last, wearied of self-destruction, men will practise virtue and abstain from sin, growing in length of life generation by generation as a reward, until the age of man reaches 80,000 years, and maidens are marriageable at 500 years. It is tempting to regard this as a picture of a Kingdom of Love ruled over by a Prince of Love (*metta*), but it would be to remodel, not to interpret the Buddhist record, which does not here develop the conception of love though it recognizes human solidarity. Nor do the many versions of the *Maitreyasamiti* known to us alter essentially the picture.[3]

[1] DN. iii. 76; cf. Beckh, *Buddhismus*, i. 132 f.

[2] The exact sense of the term is doubtful; normally it may be held to denote 'one whose existence (*sattva*) or essence is enlightenment'; cf. ERE. ii. 739. But it has also been rendered 'a being (destined to become possessed of) enlightenment' (cf. Winternitz, *Ind. Litt.* ii. 89, 367); 'one who has the will (*sattva*) for enlightenment', a result also obtainable by taking *sattva* as a misrendering of Pali *satta*, for *çakta*, 'having power', a view defended by Walleser (*Prajñāpāramitā*, p. 5, n. 3) by the analogy of Sutta, mistaken in his view for Sūtra in Sanskrit in lieu of *sūkta*, 'well said'—an implausible hypothesis. Senart (RHR. xlii. 360, n.) finds the explanation of the phrase in the Sāṁkhya idea of Sattva as the highest of the Guṇas, but essentially implicated in material existence as opposed to Puruṣa.

[3] See E. Leumann, *Die Maitreyasamiti*, Strassburg, 1919, who re-edits also the Pali *Anāgatavaṅsa*, a short poem on Metteyya, and fragments of the story in the unknown Iranian dialect styled North-Aryan by Leumann, and ascribed to the Çakas by Konow (GGA. 1912, pp. 551 f.) and Lüders (SBA. 1919, pp. 734 ff.).

CHAPTER VII

THE PLACE OF BUDDHISM IN EARLY INDIAN THOUGHT

1. *Early Indian Materialism, Fatalism, and Agnosticism*

From the Pali Canon we gather the clear impression that the systems which caused most interest and evoked most serious opposition from the Buddha dealt with life either purely materialistically, or were fatalistic, or denied the possibility of any knowledge. The glimpses we have of these doctrines is tantalizingly slight, and give no appreciation of the arguments by which they were supported. But there is sufficient evidence of the power of these beliefs in the history of Indian thought to show that the schools attacked by the Buddha were not visionary foes, but holders of doctrines popular and widespread among thinking men.

The simplest, and most hopeless from the Buddhist point of view, was presumably the creed of Ajita of the garment of hair (*kesakambalin*). It was a pure materialism; man is built up of the four elements, which at death are resolved into their native earth, water, fire, and air, while the senses, conceived apparently as in the classical form of the Cārvāka doctrine as the product of the commixture of the elements, pass into space, whose existence is also accepted. Hence, there is no true birth, whether from father and mother or fortuitous; there is no fruit of gift or sacrifice in this world or the next; wisdom avails not to prevent annihilation in the grave. An essentially similar doctrine doubtless was that of the Lokāyatas, who held that the soul was identical with the body, in the sense that it died with it, a doctrine evidently very popular in early India and persisting later, for the *Arthaçāstra* ranks the system with Sāṁkhya and Yoga as prevalent doctrines.[1]

Not much further advanced is the creed of Pakudha Kaccāyana; in it seven permanent substances, uncreated and without change, are admitted, which do not interact; the four elements, pleasure, pain, and the soul. There is, therefore, neither slayer nor causer of slaying, hearer or speaker, knower, or explainer; there is, in effect, a complete fatalism, a soul, pleasure and pain being merely thrown in to avoid the obvious difficulties of evolving them from matter.

Both these theories thus reject transmigration utterly, but Makkhali Gosāla, head of the Ājīvakas or Ājīvikas, a man well known to the Jains also, and who was once in close contact with their leader Mahāvīra, is credited with accepting transmigration, both fools and wise alike being condemned to wander for 8,400,000 periods before achieving an end of their pain. But he is entirely fatalistic in dogma; there is no cause of rectitude or depravity; men become pure or impure without reason or cause. There is no such thing as power, energy, human strength or human vigour. All is determined; it is idle by duty, penance, or righteousness to think that one can counteract the force of destiny. The pessimism of the doctrine can hardly have been diminished by the asceticism of the believers in it; we learn from the Jain scriptures of the utterly repugnant and painful practices to which they resorted, and which it seems impossible to bring into any very logical connexion with their tenets.[2]

A similarly disquieting doctrine is ascribed to Pūraṇa Kassapa; on what metaphysical basis he rested does not appear. But his view is clearly fatalistic; the committing of crime, even the making of all the creatures on earth one mass of flesh brings no guilt; in generosity, in self-mastery, in control of the senses, in

[1] DN. i. 55; cf. SN. iii. 307; MN. i. 515; DS., §§ 1215, 1362, 1364; Hillebrandt, KF., pp. 12 f., 25.; SBE. xlv. 237; SN. iii. 71; refers to casualists, deniers of the deed and deniers of existence; KV. i. 6. 60; DN., p. 56, n. 3.

[2] DN. i. 53; MN. i. 31, 198, 238, 250, 483, 512, 524; SN. i. 66, 68; iii. 69, 211; iv. 398; AN. i. 33, 286; iii. 276, 384; VP. i. 8, 291 &c; Hoernle, *Uvāsagadasāo*, pp. 108 ff.; SBB. ii. 71, n. 1; Franke, DN., p. 56; Jacobi, SBE. XLV. xxix; Mil., p. 5; Ui, VP., pp. 19, 22.

speaking truth, there is neither merit nor increase of merit. The prince who in his realm north of the Ganges gives alms and offers sacrifice reaps no reward of merit; when he slaughters and oppresses his foes to the south he acquires no guilt.[1]

These doctrines were at least definite; but Sañjaya of the Belaṭṭha clan, or son of Belaṭṭhī was agnostic pure and simple, refusing in effect to assert or deny any form of the four possible modes of framing a proposition: A is B, ; A is not B; A is both B and not B; A is neither B nor not B.[2]

It is easy to see how deeply these doctrines affected the Buddha's teaching; he opposed to them the conviction within limits of definite knowledge, while he adopted and developed a doctrine of agnosticism on a wide range of fundamental topics in the eyes of other thinkers, which in his view did not concern the essential fact of salvation. Salvation and the means of attaining it by human effort, by conduct and wisdom, he asserted as absolutely real against schemes of fatalism; he did not deny the material world, but he emphasized the essential element in life as psychic process. It was conviction of this process and its necessity, if effort were to be admitted, that produces the negation of the self regarded as something fixed and immutable as in Pakudha's doctrine.

In one point all these sages agreed; there were Samaṇas, ascetic in some degree, and they shared this peculiarity with the Jains whose leader Nigaṇṭha of the Ñāta (Nātha or Nāta) clan was evidently regarded with hostile eyes by the Buddha.[3] The Buddha himself had been a great ascetic; India admires ascetics and later Buddhist art portrays with horrible realism the emaciation of his sufferings; but, at the expense of some obloquy, he had risen superior to the excesses of asceticism and held rather that excessive asceticism was a hindrance, not an aid to the conquest

[1] DN. i. 53; SN. iii. 69; v. 126 and AN. iii. 383 attribute to him doctrines of Makkhali.

[2] DN. i. 58 f.; 27; Jacobi, SBE. XLV. xxvi; a scepticism and primitive stage of criticism of knowledge, Ui, VP., p. 23. That this Sañjaya's followers passed over to Buddhism (SBE. XLV. xxix) is implausible; Franke, DN., p. 50, n. 6.

[3] SBB. ii. 74; Franke, DN., p. 61; SBE. XLV. xxi ff.; *Sūtrakṛtāṅga*, i. 1. 1. 17; Ui, VP., pp. 19, 22. The original form was perhaps Jñātṛ.

of truth. The Jains reproached the Buddhists with a life of pleasure, and Buddhists often continued to admire penance, but the sanity of the founder of the school is undeniable.

2. *Buddhism and the Beginnings of the Sāṁkhya*

Clear as is the position adopted by the Buddha towards these aspects of thought, it is much less easy to determine the nature of his relation to the great philosophical systems then in the making, the metaphysics of the Vedānta and the Sāṁkhya. There can be no serious doubt as to the priority of the older Upaniṣads, the *Aitareya*, *Bṛhadāraṇyaka*, or *Chāndogya* to our Buddhist texts, nor need we exaggerate[1] their dates to accept this result, since we have seen no ground to place our Pali Canon in the fourth century B.C. But it is not easy precisely to determine the doctrine of the Upaniṣads; there are traces in it of an insight which gives us later the famous distinction of two forms of knowledge, the empiric, and the real, corresponding to the world of phenomena and the absolute, whose relations to the former are beyond all possibility of knowledge or expression by empirical determinations. But to accept[2] this as the oldest and fundamental Upaniṣad doctrine, of which other views are later corruptions is impossible. The main doctrine of the Upaniṣads is clearly the belief in the existence of an absolute; in the main this absolute is admitted to exist pantheistically in the world, while the destiny of the seeming individual is to be reabsorbed in release through the attainment of the saving knowledge in this absolute. It is only in the *Kaṭha Upaniṣad*, which is probably older than any Buddhist text we have, that we find a real attempt to think out the existence of the world and the self in relation to the absolute. The absolute, conceived as the person or spirit, a conception closely connected with the idea of the *Rigveda* that the world is created by the sacrifice of the primeval person (*puruṣa*) gives rise to the unevolved (*avyakta*), into which it enters as the great self (*mahān*

[1] As does Oldenberg, LUAB., p. 357, n. 185. A reference to the *Aitareya Upaniṣad*, *Chāndogya* and *Taittirīya* in Tevijja Sutta (Walleser, PGAB., p. 67) is most improbable.

[2] As do Deussen, *Philosophy of the Upaniṣads* and Schrader, JPTS. 1904-05, pp 161 f.

ātmā), and thus individualized, in a manner common in the Brahmanical speculation, develops as intellect (*buddhi*), mind, senses, and objects of sense. Beyond this speculation, elaborated in the later *Çvetāçvatara* and *Maitrāyaṇī Upaniṣads*, no progress is made in the Upaniṣads.[1]

In the classical form of the Sāṁkhya revealed in the *Sāṁkhya Kārikā* of Īçvarakṛṣṇa we find a system which differs vitally from the plan of the *Kaṭha Upaniṣad* by abolishing the universal person or spirit, and opposing to the unmanifested or nature (*prakṛti*) an infinite number of individual spirits, which, it is essential to note, are no longer conceived as in any sense enveloped in matter; from primitive matter intellect, individuation, unknown to the *Kaṭha*, mind, the senses and objects arise, but all is unconscious save through reflection in some degree[2] in the spirit, which nonetheless is a mere idle spectator of a process which concerns it not, and which will cease to be such a spectator for good, when it is realized that there is an eternal distinction and separateness (*viveka*) between spirit and matter. So artificial a structure cannot possibly be an outcome of primitive thought, and a bridge is provided in the Sāṁkhya known to the epic, where, though the later form of the doctrine begins to appear, we find also the spirit as universal, an attitude whose priority to the later idea is shown effectively by its harmony with the conception of nature as one.

That this was a form of thought existing in the period of early Buddhism cannot seriously be questioned; the precise view of the Buddha himself we cannot hope to gather, but it is interesting to examine how far the growth of the school was affected by these doctrines. There would, of course, be proof positive of influence of the Sāṁkhya on Buddhism did we take seriously the account in the *Buddhacarita* of the meeting of the Buddha with the teacher Arāḍa Kālāma and the Sāṁkhya doctrines—which have epic parallels—attributed by Açvaghosa to the latter.[3] But the

[1] Keith, *Sāṁkhya System*, chs. i and ii; Oldenberg, LUAB. ch. iii.

[2] cf. Garbe, *Sāṁkhya-Philosophie*,[2] pp. 368 f., 374 ff. with Dasgupta, *Ind. Phil.* i. 224 f.

[3] Jacobi, ZDMG. lii. 4 f.; Oldenberg, ibid. 681 ff.; GN. 1917, pp. 241 f.; Strauss. VOJ. xxvii. 257 ff. Garbe's views (SP., pp. 6 ff.) are clearly untenable; Keith, SS., pp. 22 f. (His views on Pythagoras' borrowings in Greek

Canon is silent and Açvaghoṣa a poet who would have us believe the Vaiçeṣika pre-Buddhist, so we may leave the argument aside. Less plausible still is the conjecture that the name of the Buddha's town, Kapilavatthu, retains a record of the sage Kapila, founder of the classical Sāṁkhya. The only proof available must be internal evidence.

The matter is complicated by the aversion of the Buddha to metaphysical speculations on topics deemed by him unnecessary, which explains why we have no examination of the conception of the Aupaniṣada absolute. The schematic handling of all possible theories of the continuance of consciousness after death is too formal to help, but in the *Majjhima Nikāya*[1] we do meet a passage which denounces in set terms as folly the conception of the existence of the self after death as identical with the absolute, the nearest approach—and that not in the earliest part of the Canon—to a formal attack on the absolute. This does not, however, take us necessarily to any connexion with the Sāṁkhya, and it is doubtful whether any aid is given by the attack[2] on philosophers who assert the eternity of the self and the world, bringing forth nothing new, steadfast as a mountain peak, firmly fixed as a pillar; the metaphor of the mountain top is found in epic and classical Sāṁkhya, but it applies to the spirit alone. Equally unconvincing is a Sāṁkhya origin for the distinction made by some teachers between the impermanent eye, ear, nose, tongue and body and the permanent consciousness, for the Sāṁkhya regards consciousness as equally impermanent.

It remains, therefore, to consider whether indirectly we can trace Sāṁkhya influence in its pre-classical form. More fruitful results here present themselves. There is an unmistakable similarity between the Sāṁkhya conception of the constant process of nature and the general Buddhist conception of the world as in

philosophy (pp. 126 ff.) are vitiated *inter alia* by his having overlooked Kaye, JRAS. 1910, pp. 753 ff. and are refuted by Oldenberg, GN. 1917, p. 253.)

[1] i. 138; cf. KV. i. 1. 242.

[2] DN. i. 14, 21; cf. Garbe, *Sāṁkhya-Philosophie* pp. 15 ff. That the idea of matter in Buddhism is borrowed from the Sāṁkhya, it is clearly (despite Geiger, PB., p. 81) wholly needless to assume. On materialistic tendencies in the Upaniṣad period cf. Jacobi, KF., pp. 37 ff. with Oldenberg's corrections (GN. 1917, pp. 268 ff.).

a perpetual condition of becoming. There is, moreover, a clear similarity in both systems in regard to the idea that the process is ruled by causality. True, the comparison of the Sāṁkhya system of the development of the twenty-four principles from nature downwards is a metaphysical explanation of empirical being, and therefore differs seriously from the Buddhist chain of causation of misery; hence the efforts of Professor Jacobi [1] and Pischel to work out a parallelism between the two has led to untenable comparisons, such as that of name and form with the individuation of the Sāṁkhya or of grasping with good and evil (*dharmādharmau*). But there is a real element of truth in the comparison; the idea of orderly development, which is already in the *Kaṭha*, is the source of the seeking of causal order in the Buddhist formula. But the connexion goes further than that; the vital element in the chain is the conception that ignorance of truth in the individual —not a cosmic force— produces in the substitute for a self impressions which until counteracted by knowledge, result in producing ignorance in a future birth and so on *ad infinitum*, and in the Sāṁkhya and Yoga, where the doctrine is more fully expounded, we have the same idea of ignorance—here of the non-connexion of spirit and matter—producing impressions; both systems likewise recognize the importance of the factor of desire. In both systems of thought, therefore, we have the same picture of a world of process as in a sense a self-contained and closed system; there are two differences of importance, which we may judge Buddhist innovations. The first is the disappearance of nature as an ultimate reality when evolution takes place; this obviously would have countered too violently Buddhist insistence on becoming. With it fall the Guṇas,[2] or constituents of being; indeed, the inclusion among them of the element of goodness (*sattva*) would have prevented Buddhism incorporating the conception in a system which asserted the misery of empirical reality as a ground for seeking release. Secondly, to the Sāṁkhya the whole process is unconscious save through reflection or other contact with spirit;

[1] GN. 1896, pp. 43 ff; ZDMG. lii. 1 ff.; Pischel, *Buddha*,[2] pp. 65 ff.

[2] A Sāṁkhya without Guṇas is very dubious; Keith, SS., p. 23; Oldenberg, GN. 1917, p. 242, n. 4.

this is impossible for a doctrine which denies the implication of a self in empirical reality, so that phenomena themselves appear as psychic no less than material.

There is some evidence also that Buddhism developed under the influence of the early Sāṁkhya conception of the spirit as indeed one, but not as intimately concerned with empiric reality. The doctrine expounded in the sermon on the characteristics of the not-self implies, as we have seen, the idea of a self as something utterly remote from experience, and a similar motive is seen in the sermon of Gayā on the world as enveloped in flames;[1] we seem here at the standpoint of a self which stands apart as a mere spectator of the misery of psychic existence, and the struggle for release takes the form, not of an effort within the causal series of the psychic happenings to stay its course of pain, but to realize the distinction between the self and this psychic complex. This idea, akin to the Sāṁkhya recurs quite clearly in the doctrine which makes the enlightened Buddhist say that nature is not his, he is not it, it is not his self, in terms which are a precise parallel of the recognition in the Sāṁkhya by the spirit of its distinction from nature which is the source of release from connexion with it.[2] The conclusion of borrowing is aided by a verbal similarity—rare otherwise as between Sāṁkhya and Buddhism; the conception of Nirvāṇa without residue of support (*upadhi*) is inexplicable, unless we remember the doctrine of both Vedānta and Sāṁkhya by which the spirit appears to belong to the world of becoming because of Upādhis; the transcendental in some way obtains a support and becomes transmuted into the empiric reality.

The proof of Sāṁkhya influence is obviously indirect, and not in itself complete. It is possible to argue that it is enough to assume influence of the doctrine of the absolute without the Sāṁkhya developments or to assign these developments to early Buddhism, though neither suggestion is perfectly satisfactory. But the case for influence is enormously strengthened by the

[1] MV. i. 6. 38 ff.; i. 21.

[2] Oldenberg's suggestion (LUAB., p. 319), based on MU. vi. 30, that in this proto-Sāṁkhya the spirit itself was regarded as really bound and suffering does not accord well with the Buddhist evidence, as he himself indeed admits, and is in itself improbable.

consideration that the Yoga shows with Buddhism remarkable similarities, not merely in doctrine but also in terminology, which suggest irresistibly borrowing, and render indebtedness to the kindred Sāṁkhya system extremely probable. The alternative, of Yoga borrowing from Buddhism, need not, as a factor of early development, be seriously considered; it is enough to note that Buddhists make no claim to originality in the trances which they employed, and these trances, though a popular and important feature of the discipline, favoured personally by the Buddha himself, do not in the oldest doctrine as well as later claim to be the absolutely essential elements of the process of salvation.

3. *Buddhism and Yoga*

That Yoga, that discipline, physical and mental, which procures its adepts magic powers as well as the highest reward of release or beatification,[1] is old in India is unquestioned. It is a development and rationalization of the asceticism, Tapas, which is acclaimed in the Veda as all powerful, and it stands clearly in close relation with the metaphysics both of the Upaniṣads and the early Sāṁkhya. The effort of the thinkers of the Upaniṣads to realize the absolute resulted in aiming at the divorce of the self from the things of empiric life; in such a result as was attained in deep dreamless sleep we have a condition suggesting union with the absolute, and the motive is given to adopt practices which will produce artificially a trance wherein realization of the absolute may become real. But the end is adaptable; the seeking of trance is too valuable and attractive to the Indian spirit to fail to be accommodated to any system of philosophy, and Yoga persists in close union with Sāṁkhya through the changes of that doctrine. Its first definite appearance in the Upaniṣads is, consistently enough, contemporaneous with the emergence of Sāṁkhya ideas in the *Kaṭha Upaniṣad.* By the time of early Buddhism the ascetics had perfected Yoga practices more and more energetically, and the Buddhists took them over with more than good will,

[1] Poussin, *Bouddhisme*, p. 361. See Senart, RHR. xlii. 345 f.; Oldenberg, LUAB., pp. 257 ff., 319 ff.; Beckh, *Buddhismus*, ii. 10 ff, 72 f.

regardless of the fact that the Yogin was a firm believer in the self which was denied by the Buddhist.

It is, however, an error to exaggerate the situation or to treat Buddhism as a branch of Yoga. True, the master attained the saving enlightenment by trance; the four noble truths mention trance as the last of the members of the noble eightfold path to the destruction of misery; the texts contemplate frequent use of trance. But it does not appear in the chain of causation; ignorance and intuition as the cause of misery, and of its removal are not essentially bound up with trance; and many narratives reveal the attainment of enlightenment without recourse to this means. The importance of Buddhism does not rest in its Yoga aspect, but that is not to deny the powerful influence which Yoga had upon its theory and practice.

The four ordinary meditations or trances of Buddhism correspond in general with the four stages of conscious concentration (*samādhi*) of the classical Yoga,[1] and, what is important, we have in the *Mahābhārata* a description of the first stage of concentration which expressly mentions the Buddhist features of initial and sustained application and of the separation (*viveka*) of the mind, doubtless from desire and impurity, for we cannot here read in the technical Sāṁkhya-Yoga terminology of distinction between spirit and matter. In the four or five matterless or formless meditations we have the Yoga[2] parallel of the achievement of infinity and the Buddhist conceptions of the attainment of the infinity of intelligence and infinity of space. Āḷāra Kālāma and Uddaka, two teachers of the Buddha, attained also the realms of nothingness and neither ideation nor non-ideation; the Buddha who could surpass them in this regard claims to be able to do so through the possession of the five qualities of faith, energy, thought, concentration and wisdom, and these five qualities appear in the Yoga as the necessary conditions for trance.[3] There is a precise parallel in the Yoga[4] for the series of four Brahmavihāras of friendship, sympathy with sorrow, sympathy with

[1] YS. i. 17; MBh. xii. 195. 15; Hopkins, JAOS. xxii. 357.
[2] YS. ii. 47.
[3] MN. i. 164. [4] YS. i. 33; Kern, *Ind. Buddh.*, p. 54.

happiness, and indifference, and the term Brahmavihāra is sufficient to prove Brahmanical, and perhaps Yoga origin. Significant also is the use of the terminology Citta and Nirodha of thought and its suppression in either system.

It is possible also that from the Yoga Buddhism borrowed the conception of a carefully planned regulation of psychical life in order to attain the desired end, and it is certainly interesting to recognize that the Yoga, at least in its later representatives, is conscious of the necessity of avoiding inflicting needless pain on the body. The rule to choose a pleasant spot of rest for meditation is in the *Çvetāçvatara Upanisad* as well as in Buddhism, and we hear of the feeling of lightness and gladness of the Buddhist monk as well as of the Yogin.

Much more doubtful is the question whether the Yoga influenced the development of Buddhist theory, since we do not know with any precision the form of Yoga in the centuries when Buddhism was forming its Canon. It is possible, in view of the frequency with which the epic connects the conception of Nirvāṇa with Yoga, that the term was borrowed hence by Buddhism. It is certainly remarkable that the Yoga should use of the nature of existence the terms 'impermanent, impure, misery, not-self', and the presence of ignorance at the head of the chain of causation can hardly stand apart from the fact that the Yoga with the Sāṁkhya makes ignorance the cause of the misery of the connexion of the spirit and matter, and ranks it also as the first of the five infections or defilements (*kleça*), a term taken over by Buddhism, and the ground of the others. It is far more doubtful if we can accept the idea that it is from the Yoga that Buddhism borrows the system of four noble truths; apart from the possibility of a common borrowing from medical science, the Yoga division is far too late and unimportant in the system to be accepted as the origin of the Buddhist.[1]

[1] The chain of causation may conceivably be connected with YS. iv. 11 (RHR. xlii. 359). The magic power of a Buddhist is akin to YS. iii. 27. It is less likely that the four stages of Arahantship are connected with the four degrees of Yogins, YS. iii. 51. That, in the Jhānas, Vitarka and Vicāra refer to cognition of the sensible and super-sensible (YS. i. 44 f.) is implausible, despite Beckh, *Buddhismus*, ii. 46; Geiger, PD., p. 82, n. 1.

4. *The Original Element in Buddhism*

The research of origins must not blind us to the essential fact that there was something new in Buddhism, though it must serve to warn us against too hasty conclusions as to what that new element was. We cannot, it must be admitted, claim for Buddhism the conception of causation as something new; the Sāṁkhya-Yoga had clearly mastered this conception, and had developed also the idea of the world as a process of becoming applicable to what we regard as psychic happenings; the Yoga also had reached the conception of all nature as impermanent, misery, subject to change, not-self. The further development of the idea by Buddhism was accompanied by the refusal to regard as within the sphere of legitimate inquiry the nature of what, if anything, lay behind the world we know. This agnostic element, not in itself original, leaves the way open to the mystery of Nirvāṇa, which some accept as covering nothingness, while others can treat as something ineffable, and an idea whose mere existence is enough to satisfy all desires.

Unquestionably, however, the moral training of the Buddhist system is marked by superiority to that of the Yoga, however deeply penetrated it may be by influences of the latter. The conviction of misery in Buddhism is real; it demands and receives serious treatment; both conduct and intuition are requisite for its removal, and conduct and intuition alike are aided by the development of the order in which one succours another by aid and advice. Whatever the defects of monastic organization, the root idea was valuable, and even for the laity something was done, though the Buddha had no such faith as would render it possible to lay down a doctrine applicable to all aspects of life. In the Yoga, on the other hand, the misery of spirit is after all an idle misconception; in truth there is no misery, and spirit is not bound in matter. Its philosophy remains, therefore, far less real in its influence on life and thought than Buddhism. The contrast is sufficiently seen in the missionary enterprise of Buddhism, a conception for which the cold intellectualism of the Sāṁkhya and Yoga has no place.

Yet it would be idle to suppose that these merits would have secured Buddhism its vast success and popularity save for the personality of its founder. He appeared, we must recognize, in an age when individuality had become recognized, when in India as in other lands powerful personalities were appearing and attracting respect and creating schools. Did he preach and practice love to mankind with a fervour which is almost wholly lost in the mechanical exercises of the production of the feeling of universal love which later Buddhism inculcates? Was he conscious of a mission beyond human power, and did he claim a divinity which Indian thought would readily concede to spiritual earnestness beyond normal measure? Our answer must vary with our individuality; one thing at least we must admit; despite its philosophical weaknesses and its incoherences, the founder of Buddhism must rank as one of the most commanding personalities ever produced by the eastern world.

PART II

DEVELOPMENTS IN THE HĪNAYĀNA

CHAPTER VIII

THE SCHOOLS OF THE HĪNAYĀNA

1. *The Traditional Lists*

OUR knowledge of the schools of Hīnayāna is hopelessly confused and unsatisfactory; it depends on accounts handed down in late authorities, whose sources of information are unknown to us, and who in all likelihood represent accounts given by one or other of the schools, and representing therefore, its own opinion of the course of events rather than historical fact. The Ceylonese version as presented in the *Dīpavaṅsa*, in the trustworthiness of whose sources we have every reason to put little faith, treats the Pali Canon as accepted in Ceylon by the Vibhajyavādin school of the Mahāvihāra as representing the true doctrine of the Theras or elders, and the actual teaching of the Buddha. Now even in Ceylon the Vibhajyavādins were far from holding undisputed sway; when Fa-Hian visited the island at the close of the fourth century A.D. the Mahīçāsaka school was flourishing, and would certainly have denied out and out the claim of the Vibhajyavādins.

The version of Buddhaghosa and the *Dīpavaṅsa* differing in detail even from the *Mahāvaṅsa*,[1] which is largely based on the same materials, places the first schism at the time of the Council of Vaiçālī, when, as a sequel to the condemnation of the Vajjiputtakas, the Mahāsaṅghikas broke away; from this schismatic school are two others, the Gokulikas and the Ekabbohārikas; the

[1] KV. comm., pp. 2 ff.; DV. v. 39 ff.; cf. *Mahābodhivaṅsa* (ed. 1891), pp. 95 ff. DV. has Mahāsaṅgītikas and Bahussutakas, see Minayeff, *Recherches*, ch. viii and ix; Kern, *Ind. Buddh.*, pp. 111 ff.; Rhys Davids, JRAS. 1891, pp. 409 ff.

former of these two gave rise to the Paññattivādins and Bāhulikas and later to the Cetiyavādins, apparently all these schools coming into being in the second century after the Parinirvāṇa. In the same century there arose in the Theravāda the schools of the Mahiṅsāsakas and the Vajjiputtakas, the latter giving rise to four branches, Dhammuttariyas, Bhadrayānikas, Channāgarikas, and Sammitiyas. From the Mahiṅsāsakas there arose the Sabbatthivādins and the Dhammaguttikas. The former school was prolific; it gave birth to the Kassapikas, and these in their turn gave rise to the Saṅkantikas, from whom divided off the Suttavādins. Thus, with the six Mahāsaṅghika schools and the original Theravāda, there is a total of eighteen. But the account of Buddhaghosa adds six further schools, the Rājagirikas, Hemavatikas, Siddhatthas, Pubbaseliyas, Aparaseliyas, and Vājiriyas. The Mahāsāṅghikas,[1] however, naturally did not accept the view which made the Vibhajyavādins the true representatives of the Theravāda; they themselves represented the Ācāryavāda, suggesting a learned origin for their tenets, and they claimed that the true division was threefold, Sthavira, Mahāsāṅghika, and Vibhajyavādin. The Sthaviras they subdivided into the Sarvāstivādins and the Vātsīputrīyas, omitting the Mahīçāsakas as a link between the Sthaviras and the Sarvāstivādins. The primacy of the Vibhajyavādins is also challenged in traditions from the north; the Sarvāstivādins are credited with holding that the Mūla-Sarvāstivādins were more primitive than the Vibhajyavādins, though they reckon the monks of the Mahāvihāra, but also those of the Abhayagiri and Jetavana monasteries in Ceylon, as Sthaviras.[2]

A northern view given by Vasumitra[3] accepts the first schism as that of the Mahāsāṅghikas, who gave rise in the second century after the Parinirvāṇa to the Ekavyavahārikas, the Lokottaravādins, and Kukkulikas or Kukkuṭikas, and later to the Bahuçrutīyas. In the next century there arose from it the Prajñaptivādins, the

[1] Tāranātha, *Buddhismus*, p. 271. Poussin (*Bouddhisme, Études*, p. 34) finds the Mahīçāsakas in the Mahāvihāra, but not plausibly.

[2] Tāranātha, p. 272.

[3] *Samayabhedoparacanacakra* (before A. D. 557); Wassilieff, *Bouddhisme*, pp. 227 ff. Five points raised by Mahādeva are made the origin of the trouble; Sthaviras, Nāgas, Prācyas and Bahuçrutīyas all take part in it.

Caitikas or Caityaçailas the Aparaçailas and the Uttaraçailas. The Sthaviravāda, on the other hand, in the third and fourth centuries divided into two main branches, each with further schools developing from it; the first was the Haimavatas, with the Dharmaguptikas, Mahīçāsakas, Kāçyapīyas, Sañkrāntikas or Sautrāntikas; the second the Sarvāstivādins, also called Hetuvādins or Vibhajyavādins, with the Vatsīputrīyas and their four sub-divisions of Dharmottarīyas, Bhadrāyaṇīyas, Sammatīyas or Sammitīyas, and Ṣaṇṇāgarikas. With this account there agrees fairly well that of Bhavya,[1] preserved in a Tibetan version; the Kukkulikas disappear from the Mahāsāñghika list, and the Channāgarikas from that of the Sthaviravāda, but in the latter the Mahīçāsakas reappear, and the Hetuvidyas and the Vaibādyavādins—a very bad version of Vibhajjavādin in Pali, appear as distinct, thus bringing up the number to the orthodox eighteen; in Vasumitra apparently it is intended to treat Hetu- and Vibhajya-vādins as one school. All these schools, we are led to believe, were Indian in origin; the *Mahāvaṅsa*, which confuses the issue considerably, adds that two more schools, the Dhammarucis and Sāgaliyas, arose in Ceylon.[2]

Our best source for knowledge of these sects or schools is the *Kathāvatthu* of the *Abhidharma Piṭaka*, for there is much that is unintelligible in the accounts preserved in Chinese and in modern Tibetan accounts, such as the reports of Vasumitra, Bhavya, or Tāranātha. But we are faced with the fundamental and insuperable difficulty that the text itself disdains to mention the names of the sects holding views which it refutes or discusses,[3] and we are therefore dependent on the account of Buddhaghosa, whose interest in the ideas may be creditable, but who is obviously a very poor authority on the point of what schools actually held the variant views. If we can trust his use of the present tense as indicating the actual existence of schools in his day we find only eight as

[1] Rockhill, *Life of the Buddha*, pp. 181 f; *Nikāyabhedavibhañgavyākhyāna.*

[2] Walleser (*Der ältere Vedānta*, pp. 11 f.) suggests that Mahiṅsaka denotes an Andhra school (cf. Mahiṣamaṇḍala; JRAS. 1910, pp. 425 ff.; 1911, pp. 816 ff.) whose name was misunderstood as certainly was Vajjiputtaka in the rendering Vātsī°.

[3] All the statements as to schools referred to in the KV. are derived from the comm. and are proved only for the fifth century A. D.

then active, say in the middle of the fifth century A. D., the Sammitiyas, the Sabbatthivādins, Andhakas, Gokulikas, Bhadrayānikas, Uttarāpathakas and Vetulyakas, with probably the Kassapikas, and possibly the Vajjiputtiyas and Mahāsaṅghikas; we have some corroboration of these facts in the reports of the Chinese pilgrims Fa-Hian and Hiuen-Tsang (Yuan-Chwang) who assert the existence in northern India of the Mahāsāṅghikas, while there were Mahīçāsakas in Ceylon.

The materials are wholly inadequate to attain an intelligible view of the true connexions of the schools, their tenets, or the date of their appearance. The Vajjiputtakas, Vajjiputtiyas, or Vatsīputrīyas, figure in the Ceylonese tradition as the beginners of the schism by their failure in points of discipline, and then as merging, it seems, in the Mahāsāṅghikas; the northern accounts forget this fact, or reject it, and make them an offshoot of the main school rather than of the Mahāsāṅghikas; they tell us nothing of their special views. The Gokulikas, if the Sanskrit version Kukkulika represents the original form of their name, may have derived it from their doctrine that the world is a fiery mass of misery (*kukkuḷa*),[1] but they may have really been a local school. The Andhakas, in the view of Buddhaghosa, are divided into the Pubba- and Apara-seliyas, who seem to derive their name from two cliffs facing each other in the region about Kāñcipura and Amarāvatī on the south-east coast in the Andhra country. The parallelism between the Caityikas, Uttara- and Avara-çailas as offshoots of the Mahāsāṅghika in the account of Bhavya with the Caitikas, Uttara- and Apara-çailas in that of Vasumitra has suggested that there is a real connexion between the Andhaka schools and the Cetiyavādin;[2] now there is evidence both in Sanskrit texts and late Tibetan tradition that the Caitika school was founded by a certain Mahādeva, who is credited with five heretical doctrines to decide which a council was held, apparently a confusion with the alleged Council to settle the ten points of the Vajjiputtakas. But Buddhaghosa had evidently no

[1] KV. ii. 8, where optimism is defended as orthodox.

[2] Poussin, JRAS. 1910, pp. 413 ff; *Points of Controversy*, p. xliii (corrected from p. xxxvi); cf. KV. ii. 1 ff.

knowledge of the tradition of Mahādeva, and he does not connect the Cetiyavādins with the Andhakas. Of most of the other schools our information is even less satisfactory; their names may indicate the original teachers, as Vasumitra and Bhavya assert, but we cannot place any implicit faith in so easy assertions.

Greater interest and importance attach to the tradition that the Sthaviras adopted the name of Haimavatas in the third century after the Parinirvāṇa when the Hetuvādins broke away from the main body. The fact of the connexion of the Theravāda with the north is attested effectively by the *Milindapañha*; it is impossible to question its northern origin, and there is legendary evidence of the activity of the Sthaviras in Kashmir; indeed, the suggestion [1] has been made that it was from the true fountain of tradition in Kashmir rather than from Magadha that the Council of Asoka derived its doctrines, and that the Abhidharma literature is a product of Kashmir. But this contention can hardly be taken seriously, when we reflect not merely on the dubiety of the Council, but also on the fact that the argument is based on what is now notoriously wrong, the identity of the *Abhidhamma Piṭaka* of the Pali Canon with the Abhidharma of the Sarvāstivādins, which is connected in some measure with Kashmir. But we have in the *Milindapañha* a very significant fact, which shows us that the Vibhajyavādins cannot claim full credence for their assertions of their own antiquity. The Parivāra appendix of the *Vinaya Piṭaka* is certainly a late work; it was rejected both by the Dhammarucis of Abhayagiri and also evidently was ignored by the *Milindapañha*.

2. *The Vibhajyavādins*

The origin of the Vibhajyavādins must remain obscure, though doubtless early. The exact force of the title is uncertain. But in the Canon it appears that to be an answerer in detail (*vibhajjavādin*) was one of the four rational ways of answering an inquiry. You might meet it by (1) a general proposition: (2) a number of particular propositions replying in detail; (3) a counter question; or (4) by waiving aside an unintelligible or irrelevant question. It

[1] Walleser, PGAB., pp. 145 ff.

has been contended, therefore, that, when established generalizations were being arraigned by criticism or when in the Asokan age errors springing from uncritical interpretation of doctrine were to be expunged, the way to purity of ideas lay especially in the *Distinguo* of the second of these methods.[1] This view is strengthened by the fact that once or twice in the Suttas we actually find the Buddha represented as declining to make the general assertion anxiously awaited by his interlocutor and replying instead: 'Herein I am a particularizer; I am no generalizer', and in the comment on the *Katthāvatthu* Buddhaghosa ascribes many of the disputes to want of particularization. A different origin, though one not out of sympathy with the spirit of the preceding suggestion, is ascribed in the *Abhidhārmakoça*, where the name is traced to the fact that the school answer the old question: 'Does all exist?' with a distinction; the present and the past which has not yet borne its fruit exist; the future and the past which has borne its fruit do not exist.[2]

It is reasonable to accept the view that the *Abhidhamma Piṭaka*, as we have it in the Pali Canon, is the definite work of this school, a systematic scholasticism based on the Suttas, but nevertheless often advancing in detail beyond them. The date of the Abhidharma and its redaction in its present shape are alike unknown to us, but we may reasonably believe that it was composed from the first in Pali, whereas the Vinaya and the Suttas were redacted in Pali—doubtless with many additions of original composition—on the basis of earlier work in a dialect more closely vernacular.

3. *Sarvāstivādins, Vaibhāṣikas, and Sautrāntikas*

Opposed to the Vibhajyavādins were the Sarvāstivādins, asserters of the reality of all things, and among them also we find a set of Ābhidhārmikas, who developed a philosophical literature of their

[1] AN. i. 197; Mil., p. 445; *Points of Controversy*, pp. xl. f. KV. v. 6, distinction between popular and philosophical truth; xix. 2, application of idea of the void erroneously; xi. 5, misinterpretation of term Kappa, age.

[2] Poussin, AK., p. vi., following AK. v. 25. As known to us the school is of Ceylon, but doubtless derived fr m the mainland. Later it dominated Burma and Siam; see Eliot, *Hinduis a and Buddhism*, ch. xxxvi. ff.

own, while the school possessed a Vinaya and a Sutta collection on the same lines as the Pali Canon, possibly at first written in some Prakrit, but later certainly in Sanskrit. This Abhidharma literature begins with the *Jñānaprasthāna* of Kātyāyanīputra—variously dated at three hundred or five hundred years after the Parinirvāṇa—and its six 'feet (pāda),' *Dharmaskandha* by Çāriputra; *Dhātukāya* by Pūrṇa; *Prajñāptiçāstra* by Maudgalyāyana; *Vijñānakāya* by Devakṣema; *Saṁgītiparyāya* by Çāriputra; and *Prakaraṇapāda* by Vasumitra; though it has disappeared in its Sanskrit form save for odd fragments, it is preserved in a Chinese rendering.[1] Chinese records show how that the *Jñānaprasthāna* was brought by Saṅghadeva and Dharmapriya from Kashmir (A.D. 383) possibly in a Pali-like dialect, while Hiuen Tsang (A.D. 657) used a Sanskrit version. Some of the Sarvāstivādins clung to these texts as their sole authority; Dharmatrāta, Ghoṣaka, Vasumitra, and Buddhadeva are all criticized by the Vaibhāṣikas of Kashmir and Buddhadeva is apparently the teacher mentioned in a Mathurā inscription (perhaps 50 B.C.–A.D. 10). Dharmatrāta is traditionally, but apparently in error, placed much later, being a pupil of Āryadeva the Mahāyānist (perhaps A.D. 200), and Vasumitra is assigned to the time of a son of Kaniṣka (A.D. 100).[2] These data are insufficient to help us to any very definite idea as to the date of the *Jñānaprasthāna* and its supplements; no faith can be placed on the alleged authors, the titles being manifestly intended to convey the impression of extreme antiquity. But it is clear that the Abhidharma must go back to at least a century B.C. It is impossible to prove whether it preceded, as is at least possible, or was contemporary with, or subsequent to, the compilation of the *Abhidhamma Piṭaka*.

[1] The *Prajñāptiçāstra* exists in the Tibetan and is analysed by Poussin in part as an appendix to his ed. of *Abhidharmakoça*, III, pp. 295 ff. The AKV. has Devaçarman and, for the *Saṁgītiparyāya*, Mahākauṣṭhila; Tāranātha, *Buddhismus*, pp. 56, 296; Takakusu, JPTS. 1904–05, pp. 67 ff; for the latter text, cf. DN. no. 33; SBB. iv. 200; above, ch. i. § 1.

[2] Dharmatrāta, author of the *Udānavarga* and *Saṁyuktābhidharmahṛdayaçāstra*, was uncle of Vasumitra, and his work must have been used by Açvaghoṣa; thus he probably lived under Kaniṣka; Lévi, JA. 1912, ii. 215 ff. See Lüders, SBA. 1914, pp. 101 ff.

Under Kaniṣka who presented a casket with Buddha's relics to the Sarvāstivādins, it seems,[1] must be placed the writing of a commentary, Vibhāṣā, on the Abhidharma, whence the name of the Vaibhāṣika school of Buddhism, whose centre was apparently Kashmir, although in that country itself there were Buddhists who were not Vaibhāṣikas, and although we hear of Vaibhāṣikas of the outer country, the west, and the northern borders.

To the Vaibhāṣikas and the Sarvāstivādins there developed opposition in the school of the Sautrāntikas, who insisted that the Abhidharma texts and *a fortiori* the Vibhāṣā had no authority, and that such Abhidharma as the Buddha taught was contained in the Suttas, a doctrine obviously fairly in accord with the essential facts. Therefore they adhered determinedly to the Sūtras alone, although they accepted the Sarvāstivādin and the Vaibhāṣika views save where they conflicted with their own. Of their views we have some account in the great work of Vasubandhu, the *Abhidharmakoça*, with his own commentary. The Koça itself in six hundred stanzas sets forth the views of the Vaibhāṣika school of Kashmir, but Vasubandhu was not a Vaibhāṣika or a Sarvāstivadin; on the contrary he had strong Sautrāntika sympathies, and later himself adopted the Yogācāra attitude, with which in his comment he shows himself familiar. His Bhāṣya therefore criticizes freely the views of the Vaibhāṣika, a fact which brought upon him replies from orthodox Vaibhāṣikas. The date of Vasubandhu, therefore, becomes of special interest to us; the period A.D. 420–500 suggested by Takakusu[2] on the strength of Chinese evidence may probably be taken to be superseded by the proposal of Péri which brings his death not later than A.D. 350; a date substantially earlier is impossible, if we accept the strong tradition

[1] There is confusion here between works called *Vibhāṣā* and *Mahāvibhāṣā*, in which Kaniṣka seems referred to as in the past; Watters, *Yuan Chwang*, i. 274 ff; Takakusu, JRAS. 1905, p. 415; JPTS. 1904–05, p. 123. The Vinaya of the Mūla-Sarvāstivādin is familiar with the north-west, and alludes to Kaniṣka; *T'oung Pao*, 1907, p. 115; JA. 1914, ii. 493; see JRAS. 1908, p. 1058 for casket; on Açvaghoṣa's share, see JRAS. 1905, p. 52.

[2] BEFEO. 1904, p. 37; Péri, *ibid.* 1911, pp. 339 ff; Poussin, AK., pp. viii. f.; SC. Vidyābhūṣaṇa, JASB. 1905, p. 227; Smith, *Early Hist. of India*[3], pp. 328–34; Watters, *Yuan Chwang*, i. 210, 355–9; Winternitz, *Ind. Litt.* ii. 256; Lévi, MSA. ii. 1 f.

which brings him into contact with a son of Candragupta. This is, of course, on the assumption that the Vasubandhu of the *Abhidhārmakoça* is the brother of Asaṅga, of the Yogācāra school; it is just possible to read observations of Yaçomitra in his comment on the Koça to mean that the author refers to this Vasubandhu, and he was therefore later, but this suggestion is on the whole implausible. The merits of the work are obvious, and the fact of its only partial preservation in Sanskrit has hampered greatly Buddhist studies. It covers the whole field of ontology, pyschology, cosmology, the doctrine of salvation and of the saints, and a vast proportion of its matter is common to all Buddhist belief. Hence it formed the text-book of Buddhists generally after Vasubandhu's death, whether they followed the Hīnayāna or the Mahāyāna, while it contains incidentally much evidence on the early Sanskrit Canon. It formed itself the subject of comment by Vasumitra and Guṇamati, and later by Yaçomitra whose comment is preserved to us in Sanskrit.[1]

4. *Precursors of the Mahāyāna*

Different as these schools are in view and outlook, they all are classed as within the Hīnayāna, and therefore as distinct from the Mahāyāna. The suggestion, however, has been made that the apparent distinctness is illusory and that Buddhaghosa's list at least includes sects which would by us be classed as Mahāyānist. In support of this view it is pointed out[2] that the Chinese pilgrims recognize along with Mahāsāṅghikas, Mahīçāsakas, Sarvāstivādins, Sāmmitīyas, Sthaviras, Lokottaravādins, the Pūrva- and Aparaçaila Vihāras, the Mahāyānists and Hīnayānists so that Buddhaghosa who wrote half a century after Fa-Hian (A.D. 400) could hardly fail to take account of schools of the Mahāyāna. This abstract argument is aided by the suggestion that a Mahāyānist school is to be detected in the Vetulyakas who are represented as

[1] Book III is ed. and trs. Poussin. Yaçomitra is Sautrāntika in view. Kumāralabdha, teacher of Çrīlābha, founded the school, and traditionally he is a contemporary of Nāgārjuna (c. A. D. 200); Kern, *Ind. Buddh.*, pp. 122, 127; the date, however, is clearly uncertain; cf. BEFEO. 1911, pp. 359, 375; Watters, *Yuan Chwang.* ii. 286; Eliot, *Hinduism and Buddhism*, ii. 86, n. 4, 92.

[2] *Points of Controversy*, pp. xlv. ff.

docetists, and described according to some manuscripts as teachers of the great emptiness (*mahāsuññatāvādins*), while an effort has been made to compare the description of the Mahāyāna Sūtras as Vaipulyas with their name.[1] The Uttarāpathakas, a vague title, 'northerners' must have included Mahāyānists, since they patronized the doctrine of 'suchness' (*tathatā*) in the sense of the existence of something unconditioned, while the Mahāsāṅghikas held views in some respects intermediate between the Mahā- and the Hīna-yāna. It can hardly be said that this reasoning is satisfactory. The Vetulyakas appear in history in the third century A.D. and later as a dissident sect in Ceylon, and there is nothing to show that the Uttarāpathaka doctrine of 'suchness' assumed anything like the remarkable shape which it has in the Mahāyāna.[2]

The Mahāsāṅghikas, again, though doubtless in doctrine forming a bridge to Mahāyāna ideas were clearly distinct from the Mahāyāna. To them belonged the Lokottaravādins, of whom we have a revised and altered relic in the shape of the *Mahāvastu*,[3] which purports to be the Vinaya of the Lokottaravādins, of the Āryamahāsāṅghikas; both schools are mentioned by the Chinese pilgrims, and their importance was clearly great, but the *Mahāvastu* as preserved is decidedly late, since it refers *inter alia* to Chinese and Hunnish writing and to Greek astrology.

The Sāmmitīyas have been even less fortunate, though a Çāstra was translated into Chinese between A.D. 350 and 431. They were, it is clear, closely connected with the Vātsīputrīyas, with whom the *Abhidharmakoçavyākhyā* actually identifies them.[4]

The appearance of the Mahāyāna in its developed forms as distinctive schools, Madhyamaka and Vijñanavāda, did not mean the absorption of the Hīnayāna schools, which persisted side by side with them in varying strength, the Sarvāstivādins and their

[1] SBE. XLIX. ii. 188 f; 102 f; Kern, *Vaitulya, Vetulla, Vetulyaka* (Amsterdam, 1907); Poussin, JRAS. 1907, pp. 432 f., on the strength of a blunder in a Kashgar fragment of the *Saddharmapuṇḍarīka* when Vaitulya replaces Vaipulya.

[2] Below, ch. xii. § 1.

[3] ed. Senart, Paris, 1882–97.

[4] In TRD., p. 46 they as Āryasamitīya appear as Vaibhāṣikas, and believers in a person (*pudgala*). This is untrustworthy, as regards the identification. The name may be Sammitīyas or Sāmmitīyas, and the meaning is uncertain. In MKV. (p. 148, n. 1) it stands for the Hīnayāna.

subdivisions being predominant in Northern India; in the second century A.D. we find the Caitikas at Amarāvatī, the Mahāsāṅghikas at Kārli, and the Bhadrāyaṇīyas at Nāsik. The eighteen sects are mentioned by King Guhasena of Valabhī (A.D. 559), and are known to the Chinese pilgrims, but Hiuen-Tsang obtained scriptures only of the seven, Sthaviras, Mahāsāṅghikas, Mahīçāsakas, Sāmmitīyas, Kāçyapīyas, Dharmaguptas, and Sarvāstivādins and knows the Lokottaravādins, while I-Tsing groups the eighteen under the four heads of Mahāsāṅghikas, Sthaviras, Sāmmitīyas, and Mūla-Särvāstivādins. But there were other lines of division, based on the distinction of Vinaya, Sūtra and Abhidharma, and probably these may have been more important than the school divisions proper.

While the relations of the schools among themselves were complex and varied, their relation to the Mahāyāna was obviously equally complicated; there was nothing to prevent the combination of Mahāyāna and Hīnayāna views; Fa-Hian resided at Pāṭaliputra in a Mahāyānist monastery, but found there the Vinaya of the Mahāsāṅghikas and the Sarvāstivādins; in Hiuen-Tsaṇg's enumeration of some 183,000 monks, 32,000 only were Mahāyāna out and out, 96,000 Hīnayāna, and 54,500 lived in monasteries where both faiths were studied, and he reckons some at least of the Sthaviras of Ceylon as Mahāyānists, a term which in I-Tsing covers all who read the Mahāyāna texts and worship Bodhisattvas. Neither he nor I-Tsing seems to be hostile to the Hīnayāna, but to regard it as merely an inferior stage of knowledge and practice; Hiuen-Tsang is credited with converting Harṣa (A.D. 606–48)—a very eclectic king—to Mahāyāna from Hīnayāna beliefs. I-Tsing apparently accepted as all valid the Vinaya of the Mūla—Sarvāstivādins; the Madhyamaka and Yogācāra or Vijñānavāda systems, regarded as rather complementary than opposed; and the Mahāyāna religious and ethical precepts. Eclecticism was doubtless encouraged by the existence of such institutions as the great University of Nālandā in Magadha, not far from Gayā, which appears to have come into prominence after the time of Fa-Hian; the district of Valabhī, on the other hand, was the stronghold of the Sāmmitīyas who, if we are to judge from Hiuen-Tsang's

The rest of existence is made up of eleven material compounds; one compound, mind; forty-six mental compounds; and fourteen non-mental compounds. The essential character of matter is its power of obstruction to the organs of sense, a fact which contrasts it absolutely with the ether. The unit of matter is the atom (*paramāṇu*), which is composite, as it rests on a fourfold substratum of colour, smell, taste, and touch. It is invisible, inaudible, intangible, without taste, indivisible, and unanalysable. But it is not permanent, but flashes into being; its essential feature is its action or function, and therefore may be compared to a focus of energy. Seven of these units, clustered around one as the centre, create the visible atom (*aṇu*) out of which matter, including the organs of sense, is composed. The distinctions of the elements; earth as rough, water as viscous, fire as hot, wind as movable; are due to the predominance in each of its own special characteristics and the inactivity of the others which are also present, for the unit has in itself the qualities of all the elements. The mutual attraction of material things is explained by the presence of the quality of water in each, their resistance by that of earth and so on; their collocations in nature are explicable by attraction, cohesion, heating, clustering, &c. As real, the cause never actually perishes; what happens is a change of state, when it becomes an effect, involving an alteration of name; thus the clay becomes the pot, without any real change of nature.

The relation between mental and material things is a case of causation but of a special kind since it may be said to be simultaneous, in lieu of subsequent. This raises a difficulty as suggesting the Vijñānavāda theory that there is no real externality in things, but a mistaken and illusory attribution of externality to that which is internal, as can be shown from the fact that we always experience an object and its cognition together. The Sautrāntikas reject this view; the facts are, they argue, clearly that what we see are objects, as external, not merely internal modifications of consciousness, to which in point of fact we do not in everyday life attend at all as such. The idealist admission that things appear as if external undermines their whole position, for the conception of externality could not rise without real ground. There is no real difficulty as to simultaneity between the object and the perception of it; we do not, as the objection to this possibility seems to imply, first know the object and then know the perception, but the object by contact with the sense organ impresses its form on the cognition, and then from the form we conclude by inference the existence of an external object which causes it, just as we infer nourishment from a thriving appearance, nationality from language, and love from emotion. The object moulds our knowledge without ceasing to be itself. Cognition cannot explain our objects; in itself it is the same and there would be no differentiation of objects if objects were derived from it. The diversity of cognitions in an observer, himself remaining the same, is explicable only by the operation on him of external things, a fact which gives us the realization of the self as the conscious subject (*ālaya-vijñāna*) in whom individual cognitions (*pravṛtti-vijñāna*), caused by external things, appear from time to time.

The Vaibhāṣikas, though realists, object to this doctrine of the Sautrāntikas—indeed a fanciful etymology gives them their name because of their habit of styling the doctrine of inferability 'contradictory chatter (*viruddhā bhāṣā*)'. If knowledge is thus reduced to inferability, then there is no object of perception, and, this being so, there is no basis for the observation of the invariable concomitance, which is the essential ground of inference, and we shall have a complete contradiction with all actual experience. Knowledge, in fact, is of two kinds; perception as indeterminate, that is free from the operation of imagination, which is authoritative, and determinate perception which is worked up by imagination and so is not directly authoritative, although what is inferred serves as a basis for action and common acceptance; we can verify by action the truth of inferences, and we can accept statements on authority as resting ultimately on perception.[1]

[1] SDS., pp. 14 ff.; cf. TRD., pp. 40 f., 47; SSS. IV. iii. 1 ff.; iv. 1; below, ch. xviii, §§ 2, 3. The Vaibhāṣikas appear to be credited (Wassilieff, *Bouddhisme*, pp. 280, 282) with the Mahāsāṅghika view (KV. xviii. 9) that the eye sees colour and so on, not consciousness based on the eye; cf. MKV., p. 33; Asl., p. 400; Sumaṅg. i. 183; TDC., p. 22, n. 1. The Sautrāntikas are credited

numbers, were at his date the strongest sect, though this was not the case in that of I-Tsing who assigns pre-eminence to the Mūla-Sarvāstivādins, a term which we may interpret as denoting the Sarvāstivādin school proper as opposed to its Vaibhāṣika and Sautrāntika developments.[1]

[1] See Kern, *Ind. Buddh.*, pp. 128 ff; Rhys Davids, JRAS. 1891, pp. 409 ff; 1892, pp. 1 ff; Eliot, *Hinduism and Buddhism*, ch. xxiii; Poussin, *Bouddhisme* (1898) ch. ii. Buddhaghosa, the great commentator on the Canon, and author of the *Visuddhimagga*, (c. A. D. 450-500) studied first at Gayā and may have been influenced by the Mahāyāna; Walleser, PGAB., pp. 116 f; JRAS. 1904, p. 371.

CHAPTER IX

THE DOCTRINE OF REALITY

1. *Realism*

We have seen that there is no adequate ground for attributing to early Buddhism any conviction of the ideality of the world, and the conviction that no such belief prevailed certainly gathers support from the out-and-out realism of the Sarvāstivādins, whose name is derived from their assertion: 'Everything exists'.[1] The whole of reality is comprehended under a division into seventy-five kinds of existence or Dharmas, of which three alone are uncompounded (*asaṁskṛta*), neither being produced nor dissolving. These are the ether (*ākāça*),[2] the essence of which is freedom from obstruction, and which therefore is regarded as a permanent omnipresent material substance; in other words it may be treated as space regarded as absolutely real. The second form of uncompounded existence, unplanned destruction (*apratisaṁkhyā-nirodha*), is of relatively slight importance; it is merely in one view the non-perception of objects owing to the absence of the necessary conditions as when in attending to one thing others are left unnoticed, or rather it denotes the essential character of things as ever perishing without cause. The third, deliberate destruction (*pratisaṁkhyā-nirodha*), is final deliverance from bondage which endures for ever, and which is attained by following the eightfold path as laid down in the Canon.

[1] Cf. KV. i. 6, 7. An elaborate account of the school, based on the *Abhidharmakoça*, *Mahāvibhāṣāçāstra*, &c., is given by Y. Sogen, *Systems of Buddhistic Thought*. Atomism is found in Dharmottara's *Abhidharmahṛdayaçāstra*, but the date is dubious; it is not found in the *Jñānaprasthāna* but in the *Mahāvibhāṣā*; Ui, VP., p. 26 f. Both Vaibhāṣikas and Sautrāntikas have it; SSS. IV. iii. 4; iv. 4, 13 f; the Madhyamaka rejects it; IV. i. 4; see AKB., pp. 111 ff; Ui, VP., pp. 48 f; Vasubandhu, *ibid.*, pp. 72 f; Wassilieff, *Bouddhisme*, pp. 279 f 245 ff.

[2] Or space; see § 2: and on the three non-compounds § 7; MKV., p. 176; *Album Kern*, p. 111.

2. *The Nature of Time and Space*

Though the Canon recognizes the impermanent character of existence it is devoid of any serious consideration of the meaning of impermanency. Any effective handling of the question of time is certainly missing from the Upaniṣads; the indivisible non-time of the *Maitrāyaṇī Upaniṣad* is merely a time before the actual normal time, and in the *Atharvaveda* and the *Mahābhārata*, where time appears in the light of a creator, we have nothing seriously philosophical. The explanation of the doctrine is simple enough; in the Brāhmaṇa speculation Prajāpati, the creator, is also regarded as the year; creation in time leads to the simple conception of creation by time, and there is certainly no trace even in the more advanced speculation of the *Mahābhārata* of any distinction between time as real or transcendent and time as subjective. It is hardly surprising, therefore, that early Buddhism with its clear dislike for problems not immediately tending to salvation should have left the issue severely alone; the eternity or other condition of the world is expressly included among the indeterminates.[1]

The *Milindapañha*[2] shows us a clear advance of interest in the question of time. Milinda questions Nāgasena in detail on this point, and is informed that there is past, present, and future time; time which exists and time which does not exist. This is explained in the sense that there are dispositions (*saṁkhāra*), which are past in the sense of having ceased to be, or having been dissolved, or altogether changed; to them time is not. But there are also conditions which are now producing their effect, or have in them the potentiality of producing effect, or which will otherwise lead to re-individualization; to them time is. When there

with three different views of the nature of the perception of an object. (1) All its characteristics are represented in thought form and so apprehended; (2) thought form is of the total actual presentation only, e.g. of variegated colour as such; (3) all aspects of the object are presented in thought, but it synthesizes them in one view, e.g. the different colours are made one; Wassilieff, *Bouddhisme*, pp. 275 f.

[1] Walleser, PGAB., pp. 123 ff.; Schrader, *Über den Stand der ind. Phil.*, pp. 19 f.; AV. xix. 53, 54; MBh. xii. 227. 29.

[2] pp. 50 ff. Cf. KV. i. 8, doctrine of Kassapikas.

are beings who when dead will be reborn, there is time; when there are beings who when dead will not be reborn, there is no time; and, when beings have been altogether set free by the attainment of Nirvāṇa and bodily death, there time is essentially not. The king inquires also as to the root of past, present, and future time, and is informed that it is in ignorance; the meaning of the reply is clear when the answer proceeds to enumerate the chain of causation beginning with the dispositions, for we have seen that the idea of time is illustrated by the condition of the dispositions. Were it not for ignorance, there would be no dispositions, and therefore no time; the enlightened one is exempt from connexion with time. Further, it is made clear that there is no possibility of finding a beginning to time, or ultimate point in the past; the position is made clear by the analogy of the seed, fruit, seed; egg, hen, egg; and the circle of eye, colours, sight, contact, feeling, longing, action, and, as the outcome of action, an eye in a future birth. Finally, the sage insists as against the suggestion of the king that there may be discontinuity between the present and the past and the future that there is constant continuity. That which has not been becomes, that which has begun to become vanishes away; past, that is to say, passes over to the present, and the present passes over to the future.

Prof. Walleser has deduced from these passages the conclusion that, while the existence of transcendent time is not denied, it is made clear that time is reduced to the momentary present, and that time is an ideal phenomenon, a result which follows necessarily from the reduction of time to the momentary present; past and future time, if not real, must either be absolutely nothing or phenomenal, and the latter decision is the natural one to adopt to accord with the facts. These conclusions, however, seem rather to over-estimate the degree of philosophical competence of the composer of the *Milindapañha*. There is, it must be added, no clear or probable understanding in the text of a true momentary present; indeed the true version rather emphasizes the continuity of time; the idea that the present is sharply cut off from the past and future, which appeals to the king, is rebuked by Nāgasena. A distinction between phenomenal and transcendental time is not present to the composer; his point is different, but quite clear and satisfactory; time is essentially a thing of the world of experience alone; the world exists in it, and the time is ever in motion; but in true enlightenment there is as little room for time as for anything else empirical. Of time as a mental creation of any sort there is no suggestion; the text takes it as it is found in experience, and makes no effort to analyse or explain its nature.

The ideas of the *Milindapañha* appear in a varied form in the *Abhidharmakoça*.[1] The Sarvāstivādins are there credited with maintaining the existence of everything past, present or future, while the Vibhajyavādins distinguish in their usual mode between (1) the present elements and those among the past which have not yet produced their fruition, which are existent and (2) future elements and those among the past which have produced their fruition, which are non-existent. Of the first view there are variant aspects. Dharmatrāta maintained that the essence of an element remains unchanged throughout various times, its existence alone altering, an idea made intelligible by the change of milk into curds or the breaking of a vessel of gold. The view is obviously closely akin to the Sāṁkhya in which all change is merely alteration of an existent without fundamental change of substance, and is rejected by the Vaibhāṣikas on that account, for it implies a permanent substance. In Ghoṣaka's view, when an element appears at different times, the past element retains its past aspects without being severed from its present and future aspects, and the present retains its present aspect without completely losing its past and future aspects, a view which the Vaibhāsikas very sensibly reject on the ground that it simply destroys distinctions of time, since all the aspects are to coexist. Buddhadeva adopts the view that, just as a woman can be regarded as mother, wife, or daughter, so the same entity may be described as present, future, or past in accordance with its relation to the preceding or succeeding moment; this view also the Vaibhāṣikas reject on the ground that it treats all three times as found together in one.

[1] Cf. Poussin, TDC., pp. 57 f.; AK. v. 24 ff.; Stcherbatskoi in Dasgupta, *Ind. Phil.* i. 115 f. For Sāṁkhya views, see SS., p. 73.

The view of Vasumitra, on the other hand, is accepted by the Vaibhāṣika school. It holds that difference in time is dependent on difference in efficiency; when an entity has performed its function and has ceased to act, it is past; when it is producing it, it is present; when it has not yet produced it, it is future. In all three cases there is real existence; this is obvious as regards present and future, and can be proved as regards the past by the considerations that, if the past were not real, i. e. did not exercise efficiency—this being the crucial test of reality—it could not be the object of knowledge nor could deeds done in the past produce effects in the present.

The Vaibhāṣika position is not approved by the Sautrāntika on the decidedly legitimate ground that all forms of this view really involve belief in the existence of a permanent substance persisting throughout time, the time distinctions appearing in it. If, it is pointed out, the past exercises efficiency at present, it clearly cannot be distinguished from the present, an objection which no attempt to distinguish between efficiencies will enable us to remove. Secondly, we can as experience shows know non-existing entities just as well as we can know existing entities; now non-existing entities have *ex hypothesi* no efficiency, so that it is not necessary that the past should have efficiency to be known. Again, if a distinction is drawn between an efficiency and an entity, there is immediately raised the insoluble problem why the efficiency started at any particular time and stopped at another. The true doctrine is that there is no distinction between the entity, the efficiency, and the time of its appearance;[1] entities appear from non-existence;[2] they exist for a moment; then they cease to exist. Their existence activity and action are all one. This harmonizes with the fact that, when we remember a thing as the past we do not and cannot know it as existing in the past; we know it in the same way as we knew it when it was present;

[1] Cf. the verse in BCAP. ix. 6; TV., p. 170; *Bhāmatī*, p. 361; *Upadeçasāhasrī*, p. 369; *Vedāntakalpataru*, p. 278; and see Çaṅkara, BS. ii. 2. 20: Poussin, JA. 1903, ii. 377: *Kṣaṇikāḥ sarvasaṁskārā; asthirāṇāṁ kutaḥ kriyā? bhūtir yaiṣāṁ kriyā saiva kārakaṁ saiva cocyate.*

[2] cf. Vācaspati on SK. 9. Past and future time are mere names, TRD., p. 46; MKV., p. 389; all are mere 'void; MK. xix; Ui, VP., p. 46. So as regards space; ibid., pp. 46 f.

similarly it is not true, as on the Vaibhāṣika theory, that our past passions exercise causal efficiency upon us; in point of fact they have left residues impressed which become the antecedents of the passion of the present.

The Vaibhāṣikas in their doctrine of time made a distinct change on the canonical simplicity, which recognizes merely origin and passing away[1] or the three stages of coming into being, decay, and annihilation;[2] it interpolates the moment of existence (*sthiti*), which, it asserts, was suppressed by the Buddha because of the danger which it involved to the doctrine of impermanence, but which is implicitly included in the last stage (*sthityanyathātva*).[3] What is more obvious is that the discrimination is hardly exact. These four moments of existence were evidently taken by the school as four kinds of forces, which by coming into combination with the essence of an entity produced its impermanent manifestations in life. The idea is curious and interesting; it shows how deeply rooted was the realism which converted time into a potency possessing causative force of its own.

In the *Kathāvatthu*[4] we find an elaborate, but as usual not very profitable, refutation of the Sarvāstivādin view that everything exists, understood in the sense that past, present, and future equally exist; the passages of the Suttas in favour of the former view are refuted effectively enough by other passages, without anything more than dialectical ingenuity. The conclusion arrived at is that the present alone exists, and the same doctrine is stoutly maintained against the Kassapikas, who are credited with

[1] Defended in KV. ii. 7 which denies duration of consciousness. That the Buddha accepted some duration is possible; cf. MKV., p. 283, n. 1, MK. vii. discusses origination (*utpāda*), existence (*sthiti*) and destruction (*bhaṅga*).

[2] Defended in KV. xxii. 8 against the momentary doctrine of Pubba-and Apara-seliyas. Continuity appears also in xv. 3. See AN. i. 152; KV. i, p. 61; *Compendium*, pp. 25 f., 125; the attempt to explain it away in *Points of Discourse*, pp. 374 f. is absurd. See MKV., pp. 145, 545 f., BSB. I. xvii. 15 (the characters apply to each moment; to the series, acc. AKV.) Momentariness is true of consciousness, however; KV. ii. 7; x. 1 (against the Andhakas). The Vaibhāṣikas (acc. to Wassilieff, *Bouddhisme*, p. 277) divide things as eternal and non-eternal, and ascribe all compounds to the latter category, but do not make them momentary. The Sautrāntikas reduce all to a series of moments of coming to be.

[3] The four are given in TRD., p. 46 as *jāti, sthiti, jarā, vināça*. Cf. DS., § 596.

[4] i 6 ff.

asserting that some of the past, i.e. that which is to bear fruition exists, as well as some of the future, i.e. that which is inevitably to be, as distinct from that which is only contingent. The fact is extremely interesting and raises an obvious difficulty in the face of the doctrine which is attributed elsewhere to the Vibhajyavādins[1] and which certainly appears in the *Milindapañha*; that text certainly admits the existence of past potentialities of future action, though it denies the existence of the future and the past that has performed its activity. We have in fact in this point a suggestion that the *Kathāvatthu* as we have it cannot be regarded as representing always Vibhajyavādin views, and with this concurs the obvious consideration that in not a few cases the argument is very obviously much the better in the case of the opponent than of the Vibhajyavādin, and, for example in the case of the discussion of time itself, we find in the work two distinct doctrines. The true momentariness of all consciousness is on the one hand asserted, while on the other hand it is denounced as a heresy to hold that all existence is to be reduced to conscious moments, the case of the elements, trees, &c., being adduced against such an idea, and stress is laid on the fact that the Canon assumes the more or less permanent existence of external sense matter, of the sense organs as material, and objects to any attempt to identify either with actual consciousness.[2] We may derive from these views the conception that for the *Kathāvatthu* consciousness was momentary—this is asserted even of the consciousness of a god—but that material things had some endurance, though they were not permanent, and this view is in accord with the relative permanence of body admitted in the Canon. But the *Kathāvatthu* certainly does not make explicit the doctrine.

Of space we have in the *Milindapañha*[3] two interesting notes. In the first place it is classified with Nirvāṇa as being uncaused by any of the three causes, action, seed-cause, or season-cause; apparently also, like Nirvāṇa, it is to be deemed unproduced, out

[1] AK. v. 25. [2] KV. ii. 7; xxii. 8; MN. i. 190.

[3] pp. 271, 388; DS., § 638; KV. vi. 4, 6, 7. That space is a mental construction without objective reality (*Points of Controversy*, p. 394) is clearly not meant; it is real and perceived by mind; so ADS. vi. 6. 4, contradicting the assertion in *Compendium*, p. 16. It is a mere name acc. TRD., p. 46.

of time, and imperceptible by any sense organ, except the mind. In the second passage, also late, it is described as impossible to be grasped; the resort of seers, ascetics, gods, and birds; infinite, boundless, immeasurable; not stopped by anything; and resting upon nothing. This is certainly a more philosophic view than is found in the *Dhammasaṅgaṇi* of the *Abhidhamma Piṭaka* where it is classified as a material derivative. The contrast between this view and that of the Sautrāntikas which treats ether or space as unconditioned and therefore on a parallel with Nirvāṇa itself is explained by the discussions in the *Kathāvatthu*. To the identity of the infinity of space, attained in meditation, with Nirvāṇa, it is objected that there is birth and death in that sphere, but not in Nirvāṇa. The more general view, of the Uttarāpathakas and Mahiṅsāsakas, that space is unconditioned, is met in a similar way; if so, it must be Nirvāṇa, since two unconditioned things must be identical; again, when a well is dug, there is creation of space, which is absurd if it is unconditioned, and similarly it is destroyed when a pitcher is filled, equally absurdly. The last word here is given to the heretics with some reason; Buddhaghosa helps out orthodoxy by distinguishing occupied space as conditioned, and empty space or space abstracted from objects as mere abstract ideas, which cannot be styled unconditioned. Finally, the *Kathāvatthu* rejects the Andhaka doctrine that void space is visible, because then it must be coloured matter, and visual consciousness according to scripture is not produced by the eye and space. The argument again leaves the last statement to the heretic; Buddhaghosa supplies the answer by asserting the mental comprehension of space, the doctrine probably intended in the *Milinda*.

3. *The Ego as a Series*

It is in the Sautrāntika, to all appearance, that the doctrine of the self as a continuum first definitely takes shape, but the idea is certainly contained in germ in the *Milindapañha*.[1] The point is there quite explicitly raised; is the infant the same as the man? Is the mother of the child the same as the mother of the man? The boy before and after his course of school? The man who

[1] pp 40 f.

commits crime and he who has suffered punishment? The answer is given by the simile of the flame of a lamp which burns throughout the three watches of the night, and yet the lamp remains the same. Just so is the continuity of a person or thing maintained; one comes into being, another passes away, and the rebirth is, as it were, simultaneous. Thus neither as the same, nor as another does man go on to the last phase of his self-consciousness. So milk turns into curds, but the purchaser who has left it in the hand of the seller cannot next day repudiate the purchase; the thief of a mango cannot escape mutilation because the mango he stole was not the mango the owner planted; if a girl is given in marriage for a price when a child, and her husband goes abroad, he is entitled on his return to demand her back from another who has married her, nor will he be allowed to evade his obligation by pleading that the maiden is quite other than the girl.

This idea of continuity (*saṁtati*) is to be found occasionally in the Abhidhamma, Buddhaghosa, and in the *Nettipakaraṇa*;[1] it is freely found in the Sanskrit texts, the *Çikṣāsamuccaya* has *svasaṁtāna* and *parasaṁtāna* as equivalent to the self, and the self of others. Things in the Sautrāntika are reduced to mere moments (*kṣaṇa*), a refinement on the earlier conception of impermanence (*anitya*), and these moments are denied activity in the true sense of the term, though they are regarded as caused and causes, results and antecedents. 'How can there be action on the part of that which is not enduring? The action and activity of the moments, that is their mere existence.'[2] The continuity involved is real; not only does it take place throughout life, which is easy to recognize, but it continues on death; the consciousness which appears at birth (*aupapattyaṅçika*) and the consciousness on death (*māraṇāntika*) are in essential relation;[3] the one is in a sense contem-

[1] DS., §§ 585, 643, 734; KV. x. 1; xi. 6; xxi. 4, and comm.; ADS. v. 12, 15, 16; NP., p. 79; Ç., pp. 23, 126; NB., pp. 13 f.; AK. v; NBh. i. 1. 2; BCAP., pp. 237, 255, 307, 309, &c.; MKV., pp. 85, 281, 283, 310, 312 f., &c.; SSS. IV. iv. 5–8; Poussin, JA. 1902, ii. 284; 1903, ii. 359; TRD, p. 39; Buddhaghosa, JRAS. 1904, pp. 370 f.

[2] See § 2; Wassilieff, *Bouddhisme*, pp. 277 f.

[3] Mil., p. 47; cit. in MKV., p. 53; *Çālistamba Sūtra*, JA. 1902, ii. 272; Ç., p. 226; BCAP. ix. 78.

poraneous with the other, the idea being illumined by the comparison of the two with the movement of the scales of a balance. Hence we see at once how the last thought on death has an essential influence on the form of rebirth.[1] Moreover, the idea of the series of cause and effect presents a great advantage from the point of view of the explanation of the effect of the act (*karman*). Each moment is to be regarded as impressing itself on all that follows, perfuming it, as the phrase (*vāsanā*) specially affected indicates, just as the jasmine flower assumes various hues if it has, when in seed form, been imbued with a dye. Man, therefore, carries with him at every moment his future; his death and his fate are implicit within him; the fruit of some good deed done long ages ago may come to action, and reward even with the Tuṣita heaven the man whose sins have previously condemned him to the agonies of the peculiarly horrid hells imagined by Buddhist piety; or his sins may even carry him to hell in his life.[2] The theory affords, moreover, an easy explanation of memory;[3] when any object has been experienced a seed of memory is implanted in the consciousness continuum, and in the course of time on the ripening of the seed memory comes causally into being without the intervention of any needless entity like a thinker, and so we can explain recognition. It is easy also to understand how such a series may be continued in a life even in the world without form.[4] Nor is it difficult to appreciate that it is possible to bring this stream of consciousness to an end; or at any rate, if it is perhaps difficult, it does not require too great a strain on the faith of the believer. But the possibility is also open, to become of importance in the Mahāyāna, that the saint may impress on his series the determination to save all creatures, to be a Bodhisattva rather than become an Arhant. The theory has, moreover, the obvious benefit that it avoids the difficulties either of permanence or destruction; it follows a mean, for the series is in constant change and therefore there is no permanence, but it is a series, a line which is without beginning, though it

[1] The Sabbatthivādins and Uttarāpathakas even hold that concentration (*Samādhi*) is continuity of consciousness (*citta-saṁtati*); KV. xi. 6.

[2] Mil., pp. 101, 115.

[3] BCAP. ix. 24, 101; AKV. (Burn. MS. 477 a).

[4] AKV. (Burn. MS. 185 a); JA. 1902, ii. 278, n. 1.

may come to an end through liberation, and there is not, therefore, the fatal possibility of destruction by any other cause than liberation.

So far we seem to be on sufficiently assured ground; but is it possible to attribute to the school two further doctrines, each of great promise for the rendering logical and complete the Buddhist conception of the self? In the first place, it may be that the Sautrāntika deserves the credit of having determined to break away from the doctrine of the possibility of the intervention of external accident in the course of life.[1] The Canon, it must be remembered, has no such assertion; it certainly does not teach the universal reign of cosmic and psychic law, and the list of indeterminates includes the issues of the causation of pleasure and pain. Moreover, we have in the *Kathāvatthu* emphatic testimony to this effect; the Rājagirikas and the Siddhatthikas are credited with maintaining that all in the world is due to Karman, and this view is rejected in an argument which can hardly be called satisfying. The points raised seem to be, first that to say that Karman is the result of Karman is to confuse action with its effect, and, second, that the theory reduces the present to a mere effect, without initiative of any sort. The same idea occurs in a further polemic against the Andhakas and the Uttarāpathakas, who assert that things are by nature immutable, e.g. matter cannot become one of the spiritual aggregates or *vice versa*, and that all actions are inflexible. The answer given is an appeal to the fact that the master's teaching provides for two uniformities in life; the one by which the worst offenders are assured of immediate retribution after death, and the other by which the pathwinner is assured of final salvation, while there is another group in which there is no such fixity. The opponent in these arguments is allowed to have the last word, and certainly the better of the

[1] Poussin, *Bouddhisme*, p. 181, who admits that there is no decisive proof. Later see BCA. vi. 43; TRD., p. 26; Mrs. Rhys Davids' objections (JRAS. 1903, p. 590) clearly carry us too far in the opposite sense, by reducing consciousness to an epiphenomenon of sense and object contact. There is, *per contra*, no ground to attribute the doctrine to the Canon (JA. 1903, ii. 371 notwithstanding). The Mahāsāṅghikas appear to have held this view as regards sounds and sense organs and generally (KV. xii. 2 ff.) Cf. p. 286.

contention.[1] Yet in the *Milindapañha* also there is no attempt to assert the all-pervading power of Karman in any consistent way; on the one hand, to its force is traced the fact that the hard things consumed by lions perish in digestion but the soft embryo survives; on the other hand, in a decidedly late passage, it is expressly asserted that the Arahant suffers bodily pain, over which he has no mastery, and the whole treatment makes it clear that the body, without regard to Karman, is considered as affecting the mind.[2] The Sautrāntikas, as we have seen, accepted the reality of an external world, as inferred from our sensations, but they seem, it has been suggested, to have adopted the view that the form of the world is the result of Karman; the sins we have done in the past provide the physical environment and circumstances of our punishment; the murderer by his action creates in due course the hell in which he suffers the penalties of the damned. But it must be admitted that on this point we have no certainty; the logical conclusion may not have been effectively drawn.

The second advance may be attributed more surely to a section of the school.[3] It appears to have faced the problem of self-consciousness with more than usual boldness, and to have discarded the old and complicated effort to hold that in some manner, decidedly difficult to understand, the succeeding moment was conscious of the preceding moment and so generated a sort of self-consciousness.[4] The arguments by which they established their view seem to have been based on similes, whence their style 'masters of similes' (*dārṣṭāntikas*). The fact of the experience of

[1] KV. xvii. 3; xxi. 7, 8. There are acts without fruit, xii. 2; xvii. 1. But another cannot bestow happiness or the reverse, xvi. 3; JA. 1903, ii. 444. The orthodox view evidently desired to maintain the freedom of the will, however illogically and inconsistently with the doctrine of the non-self.

[2] Mil., pp. 134 ff.; 180 f., which expressly asserts chance (*animitta*); 253, the Arahant cannot control his body. For interaction cf. KV. vii. 8; ADS. viii. 9, natural causes co-operate with moral; Buddhaghosa, KV. vii. 8.

[3] Poussin, *Bouddhisme*, p. 182, citing MA., p. 267; AKV. (Paris MS.) f. 309^b. Not all are users of similes (AKV. Paris MS. 309^b). Cf. Wassilieff, *Bouddhisme*, pp. 112, 277; Tāranātha, *Buddhismus*, p. 274.

[4] KV. xvi. 4 denies the view of Apara—and Pubba-seliyas that attention to consciousness is simultaneous. For the later doctrine see NB., p. 103; NBT., p. 14; TRD., p. 40; BCA. ix. 101, 15 ff.; Ç., pp. 234 f.; MKV., pp. 61 f., 114, vii. 9; *Vedāntakalpataru*, p. 293; the Vijñānavāda accepts, the Madhyamaka denies the doctrine. Some Sautrāntikas at least (Wassilieff, p. 285) accepted the relation of temporal succession. Cf. Wassilieff, *op. cit.*, p. 307.

memory: 'I have seen' suggests the possibility of knowledge of the self; the lamp sheds light on the jar, but equally lights up itself; the word at one and the same moment conveys the sense, which it has, and the sounds, of which it is composed. Consciousness, therefore, can be and is self-conscious, and this fact explains the doctrine that perception of external things is only indirect. The naïve idea that consciousness is in direct contact with reality is discarded for the more complicated conception that the external reality is known because consciousness takes through the medium of the sense organism the form of the object, and then is conscious of itself; that objects are external is recognized because of the temporary and accidental character of the objects of consciousness, which shows that they are not essentially parts of consciousness itself.

We have thus attained some measure of effective personality without departure from orthodoxy; indeed, the Saṁtāna seems to have achieved acceptance widely as the equivalent of personality. We hear phrases such as 'Çākyamuni's Saṁtāna was then Sunetra'; 'the Saṁtāna of a multitude of people'; 'when one speaks of consciousness as reincarnating, one means the series of thought'; and even in popular form 'their Saṁtāna is feeble'. Indeed, the school seems to have gone so far as to treat the series as possessed of freedom of the will, for we are told of the difficulty of directing the intellectual series (*cittasaṁtāna*) against the current and of keeping it away from things of sense.[1] Here again we see how readily popular conceptions were accepted without investigation of their compatibility with the main tenets of the school. If, as seems to have been the case, the school was impressed with the conception of the rule of Karman, then it must have been obvious that in no true sense was any freedom of the will even conceivable. If there is a series, each of which is in the relation of cause, effect, cause and so on, then, while it can be said that the series as a whole is uncaused, it is equally clear that every single link in the chain is caused and without possibility of freedom.

The conception of a Saṁtāna was clearly not acceptable to all the Hīnayāna schools; we have a decidedly emphatic denunciation

[1] AKV. (Paris MS. f. 372a) in Poussin, *Bouddhisme*, p. 183.

of it in a passage of the *Saṁyutta Nikāya*[1] where it is denounced as an illusion and idle talk, while in the Brahmanical texts energetic criticism is directed against the whole conception. Either, it is argued, the plan means that there is a Saṁtānin, or subject, under the moments, which means that the Buddhist is throwing aside his doctrine of non-ego and momentariness, or there is no real continuity at all and the Saṁtāna leaves us with nothing to solve the problem of individuality.

The new theory is used by Vasubandhu[2] to discredit the doctrine of the existence of a person (*pudgala*) as maintained by the Vātsīputrīyas against the more orthodox denial of any person. The denial of a soul is based on the absence of any cause which would lead us to accept the idea as necessary, just as for instance the sense organs are necessary to explain perception. Moreover, any self which really exists must be something over and above the impermanent factors of empiric individuality. But such a self, which must be uncaused, eternal, and without change, would be without activity or practical efficiency (*arthakriyākāritva*) which is the essential characteristic of reality. The Vātsīputrīyas object to this train of thought that the person is certainly implicated in the elements of empiric individuality or personal life, but though implicated is separate, and cannot be said either to be the same as, or different from, the personal elements, just as fire is neither the same as, nor different from, the burning stick, and yet is something more than it. They support this contention by the facts of action, e.g. of walking, which imply a personal agent, and of consciousness which imply an actor. Vasubandhu objects that the appearance of continuity in motion is a misleading result of analogy from one's own experience; what is true is that there is a series of new productions of motion in different places just as in the case of moving fire. Similarly there is in consciousness nothing more than the fact of a series of thought moments which are in causal

[1] iii. 142; cited MKV., p. 41. Cf. Ç., p. 359; BCAP. ix. 73; Poussin, JA. 1902, ii. 287. Mrs. Rhys Davids (*Psych. Ethics*, p. LXXXI) appears to attribute to Buddhism the denial of free will, but determinism is unorthodox, KV. xxi. 7, 8: presumably in *Buddhism*, pp. 221 ff., the older view is abandoned.

[2] See the *Pudgalaviniçcaya* in the AK. viii, rendered by Stcherbatskoi (*Bulletin de l'Academie des Sciences de Russie*), in Dasgupta, *Ind. Phil.* i. 117 f. Cf. TRD., p. 46 where the Pudgala is attributed to the Vaibhāṣikas, alias Āryasamitīyas.

relation. Memory is explained by this fact; it requires no agent, merely an earlier experience, and arises when suitable conditions of attention, freedom from pain, &c., are present.

The conclusion, therefore, is that there is no real self; the term is accordingly merely a convention; we never know the self as such, but merely have knowledge of psychic happenings, sensations, perceptions, feelings, and so on. The same consideration applies equally to material things; milk, for instance, is a designation given to certain momentary colours, tastes, &c., fictitiously unified under the term milk. But there is continuity in the individual[1] though not a self, and thus we understand why the Buddha did not lay down either the identity or difference of the soul (*jīva*) and the body, since the conception of a soul is a mistaken one.

4. *The Doctrine of Causation*

The later texts show a decided development in the investigation of the theory of causation generally. They make the important distinction between causes generally (*paccaya*) and the cause proper (*hetu*), which is the real producer of the result, the other causes being conditions, coefficients or auxiliaries. In the *Paṭṭhāna* of the *Abhidhamma Piṭaka* there occurs a very elaborate classification of conditions under twenty-four heads: position, object, dominance, contiguity, immediate contiguity, coexistence, reciprocity, dependence, sufficing condition, antecedent, consequence, succession, action (*karman*), effect, support, control, Jhāna, means, association, dissociation, presence, absence, abeyance, continuance. The modes of relation vary according to the things related; thus mind content bears to mind content the six relations of contiguity, immediate contiguity, absence, abeyance, succession, and association. But in all cases the conception is that the condition or cause renders service to the effect; each thought is influenced by those related to it, and in very late Buddhism the power of one idea to affect another becomes styled its ability (*satti*). The essence of the theory in its application to mental states is

[1] This is expressed in the conception Jīvitindriya of the Pali Abhidhamma, applied both to immaterial and material series; see DS., §§ 19, 635; KV. viii. 10; *Vibhaṅga*, p. 123; *Compendium*, pp. 17, 156. The idea is not, however, worked out.

interesting; it is the parallel of the Sautrāntika view which sees a complete continuity of consciousness, in which each moment is charged with all the past, and it offers, if not an explanation, still the possibility of an explanation of the facts of memory. We need not assume that the doctrine is any older than the Sautrāntika school.[1]

But the elaboration of twenty-four with its obvious weaknesses as we can see them in their exposition in the *Abhidhammatthasaṁgaha* is opposed by others, who give four causes only, while one set of Sarvāstivādins made seven.[1] The four are the true cause (*hetu*), which engenders a thing, like the seed; the support (*ālambana*) which serves to engender thought and its sequels (*citta-caitta*) born of the true cause; the immediately contiguous (*samanantara*) cause, which is either the destruction of the cause,[2] as the seed is destroyed to produce the shoot, or the stream of thought which gives room for the presentation in question; and the dominant (*adhipati*), denoting that on whose existence the other depends. The last of these is styled also the means, and the second and third are classed as embracing (*parigrahaka*) causes, since they envelop the true cause, and further its maturity.

Simpler is the series also of four found in the *Nettipakaraṇa* in explaining sight perception in elaboration of the old canonical doctrine of the collision of organ, object, and attention; we have the act of attention as cause proper; the eye as dominant cause; coloured matter as the support or object; and light as a dependent (*sannissaya*) cause. The act of attention (*manasikāra*) is of the same character as the resulting visual consciousness; hence it is its true cause.[3]

The Vaibhāṣikas have a sixfold division of causes which marks

[1] *Duka*, pp. 3 f.; KV. xv. 1 f.; NP., p. 78; VM. in JPTS. 1893, pp. 109, 138; *Vibhañga*; Poussin, TDC., p. 52; *Compendium*, pp. 42 f., 187 f., 259 f., 279 f. The attempt in *Points of Controversy* (pp. 294, n. 3, 390 f.) to see an important contribution in this doctrine is erroneous.

[2] Mvy. 115; MK. i. 2; MKV., pp. 77 f.; MA., pp. 87 f.; AKV. in TDC., p. 54, n. 2; Bhavya (Rockhill, *Life*, p. 196); the extra three are Karman, Āhāra, Niçraya. Lañk., p. 85 has six—*bhaviṣyat*, *sambandha*, *lakṣaṇa*, *kāraṇa*, *vyañjana*, and *upekṣā*.

[3] MKV., p. 85; NBh. iv. 1. 14; SDS., p. 16. See KV. x. 1, negativing the Mahāsāñghika view of continuity of the aggregates. See AKV. in MKV., p. 77; TRD., p. 39.

no special advance: they reckon the efficient (*kāraṇa*) cause, which does not impede the effect, e.g. the objects and other causes of vision; co-operative causes (*sahabhū-hetu*), e.g. in producing merit, correct views, &c.; causes of the same nature (*sabhāga*), merit producing merit; united (*saṁprayukta*) causes, e.g. faith and intelligence; omnipresent (*sarvatraga*) causes, like false views which affect every act; and causes of fruition (*vipāka*), distinguished as having effects, that is, feelings different in character from the cause which is an action.[1] There is more that is useful in the fivefold division of some schools which reckon efficient causes, e.g. seed; causes of knowledge, e.g. smoke showing flame; causes of manifestation (*vyañjaka*), the lamp, the jar; causes of destruction (*dhvaṅsaka*), denied by some as heretical as all things are momentary; and causes making one attain (*prāpaka*) such an object as Nirvāṇa.[2]

There is more originality in a theory which expresses satisfactorily in one aspect the point of view of the Sautrāntikas; the nature of things is eternal causation, unsubstantial, momentary (*kṣaṇika*); things exist only in virtue of dependence (*idaṁpratyayatāphala*). Causation or the relation of cause and effect (*kāryakāraṇa-bhāva*) is not a process of the evolution of the cause into the effect, as in the Sāṁkhya doctrine (*satkārya-vāda*), nor of the creation by the cause of an effect differing from itself, but is the necessary succession of determined effects (*niyāmatā*); its dependence constitutes the whole nature (*dharmatā*), suchness (*tathatā*), of things; they have no other reality. Their production is in the nature of magic (*māyā*); no real causality can be attributed to the impermanent; their action and causality are merely their becoming and *vice versa*. Hence we cannot talk rationally of the destruction of things by a cause.[3]

The idea here expressed is not uncanonical, in so far as it deals with the conception of order (*niyāmatā, dhammatā*), and we find in Buddhaghosa[4] an interesting fivefold division of the principle

[1] NP., p. 80; SDS., p. 16; cf. NBT., pp. 13, 18; *Bhāmatī*, ii. 2. 21; *Vivaraṇaprameya*, p. 34; TRD., p. 39.

[2] Mvy. 114; AKV. (Burn. MS. f. 133); TDC., p. 55. [3] AKV. f. 156.

[3] *Çālistamba Sūtra*, TCD., pp. 62 f.; *Bhāmatī*, ii. 2. 19; *Vedāntakalpataru*, p. 273; MKV., p. 9; SDS., p. 17. Cf. KV. vi. 2; xi. 7; trs. pp. 386 f.

[4] Mrs. Rhys Davids, *Buddhism*, pp. 119 ff. See Mil., p. 268.

of order: the order of act and result; the physical order (*utu-niyama*), e.g. winds and rains; the order of seeds, physical organic order, e.g. sugary taste from the cane; the order of thought (*citta*), the relation of antecedent and subsequent states of consciousness; and the order of the Law, the phenomena which herald a Bodhisattva's advent to earth for the last time, cosmic conditions of production of the norm.

5. *The Chain of Causation, Internal and External*

It was in this period that the orthodox interpretation of the chain of causation, conceived as the wheel of the Law came into being. This view was confronted by, but easily triumphed over, in the scholasticism, though hardly in the popular idea, a variant which is preserved in pictorial form at Ajaṇṭā as well as in Tibet and has textual authority. The interpretation rests on the conception of the being in an intermediate state (*antarābhava*) which some schools regarded as existing between one birth and another: that is the consciousness, which, defiled by ignorance and previous dispositions, seizes on name and form and the six organs; observes a pair—human or animal according to his previous desert—in union, feels love for the mother, in desire enters the father's head, fixes itself on his thought, grasps the organ of enjoyment, becomes an embryo (*bhava*) and is duly born.[1] Even cruder is another theory known from Brahmanical sources only which places in the embryo the development from consciousness to grasping.[2]

The *Abhidharmakoça*[3] presents us with a scholastic view of the chain which has obvious merits. It is clear that the succession of the factors cannot be taken too seriously; contact, feeling, thirst, grasping, are ever renewed in our life; grasping arises from ignorance and dispositions, which must be ever present to make feeling lead to it; contact presupposes the existence of organs, name and form, and consciousness; the whole therefore

[1] *Caṇḍamahāroṣaṇa Tantra*, ch. xvi (JRAS. 1897, p. 463); Waddell, JRAS. 1894, pp. 367 ff.; *Lamaism*, pp. 108 ff.; Poussin, TCD., p. 39.

[2] *Brahmavidyābharaṇa*, ii. 2. 19 (SBE. xxxiv. 404 f).

[3] AK. iii. 21 ff. See also *Çālistamba Sūtra*, in MKV., p. 566; Ç., p. 225; Oltramare, FBDC., pp. 42 f.; TCD., pp. 40 ff.

are rather simultaneous coefficients of existence (*bhavaṅga*). The vital element, as is clear from the Canon where consciousness appears as sixth element, and where it clearly dominates matter in name and form, is consciousness, and accordingly it is existence (*bhavaṅga*) par excellence; it is the seed which grows, watered by thirst, opened up by ignorance in the field of action, which with thirst engenders it; these three, therefore, are coefficients to the cause as consciousness, an idea exactly in harmony with the revised estimate of causes. The chain, therefore, can now be regarded properly as a series of states (*avasthā*) of consciousness under the influence of these factors. Determined by previous dispositions produced by ignorance, it is incarnated as rebirth consciousness, or mind, confused however by the process of birth renewal. Then it assumes with matter the form of the five aggregates, possessing the senses of mind and body, that is touch.[1] Then the other four senses develop, and actual birth takes place. Then comes a period of contact, marked by feeling but without appreciation of the causes of feeling which is obtained in the next stage of feeling; then comes thirst viewed as especially sexual desire; then grasping in the shape of the four infections, desire, heresy, ritualism, belief in the self; then the act which produces a future birth, and ultimately that birth with death to follow.

The Sautrāntikas give four aspects of the cause of the production of misery as taught in the chain. They hold that things must be looked upon by one who understands them truly as caused (*hetutas*): it is false that there is no cause; as resulting from several coefficients: it is false that there is one cause, the Lord of the deists or the nature of the Sāṁkhya; as produced: it is false that things merely develop, and do not have a true beginning; and as arriving for this reason and that: things do not come to pass from a deliberate plan, there are many causes in the world.[2]

A further departure of interest[3] is made by the application of the conceptions embodied in the chain of causation to external

[1] KV. xiv. 2 agrees with this view against the Pubba—and Apara-seliyas who accept all six senses in the embryo.

[2] MVy. 54; *Dharmasaṁgraha*, 98; AKV. vii; TDC., pp. 56 f.

[3] *Çālistamba Sūtra* in TCD., pp. 68 ff.; Laṅk., pp. 85 f.; NP., pp. 78 ff.; Ç., pp. 219 ff.

reality; it develops parallel with a formal distinction between two kinds of the chain, the one viewed from the point of view of the true cause, the other from that of the coefficients, understood here, however, is the limited and narrow sense of the four elements and space which the Canon gives as cause of the descent of the embryo into the womb. This idea is developed in full, one aspect being the ordinary list of cause sequence, the other dealing with the part played by these external elements in the process. There is also given the series of states of the seed from the first to the development into the flower, which constitutes the true causal combination (*hetūpanibandha*) of the external chain of causation (*bāhya pratītya-samutpāda*); the coefficient series (*pratyayopanibandha*) contains earth, water, fire, wind, ether, and the season, these co-operating to bring the seed to fruition. The transition from this view to the parallel conception that in the case of the development of consciousness the true coefficients are to be found not so much in the elements as in ignorance, action, and thirst, was obvious and was easily made.[1]

The doctrine, though usually illustrated by the case of the seed, was capable of extension to other material objects, despite their like of life; we find in the *Nettipakaraṇa* as well as the seed the case of the lamp; the true cause of the flame is itself, the oil, wick &c., are but coefficients, an interesting example of the conception of formal cause.

6. *The Later Doctrine of Momentariness and Causal Efficiency*

The Sautrāntika doctrine of momentariness received no substantial development in the school, but was energetically defended by Ratnakīrti (A. D. 950)[2] from the attacks made upon it by the Nyāya-Vaiçeṣika school which declined to accept the denial of substance and true causation which it involved. The production of effects, he maintains, can be explained on the doctrine of momentariness and causal efficiency as the characteristics of existence, and not otherwise. Take any existent object, such as

[1] VM. xix (Warren, HOS. iii. 242 f).

[2] *Kṣaṇabhaṅgasiddhi*; *Six Buddhist Nyāya Tracts*, ed. Haraprasād Shāstrī (BI. 1910), pp. 20-77. Cf. TRD., pp. 28-31; 40 explains how momentariness is not perceived.

a jug at present perceived; it exists in the production of the effect of my perception of it; it is manifestly absurd to say that this effect is identical with the past or future, and it is equally absurd to hold that in the past and future it produces no effect; if it has any capacity to be effective, it must manifest it always, or there is no reason why it should do so now. What now exists, therefore, is essentially momentary; the jug which now affects my senses is not the same as the jug which formerly existed, for they differ essentially in capacity, and capacity is the essence of existence.

There are two obvious Nyāya objections to such a statement which Ratnakīrti seeks to meet. The first is that, as capacity is regarded as existence, it becomes impossible to know anything, since capacity cannot be known until the effect is known, and the effect in turn cannot be known until its effect is known and so on to infinity, a fatal objection in the Nyāya view. Secondly, momentariness negates the existence of any permanent perceiver of change, and destroys the possibility of inference which the Buddhists admit. The reply to the former contention is an appeal to the facts; the existence of seeds means no more than the capacity of producing shoots; even if the capacity is itself dependent on a further capacity, still the fact is undeniable, and there is no objection to an infinity which is in accord with reality. Nor is there any force in the objection that a cause such as a seed must wait for a number of subsidiary conditions, e.g. water, earth, &c., before it can produce the shoot; the true view is that the seed-moment produces the conditions as well as the shoot, its potency to do so being explained by earlier causal moments on which it depends; this comprehensive power may be illustrated by the analogy of the single perceptual moment which reveals a large number of objects. The second set of objections is rejected as equally unsound. Facts show that under certain conditions there is knowledge of concomitance either positive or negative; granting that the knowledge is subsequent to the concomitance, nevertheless it holds within itself the experience of the preceding moment, and this serves to supply the place of a permanent observer. The existence of concomitance also is possible, not because there are permanent entities, but because of the extreme similarity of the momentary existences concerned.

These discussions clearly leave unsolved the essential difficulties of the conception of momentariness and causal efficiency. The mental series which gives the only self allowed is clearly possessed in some sense of a causal continuity, each state taking up in itself the results of previous conditions. But causation in regard to the external reality accepted by the school is not rendered intelligible, and still less the interrelation of the two disparate forms of reality.

The Buddhist argument for momentary activity is presented with special care in the *Sarvadarçanasaṁgraha*.[1] Whatever exists is momentary, because it exists; existence is admittedly practical efficiency or activity, and activity has only two possible forms, successive and non-successive, on the principle of excluded middle. These two are both inconsistent with permanency, and therefore activity and existence are momentary. If this inconsistency with permanence is called into question, it can be established by a simple dilemma; does the permament object possess at present the capacity of past and future activity? If it does, then it must produce these effects now, since that, which has capacity, like a collection of causes, cannot fail to act. If not, then it will never have the power, and the theory that it has true existence is overthrown. Nor is it any use to assume successive subsidiaries with which the permanent object accomplishes results. If these subsidiaries do not assist the thing, they are idle; if they do, are they different from the thing or not? If they are different, then it is they that bring about the result, not the non-changing object, nor can this fact be avoided by any attempt to argue that it is the permanent entity that produces with the subsidiaries. If, on the other hand, it is the case that the subsidiaries are identical with the original thing, then it is clear that the permanent thing has changed its nature, which means that it is not permanent. It is equally impossible that a permanent thing should have activity as simultaneous; we have the dilemma: does this permanent entity after producing these effects at once survive or

[1] pp. 7 ff. See Aniruddha on SS. i. 33-41 who uses the *Sarvadarçanasaṁgraha*. In SS. v. 92 f. we have an attack on the Buddhist denial of genus. See also § 7.

not? If it does, then it will go on for all time producing these effects; if it does not, its permanence is *ex hypothesi* non-existent. Hence the permanent can never be active, and, as existence is activity, the permanent is never existent, and all is momentary.

7. *Vedānta Criticisms of Realism*

Çañkara in his exposition of the *Brahma Sūtra*[1] is explicit in his refutation of the whole Sarvāstivādin doctrine, which he summarizes with sufficient practical accuracy. He points out that there is no possible explanation of the aggregates which make up the empiric individual; the material aggregates are unintelligent; they cannot, therefore, unite themselves with the psychic elements, and the lighting up of intelligence is dependent on the prior existence of a body. The denial of the Lord deprives the Buddhists of any means of explanation *ab extra*; the series of consciousness as momentary cannot be the cause of motion in the atoms; the atoms and the aggregates cannot be self active, else they could never be brought to rest and release would be impossible. It is impossible to avoid this difficulty by reference to the chain of causation as sufficient explanation; even admitting that each member of the chain explains the next, still there is no explanation of the formation of aggregates. Moreover, the chain itself is open to grave criticism; as its elements are momentary, release itself subserves no purpose save itself, and, therefore, is in no sense true release. Further, it is really quite impossible for anything truly momentary to have any causal efficiency at all; that involves its persisting into the effect, which is wholly incompatible with momentariness. The Buddhists, indeed, abandon the doctrine of momentariness in admitting stages of origination, duration, and destruction, for these assume a certain degree of permanence. Nor will it avail to deny origination and destruction, for that will mean that the thing is everlasting. Similarly it is useless to deny causality, thus saving momentariness, for then there would be no regularity in the universe, and the view contradicts the whole Sarvāstivādin theory of causation. The whole doctrine, however, is ruined by the facts of experience which no philosopher can

[1] ii. 2. 18–27; cf. Rāmānuja, *Çrībhāṣya*, ii. 2. 17–26.

dispose of. All memory and recollection need a permanent and abiding subject, of which we are conscious in fact as every one admits, and the judgements 'this is similar to that' and 'this is the same as that', if analysed, reveal equally the existence of permanent objects.

The three uncompounded things of the Sarvāstivādins receive equally short shrift.[1] These entities are represented as non-substantial, merely negative (*abhāva-mātra*), devoid of positive characteristics. Cessation, dependent on a sublative act of mind, or not so dependent, denotes destruction preceded by an act of thought and not so preceded,[2] and either is absolutely impossible of acceptance. For both forms must refer either to the series of momentary entities as destroyed or to the entities themselves. The former is impossible; analysed, it means that the last link in the series has no effect; that means, on the Buddhist doctrine of causal efficiency as existence, that it does not exist; if so, the preceding member of the series equally does not exist, and so the whole series is reduced to nothingness. The second alternative is equally impossible; utter destruction of a momentary existence is inconceivable; experience shows us always persistence amid change, and, even where empirical investigation does not actually reveal the permanent element, analogy proves that it is still in existence, an argument possibly suggested by the case of light or chemical compounds. Moreover, the destruction of nescience, which is included in the cessations above-mentioned, must either take place in consequence of perfect intuition or without such intuition. In the former case then it is caused, and destruction can no longer be assigned to a special class of uncompounded and uncaused things; in the latter, the Buddhist teaching is waste of words.

Space is equally unable to sustain examination as conceived by

[1] Acc. to TRD., p. 46 space or ether (*ākāça*) and caused destruction (*sahetuka vināça*) are mere names (*saṁjñā, pratijñā, saṁvṛti, vyavahāra*). The same doctrine is asserted of space and Nirvāṇa in MKV., p. 389, a remodelling of the citation. Cf. *Çrībhāṣya*, ii. 2. 21 ff.

[2] On uncaused cessation see NB., p. 106; NK., p. 78; *Bhāmatī*, p. 360; *Tantravārttika*, p. 171; *Çlokavārttika*, p. 736; NVT., p. 383: MKV., pp. 29, 414; AKV., JRAS. 1902, p. 371.

the Buddhist; it must be real in view of the quality of sound belonging to it, for earth and other things with qualities are real. It is useless to maintain that it is really the absence of any covering or occupying body, for what is it that enables us to declare that there is the absence of a covering body in one place, and not in another? The answer can only be space, or rather ether, on which in point of fact the Buddhists themselves assert air to rest,[1] implying its material character and its positive nature. Moreover to the case of space, and the two forms of cessation or destruction alike the objection applies that the Buddhists treat them as not positively definable, and yet as eternal, an impossible position, for eternity or non-eternity can be asserted only of real entities, not of mere negations.

[1] Cf. DN. ii. 107; Mil., p. 68; MKV., p. 166; AKV. in Burnouf, *Introd.*, p. 448.

CHAPTER X

THE PSYCHOLOGY OF CONSCIOUSNESS

1. *The Abhidhamma Piṭaka*

SAVE as regards the development of a doctrine of relations, there is practically no advance in the *Abhidhamma Piṭaka* on the psychology of the two earlier Pitakas as regards anything save classification and analysis, and this advance is often a doubtful improvement. Formulae and definitions make up the stock in trade of the Abhidhamma books, which, if ever they served any effective purpose, must have been supplemented by oral discussions, and which are largely intelligible to-day, in so far as they have any definite meaning, merely in the light of the explanations of Buddhaghosa, which need not always reflect the views of the compilers.

The analysis of consciousness in the *Dhammasangaṇi*[1] is essentially motived by ethical considerations. Consciousness is analysed into eight types of good consciousness, and twelve types of bad consciousness, which are applicable to human beings *in primis* but also to infra-human beings, the gods, and other celestials, but not to beings in the more ethereal Brahma- or Rūpa-lokas, worlds of attenuated matter, or the sphere in which matter no longer has any existence (*arūpaloka*). Thirdly, there is ethically indeterminate consciousness. In each case the consciousness is judged ethically not as causing a result, but as the effect (*vipāka*) of earlier action, and a curious result is thus developed, which is not known to the *Sutta Piṭaka*. The term good is restricted to felicific or causing welfare; the welfare caused is reckoned, wherever and whenever experienced, as neutral, and is not treated as

[1] In addition to the Intr. see *Buddh. Psych.* ch. vii. That the Piṭaka is earlier than the bulk of the *Milindapañha* as those assumed is neither probable or proved save as regards the later parts.

itself felicific, but is classed as neutral or indeterminate (*avyākata*,) being neither good or bad.[1]

There is not much psychological insight here, nor much more in the distinction between phenomena of the self and those that are external (*bāhira*, *bahiddhā*), which merely places the spheres of the six senses, including mind, against the spheres of the six sense objects, including mental objects, or the distinction of aggregates of the self as against those which are external, which merely sets the five aggregates making up the individual against the aggregates which are referable by other persons to their selves, but the distinction deserves notice as it is the nearest approach made to that between subjective and objective, from which it obviously differs in essentials. Attention (*manasikāra*) is mentioned among neutral states, but it is only from Buddhaghosa that we have a threefold aspect, the adverting of sense; the adverting of mind, ensuing on sense; or the linking of mind with object as a charioteer links the horse and the chariot, an interesting echo of an Upaniṣad reminiscence. Memory is mindfulness, bearing in mind, the opposite of superficiality and obliviousness, but no light is shed on the problem of forgetfulness or reinstatement, and we are left merely with the suggestion that consciousness reminds itself of what it has, implying the involution of the past in the present, as a treasurer details his revenue to the King.

The distrust of the value of these lucubrations is increased when we come to the elaboration of a distinction between Rūpa, material form or matter,[2] which is underived (*no upādā*) and which is derived (*upādā*). The topic gives us as underived Rūpa the sphere of the tangible, that is those elements which are appreciated

[1] As indeterminate rank also matter and Nirvāṇa, and Kiriyā, action as consciousness leading to no results; it arises during the actual process of sensation (Asl., p. 294); its characteristic form is the consciousness of the Arahant which is unproductive of Karman (pp. xci. ff. 156 ff). The Mahāsaṅghika doctrine that all Karman entails moral result (*vipāka*) is refuted (KV. xii. 2) as is the Andhaka and Uttarāpathaka view that error is unmoral (KV. xiv. 8), and the Uttarāpathaka view that dream consciousness is unmoral (KV. xxii. 6). Cf. KV. xxii. 3 (p. 360, n. 1); *Compendium*, pp. 19, 235 f).

[2] That matter is meant in a Berkeleian sense (*Compendium*, p. 272) is quite absurd; see above ch. ii. § 1. It is contradicted by DS., §§ 1185 ff.; KV. xxii. 8 (citing MN. i. 190).

by touch, namely the earthy or solid, the lambent or fiery, and the gaseous or aerial elements or Mahābhūta, 'great beings' in the traditional phraseology, and the fluid or moist elements. This simply denotes as ultimate realities, grasped save water by the sense of touch, these four elements, and is clearly simple and natural. But the dependent Rūpa includes (1) the senses, vision, hearing, smell, taste, body sensibility (replacing the skin of the Upaniṣads as regards touch); (2) sights, sounds, odours, tastes, but not the object of touch; (3) the faculties of femininity, masculinity, and vitality;[1] (4) intimation by act and by speech; (5) the element of space; (6) buoyancy, plasticity, wieldiness, three qualities of matter, and integration, maintenance, decay, impermanence,—four phases in the coming into and going out of being of matter; and (7) bodily nutriment. The simple explanation of the classification is that these various classes have all something to with matter, and in that sense are matter *qua* derived. The senses themselves are subtle matter, and invisible; their objects are immediately bound up with matter; the faculties bound up with life are an aspect of matter as it appears in the matter aggregate of the individual, and intimation by act and speech are introduced into the classification on the same ground of connexion with the material side of the empiric self, while bodily nutriment is explained in the same way. The inclusion of space[2] is interesting, and a novelty; it appears in the Canon as if it were a fifth element, and, of course, it would be absurd to imagine that it appears as derivate matter, because it was a pure form of intuition or a mental construction. But the difficulty disappears when we consider that the element of space like the following seven items is intimately connected with matter. Space is necessary for the movement of matter, and can just as well be placed under derivate matter as can the qualities of matter and the four stages of its coming into being, state of being, decay, and impermanence, which it may be noted agree with the Sautrāntika doctrine of the four, not three stages, in being.

The most interesting point undoubtedly is the suggestion that touch is in some way more directly in connexion with matter than

[1] See ch. ix. § 3. [2] See ch. ix. § 2.

the other senses, although it is asserted not to perceive the cohesion of water, but only the other three characteristics, so far as present in it. But the idea is not explained or developed, further than by Buddhaghosa's illustration which makes the other senses and their objects relatively speaking cotton balls striking on cotton balls on the elemental anvils, while touch is the hammer which smites through the cotton balls to the anvils. To claim this as an anticipation of the doctrine of the development of the other senses from touch is clearly unwise.

We owe to the *Dhammasaṅgaṇi* an attempt to make concrete the vagueness of the term dispositions (*saṁkhāra*) by a long list of states classified under it, to which we have already alluded.[1] The term comprehends in effect every mental condition, including attention and volitional states which is or may be aroused as the result of past experience on the occasion of any impression of sense or idea. Such an understanding, it is plain, is without psychological value, and it is a proof of the lack of investigation on an empirical basis that no serious attempt is made to dispense with the perfectly indefensible doctrine of the five aggregates. But a beginning is being made to express more intelligibly the problem to the extent that a division of mental phenomena into those of thought (*citta*) and thought properties (*cetasika*) is found;[2] under the former rank the five forms of sense cognition, the activity of mind (*manas*) cognition, and representative cognition, while the latter covers the other three aggregates of feeling, perception, and dispositions. Matter, and the uncompounded element, Nirvāṇa, which agree with the three aggregates mentioned as not being of thought, disagree with them in not being thought properties; we thus have the aggregate of intelligence set up definitely as thought; the other three aggregates as thought properties; and independent of either category the classes of matter of all kinds, including the matter aggregate of the individual, and the uncompounded

[1] Above, ch. v. § 3; see ch. x. § 4.

[2] The term occurs first in DN. i. 213; the later use appears in the *Paṭisambhidāmagga*, i. 84; *Vibhaṅga*, p. 421; DS., §§ 1187 ff. The Rājagirikas and Siddhatthikas deny *cetasikas*; KV. vii. 3. The Vaibhāṣika view ingeniously makes *citta* as Vijñāna the grasping of bare fact (*vastumātra*), *caitasa* as grasping particulars; AKV (Burn. MS.) f. 28ᵃ, MKV., pp. 65, n. 3; 74, n. 6.

element, Nirvāṇa, and from this is derived the fourfold division which is accepted in mediaeval Buddhist texts, such as the *Abhidhammatthasaṁgaha* (12 cent. A. D.). In the Abhidhamma itself the *Kathāvatthu* gives a list of states which evidently are intended to cover the sphere of the other three aggregates and to be treated—whether all or some of them is not stated—as coexistent accompaniments of thought. The separateness of the four aggregates is thus being undermined, the intelligence aggregate being given the central position and designated as thought while the others are made its accompaniments.

The love of generalization and definition of the Abhidhamma writers leads inevitably to the extension of their statements to those worlds which are above man; the study of the animal mind is neglected, though its importance is obvious, since rebirth as an animal in consequence of previous sin is a very frequent occurrence, and only a little less unpleasant than rebirth in a hell or purgatory. But animals though capable, the *Milindapañha* tells us, of reasoning in a discursive way, cannot attain intuition and therefore are debarred from salvation. On the other hand, the gods are essentially sublimated men, and rebirth as some sort of god in one or other of their worlds is the legitimate desire and end of the ordinary man who desires longer, more serene life, and is not yet worthy of seeking to become delivered as an Arahant. The doctrine is early, but the details are reserved for the idle theorizing of the Abhidhammas Sanskrit and Pali, though in strictness what is recorded is as in the case of the rest of the system not theory, but the account given by that intuition which is the source of enlightenment and of all our insight into the things, which are hidden to the ordinary powers of reason. Matter and feeling are found together in the world of desire; matter still persists in the sphere of unconscious beings, which is attained in the third Jhāna by adepts; feeling is there absent, but alone is found in the sphere of the immaterial world (*arūpaloka*).

2. *The Milindapañha*

The *Milindapañha* which is interesting for its strict adherence to the denial of any true soul (*jīva, puggala, vedagū*) incidentally insists on the separateness and necessity of the senses;[1] the alleged soul is repudiated precisely because it, in theory autonomous, can only use a specific sense to obtain the corresponding sense experience, while, if it were really autonomous, it could use any of the senses or dispense altogether with the use of any of the sense organs while in fact there can be no sense experience if the sense organ is removed, a contention which may conceivably have been directed against the contemporary Sāṁkhya school. The relation of sensation to the functions of mind is then investigated, the issue being whether sensation issues commands to ideation or ideation bids sensation to act. The question is quaint, and the answer negates either view; in place we have the explanation of the constant succession of the activity of mind on sense perception in inclination or natural tendency, as when rain water runs away down a slope; in existing structure as when in a walled city there is but one means of ingress and egress; in habitual process, as in the order followed by the wagons of a caravanserai; and in practice, as skill is gained in the arts of writing, arithmetic, and valuation.

As regards cognition the ideas of initial and sustained mental application (*vitakka*, *vicāra*) are illustrated by similes pointing to the application of attention followed by the repeated pulsations of attention thus applied. The analysis of cognition is of importance in emphasizing the simultaneity of the elements involved; the contact, feeling, perception, conceived intention or volition (*cetanā*), initial and sustained attention, which are here united as supervening on the three factors—once reduced to two—of sense organ, object, and intelligence directed to the sense, are asserted to be simultaneous, the factors being capable of distinction but not experienced successively or in isolation any more than the flavours employed in the making of a sauce by the royal cook. Later analysis denied the simultaneity, substituting instead swift succession, doubtless in accord with the Nyāya view.[2]

On the subject of higher knowledge an interesting development

[1] Mil., pp. 55 f.; 86 f.; 57 ff.
[2] Mil., pp. 62 f.; 56, 63. For the later view, see Ledi Sadaw, JPTS. 1914, p. 149, and cf. KV. ii. 7; xvi. 4.

is made in the exposition of a series of types of minds, as a reply to the difficulty suggested by the fact that, though omniscient, the Buddha was not always consciously so, but had the power to know anything to which he might direct his attention. The seven stages are those of the ordinary sensual man; the man who has entered on the path to salvation; the man who has so far progressed that he has but one more life on earth to live before he will attain the end; the man who will attain the end in heaven; the Arahant or enlightened man; the Pacceka or individual Buddha who knows but does not preach enlightenment; and the omniscient Buddha, who is actually or potentially all-knowing. Insight again is discriminated from reasoned thinking (*yoniso manasikāra*) as elimination as opposed to mental grasp; the latter is ascribed to sheep, goats, oxen, buffaloes, camels, asses, but these representatives of animals are denied insight or intuition. Again, awareness is attributed to intelligence (*viññāna*), discernment to intuition (*paññā*), and among the results of intuition are placed as assured miracles like the power to move through the air, or travel in an instant to the Brahma-world, situated at four months' journey of a falling body from the earth.[1]

Mindfulness (*sati*) appears definitely here in one place as equivalent to memory, and the grounds of it are given as sixteen,[2] in a manner which exhibits no trace of any serious investigation. They are (1) extraordinary effort, as when former births are called to mind; (2) outward aid, that is, being reminded by others; (3) impression caused by importance of the occasion or pleasure; (4) impression made by pain; (5) similarity of appearance; (6) difference of appearance; (7) knowledge of speech which produces memory on being reminded by others; (8) a sign, e.g. a mark on a bullock; (9) effort to recollect on the prompting of others; (10) calculation, as in the knowledge acquired in writing that such and such a letter follows another; (11) arithmetic, as when accountants do big sums by their knowledge of figures; (12) learning by heart, as in the case of reciters of the scriptures; (13) meditation, as

[1] Mil., pp. 102 ff.; 32, 39, 82.

[2] Mil., pp. 78 ff. There are actually seventeen causes, which are to be reduced to sixteen. Cf. KV. i. 8; the Uttarāpathakas hold that mind in recalling is without object; ix. 6. For the Nyāya view. cf. NS. iii. 2. 44.

when a monk recollects a temporary earlier experience; (14) reference to a book, as to a law; (15) a pledge, as when a man recollects from seeing pledged goods the occasion; and (16) actual experience, as when one remembers what one has seen, heard, tasted, &c. There is, it is clear, practically no appreciation whatever of the nature of the problem.

There is also given out in a late chapter a theory of dreams, which describes six kinds of men who experience them, he who is of a bilious, windy or phlegmatic humour, he who is influenced by a god, he who habituates himself, and he who does so in the way of prognostication, the last sort only of dreams being true. The prognostication comes about not by the action of any person, god or man, but it enters the mind of the sleeper of itself, and is explained to him by one skilled in omens, just as such a person prognosticates from external signs such as pimples. Dreams take place in 'monkey-sleep', a state between waking and deep sleep. But the theory, naïve in its acceptance of popular belief in divine action and in the autonomy of prognostication, is interesting incidentally; it is explained that there is no dream in deep sleep for thought (*citta*) has then entered into, and become one with the Bhavañga, and in that state thought does not act, and, being inactive, it does not experience pleasure or pain, and dreaming is impossible in such a condition. The Bhavañga, or stream of being, is a conception barely known in the Abhidhamma, and there not explained, but it evidently has already here the sense of a continuum which is not conscious, but from which consciousness emerges, and which may therefore be reckoned as sub-conscious.[1]

Volition [2] receives little further explication. The term Cetanā is defined as having the characteristic of being conceived and the being prepared, but the terms are obscure; the illustrations of one who prepares and gives poison to others with the result that both suffer pain suggest that it denotes deliberate intention

[1] Mil., pp. 297 ff.; on Bhavañga, NP., p. 91; *Tika-Paṭṭhāna*, in *Compendium*, p. 267, n. 1; ADS. iii. 8. In AN. ii. 79 *bhava* appears with the other three aggregates, matter, feeling, ideation, covering perhaps consciousness and the dispositions. On the Nyāya view of dreams cf. ILA., pp. 66 f.

[2] Mil., p. 61. Conation (*viriya—indriya*) is recognized in DS., § 13. On Cetanā cf. *Compendium*, pp. 235 ff.

followed by effectual action. The doctrine also occurs that involuntary evil is more blameworthy than voluntary, as a man who intentionally seizes a mass of hot metal suffers less than he who does so unawares.

3. *Buddhaghosa and the Sarvāstivādin Schools*

In the scholasticism of Buddhaghosa and of his contemporary Buddhadatta, as well as more developed in mediaeval Pali texts, we find the doctrine of the Bhavaṅga elaborated. In describing the process of consciousness (*viññāna*), Buddhaghosa enumerates fourteen modes of process,[1] namely, in reconception; in subconsciousness (*bhavaṅga*) as in sleep, &c.; in adverted attention (*āvajjana*); in the five modes of special sense impressions; in recipience of them; in investigation; in determination; in complete apprehension; in registration; and finally in death. At the end of registration, then, the process once more becomes that of the stream of unconscious being, until circumstances arise to cause adverting once more to supervene. The lapse of the last subconscious thought (*citta*) is decease, but immediately there arises conception and the stream of being flows on uninterrupted unless a man attains enlightenment. The *Abhidhammatthasaṁgaha* presents us with a complex theory by which in an act of perception seventeen moments in succession are involved, but its psychological value is minimal. On the part of mind in sense cognition Buddhaghosa has much to say, but with decided inconsistence; at one time he maintains the simultaneity of the action of mind and of the sense, at another makes the sense impression the necessary basis of the action of mind.[2] He does not raise any question of the existence of a medium for sense impressions other than touch, and he is naïvely realistic in conception as to the action of matter on spirit. The doctrine that like must be known by like is first recorded by him, but as old, and he indicates that the practice of saying that one sees length or shortness is derivative, the truth being that touch gives us these matters, and sight

[1] VM. xiv; Buddhadatta, *Abhidhammāvatāra*; *Buddh. Psych.*, p. 179; *Compendium*, p. 126.

[2] Asl., pp. 73, 263; *Compendium*, p. 259, n. 1.

colour alone.[1] The organ of touch, he insists, is diffused through the whole body, for otherwise we could not have the great variety of tactile experience which we actually do possess. He first records the heart as the seat of the mind.

In the realm of thought Buddhaghosa has an interesting doctrine of the relations of perception (*saññā*), intelligence (*viññāna*), and intuition (*paññā*). He compares them[2] to the different reactions provoked by the sight of precious metals in a child, which sees in them coloured objects; in a citizen who recognizes in them utilities with exchange value; and in an expert who can tell their origin and fashioner. On the topic of zest or interest (*pīti*) he has much to say,[3] and he illustrates the superhuman powers which are possessed by a person in such a state.

Interest attaches to the suggestion that by Buddhaghosa an idealistic interpretation was given to aspects of sensation and feeling, in which earlier views saw the interaction of material and psychical factors; the Sautrāntikas as well as the Vaibhāṣikas, as we have seen, accepted the real interaction of matter and spirit. Is it possible that Buddhaghosa, who was, we know, trained in the traditions of India before he came to Ceylon, adopted a more idealistic position, and accepted in effect the Vijñānavāda doctrine of the object of perception as wholly ideal? It has been suggested[4] that this is the sense in which we are to read his exposition of the old formula: 'Because of the eye and visible matter there arises visual consciousness; the collision of the two is contact; conditioned by contact arises feeling; what one feels, one perceives, &c.' In Buddhaghosa[5] we have the explanation that in the phrase 'matter strikes on form' the latter words are 'a term for the eye (i.e. the visual sense) being receptive of the object of consciousness.' This is held to be 'a clear attempt to resolve the old metaphor, or, it may be, the old physical concept into terms of subjective experience.' Again in dealing with the simile of the *Milindapañha*, which

[1] Asl., pp. 317 f.; 311 f. Cf. ILA., p. 191. That the doctrine of like by like was borrowed by Greek thought from India (*Buddh. Psych.*, p. 143, n. 2) is absurd.

[2] On MN. i. 292.

[3] Asl., p. 115; VM. iv.; *Buddh. Psych.*, pp. 187 ff.; *Compendium*, p. 243.

[4] *Psych. Ethics*, pp. liv ff.; 5, n. 2.; Walleser, PGAB., p. 117.

[5] Asl., p. 309.

compares the clash of object and organ with the impact of two cymbals and the butting of two goats, 'we are told by Buddhaghosa to interpret eye by visual cognition and to take the concussion in the sense of function (*kiccaṭṭhen' eva*)', and he tells us that when feeling arises through contact the real causal antecedent is mental, though apparently external.[1]

It would not appear from these arguments that Buddhaghosa did more than recognize in cognition and feeling that there was always present a stream of consciousness which was subject to modification by external reality, the Sautrāntika doctrine, and this realism of Buddhaghosa is supported by the absence of any other suggestion that he regarded the world as ideal any more than did the Vibhajyavādins generally. We have indeed a remarkable proof of the realism of his thought in the fact that, whereas the Canon is silent on the point, he is express in asserting the existence of a heart basis which bears to mind the same relation as the sense organ does to the sense as psychic activity; it is the place where the door objects or sense impressions come, and are assimilated or received into unity.[2] Buddhaghosa thus is punctilious in insisting on the physical basis of mind as the most important of sense organs, and this contradicts any idea of his being prepared to deny the reality of the external world. Further doubt is thrown on the interpretation of Buddhaghosa's view by the attempt to find in the *Dhammasaṅgaṇi* itself the view that the process of sense perception is not materialistically conceived. We are not told, it is pointed out, where the mutual impact takes place nor with what a distant object impinges. If Dhammas are conceived as states of consciousness, and Rūpa is conceived as a species of Dhamma, it follows that both the Rūpa, which is external and comes into contact with the Rūpa which is of the self, and also this latter Rūpa are regarded in the light of the two mental factors, necessary to constitute an act of sensory consciousness, actual or potential. But it is plain that the reasoning rests on wholly false assumptions, namely that Dhamma is conceived as

[1] Asl., p. 108; Mil., p. 60; Asl., p. 109.

[2] *Psych. Ethics*, pp. lxxviii ff.; *Compendium*, p. 277, where the attempt to claim for the Buddha knowledge of the function of the brain is ludicrous.

a state of consciousness and Rūpa as a species of it in that sense; Dhammas include all things of every kind, material and spiritual, and Rūpa is matter. The simple sense of the *Dhammasaṅgaṇi* and the Canonical tradition appears to be that consciousness is directed towards the eye and object and assists, therefore, as a third element in the contact which produces feeling, perception, &c. The *Majjima Nikāya*[1] indeed gives the three factors as the objects, the senses, and the act of attention, and this sense will adequately fit the views of Buddhaghosa and is entirely in keeping with the references in the *Milindapañha*.

The true theory, therefore, seems to be that the Sautrāntika doctrine, whether deliberately or not, takes effective cognizance of the difficulty, which the Canon ignores, of the nature of attention. In the anxiety to deny the existence of anything permanent, the Buddha in his response to Sāti[2] seems even to deny the existence of any such thing, by asserting that visual consciousness arises from the eye and the object; it is, of course, clear that no such doctrine was intended, for that would be in effect a materialism of which the spiritual is an epiphenomenon, but that the point of the Buddha's rebuke is that the doctrine asserted by Sāti affirmed the persistence unaltered (*anañña*) of the consciousness (*viññāna*). The Buddha's reply insists that, because of the dependence of the content of consciousness on the sense and the objects of sense, it is constantly changing. The Sautrāntika view fills the lacuna of explicit exposition of continuity by adopting a theory which enables it to appreciate the true sense of the Buddhist doctrine of perception.

We find also among the Sarvāstivādins a view of the nature of the process styled perception or ideation (*saṁjñā*), which gives that category a more effective content than it sometimes has in the older psychology.[3] We must distinguish between the mere actual perception, for example, of blue, and the judgement 'this is blue' when the object is fixed by being given a name, so that we may treat perception as involving two kinds of contact,

[1] MN. i. 190. [2] MN. i. 256. Cf. on the causation of cognition, ch. ix. § 4.

[3] AK. iii. 30 with Bhāṣya (p. 50). Contra *Vibhaṅga*, p. 6 with comm.; SBB. iii. 59, n. 1; DN. ii. 59; *Buddh. Psych.*, pp. 49 f. Cf. AKV. in *Dharmasaṁgraha*, 28 (p. 41); (Paris MS. f. 241[a]) in MKV., p. 74, n. 6.

the simple one of resistance and one of denomination; it is tempting to assume that some such idea really underlay the distinction of resistance-perception and denominative-perception (*paṭigha-* and *adhivacana-saññā*) in the *Vibhaṅga*, but the view of Buddhaghosa is different.

In general there is nothing very novel in the Sarvāstivādin psychology; the senses are material, each being divided into a principal consisting of a combination of pure and minute units while the accessory is made of flesh; the differences between the five depend on the difference of their atomic combinations. They possess each the power of natural perceptual discrimination, but it lies with intellect (*mano-vijñāna*) to exercise the function of discrimination of things as past, present, and future, and the power of recollection and recognition. Mind (*manas*), here appears in its usual rôle of co-ordinating intellectual activity, but the conception of the relation of sensation and mind is by no means clear of confusion. In its capacity as will the mind appears as Citta. Every act, feeling, or thought is accompanied by a latent state, which later comes to fruition, and thus bridges the gulf between the cause and the effect in the working of the principle of action. In the case of verbal or bodily action the impress is quasi-material (*avijñapti*).

The details of the scheme are occasionally interesting; the sense of sight grasps not merely colour, but also configuration (*saṁsthāna*); e.g. long, short, round, square, high, low, straight, and crooked. The sense of touch appreciates the four elements, and also the qualities of smoothness, roughness, lightness, heaviness, cold, hunger, and thirst. These qualities fall under touch, because they represent the feelings generated in sentient beings by objects; thus thirst is caused by a touch which excites the physical body when the element of fire becomes active and predominates over other energies. In some of these dicta and in the general view the closeness of connexion with the Nyāya-Vaiçeṣika system is obvious.

4. *The Classifications of Phenomena*

In all the schools great attention was devoted to classification[1] and division of phenomena, material and psychic, a process indicating in the view of the Mahāyāna some failure to realize the truth of the doctrine of momentariness, since the theories took the aspect of regarding existence as made up of temporary complexes, indeed, but of complexes derived from a number of irreducible factors, a conception really heretical.

The Theravādin classification, as we have seen, is based on the old doctrine of the five aggregates; it reckons under matter (*rūpa*) the strange miscellany recited above; under feeling it accepts the three classes of pleasure, pain, and neutral feeling, adding sometimes mental and physical sensation; under perception or ideation (*saññā*) we have the ideas corresponding to the five senses and to mind as the sixth; of dispositions or mental qualities (*saṁkhāra*) there are fifty-two divisions and of consciousness or intellect (*viññāna*) there are eighty-nine, classed from the point of view of the merit or demerit resulting. Of these the mental qualities alone are of sufficient interest to deserve mention. Seven mental qualities are common to every act of consciousness: mental contact, feeling, ideation, volition (*cetanā*), concentration, (*ekaggatā*), alertness (*jīvitindriya*), and attention (*manasikāra*). Six mental properties may or may not be present: initial and sustained application, deciding (*adhimokkha*), effort, zest, and impulse or conation (*chanda*). These thirteen are unmoral. There are fourteen evil mental qualities: dullness, impudence, recklessness, distraction, greed, error, conceit, hate, envy, selfishness, worry, sloth, torpor, and perplexity. There are nineteen virtuous mental qualities: faith, mindfulness, shame or prudence, modesty, discretion, non-covetousness or disinterestedness, amity or non-hatred, balance of mind, composure of body[2] or of mind, buoyancy of body or of mind, pliancy of body or of mind, adaptability of body or

[1] Cf. McGovern, *Mahāyāna Buddhism*, ch. vii; DS. and AK.; for the developed Theravāda, ADS.; *Compendium*, pp. 237 ff.

[2] That *kāya* here means the aggregates other than *citta* (*Compendium*, p. 96, n 3; Asl., p. 150 on DS., § 40) is very dubious. The contrast between ADS. and DS., § 62 as to Saṁkhāras is interesting as a token of elaboration.

of mind, proficiency of body or of mind, rectitude of body or of mind. There are three forms of propriety or abstinence (*virati*), right speech, right action, and right livelihood; two illimitables, pity and appreciation; and one supreme possession, intuition.

The Sarvāstivādin divisions, based on the distinction between uncompounded and compounded things, recognize seventy-two of the latter. Under matter they class five sense objects, five sense organs, and latent matter (*avijñapti*), the impression left by vocal or bodily action on the bodily organism. The mental element is single, though there are six forms of consciousness, the five senses and mind consciousness. There are forty-six divisions of mental qualities, corresponding to the dispositions of the Theravādins. Ten neutral elements are always present: sensation or feeling, ideation, volition, contact, impulse, intellect (*mati*), memory, attention, deciding (*adhimokṣa*), concentration (*samādhi*). There are ten good elements which are always present: faith, diligence, indifference, shame, modesty, non-covetousness, non-hatred, harmlessness, serenity, temperance or non-slackness. There are six great evil elements: dullness or nescience, intemperateness, indolence, disbelief, sloth or idleness, distraction or rashness. There are two non-virtuous great elements: shamelessness, immodesty. There are ten lesser evil elements, not present in all forms of sentiency, but only in those forms of life which are possessed of self-consciousness: wrath, hypocrisy, envy, jealousy, anguish, injury, rancour, deceit, trickery, and arrogance. Finally, there are eight miscellaneous minor (*aniyatabhūmika*) mental qualities: repentance, torpor, judgement (*vitarka*), investigation (*vicāra*)—that is initial and applied attention, cupidity, anger, pride, and doubt. Finally, there are fourteen miscellaneous elements classed as non-mental compounds (*cittaviprayukta dharma*). They are attainment, non-attainment, general characteristics (*sabhāgatā*), unconsciousness (*asaṁjñitā*), ecstacy with loss of consciousness (*asaṁjñisamāpatti*), continuation of this, equivalent to cessation of existence (*nirodhasamāpatti*), life, birth, continuance (*sthiti*), decay (*jarā*), impermanency (*anityatā*) words, sentence, and letters.

This not very happy attempt at an objective description is

accompanied by a subjective classification ; this recognizes the five aggregates making up the individual, which correspond with the seventy-five things of the objective classification and the twelve bases (*āyatanas*) of mental action, namely the five senses, the five sense objects, the mind and ideas,[1] being the necessary materials for the functioning of consciousness, while the eighteen factors (*dhātus*) of consciousness consist of the twelve bases together with the six forms of consciousness, the five senses and mind. In the whole scheme as in that of the Theravādins we find little of philosophical insight or importance in this, clearly a very important side in its own eyes of the activity of the school.

[1] TRD., pp. 31 f. ; ADS. vii. 8, *Compendium*, pp. 254 ff. For the relation of the Pudgala to them in the Vātsīputrīya view see Wassilieff, *Bouddhisme*, pp. 252 f. Cf. above, ch. iv, § 4.

CHAPTER XI

THE THEORY OF ACTION AND BUDDHOLOGY

1. *The Mechanism of the Act*

To the *Abhidharmakoça* we are indebted for a full development of the theory of the mechanism of the act and its fruition, which unites into a more or less coherent whole the vaguer hints of the earlier texts. Insistence is laid on the necessity of volition for action; the accidental destruction of a human being when aiming at a pumpkin is no murder, and issue on this point is taken with the Jain view, which curiously enough is repeated in the *Milindapañha*. The Jain argument is that the man who slays, however unwittingly, is guilty of murder, just as the man who touches fire, however unknowingly, is burned. But this is rejected as absurd; the mother and the embryo would each be guilty of injuring the other; a murdered man would be guilty as the cause and origin of the slaying; if the analogy of fire is pressed, it results in holding that a man who induces another to kill is no murderer, since he did not strike the blow, while unconscious sin would be graver than conscious sin, just as the man who incautiously touches fire suffers more than he who does so knowingly.[1]

The element of intention is differentiated from bodily or verbal action by its effects; it leaves only an impression (*vāsanā*) on the mental series, while bodily and verbal actions as material create something also quasi-material styled by the scholastics Avijñapti, which persists and develops without consciousness on the part of the individual. This curious doctrine contains in itself the recognition of a real fact; the taking of a religious vow impresses on a man's character a peculiar bent, which is not consciously

[1] MKV., pp. 306 f.; AK. iv; Poussin, *Nirvāṇa*, p. 69; cf. Mil., p. 158.

present but none the less must definitely affect the trend of his actions.[1]

The criterion of action remains dubious, for the doctrine that a good act is one that benefits a neighbour is incidental only, and the general rule is merely that a good act is one which matures into a pleasurable existence in future, while a bad act leads to pain. Or again, an act is good if it aims at pleasure in a future existence, but not if it seeks happiness in this, a doctrine which has obvious limitations, since it may lead, as in the case of Nanda, a kinsman of Çākyamuni, to acceptance of the tonsure and separation from his wife, merely to gain the delights of celestial brides in the world of heaven.[2] The system allows also excessive room to the inculcation of the virtue of generosity; even if a man sins not, and thus secures rebirth as a man, he will be poor if he has failed in generosity; if he sins, but is generous, he will pay for the sin by rebirth in hell or as an animal or ghost, but thereafter he will reap the reward of birth on earth as a rich man or as a god in heaven. It accords with this that the casuistry of the gift is elaborated. A gift depends for its value on such factors as the faith, learning, morality, and intention of the giver; the manner and moment of donation; the qualities of the object given; and, last not least, the qualities of the recipient or field (*kṣetra*) of donation. A man, however wicked, is a more worthy object of favour than an animal; gifts to the poor and sick are especially fruitful; gifts in return for services are laudable, and gifts to a virtuous and enlightened saint are best of all. In every case of course desire of immediate reward in this life is excluded.

The mechanism of transmigration, vaguely conceived earlier, is now brought into effective connexion with action. Normally a being, god, man or animal, lives its life without essential physical change, though occasionally punishment for crime may change a man into a woman or transfer him into a hell being

[1] Poussin, *op. cit.*, pp. 71 f. The gift does not, however, exist in intention alone, as the Rājagirikas and Siddhatthikas hold; KV. vii. 4.

[2] Poussin, *op. cit.*, p. 76, n. 2; *Saundarananda Kāvya* (JA. 1912, i. 79): *aihikasukhārthaṁ karmāpuṇyam*, AKV. (Paris MS.) f. 236[b]. That Buddhism is hedonistic is admitted in *Psych. Ethics*, pp. lxxxiii ff.; the attainment, or even the seeking after, enlightenment is pleasant beyond other pleasures; *Buddhism*, pp. 230 ff.

without the intervention of death. But death is normally the portal to the next existence and the last consciousness of life is determined in form by appropriateness to the new birth to be achieved, which in its turn depends on the action to be rewarded or punished. If the fate of the man on death is to be hell, he hears the cries of the tormented, and his rebirth or conception consciousness (*pratisaṁdhi-vijñāna*) is a continuation of this last consciousness before death. An animal is incapable of action proper; but an ancient deed may reward it with rebirth as a man, and its dying consciousness takes the form of ideas, desires or images which are continued in an infant birth. The process is complex, since each individual series extends indefinitely into the past, and the future rebirth cannot be predicted, though a meritorious person may often secure the kind of rebirth he desires by intense thought of it before death.[1]

The process of rebirth may be immediate; thus gods and beings of hell are not conceived, but the last consciousness of the dying man creates in some fashion for itself the necessary divine or infernal body out of unorganized matter. In the case of men, animals or ghosts there may be delays in rebirth if circumstances are not propitious, and in the meantime it may exist as a Gandharva, for seven or forty-nine days, before it finds its way to fashion with the aid of the conceptional elements the necessary embryo, and errors are possible in detail at least; the consciousness may be born in jackal, not dog shape.

There is obviously a difficulty in determining the time of the reward or punishment of action, which the scholastic states without explaining. We must distinguish between acts which are supernatural (*lokottara*), leading to release, neither born of desire nor leading to it, and destructive of the reward of earlier deeds, and those acts which, born of desire, lead to rebirth or reward. Some of those acts need not be rewarded; a saint may obtain release without the tedium of enjoying in heaven the reward of his good deeds, and he who has won the position of a non-returner (*anāgāmin*) has not to suffer in hell or on earth or

[1] Poussin, *Nirvāṇa*, pp. 85 ff. Cf. the mediaeval Ceylonese doctrine, *Compendium*, pp. 73 ff.

in an inferior heaven the fruits of past deeds. Of those deeds that bear reward some may be requited in this life; a good man if he commits some minor sin will pay the penalty ere his death, while a bad man who committed the same fault would suffer torment in hell. On the other hand such grave crimes as parricide receive inevitably punishment in the next life. But most serious sins may be punished then or their retribution may be delayed to permit the retribution of other acts, or in rare cases by the attainment of sanctity they are turned into deeds to be requited in this life.

Artificial as the theory is, it serves to explain the whole nature of existence of sentient beings. An evil deed results in birth as a hell being, and if wicked enough the sin may compel long periods of rebirth in such a state. The birth and the sufferings undergone are the fruit of ripening of the sin (*vipākaphala*). But at last the force of birth projection by the sin is lessened; an animal existence or existences follows, whose sufferings are again the fruit of ripening, while the character of the birth is the fruit similar to the action (*niṣyanda-phala*) as when the murderer is reborn as a tiger. The power of birth projection is at last exhausted, and the way is open for some deed done in a former birth which had merit, and which now projects a human birth, but the life that follows will be coloured by a fruit similar to the ancient sin; the murderer will be crushed to death,[1] the thief poor. Moreover, he will have a character tinged by the nature of his son; the murderer will be evil disposed.[2]

But it is not merely each organism which is brought into being by the effect of action. The world in which the organism is to exist owes its existence to the same cause; it is material indeed, but its actual condition is not due to any nature of its own; it is the fruit of mastery (*adhipati-phala*) of the acts of beings. This is seen most clearly at the beginning of a cosmic age;[3] the whole material universe is the fruit of mastery of all the deeds of the

[1] A thorn which pricks the Buddha's foot is the fruit of a slaying of a man in the 91st Aeon hence; TRD., p. 26.

[2] Can one in hell do good? KV. xiii. 2 does not deal with this, but with good done by one who has already committed a crime dooming him for a Kappa.

[3] On this topic, see AKB., pp. 99 ff.

world of living beings. The rule is universal, and applies to the divine sphere with a completeness and boldness unknown to Brahmanical thought. In the cosmic evolution the acts of the being whose merits are to secure his appearance as the Brahmā of the age produce his divine palace, in which the god comes into being, to delude himself into the belief that he is self created (*svayam-bhū*). By a similar delusion he imagines that the other beings who come into existence as his companions in his heaven are creatures of his desire for companionship, instead of being produced by the merits of ancient days, and hence is derived the worship of Brahmā as creator and overlord, ideas merely idle;[1] Brahmā in truth like gods of inferior rank has come into being as the reward of noble actions and deep meditations, the Brahma-vihāras, in previous existences, but power he has none, and he differs from the monk set on release in that his acts in the past have aimed at wordly motives.

2. *The Mode of Transmigration*

On one point in special in the process of the working of action, we find an interesting divergence in the schools, on the precise mode of transmigration. Popular ideas attributed birth to the co-operation with the parents of an entity, the Gandharva,[2] representing in some vague way the soul which was to be born. Acting on this doctrine the Sammitiyas and Pubbaseliyas held that after death there was an intermediate state before rebirth, a view with which we may connect the opinion of both the Pubba- and Apara-seliyas that the embryo was immediately provided with a full sense apparatus.[3] The Sarvāstivādins adhered to the view as regards all those to be reborn in the worlds of desire and matter as contrasted with those to be reborn in the world of non-matter, a distinction suggesting that the intermediate being must be treated as quasi-material, with a

[1] DN. i. 17 ff., 220 ff.

[2] Cf. MN. ii. 137; Mil., p. 123; J. v. 330; Divyāv., pp. 1, 440; AK. iii. 12 (pp. 18, 23, 25, 65, 234). For the Vedic idea see Oldenberg, *Rel. des Veda*², pp. 252 ff.

[3] KV. viii. 2; xiv. 2; Wassilieff, *Bouddhisme*, pp. 242, 249, 255; Poussin, JA. 1902, ii. 296 ff.; BCAP. ix. 73; *Çlokavārttika*, p. 704; SS. iii. 10 with comm.; Keith, SS., pp. 36, 82; KM., pp. 59, 65.

transporting (*ātivāhika*) body, analogous to the subtle body of the Sāṁkhya. The Vaibhāṣikas seem to have accepted the intermediate being, supporting the view by the consideration that it is not always possible for the suitable rebirth to be obtained immediately on death.

On the other hand the idea is rejected by the Mahāsāṅghikas, the Ekavyavahārikas, Lokottaravādins, and Kukkuṭikas, and the *Milindapañha* [1] clearly has no belief in any body to transport the consciousness from one destiny to another; the difficulties of the king are resolved by the reflection that one can as rapidly send one's thought to Kashmir as to Kalasi, 200 leagues as against twelve. We learn also from Çaṅkara that the passage of the soul into a new life was conceived as taking place without any body by the Buddhists whose views he combats. If for soul we say series of consciousness, this may stand for the Sautrāntika view, but it is possible that, realists as they were, they were willing to accept some subtle matter as accompanying consciousness; the important fact, however, is that their doctrine of continuity enables them to meet adequately the difficulty of continued existence. In any case from their standpoint it is clear that the consciousness is the essential element which determines the new life; whether or not it takes a body with it, it is the seed of consciousness, which through the physiological apparatus of the union of the parents produces the shoot of name and form, the concrete individual.

3. *The Nature of the Buddha*

Whatever the element of divinity asserted for himself or accorded to the Buddha by his early disciples, the Pali Canon undoubtedly is sincere in emphasizing the humanity of the Buddha; his epithet of 'superior to the world (*lokuttara*)' denotes him merely as one who has attained a perfection of enlightenment and release from the cycle of rebirth. But we learn from the *Kathāvatthu* that other philosophical schools took a distinctive view of the nature of the Buddha, and were supernaturalists in the sense that they did not admit the true or complete humanity of the teacher. There was, indeed, an obvious difficulty in the

[1] p. 83; Çaṅkara, BS. iii. 1. 1.

orthodox view; the attainment by the Buddha of enlightenment is accomplished by the same processes as that by which he enters into the state in which he absolutely passes away. It becomes, therefore, obviously not a little difficult to accept the ordinary version of the life of the Buddha; how can a person who has attained in becoming a Buddha the same state as is attained on the final Nirvāṇa be supposed to have been accessible to mere mundane emotions like pity, and the Uttarāpathakas[1] are recorded as denying that the Buddha felt pity. There is the same difficulty regarding the preaching of the law; the older tradition asserts that from the night of the illumination to his passing away the Buddha said nothing false; for this, is substituted the idea that he said nothing at all.[2] But some explanation of the teaching of the law is required, more satisfactory than picturesque conceptions of the enlightenment being imparted by the bright hairs on the Buddha's forehead, or the eloquence of the walls of the place of instruction, and a solution for the difficulties is found by the Vetulyakas, a mysterious school, in the doctrine that the Buddha never lived in the world of sense but displayed himself on earth in a specially created form, while the doctrine was preached by the disciple Ānanda.[3] This is to carry the matter further than is necessary, and we find among the Lokottaravādins of the Mahāsāṅghikas a more modified concept.[4] Çākyamuni there is represented as having taken, long ages ago in the presence of a Buddha of the same name, the vow to become a Buddha and to have followed up his purpose through the elaborate process of the acquisition of the ten perfections. Then incarnating himself for the last time he enters into the womb of the virgin Māyā, in a mental or spiritual (*manomaya*)[5] form in which he is able to give instruction to mankind. A difficulty

[1] KV. xviii. 3; see Mil., p. 110.
[2] KV. ii. 3; xviii. 8 (Poussin, *Bouddhisme*, p. 253); AN. ii. 24; BCAP. ix. 36; MKV., p. 366.
[3] *Çlokavārttika*, p. 86; KV. xviii. 1; Kashgar frag. of *Saddharmapuṇḍarīka*, JRAS. 1907, p. 434. Cf. Ç., p. 284.
[4] *Mahāvastu*; Poussin, *Bouddhisme*, pp. 248 ff. See also Oltramare, *Muséon*, 1916, pp. 3 ff.
[5] Or, 'mind made' possibly; Mhv. i. 218, but this lacks plausibility in view of the regular use, DN. i. 34, 77, 187. Cf. ERE. viii. 329; above, p. 129, n. 4.

for the school obviously here presents itself; the traditional account of the Buddha gave him one—or three[1]—wives, and in order to enhance the glory of his self-sacrifice in becoming a Buddha, insists on the pleasures of sense which he enjoyed in the harem; a son Rāhula is also attributed to him; he is converted to a sense of the futility of life by the spectacle of a sick man, a corpse, and a monk, but performs vain and prolonged austerities before he attains the desired end. Clearly it is impossible to attribute such actions even to the spiritual form; complaisance with the world (*lokānuvartana*) may be carried too far, and therefore these matters are treated as mere edifying stories, or, at any rate, if they represent fact, the acts were done merely for our edification. Certainly, however, the Buddha in his earthly life was wholly exempt from physical desires and his wife, whose existence is admitted, was a virgin. On the other hand, it is clear that the Nirvāṇa of this spiritual Buddha cannot be treated as imaginary, nor are we to regard his form as merely spiritual. This view asserted by Udāyin is expressly contradicted; the body, if subtle, belongs to the world of matter; it is visible because it is material, spiritual because it is not generated according to the law of physical desire but comes into being spontaneously; indeed, it appears that from the eighth state of their advance in the perfections, future Buddhas possess a body of this kind.

There is obviously much confusion of thought apparent even in the scant sources available. The evidence, however, is interesting as suggesting that the Mahāsāñghikas represent a strong and early belief in the divinity of the Buddha, although it is only in a fragmentary and late form that their views are preserved to us.[2]

A question of importance is presented by the attitude of the *Milindapañha*[3] to the difficult problem of the efficacy of gifts to

[1] Péri, BEFEO. 1918, no. 2.

[2] The Vaibhāṣikas treated the Buddha as essentially human; the Sautrāntikas seem to have recognized a large number of Buddhas and the doctrine of the Dharmakāya, body of the law, of each; Wassilieff, *Bouddhisme*, pp. 272, 285 f.

[3] pp. 95 ff., 177 f.; KV. xvi. 1–3. Gifts to the dead are approved, Mil., pp. 294 ff.; disapproved as a Rājagirika and Siddhatthika heresy; KV. vii. 6.

the Buddha. The issue is clear; the Buddha is absolutely departed; neither in life, nor yet more in death can he accept gifts; if there be no recipient, how can homage to him avail? But Nāgasena insists on the merit of acts of homage and seeks to explain this quality by similes; if a great fire goes out, men kindle one for themselves; so men by erecting a shrine do homage to the supreme god under the form of the jewel treasure of his wisdom and win rebirth as a man, or god, as even release. Seed sown on the earth grows into trees, though the earth is unconscious. Diseases come to men without their consent from former evil deeds; hence, it follows that a good deed must bear fruit apart from consent, just as ill deeds done to a saint bring retribution without his desire. But we have also in the text a reference to the beautiful doctrine that a man may transfer his merit, instead of keeping it to himself alone; if a man were to keep on transferring the merit of his good deeds to others, still he would only increase himself in merit; the stress laid is on the latter part of the proposition but the existence of the former conception is clearly indicated. It is, however, clearly unorthodox, for the *Kathāvatthu* delivers a polemic against the Mahāsāṅghika doctrine that the attainment of power in this world must include the control of the consciousness of others, so that what one man does another may enjoy. It condemns also the kindred topic that one can help the mind of another, and the Hetuvādin doctrine that one can cause happiness to another, except in the indirect sense of promoting conditions—as did the Buddha by his teaching—whence happiness may be produced, each for himself, by every one.

The *Kathāvatthu*[1] also is strictly orthodox regarding the career of a Bodhisattva. The idea encouraged by the Jātaka literature that the Buddha adopted deliberately in the past for the benefit of men such evil dooms as existence in hell, rebirth, the performance of hard tasks, and of penance under alien masters, is emphatically rebuked as a heresy of the Andhakas. The reality

[1] xxiii. 3 (J. no. 514); iv. 8 (MN. ii. 46 f.). An anticipation of the later doctrine may be seen in the legends of Piṇḍola and Kāçyapa, which contemplate Arhants awaiting Maitreya's advent; JA. 1916, ii. 196, 270.

of the experiences of the Bodhisattva could not, of course, be denied without repudiating the tradition, but to claim that these experiences were voluntarily undergone implies a doctrine which is wholly unacceptable to the Vibhajyavādins. The school denies also the belief of the Andhakas founded on a Sutta that Çākyamuni entered on the path of assurance under the dispensation of the Buddha Kassapa; if this were true, then he must have been a disciple of Kassapa, and this contradicts the essential nature of a Buddha which is to be self-developed.

4. *The Perfections of the Saint*

Especial stress was laid in the schools on the development of the view of the character of the Arhant, which assumed in the opinion of the Vibhajyavādins a rigidity, excluding human weaknesses and imperfections. Thus they deny strenuously the possibility of the falling away of an emancipated one, even in the case of one who attains only occasionally in meditation full emancipation, against the view of the Sammitiya, Vajjiputtiyas, Sabbatthivādins and some Mahāsaṅghikas that the Arhant is liable to fall away. They deny also the doctrine of the Pubba- and Apara-seliyas that the gods of the Māra group can impose physical impurities on saints.[1] As against the Andhakas it is maintained that the saint has complete knowledge, that he cannot doubt, and that he cannot be surpassed in knowledge by others, while against Mahāsaṅghika and Andhaka views it is claimed that he casts aside every fetter of ignorance and doubt in attaining his end.[2] But the saint is human; the Uttarāpathakas, who hold that he is entirely free in every regard from any connexion with the four intoxicants, desire, lust for rebirth, false opinion, and ignorance, are reminded that his body and his sense organs cannot be deemed uncontaminated by these intoxicants, and that only the path, its fruits, Nirvāṇa, and the factors leading to insight are really free from connexion with the intoxicants. Similarly, though the saint is indifferent as to sense impressions as part of his character, his indifference is manifested under

[1] KV. i. 2; ii. 2; possibly one of Mahādeva's five points, JRAS. 1910, p. 418; Wassilieff, *Bouddhisme*, pp. 223 ff.

[2] KV. ii. 2-4; iv. 10; xxii. 1.

human conditions; he cannot attend to more than one sense impression or idea at the same time, for his consciousness is essentially momentary, as also is that of a god.[1] The gods also are forced into human mould; it is a mistake to hold, as the Sammitiyas do, that there is no self culture among the gods of the higher heavens of the worlds of desire and matter, save, of course, in the realm of the unconscious gods, for the Andhaka doctrine that consciousness really exists there is absolutely rejected.[2] Again, the progress to sainthood must be carried out in strict accordance with the stages marked out; the Andhakas are wrong in defining saintship, so as to cover the simultaneous putting aside of all the fetters; in the first three stages five of the fetters are removed; in the last the aspirant rids himself of the desire for rebirth either in the world of matter or of non-matter (*rūpa-*, *arūpa-*, *rāga*), conceit, distraction, and ignorance. The Uttarāpathakas are also wrong in ascribing to a learner the insight of a saint.[3]

The saint by his actions, gifts to the order, saluting shrines and so forth does not accumulate any action to continue to bear fruit; if he could win merit he could also win demerit, which is impossible.[4] Nor is it necessary that he should experience the results of all his former action before his death, so that he cannot die an untimely death, as asserted by the Rājagirikas and the Siddhatthikas, in accordance with their general doctrine that all is derived from action. Still less can a saint fall away from sainthood because, as held by the Pubbaseliyas and the Sammitiyas, in a previous birth he has calumniated a saint.

The state of the saint in passing away raises difficulty; it is denied that he possesses an ethical consciousness at such a moment, which is contrary to the extinction of ethical considerations for the sage, though asserted by the Andhakas. Nor is the Uttarāpathaka doctrine right, under which the saint attains the

[1] KV. iv. 3, 5; doubt and ignorance of Arhatship are two of Mahādeva's points; contrast MN. iii. 110; AN. v. 155, 162; ERE. i. 744.

[2] KV. i. 3; iii. 11; they do not practise moral control, iii. 10.

[3] KV. iv. 10; v. 2.

[4] KV. xvii. 1; 2; viii. 11. The Prajñaptivādins deny untimely death; Wassilieff, p. 244.

completion of existence in imperturbable absorption of meditation; on the contrary in accordance with the Canon we must recognize that he passes out of meditation before death, and that therefore he dies with possession of that sub-consciousness (*bhavaṅga-citta*) which is the normal characteristic of life, and which is non-ethical and purely resultant.[1]

No person may become a saint unless he has laid aside the life of a layman, canonical texts to the contrary and the views of the Uttarāpathakas notwithstanding; it is impossible also for any embryo to become a saint at the moment of rebirth nor can a dreamer attain this state.[2]

4. *Nirvāṇa as the Unconditioned*

There is comparatively little development in the schools of the conception of release. The *Milindapañha*[3] in the older portion insists on the conception of release as cessation of birth, old age, death, and the attendant woes of life; it is held that he who has overcome the tendencies to rebirth is aware of his success in producing cessation of craving leading to it, while those, who have not, still know the excellence of release by hearing of it from those who have experience of it, precisely as the pains of mutilation are known by listening to the moans of the sufferers. In the later portions we have, after an assertion of the non-existence of any true being in the world, a discussion of space and Nirvāṇa as uncaused by any of the recognized causes; there is a cause of the realization of Nirvāṇa, but not of its origin, just as one can go to the Himālayas, but cannot bring them to oneself. Nirvāṇa is uncompounded; it cannot be said to have been produced, or not to have been produced, or to be possible of production, to be past, future, or present, or perceptible by any sense organ. Nirvāṇa exists and is perceptible by the mind; with a pure heart, free from obstacles and cravings the disciple can see Nirvāṇa. Its nature can be explained only by similes, just as wind cannot be grasped, though it most assuredly exists.

[1] KV. xxii. 2, 3.

[2] KV. iv. 1, 2; xxii. 5; xxiii. 1 may sanction married life according to the Andhakas and Vetulyakas.

[3] pp. 50, 69; 268, 271 f., 313 ff.

Nirvāṇa is utter bliss, without pain; though its form, figure, duration, or size cannot be explained, yet something may be said of its qualities. It is untarnished by evil dispositions; it cools the fever arising thence; it is boundless, full of saints; it blossoms with the flowers of purity, knowledge, and emancipation. It is infinite, is satisfying to all desires, it is very exalted, and immovable. It can be realized by freedom from distress and danger, by peace, calm, bliss, delicacy, and purity. There is no place where Nirvāṇa is stored up, save only right living.

The *Dhammasangaṇi* almost ignores the term Nibbāna, but in the ancient supplementary exposition or comment (*atthuddhāra*) Nibbāna is invariably substituted for the term uncompounded element. Yet it is noteworthy that in the text itself the uncompounded element is never identified with the fruit of sainthood which is certainly one aspect of Nirvāṇa. This uncompounded element is described by a long series of negatives; it is not connected with thought in any form, nor with the fetters, the contagions, the ties, corruption, grasping, joy, ease, disinterestedness; it is, however, positively described as supra-mundane; it is invisible, non-impinging, without material form; uncaused; it cannot be affected by insight or culture; it is indeterminate and produces no result.[1]

In the *Kathāvatthu* we meet the Andhaka conception of Nirvāṇa as morally good, but this view is rejected, since morally good means positively that which will produce a good rebirth, and this is inappropriate to Nirvāṇa. An interesting discussion arises on the dictum on the *Majjhima Nikāya* that the enlightened man does not think about Nirvāṇa. This leads to the Pubbaseliya doctrine that Nirvāṇa as an object of thought is really a hindrance, a view very imperfectly refuted by the Theravādin, while Buddhaghosa is so perplexed by the issue—the Pubbaseliya being accorded the last word in the discussion—that he falls back on the quite impossible solution that Nirvāṇa here is simply temporal well being, a matter connected with the satisfaction of natural desires only.[2]

[1] *Psych. Eth.*, pp. 359, 361, 367 ff. There is nothing new in ADS. vi. 14; ix. 9.
[2] xix. 6; ix. 2; MN. i. 4. On Nirvāṇa as void, see ch. xiii, § 1.

PART III

THE PHILOSOPHY OF THE MAHĀYĀNA

CHAPTER XII

MAHĀYĀNA ORIGINS AND AUTHORITIES

1. *The Origin of the Mahāyāna*

Is it possible to deduce the origin and development of the Mahāyāna from factors immanent in the Hīnayāna, or must we allow for the introduction of an element of influence of foreign thought on India? There are facts which tell in favour of the latter hypothesis. It is clear that the rise of Mahāyāna was rapid in the first and second centuries A. D., and this was the time when after Greek and Parthian and Çaka princes the Kuṣan dynasty was reigning in India. Matters had greatly changed since the days of the Buddha; foreigners had freely penetrated the country, commerce had grown, and it is not without importance that the most metaphysical of the treatises of early Buddhism the *Milindapañha* purports to be a dialogue between an Indian sage and a Greek ruler. The most important of all Madhyamaka texts, the foundation in a sense of the Mahāyāna is the *Prajñāpāramitā*, the book of the perfection of intuition or knowledge, twin sister of the Sophia or the Gnosis of Asiatic Greece. The doctrine of the Trikāya, the three bodies of a Buddha, seems to appear so abruptly as to suggest borrowing from without. Moreover, the sudden activity of the Mahāyāna, its conviction of the necessity of the preaching of salvation, and the doctrine of the duty of man to lay aside the dream of swift release from transmigration for himself, and to choose instead the career of a Buddha to be for the sake of the release of the world from tribulation, suggest the introduction of a new spirit, which India was eager and able to assimilate, but which could not have arisen in such a form unless there had been external influences at work.[1]

Such in effect is the case which can be presented for foreign influence, nor is it possible to deny that such influences may have been at work. The fact of the introduction of new peoples and new ideas to India is obvious enough in the field of art where actual remains exist to tell a conclusive tale. To deny the same influence in other spheres, because it is less easy to prove it, is clearly illegitimate. The development of the Mahāyāna was parallel with the introduction of Greek astrology[2] into India; we cannot assert that Āryadeva who apparently knew the latter must have been ignorant of any other side of Asianic thought. What we can establish, and that with a considerable degree of probability, is that there existed in India itself, partly even in early Buddhism the germs of the results which are revealed in the Mahāyāna; we cannot deny that these seeds may have been stirred to active life by the intellectual ferment which must have been caused by the introduction of new peoples to India. History has shown us how able are Indians to assimilate in their own distinctive manner foreign conceptions, in ways which it is difficult or impossible effectively to trace, and from this fact we may be warned not to deny foreign influences in the past, because the traces of them are slight. When India appropriated, it was with an activity of its own, which made the borrowing appear an integral part of the ancient thought.

The view of the Mahāyāna itself is simple; it wholly denies that it is anything save the true doctrine of the Buddha, which, however, as too important and abstruse, was not made known generally by the master, a fact which accounts for its non-appearance in the Pali Canon or at least for its comparative insignificance. In point of fact it is present even there; the

[1] S. Lévi, MSA. ii. 16 ff. Manichaean influence on the doctrine of defilement of thought and Neoplatonic on the idealist system are suggested. Contrast Kennedy, JRAS. 1902, pp. 377 ff.; Eliot, *Hinduism and Buddhism*, iii. 445 ff.

[2] As to the drama cf. Lindenau, *Festschrift Windisch*, pp. 38 ff.; Lévi, JA. 1902, i. 123; as to logic, Keith, ILA., p. 18; as to romance, Keith, JRAS. 1915, pp. 784 ff.

Kātyāyanavāda in the *Saṁyutta Nikāya*[1] is acclaimed as asserting the doctrine of the vacuity of things, since it denies the reality of either existence or non-existence. Moreover, the Pūrva- and the Apara-çaila schools are asserted to have had the Prajñāpāramitā Sūtra and other Mahāyāna texts written in Prakrit. The *Mahāvastu*, again, which is a Mahāsāñghika text, contains the essentially Mahāyāna doctrines of the ten stages of the Bodhisattva's progress as well as of the perfections. The doctrine of the magic body of a Buddha, and therefore also of the three bodies, is necessitated by the stories related of the Buddha by the Hīnayāna itself; how else could he have acted, as is there reported of him? On the contrary, their own doctrine does not in any way depart from the true teaching of the Buddha; the systems of the Hīnayāna need not be utterly rejected, but they represent merely an inferior stage of truth, suited for minds unable to appreciate the true reality.[2]

The defence of the Mahāyāna cannot be accepted as wholly convincing. As regards their allegation of early Mahāyāna Sūtras in Prakrit certainty is unattainable, but we have no possible reason to treat the Pūrva- or Apara-çaila schools as early, and the existence of a Prakrit *Prajñāpāramitā* at an early date is quite unproved. The insistence of the school on attributing to a Bodhisattva like Maitreya its most important texts suggests an uneasy consciousness of posteriority, and, unless we are devout Buddhists, we are not called on to believe that the teaching of Nāgārjuna is inspired by the Buddha himself. Historically we may reasonably say in view of the Chinese translations of the second century A. D. that the Mahāyāna movement became effective in the first century A. D.[3] and, as will be seen, it rested largely on elements present in primitive Buddhism.

It is clear, indeed, that the doctrine of vacuity or in the Vijñānavāda of empty thought is a development, natural and

[1] ii. 17; MKV., p. 269.

[2] Wassilieff, *Bouddhisme*, pp. 264 f.; MA., pp. 21, 134; Çañkara, BS. ii. 2, 32; SDS., p. 7; BCA. ix. 45–7; MK. xxvii.

[3] *Ratnakūṭa Sūtra* before 170 A. D.; *Akṣobhyavyūha*, *Daçasāhasrikā Prajñāpāramitā*, *Mahāsukhāvatī* before 186 A.D.; Poussin, *Bouddhisme*, p. 260, n. The earlier work (trs. 67 A. D.) of Kāçyapa Mātañga, Sūtra of 42 sections, does not clearly contain any Mahāyāna doctrine; Eliot, *Hinduism and Buddhism*, ii. 71, n. 2.

perhaps inevitable of the insistence of primitive Buddhism on the transitory character and non-substantiality of all things, and of the Buddha's long list of indeterminates. Granted that early Buddhism was realistic in a naïve way, it contained within itself the seeds of negativism; if the chain of causation, as the *Saṁyutta Nikāya*[1] boasts, overthrows the doctrine that the misery of existence is made by self, by another, by both or by neither, it is not a difficult step to assert the invalidity or vacuity[2] of every possible idea, as does the *Prajñāpāramitā*, with an elaboration of repetition which suggests the fascination of the theorem for philosophically immature intellects. There was a sense also in which this negativism has more affinity to early Buddhism that the Sautrāntika doctrine, which doubtless most nearly affected the growth of the Mahāyāna. The Sautrāntika and Sarvāstivādin theory accepted the world as the product of the unstable combinations of seventy-five stable elements; they had thus indirectly assailed the true doctrine of impermanence, for, though they admitted constant change, they recognized the changing forms as having beneath them something real and permanent.

The Vijñānavāda again could fairly argue that its doctrine was a mere legitimate development in an improved form of the conception of the ego-series of the Sautrāntika. The receptacle intellect or consciousness (*ālaya-vijñāna*), as contrasted with the individual intellectual acts (*pravṛtti-vijñāna*), expressed more clearly than could the Sautrāntika the fundamental fact that each moment in the intellectual series is charged with the whole accumulated experience of the individual from endless time. Nor could it be said that the metaphysical conception of the void intellect as the *prius* of all things was wholly incompatible with the Hīnayāna; the earlier Buddhist thought would have denied the possibility of such an assertion, but it did not wholly exclude it.

It is less easy at first to trace the transition from the narrow

[1] ii. 113.

[2] In KV. xix. 2 void as a synonym of Nirvāṇa is assumed by the Theravādin, who rejects vacuity as part of the dispositions aggregate; so also iii. 2; x. 3. The world, however, is only void of soul; i. 1. 241 (SN. iv. 54); Nirvāṇa allows of no positive concept, but voidness in the Pali texts seems to have specific reference to soul; DN. iii. 219; DS., §§ 121, 344 ff., 514 ff.; KV. i. 1. 241; SN. iv. 54; ADS. ix. 9; vi. 14.

ideal of the Arhant to the generous conception of the Bodhisattva who seeks not Nirvāṇa, but Buddhahood for the salvation of the world. But we cannot doubt that from the first there was a party in the faith which felt that the ideal of the Arhant was narrow and rather selfish; that some doubted whether true release could so easily be won; that some were by no means assured that release was what they desired, and would have preferred to be assured of a life of greater bliss in the future. India has always been the home of fervent devotion[1] and we find in the *Jātakas* the lively expression of the conception of the Buddha as one who in a series of past lives has practised with devotion the highest perfections; granted that the Bodhisattva ideal did not penetrate deeply into the Pali Canon in its older parts, it was too strong to be entirely excluded, and the Mahāyāna conception cannot be said to be inconsistent with a natural development of the idea. The argument is all the stronger when it is remembered that in the period of the growth of the Mahāyāna there must have been developing the doctrine of the Avatārs of Viṣṇu, animated by the desire to bring succour to mankind. It is possible also that the doctrine of the stages of Bodhisattva's advance are really borrowed by the Mahāyāna from the Mahāsāṅghikas, and not a Mahāyānist interpolation in the *Mahāvastu*, and the Sautrāntikas may have entertained the doctrine independently.

The break between the Buddhology of the Hīnayāna and that of the Mahāyāna at first presents a graver problem, but there is a real sense in which the Mahāyāna returns in its Buddhology to a position in closer harmony with the views of the Buddha than was the developed Hīnayāna school. We certainly have the impression in the early texts that there is no very essential difference between the disciples and the master so far as attaining the goal of release is concerned, although the master has the inimitable privilege of revealing the way. But the later Hīnayāna seems to place a great gulf between the mere Arhant and the Buddha, a distinction which the Mahāyāna in a sense minimizes by encouraging every one to aim at Buddhahood as

[1] The parallelism of the Bhakti of the *Bhagavadgītā* and the *Saddharmapuṇḍarīka* is patent; Kern, SBE. XXI. xxv. ff., *Ind. Buddh.*, p. 122.

a just endeavour. In general, however, the Mahāyāna, perhaps in accord with a very early movement in Buddhism, is intent on magnifying the personality of the Buddha, and in minimizing his humanity. There are for this obvious precedents in the Hīnayāna itself. We have the out-and-out docetism of the Vetulyakas, who hold that the Buddha abode in the Tuṣita heaven while a magic shape taught to Ānanda the doctrine on earth.[1] We have the claim of the Andhakas that in all his speech the Buddha was ultra-mundane, and that he had power (*iddhi*) to reverse even the rules of causality, while the Mahāsāṅghikas held the doctrine of the omnipresence of the Buddha.[2] The Sautrāntikas agree with the Mahāyāna in the doctrine of the ten powers peculiar to the Buddhas and are asserted to accept the theory of a body of bliss (*sambhoga kāya*), which is an essential element of the doctrine of the Trikāya.[3] Moreover, the conception of the law as the body of the Buddha is foreshadowed in the Canon, so that in germ the whole conception of the three bodies of a Buddha, which certainly at first sight seems strange, is latent in the Hīnayāna. The motive power which accounts for this development of theism is simple; the age was one of the predominance in the popular mind of the great sectarian gods with the doctrine of devotion and salvation by grace, and it was inevitable that a faith which sought to be popular, since its votaries essentially depended for their subsistence and all their comforts on the generosity of lay supporters, should find it necessary to supply the need of its adherents. We may surmise that at no time was the popularity of Buddhism unaffected by its religious associations, and in the Mahāyāna we find this element frankly and effectively developed in the doctrine of the grace of the Bodhisattvas and Buddhas, and the possibility of the transference of merit. It is characteristic that in the new faith the deity Amitābha assumes a high place; he is clearly a sun god transferred to Buddhist use, a striking sign of the interpenetration of Buddhism with popular religion. It is important to remember also that, side by side with the doctrine of the Arhant, there existed the

[1] KV. xviii. 1, 2; Kashgar fr. of *Saddharmapuṇḍarīka*, JRAS. 1907, p. 434.

[2] KV. ii. 10; xxi. 4; 6.

[3] Poussin, *Bouddhisme*, p. 290. Cf. ch. xvi. § 2 for the doubt on this point. They accepted the Dharmakāya which is preluded in the Canon.

devotion of the people to relic and shrine worship, attested in art, which in the Gandhāra sculpture passes into the open veneration, not of symbols merely, but of representations of the Buddhas and Bodhisattvas. The practice of personal representation was doubtless borrowed from Greek art,[1] but it proved acceptable because the idea of the divinity of the Buddhas was already prevalent.

There are also in minor details coincidences between the Hīnayāna and the Mahāyāna which show the continuity of development of Buddhist thought. The doctrine of the double form of teaching of the Hīnayāna[2] is repeated in the strengthened form of degrees of reality and truth in the Mahāyāna. While the Hīnayāna is not convinced that everything is void, it permits meditations on things as void,[3] and the Vetulyakas, that mysterious sect, even appears on one reading as champions of the great void.[4] Moreover, the Uttarāpathakas are credited with a doctrine of thusness[5] or suchness (*tathatā*, from *tatha*, 'true') as indicating the unconditioned element at the bottom of things which may well be a precursor of the system of the *Mahāyānaçraddhotpāda*.

2. *The Literature*

Of the literature of the Mahāyāna itself and of schools with Mahāyānist leanings much indeed has been preserved, but infinitely more has disappeared, and of what has been left a great part as yet exists only for us in Chinese or Tibetan versions. Unfortunately, the Chinese records render it extremely difficult to determine the precise condition of the texts translated and, despite the numerous

[1] Foucher, RHR. xxx. 340; JA. 1903, ii. 208 f., 319 f., 327; *L'Art gréco-bouddhique du Gandhāra* (1905); *Beginnings of Buddhist Art*, pp. 111 ff.

[2] The person (*pudgala*) is thus taught; it is a *sammuti-sacca*, truth by general consent, but really erroneous; Poussin, JA. 1903, ii. 262, n. 3; KV. comm. i. 68.

[3] DN. ii. 319; DS., §§ 121, 344, 514 ff.; ADS. ix. 9; cf. vi. 14 and p. 67.

[4] Comm. on KV. xvii. 6, v.l. Mahāpuṇṇavādins. We cannot prove them, or KV. xvii. 6, to be pre-Mahāyāna.

[5] KV. xix. 5. Hints of the receptacle consciousness, Ālayavijñāna, are to be seen in the Mahāsāṅghika doctrine of a root (*mūla*) consciousness and the Mahīçāsaka doctrine of something over and above the aggregates; Suzuki, *Muséon* v. (1904) 376 f. An interesting example of the way of changing alleged Sūtras is seen in MKV., p. 389 as against TRD., p. 46; Nirvāṇa being made unreal. Cf. MKV., p. 176, n. 3; SN. v. 430.

notices which we have of the dates when translations were made, it is not always easy to ascertain to what precise text the date is applicable. The texts, which are preserved in mixed Sanskrit, or Sanskrit, present also grave difficulties of chronology; the impression is often inevitable that they are conglomerates, in which old matter and new are confused, and to which therefore it is impossible to ascribe any one period.

The most important text to shed a light on the origin of Mahāyāna ideas is doubtless the *Mahāvastu*,[1] claiming to be the Vinaya of the Lokottaravādin school of the Mahāsāṅghikas, a style which it deserves only in so far as, like the *Mahāvagga* of the *Vinaya Piṭaka* it does give an account of the first conversions and of the founding of the community of monks, following upon an immense narrative of the life of the Buddha, in the main in accord with the Pali tradition. Distinctively Mahāyāna is undoubtedly the account of the ten stages of the Bodhisattva's progress to Buddhahood; we find also the doctrine of the existence of many Buddhas, and the view that the worship of the Blessed One is sufficient to win Nirvāṇa. Unhappily, we cannot ascertain the date of the text; its Hunnish and Chinese references, its recognition of the halo, introduced from Greek art into the art of Gandhāra, prove comparatively late redaction, though much may be older, as is suggested by the fact that the whole is composed in mixed Sanskrit without the addition of passages in purer Sanskrit as in the Mahāyāna Sūtras proper.

Equally vague in date is the famous *Lalitavistara*,[2] whose title, 'Full account of the Play' of the Buddha marks its full acceptance of the supramundane character of the Buddha. It is clearly the biography of the master according to the Sarvāstivādin school, remodelled finally as a Mahāyāna Vaipulyasūtra as it expressly calls itself, in which the humanity of the founder of the faith has disappeared. Its date is uncertain, since we do not know how far

[1] Ed. É. Senart, Paris, 1882-97; Barth, *Journal des Savants*, 1899, pp. 459 ff., 517 ff., 623 ff.; E. Windisch, *Die Composition des Mahāvastu* (1909); Oldenberg, GN. 1912, pp. 123 ff.; Winternitz, *Ind. Litt.* ii. 187 ff. (the reference, p. 193, to Yogācāras (i. 120) as a sect is erroneous).

[2] Ed. S. Lefmann, Halle a. S. 1902-8; trs. Ed. Foucaux, Paris, 1884-92; Winternitz, ii. 194 ff. Possibly originally composed in language akin to that of the *Mahāvastu*; F. Weller, *Zum Lalitavistara*, Leipzig, 1915.

our text represents what was translated into Chinese about A. D. 300. But the parallelism between the text and Gandhāran art [1] suggests that Buddha worship flourished in the second century A. D. and much of the *Lalitavistara* may go back to that date; it contains probably still older material. More precise dating would be possible, if we could be sure that it was from it, as it stands, that Açvaghoṣa derived the material for his *Buddhacarita*, but that is far from certain.

Of the Mahāyāna or Vaipulya Sūtras proper, vasts texts of which some were probably first written in Prakrit but later turned into Sanskrit, while others from the first were composed in the language which had become dominant for all literary purposes, the most important for the doctrine of negativism or the void (*çūnyatā*) is the series of *Prajñāpāramitās*,[2] extolling the perfection of intuition, the highest perfection which a Buddha can have. The texts are of various size; tradition asserts on the one hand that the original was in 125,000 çlokas or lines of thirty-two syllables; then was reduced to 100,000, 25,000, 10,000 and 8,000, while another version makes the 8,000 line text the original of which the others are mere amplifications; a large variety extending from 100,000 lines to 700 lines is indeed known to us. The length in fact is unimportant; the substance is given in the short *Vajracchedikā*, the intuition 'which cuts like a diamond', which translated into Chinese in A. D. 401 forms with the *Prajñāpāramitāhṛdaya*, in which the metaphysics is neatly packed into a magic formula, the leading text of the Shin-gon sect in Japan. It is impossible to extricate the real facts of the composition of the text; some form in 10,000 lines existed in Chinese by A. D. 179. The doctrine of the void is here taught without argument merely in the form of the dogmatic negation of every concept both in its positive and in its negative form on the authority of the Buddha.

[1] Foucher, *L'Art gréco-bouddhique du Gandhāra*, i. 324 ff., 616 ff.; for dates, i. 40 ff.; Grünwedel, *Buddh. Kunst*, p. 81; Waddell, JRAS. 1914, pp. 140 ff. dates the art earlier, but on dubious grounds.

[2] See Walleser's trans. of the *Aṣṭasāhasrikā* and *Vajracchedikā*, Göttingen, 1914, pp. 15 ff. The latter is trans. Max Müller, SBE. XLIX. ii. 109 ff.; the former ed. BI. 1888; the *Çatasāhasrikā*, ibid. 1902 ff.; the *Vajracchedikā* in *Buddhist texts from Japan*, I, Oxford, 1881; it exists in whole or part in many renderings; Winternitz, ii. 249, n. 1.

The *Samādhirāja*[1] deals with the supreme meditation which produces the highest knowledge, the recognition of the vacuity of all things; in meditation the Buddha is to be conceived as the law, the beginning of all things, of endless might and goodness. The *Suvarṇaprabhāsa*,[2] rendered into Chinese in the fifth century (*c.* 420), A. D., maintains the doctrines of the void and the law as the true body of the Buddha as against the search for corporeal relics of a human Buddha, but its great renown in Nepal, Tibet, and Mongolia is due to its character as a glorification of the power of spells (*dhāraṇīs*) in the style of the Hindu Purāṇas and Māhātmyas. The *Rāṣṭrapālaparipṛcchā*,[3] translated into Chinese between 589 and 618 A. D., describes the characteristics of a Buddha, illustrating them with Jātaka tales, and is interesting for the censure it conveys on the degeneracy of a Buddhism in which celibacy has disappeared.

For the idealist or Vijñānavāda or Yogācāra school of Buddhism there is important evidence in the *Laṅkāvatāra*[4] which was rendered into Chinese in 443 and 513 A. D., though perhaps our text was later interpolated. It is, indeed, our best authority in Sanskrit for the Vijñānavāda, together with the *Mahāyānaçraddhotpāda* which, however, possesses individual features of its own. Moreover, it is important in giving us polemical disquisitions on the doctrines of the Sāṁkhya, Vaiçeṣika and Pāçupata schools among others. Its quaint title is derived from the fiction that the discourse was delivered by Buddha to the demon Rāvaṇa, lord of Laṅkā, both, of course, as the Sūtra is careful to remind us, utterly non-existent. The ten stages of the progress of the Bodhisattva described here are also expounded in a form accepted by both the Madhyamaka and the Vijñānavāda schools in the *Daçabhūmaka*,[5] styled in one version *Daçabhūmīçvara*, translated into Chinese between 265 and 316 A. D.

[1] NBL., pp. 207 ff.; or *Candrapradīpa Sūtra*; cited in MKV.; Ç.; and BCAP. viii. 106.

[2] Ed. Sarad Chandra, Calcutta, 1898; NBL., pp. 241 ff.; Winternitz, ii. 245.

[3] Ed. L. Finot, Petrograd, 1901; Poussin, *Muséon*, iv (1903), 306 ff.

[4] The ed. of the Buddhist Text Society (1900) is very imperfect. Cf. NBL., pp. 113 ff.; JASB. 1905, pp. 159 ff.; JRAS. 1905, pp. 831 ff.

[5] NBL., pp. 81 ff.

Definitively religious is the famous *Saddharmapuṇḍarīka*,[1] the Lotus of the Good Law, translated in the same period, written in Gāthās, verses in mixed Sanskrit, and in moderately correct Sanskrit prose, which is often later than the Gāthās, though in some cases the Gāthās are themselves mere late patchwork based on the older style. Çākyamuni here appears deprived of his humanity, as a great god, who teaches Buddhahood as the best of paths, in preference to the Hīnayāna, and inculcates every form of worship, even in play, as leading to Nirvāṇa. Chapters XXI to XXVI are later additions, though included in the Chinese rendering, and in chapter XXIV is a eulogy of the Bodhisattva Avalokiteçvara, the saviour of creatures *par excellence*. His merits form the subject of the *Avalokiteçvaraguṇakāraṇḍavyūha*, usually shortened to *Kāraṇḍavyūha*,[2] 'full account of the basket' of the virtues of the lord which exists in a prose and a verse tradition, and was rendered into Chinese by A. D. 270. This text is remarkable for its patronage of the doctrine of an Ādi Buddha, the *prius* of all things, while the cult of Avalokiteçvara was known to the Chinese pilgrim, Fa-Hian, in A. D. 400. Another Bodhisattva, the incarnation of knowledge is Mañjuçrī, whose merits are the subject of the *Gaṇḍavyūha* or *Avataṅsaka Sūtra*,[3] translated between 317 and 420 A. D. The *Sukhāvatīvyūha*,[4] translated in some form between 148 and 170 A. D., and preserved in two Sanskrit versions, is devoted to the praise of the Buddha Amitābha or Amitāyus, and his paradise; the *Amitāyurdhyāna Sūtra*[5] inculcates mediation on Amitāyus as the mode of gaining this paradise, and the three texts are of historical importance since they are the scriptures of two Japanese sects, the Jo-do-shū and the Shin-shū, of which the latter claims the largest number of adherents of any Japanese Buddhist sect. The *Karuṇāpuṇḍarīka*,[6] translated in the sixth century,

[1] Ed. H. Kern and B. Nanjio, BB. x, Petrograd, 1908 ff.; trans. SBE. xxi; cf. JRAS. 1916, pp. 269 ff.

[2] Prose version ed. Satyavrata Sāmaçrami, Calcutta, 1873; NBL., pp. 95 ff.; Burnouf, *Intr.*, pp. 196 ff.; ERE. ii. 256 ff.

[3] NBL., pp. 90 ff.; a section, the *Bhadracarī*, is ed. K. Watanabe, with trans. by Leumann, Leipzig, 1912; cf. Pelliot, JA. 1914, ii. 118 ff.

[4] Ed. Oxford, 1883; trans. SBE. XLIX. ii.

[5] Trans. from Chinese, SBE. XLIX. ii. 159 ff.; Walleser, Heidelberg, 1916.

[6] Ed. Calcutta, 1898; NBL., pp. 285 ff.

similarly glorifies the Buddha Padmottara and his paradise, while the Buddha Akṣobhya is the theme of the *Akṣobhyavyūha*, translated before A. D. 186. But the number of Sūtras known by name and citation or existing in Chinese versions is extremely large; the *Ratnakūṭa Sūtra* is said to have been translated before A. D. 170, and, without paying too great attention to the exact dates, there is sufficient evidence that the Sūtra literature must have been abundant by the second century A. D. and presumably somewhat earlier.

Apart from the Sūtras, and of not less importance, are works by authors whose personality is more or less known to us. The earliest in time perhaps is Açvaghoṣa, son of Suvarṇākṣī, educated as a Brahmin, then an adherent of the Sarvāstivādins and later a precursor of the Mahāyāna. His date is obscure, for the tradition of his connexion with Kaniṣka is not altogether supported by the tone of the references to that king contained in the *Sūtrālaṁkāra*, but it is not improbable that he flourished under or shortly after that prince, whose own date, however, still remains in controversy; a date about A. D. 100 is not improbable for the poet. His great epic, the *Buddhacarita*[1] is based either on the *Lalitavistara* or on the same materials, and, save in its spirit of devotion to the Buddha, is not markedly different from the Hīnayāna. The *Sūtrālaṁkāra*,[2] even through the medium of a translation from the Chinese, shows much merit; it is a collection of edifying legends of the Jātaka type, in which Açvaghoṣa applies the resources of his poetic spirit to adorn the teachings of the faith. The *Vajrasūcī*,[3] a polemical tract in which the author seeks to overthrow the Brahmanical caste system on the score of citations from the Veda, the *Mahābhārata* and the *Mānava Dharmaçāstra*, is of dubious origin, for by one source it is attributed to Dharmakīrti. Far more

[1] Ed. Cowell, Oxford, 1893; trans. SBE. XLIX. ii.; Formichi, Bari, 1912; *Über die chinesische Version von Aśvaghoṣa's Buddhacarita*, Leipzig, 1916. On Kaniṣka's date see reff. in Winternitz, ii. 375; Rapson, CHI. i. 583 ff. The Rāja Açvaghoṣa (EI. viii. 171 f.; JRAS. 1912, pp. 701 ff.) is probably different.

[2] Trans. Ed. Huber, Paris, 1908; Lévi, JA. 1908, ii. 57 ff. Sanskrit title, *Kalpanāmaṇḍinikā*, acc. to Lüders, DLZ. 1919, p. 474; cf. *Bruchstücke buddhistischer Dramen*, p. 63; Poussin, *Muséon*, x (1909), 86 ff.

[3] Weber, *Über die Vajrasūcī* (1859); Lévi, JA. 1908, ii. 90 ff.

important is the issue regarding the *Mahāyānaçraddhotpāda*,[1] the Rise of Faith in the Mahāyāna, which is one of the best of Buddhist philosophical treatises, and worthy even of Açvaghoṣa's fame. The doctrine in this work, however, distinctly advanced; it represents a form of the Vijñānavāda in which the ideas of suchness and the Tathāgatagarbha, womb of the Tathāgata, are developed in an absolutist sense. It is, of course, illegitimate *a priori* to hold that such doctrines could not be adopted or promulgated by Açvaghoṣa, but the evidence for his authorship is not very convincing; the work was rendered into Chinese in 554 and 710 A. D. and our knowledge of it is derived from a translation of this later version. An older Chinese tradition does not contain the attribution to Açvaghoṣa, and it is easy enough to understand how the work was attributed to him later, while it is remarkable, if he were the true author of it that we should not have more convincing evidence of his authorship. We have possibly some ground for doubting the attribution in the fact that we find the doctrine of vacuity alluded to in the *Saundarananda*[2] which deals with the conversion of Buddha's half brother Nanda very much against his will, and incidentally gives much information on the faith, and the same doctrine, together with the distinction of absolute and apparent truth, is found in another treatise attributed on Chinese authority to Açvaghoṣa.[3] The question is of some historical importance; if Açvaghoṣa were really the author of the *Mahāyānaçraddhotpāda*, then we must assume that the doctrine of idealism developed effectively before that of vacuity. This seems contrary to tradition, and even to probability; the idealism of the Vijñānavāda presents rather the appearance of an effort to render more plausible the negativism of the Madhyamaka. But the material is clearly inadequate to permit of certainty.

Açvaghoṣa's literary efforts on behalf of Buddhism extended also to the sphere of drama; fragments of his works are preserved

[1] *Discourse on the Awakening of Faith in the Mahāyāna*, by T. Suzuki, Chicago, 1900. Cf. Winternitz, ii. 211; Ui, VP., p. 44, n. 3.

[2] Ed. Haraprasād Shāstrī, BI. 1910; cf. Baston, JA. 1912, i. 79 ff.; Hultzsch, ZDMG. lxxii. 111 ff.; lxxiii. 229 ff.

[3] Cf. Vidhushekhara, JRAS. 1914, pp. 747 f.; Keith, ibid., p. 1092; he knew the Prajñāpāramitā doctrine, Ui, UV., p. 44, n. 3.

to us, in sufficient extent to show that he was master of the technique of the art and that his drama already manifests most of the characteristics of the Indian theatre.[1] His lyrics were famous, and we possess in the *Gaṇḍīstotragāthā*,[2] restored from Tibetan, a curious specimen of his literary genius. Of literary rather than philosophical interest is the complex question whether Açvaghoṣa is really identical with the poet Mātṛceṭa, to whom I-Tsing attributes the *Çatapañcāçatikanāmastotra*, or with Maticitra, author of a letter to a king Kanika, the question of whose identity with Kaniṣka is no less obscure. Fragments of Mātṛceṭa's work are now in our possession, while his *Varṇanārhavarṇana* is preserved in Tibetan. Of the same type of elaborate Kāvya poetry is the *Jātakamālā* of Āryaçūra or Çūra celebrating the perfections of the Buddha.[3]

Serious doubt exists also as to the date of Nāgārjuna,[4] who passes for the founder of the Madhyamaka system of the Mahāyāna; the most certain fact, perhaps, is that Āryadeva, who was apparently a younger contemporary, uses in a poem, *Cittaviçuddhiprakaraṇa*, the words *rāçi* and *vāraka*, showing therefore a knowledge of Greek astrology which can hardly be supposed to have reached India in this form before A.D. 200, and may possibly be placed later; the argument is not conclusive, since we cannot absolutely prove that the new system of naming days of the week did not spread to India by A.D. 100, since it existed before the end of that century in Italy, but it agrees well enough with tradition to make A.D. 200 a reasonable date for Nāgārjuna. What is certain is that we may regard as his the *Mūlamadhyamakakārikās* memorial verses in which he sets out the doctrines of his system, an absolute negativism. His own comment, the *Akutobhayā*, exists in Tibetan, and in a revised version by an unknown hand was rendered into Chinese by Kumārajīva to whom (*circa* A.D. 405)

1 Lüders, *Bruchstücke buddhistischer Dramen* (1911) and SBA. 1911, pp. 388 ff.; Konow, *Das indische Drama*, pp. 50 ff.

2 Ed. A. von Stael-Holstein, BB. xv. Petrograd, 1913; Thomas, JRAS. 1914, pp. 752 ff.

3 Cf. Thomas, *Kavīndravacanasamuccaya*, pp. 25 ff.; Winternitz, VOJ. xxvii. 43 f.; Lüders, SBA. 1914, p. 103.

4 JAOS. xxxi. 3; Kern, *Ind. Buddh.*, p. 122. Poussin, (*Bouddhisme*, p. 383, n. 1) queries the attribution to Āryadeva of the *Çittaviçuddhiprakaraṇa*.

we owe a legendary biography of the sage.[1] The work evoked not merely great praise but many commentaries; those of Buddhapālita and Bhāvaviveka exist only in Tibetan, but that of Candrakīrti, the *Prasannapadā*, is preserved in Sanskrit and may be ascribed to the seventh century A. D. We need not, of course, take seriously the conception of Nāgārjuna as the creator of the Çūnyavāda philosophy, though the Hīnayāna ascribes to him the *Çatasāhasrikā Prajñāpāramitā*. He must rather be counted as the great dialectician who effectively presented and won fame for the school, and whose work therefore threw other authors in the shade. The relation of his work to the various versions of the *Prajñāpāramitā* is wholly indeterminable with the evidence available; these texts are merely dogmatic assertions of the essential character of vacuity, and could be elaborated after Nāgārjuna or exist before him. Of other works of Nāgārjuna we have the *Dharmasaṁgraha*,[2] a collection of technical terms, which may or may not be his, and the *Suhṛllekha*,[3] addressed to an unknown king, also of dubious authenticity.

Of Āryadeva we now have beside fragments the *Catuḥçataka*,[4] the *Hastabālaprakaraṇa*,[5] and the *Cittaviçuddhiprakaraṇa*;[6] the latter concludes that the mind, when without a touch of imagination, is the true reality, the apparent diversity which it exhibits being explained by the coloration of imagination, just as the limpid crystal is discoloured by the reflection of a coloured object, a doctrine which shows that Āryadeva[7] was approximating to the views of the Vijñānavāda or the *Mahāyānaçraddhotpāda*. The foremost authority on the Vijñānavāda, though not necessarily or probably its founder, is Āryāsaṅga, or Asaṅga, the real author of the *Yogācārabhūmiçāstra*, of which the *Bodhisattvabhūmi*[8] is pre-

[1] Text ed. with *Prasannapadā* by Poussin, BB., iv. Petrograd 1913; comm. from Tibetan and Chinese by Walleser, Heidelberg, 1911 and 1912. The author of the latter was certainly not Āryadeva, but possibly Piṅgalākṣa, or Vimalākṣa; cf. Ui, VP., p. 45, n. 2.

[2] Ed. Oxford, 1885. Cf. H. Stönner, SBA. 1904, pp. 1282 ff.

[3] H. Wenzel, JPTS. 1886, pp. 1 ff.

[4] Haraprasād, JASB. vii. 431 ff.

[5] JRAS. 1918, pp. 267 ff.

[6] JASB. lxvii (1898), pp. 165 ff.

[7] On his identity, cf. Péri, BEFEO. xi. 366 ff.

[8] *Muséon*, vi (1905), 38 ff.; vii (1906), 213 ff.; U. Wogihara, *Asaṅga's Bodhisattvabhūmi*, Leipzig, 1908.

served in Sanskrit. This text, which with others is ascribed to Maitreya, in the manner of the Mahāyāna, attempts to prove the authenticity of its doctrine ; it rests on the belief in enlightenment as the supreme reality to be attained by the Yogācāra, the monk who practises the Yoga mysticism which is an essential part even of the Hīnāyana, but is now incorporated definitely in the Mahāyāna, giving the idealist school the alternative name of Yogācāra. The ten stages of the progress of the Bodhisattva to enlightenment are described in the *Mahāyānasūtrālaṁkāra*, in verse with a prose comment by the author. Other works by Asaṅga are enumerated, *Mahāyānasaṁparigrahaçāstra*, *Madhyāntavibhāga*, *Mahāyāna Sūtra*, various *Upadeças*, *Saptadaçabhūmi Sūtra* &c., but it is difficult to ascribe to him any high rank as a philosopher. It would be interesting to ascertain his precise relation to the *Laṅkāvatāra* ; if we could accept the ascription of the *Mahāyānaçraddhotpāda* to Açvaghoṣa and the identification of a citation in it with the *Laṅkāvatāra*, we could be sure that Asaṅga was later than the Sūtra, in which case his claim to originality would be very slight. In point of fact, however, originality was not the aim of these writers, but rather effective exposition of a doctrine already in circulation.[1]

Asaṅga's brother, Vasubandhu, originally like him an adherent of the Sarvāstivāda, and author of the *Abhidharmakoça*, was converted in late life by Asaṅga to belief in the Mahāyāna, which he illustrated by commenting on the *Saddharmapuṇḍarīka*, the *Prajñāpāramitā*, the *Vimalakīrti*, the *Avataṅsaka*, the *Çrīmālāsiṅhanāda* &c., and by composing the *Ratnatraya* and *Vijñānamātrasiddhi*. His fame seems to have been extraordinary, and his works to have been studied by both the Hīnayāna and the Mahāyāna schools and to have spread far beyond India. He also wrote a *Paramārthasaptati* attacking the *Sāṁkhyasaptati* of the mysterious Vindhyavāsa, whose identity with Īçvarakṛṣṇa is still in doubt. The date of the brothers is uncertain, but the Chinese evidence suggests strongly that they flourished up to the middle of the

[1] *Mahāyānasūtrālaṁkāra* in ed. and trans. S. Lévi, Paris, 1907-11. The *Abhisamayālaṁkāra* appears to be by a real Maitreyanātha ; Haraprasād, JASB. vi. 425 ff. before A. D. 265, but cf. Walleser, PP., pp. 27 ff.

fourth century A. D., a date which suits well all the evidence available.[1]

Of later works importance attaches to the *Madhyamākāvatāra*[2] of Candrakīrti (sixth century A. D.) the commentator on Nāgārjuna's Kārikās, and to the *Çikṣāsamuccaya*[3] and *Bodhicaryāvatāra*[4] of Çāntideva, who lived probably in the seventh century A. D. The former of Çāntideva's works is in the main a mass of citations, often of some length, from texts not otherwise available to us in Sanskrit form; the latter is a poem of great religious merit, worthy of comparison in its own way with the *Imitatio Christi.* In a sense it is a *tour de force*, for the author is devoutly convinced of the nothingness of things, but his philosophy does not forbid him to exhibit a fervour of pious devotion. It is accompanied by a comment by Prajñākaramati, which contains valuable notices bearing on the text.

Mahāyāna doctrines appear also in many other texts; even in the *Divyāvadāna* one section claims to be a Mahāyāna Sūtra, but these contain little of philosophical importance, and indeed of the literature mentioned comparatively small portion is concerned with philosophic issues, while many texts are still unavailable, existing only in Chinese or Tibetan versions. The result is inevitably that on many points it is extremely difficult to secure any clear view of the Mahāyāna position in detail; we can, however, ascertain some general principles, and from these we may be assured that what is lacking is not of special value even for the history of Indian philosophy.

Of the later history of Buddhism as a philosophy in India comparatively little is important. The commentators on the

[1] His *Viṅçakakārikāprakaraṇa* is trans. from Tibetan by Poussin, *Muséon*, 1912, pp. 53 ff. On the date see esp. Péri, BEFEO. xi. 339 ff.; Lévi, ii. 2 n.; Winternitz, VOJ. xxvii. 36; Keith, JRAS. 1914, p. 1091. On Yogācāra literature see Stcherbatskoi, *Muséon*, vi (1905), 144 ff.; Garbe, (*Sāṅkhya-Philosophie*,[2] p. 74) and Pathak, IA. xli. 244 maintain the older date but idly; see Smith, *Early Hist.*,[3] pp. 328 ff.

[2] Trans. from Tibetan by Poussin, *Muséon*, viii (1907), 249 ff; xi. (1910), 271 ff.; date, Winternitz, ii. 259, n. 3, 379; Wassilieff, *Bouddhisme*, p. 208.

[3] Ed. Bendall, BB. i, Petrograd, 1902; trans. by him and Rouse, London, 1922; for his life, Haraprasād, IA. xlii. 49 ff.

[4] Ed. Poussin, BI. 1901 ff.; trans. Paris, 1907. Cf. Foucher, RHR. lvii. 241 ff.

Madhyamaka and the Vijñānavāda contended against one another, without either school ousting the other; the Mīmānsā, Vedānta, and Nyāya-Vaiçeṣika criticized severely Buddhist views. It is, however, significant that, while Kumārila makes strong play against the Madhyamaka, Çañkara who refutes elaborately the Sarvāstivādins and the Vijñānavāda disposes summarily of the Madhyamaka. The polemics of Uddyotakara and Vācaspati Miçra are of special interest as showing the lively controversies of the schools. The Buddhists, for their part, were keen controversialists, invading the field of their enemies; we have fortunately good specimens of their controversial style in the treatises of Açoka and Ratnakīrti, both about the close of the ninth century A. D. In the *Avayavinirākaraṇa* the former makes an onslaught on the Nyaya thesis that the whole is something over and above the parts to which it stands in the peculiar relation of inherence (*samavāya*); in truth the whole is nothing apart from the parts and the relation is a myth. In the *Sāmānyadūsaṇadikprasāritā* equal havoc is made with the conception that we experience generals or universals as real; we see the five fingers of the hand, not a sixth universal, which is as unreal as a horn on one's head. Ratnakīrti established by two treatises, both positively and negatively, the doctrine of momentariness. The general decay of Buddhism from internal causes was accelerated by the havoc wrought by Mahomedan invaders, whose destruction of the monasteries and their inmates uprooted a faith in which the laity were only loosely attached to the Church, and from the twelfth century onwards Buddhist theories cease to attract much living attention in the schools.

In China and Japan, on the other hand, the doctrines of the Mahāyāna were destined to have a great vogue and to develop into systems in which the nothingness of Nāgārjuna is transmuted into a very positive absolute; it is easy to interpret in the light of such developments our texts, but the result is undoubtedly in large measure to falsify the true signification.[1]

[1] T. Suzuki's *Outlines of Mahāyāna Buddhism* is written from this point of view; it seems in fact to represent the attitude of the Shin-gon-shū school which is permeated with Tantric philosophy and is said to be derived

Interesting light on the systems is thrown in a large number of works of other schools such as the *Nyāya* and *Vedānta Sūtra* and their commentaries, Kumārila's *Vārttika*, Jayanta's *Nyāyamañjarī*, Varadaraja's *Tārkikarakṣā*, and Çrīdhara's *Nyāyakandalī*, and in sketches of philosophical schools such as the *Sarvasiddhānta-saṁgraha*, *Sarvadarçanasaṁgraha*, and Guṇaratna's *Tarkarahasya-dīpikā* on the *Ṣaḍdarçanasamuccaya*.[1]

from the *Mahāvairocanābhisambodhi Sūtra* (translated A.D. 724) and other Tantric works, but unfortunately it treats the Mahāyāna as a unity; see de la Vallée Poussin, JRAS. 1908. pp. 885-94 ; 1910, p. 133.

[1] For controversies with the Mīmāṅsā see Keith, KM. esp., pp. 46 ff. ; for logical discussions ILA. (reff., p. 275). The *Sāṁkhya Sūtra*, a late text deals with many Buddhist doctrines, and in i. 42–7 specifically with the Mahāyāna doctrines ; see Garbe, *Sāṁkhya-Philosophie*,[2] p. 146, n. 1. On its age see ZDMG. lxii. 593 ; Keith, SS., pp. 91 ff. From Chinese sources alone do we know of Harivarman, author of the *Satyasiddhiçāstra*, perhaps c. 250 A.D.; Ui, VP., pp. 4 f., 42 f., 45, 50, 55 f.

CHAPTER XIII

THE NEGATIVISM OF THE MADHYAMAKA

1. *The Doctrine of Knowledge*

In the Madhyamaka appears a new conception of kinds of truth which advances far beyond the simpler ideas of the Hīnayāna. In the latter we find only a simple distinction between the absolute truth, which is contained in the dogmas of the denial of the self, the reality of the chain of causation, and of the operation of the act, and a form of truth which may be called conventional or relative (*saṁvṛti-satya*), which is indeed absolutely false since it asserts such ideas as the self or person, but which may be admitted as truth because it passes as such in ordinary life, is useful, and is sometimes employed by the Buddha in his teaching. The Buddha, it is recognized, employed in his discourses two forms of instruction, the one conforming to absolute truth (*pāramārthikā*), and the other provisional and introductory (*ābhiprāyikī deçanā*).[1]

In the Madhyamaka[2] the matter is carried one step further; the absolute truth is a negativism or doctrine of vacuity (*çūnyatā*), established by the application to the ideas accepted by the Hīnayāna as absolute truth of a logic, which insists that any contradiction is an infallible proof of error, and which finds contradiction in every conception, and, determining *a priori* what is impossible, denies its existence on that ground in the face of facts. Inferior in essence to this is the knowledge of obscurity or inaccuracy (*saṁvṛti-satya*), which is knowledge based on the

[1] Cf. Mil., p. 28; KVA., pp. 33 ff.; Poussin, JA. 1902, ii. 250; 1903, ii. 360; KV. v. 6, brings out clearly the distinction; cf. JPTS. 1913-4, p. 129.

[2] BCA. ix. 2 f.; v. 62. For the two truths see MK. xxiv. 8, discussed *Çlokavārttika*, p. 218; MA. p. 70; BCA. ix. 107-11, 139 f.; Wassilieff, *Bouddhisme*, pp. 328 ff.

facts of experience, and which may be reckoned as true, both because appreciation of this truth is a necessary element in the acquisition of the absolute truth, and because it corresponds to the actual facts of thought and reality. Both are indeed in the ultimate analysis unreal and cannot be sustained, but they are solid facts which cannot be ignored. This form of truth may be subdivided into the knowledge of Yogins or sages, who interpret correctly the nature of existence in the sense adopted by the Hīnayāna, and that of the world (*loka-saṁvṛti*) which does not appreciate the true character of such matters as the momentary nature and misery of things, and believes in entities such as god or the soul. This latter form of knowledge is false from the point of view of that of the Yogin, and even among Yogins there are differences in accuracy of knowledge. From another point of view this realm corresponds with the sphere of things casually produced (*pratītya-samutpanna*), above all the momentary series of ideas which constitute the self. These things are not indeed real, but they have the seeming of reality and of producing effects. They are thus contrasted with the third form of knowledge, which is of imaginary (*parikalpita*) things, a term covering such false interpretations of experience as the water seen in the mirage, or the nacre mistaken for silver, or the rope thought to be a snake. Ordinary perception and reasoning are enough to rid us of these delusions, and the riddance at once enures to our practical advantage. But it is a matter for deep investigation (*vicāra*) to shake ourselves free from the delusion of the knowledge of obscurity, and at first sight we do not seem to gain anything by learning that it is not in reality true knowledge at all, although later we recognize that such recognition is the necessary preliminary to full enlightenment. Yet there is here an obvious difficulty, not disposed of by the school; a dream, let us say, is imaginary; none the less it cannot be denied to have been caused, and still less can it be asserted that such an imaginary thing cannot lead to action; the rope mistaken for the snake evokes the backward movement as surely as the reptile itself.[1]

[1] Poussin, JA. 1903, ii. 381, n. 5.

2. *The Doctrine of Negativism and the Void*

As the doctrine of knowledge of the Hīnayāna presented a fatal temptation to further depreciation of our powers of knowing, so the Sautrāntika conception of the doctrine of the momentary series of states in lieu of the self, encouraged the Madhyamaka to proceed to further dissection. To reduce the self to such a series, to assert the act but not the agent,[1] was to produce something essentially obscure and doubtful, and to open the way to the suggestion of an absolute self underlying the series such as the person (*puruṣa*) of the Sāṁkhya; and, even if the momentariness of each state were insisted on, that would merely mean the imagination of a series of substantial though momentary selves, a re-introduction of the hateful doctrine of the self. Yet the orthodox alternative, to insist on the absence of any thing save a causal series, is fatal to the essential doctrine of action. There can be no true act if there is no freedom of the will, and without a true act there can be no enjoyment of fruits. To assert the act and deny the agent is therefore impossible; you must admit both, in that case merely from the standpoint of common sense (*vyavahāratas*),[2] or deny both from the standpoint of absolute reality. There is no room for a moral agent or responsibility in the mere potency into which the Sautrāntika doctrine in effect reduces existence.

The idea of consciousness and knowledge is equally unable to bear serious examination; it is as unreal as the belief of a man with ophthalmia that there are hairs floating before his vision.[3] Knowledge is impossible, and therefore[4] cannot exist; examined, it proves out of the question to know anything external or even internal; the point of the sword cannot pierce itself or the finger touch itself. Consciousness cannot know anything either ante-

[1] Ç., p. 262; BCAP. ix. 73; AKV. (MS. Burn. f. 475[a]) in JA. 1902, ii. 255, n. 2; against Sāṁkhya views, BCA. ix. 60-8.

[2] *Kartā svatantraḥ karmāpi tvayoktaṁ vyavahārataḥ*, BCAP. *l.c.*; cf. BCA. viii. 97 ff.

[3] MKV., p. 58.

[4] MKV., p. 210 (x. 12). See Çaṅkara's critique, BS. ii, 2. 28; ch. xv. § 3.

cedent, simultaneous, nor subsequent to itself.[1] But the matter can be carried further; there is no such thing as causation of consciousness or of anything else. The Pali Canon[2] already recognizes that the chain of causation is opposed to the doctrine that anything is produced either by itself, by another, by both or neither, and this is confirmed by reasoning. If a thing already exists, it cannot come into being through itself. To say that it is originated by others implies the production of something already existing, or we should have the absurdity of darkness producing light. Since neither itself nor other things can produce anything, it cannot be the effect of both, and to deny any cause would mean that any thing could come into being at any time. The doctrine of causation, therefore, must be taken as referring only to the world of ignorance. How again can that which is momentary have any effect? Is it anterior, simultaneous, or posterior? The two latter views are absurd, but so is the former which makes out the disappearance of one moment the cause of the appearance of another. Moreover, the very idea of production by another contradicts the fundamental doctrine of the non-existence of the self, since there can be another only when a self is admitted. More generally there is no such thing as the true independent nature of any object; heat is not the nature of fire, for each depends on a variety of conditions and so indefinitely; we cannot attain any idea which can be said to be the true nature of any object, and therefore we are equally unable to assert the essence or existence of other things which have meaning only when we grasp the nature of any object.[3] Similar difficulties affect every recognized conception; the characteristics cannot exist before the thing characterized, since without them it has no existence and cannot therefore come into being, while the thing characterized cannot take on the characteristics.[4] Movement is impossible; he who has gone is not going, nor is he who will go; while the goer does

[1] Cf. the Vijñānavāda argument in SDS., pp. 12 ff. against external reality with MK. xiv; against self-consciousness, MKV., pp. 61, 62 (*Ratnakūṭa*); BCAP. ix. 18; Ç., p. 235; *Bhāmatī*, p. 379; NVT., pp. 255, 466; against perception, Āryadeva, MKV., p. 71 (inference, p. 75); BCA. ix. 94 f.

[2] SN. ii. 113; cf. MKV., p. 77 (i. 2).

[3] MK., p. 78; ch. xv; i. 10; xiii.

[4] MK. v.

not go, since that would need two forms of action, one to give him the style of goer, and one to be attributed to him in saying that he goes. The goer does not stand, but neither does the non-goer, since he is *vi termini* not connected with going, and he who stands is connected negatively with going.[1] Every conceivable relation yields to such dialectic; subject and object; actor and action; fire and fuel; existence and non-existence; extension or matter; sensation and perception; origination, duration, and disappearance; unity and plurality; whole and part; time; the aggregates; the six elements; the dispositions; the senses; as well as all the deepest doctrines of Buddhism, including misery, the Tathāgata, the noble truths, the chain of causation, bondage, and release itself, prove incapable of sustaining the searching examination or *reductio ad absurdum* (*prasañga*) which establishes that they neither exist of themselves, nor by others, nor by both, nor by neither.[2]

It follows, therefore, that we cannot really make any affirmation regarding anything; all is merely appearance, the result of ignorance of the truth. Absolute reality, Çāntideva[3] points out, does not fall within the domain of the intellect (*buddhi*), for that moves in the realm of relativity and error. Nāgārjuna[4] denies consistently that he has any thesis of his own, for to uphold one would be wholly erroneous; the truth is silence, which is neither affirmation nor negation, for negation in itself is essentially positive in implying a reality. He confines himself to reducing every positive assertion to absurdity, thus showing that the intellect condemns itself as inadequate just as it finds hopeless antinomies in the world of experience. Whence, however, comes this illusion which appears in the form of the world of spirit and matter? There are two replies possible; in the first place, it is pure unreality, and it is needless to explain the unreal. Secondly, it has its origin in a previous state of illusion, and so on *ad infinitum*, rendering any further explanation needless.

The conception thus presented is difficult and obscure; on the one hand, we have the constant insistence on the vacuity of every

[1] MK. ii.

[2] MKV., pp. 23, 36; cf. Çrīdhara, NK., p. 198; NVT., p. 407. On time see MK. xix.; on whole and part BCA. ix. 79–88.

[3] BCA. ix. 2.

[4] *Vigrahavyāvartanī* in MKV., p. 16.

conception, reiterated *ad nauseam* in the *Prajñāpāramitā*;[1] the self is in reality the not-self; the sensation is void of sensation, and thence is called sensation; Nirvāṇa is without origination or cessation, neither one nor many, without motion or absence of motion, neither eternal nor ceasing; it is identical with the round of existence (*saṁsāra*)[2] since both are unreal, and the clearing away of illusion (*vyavadāna*) in the same way is identical with the infections of illusion (*kleça*). On the other hand there is accepted the existence of the possibility of release through the removal of the obscuration of Nirvāṇa, which in reality is eternally realized by means of the destruction of the veil of illusion. Were it not that the veil was illusion pure and simple, such release would be impossible; it is a fault of the Sautrāntikas that they imagine the possibility of the utter destruction of a series really existing. There is, however, here a difficulty hardly disposed of by the school; if illusion persist in its generation of things that are void, how can it be made to desist from this evil habit?[3] There is no obvious reply; granted that the states are recognized as void, still there is no conceivable reason in that why they should not continue their unreal existence. Even more fatal, of course, is the obvious difficulty of the introduction of the conception of the intelligence which recognizes the unreality of all the categories of the intellect, including the Tathāgata himself; but it finds its origin in the conception of early Buddhism, which discriminates the ordinary work of the intellect and the intuition (*prajñā*) of the Buddha.[4]

There is, however, an obvious difficulty in pressing to the uttermost the doctrine of the unreality of the empiric world of illusion. If we accept the strict doctrine of Nāgārjuna, as interpreted by Buddhapālita and Candrakīrti, and accepted by Çāntideva, we must admit that the phenomenal world has not merely no existence in absolute truth, but has even no phenomenal existence, difficult as this conception is, and numerous as are the

[1] 'Even the smallest thing is not known or perceived there, therefore it is called the highest perfect knowledge'; SBE. XLIX. ii. 138.

[2] MK. xxv. 19 ff. [3] Cf. BCA. ix. 77 f.

[4] Candrakīrti's relation to Buddhapālita is recognized by Tāranātha, *Bouddhisme*, pp. 137. 148.

failures of its holders exactly to express it. In Bhāvaviveka's exposition of Nāgārjuna we find a more reasonable view; just as he rejected the view that silence was the only proper attitude of the Madhyamaka,[1] so he held that the world of phenomena was phenomenally valid, though from the point of view of absolute truth unreal.[2] The views of his rivals thus are closely parallel to the Vedānta of Çaṅkara, while his own show traces of realism comparable to the more directly realistic attitude of Rāmānuja as foreshadowed in Bādarāyaṇa.

Illusion absolute or illusion relative, the world has an enormous importance for the Madhyamaka and for the Mahāyāna generally; whatever it be in ultimate analysis, it must be practically treated as if it were real, and the narrow conception of an individual struggle for release gives place to a grandiose conception of efforts to bring salvation to the world and an elaborate theology worthy to rival the best products of Indian sectarian belief.

[1] Hence he attempted to establish by positive arguments the views of the school, and hence he and his followers are Svātantrikas as against the Prāsaṅgikas; MKV., p. 23, n. 3; cf. Wassilieff, *Bouddhisme*, p. 320 who gives (pp. 330 ff.) eleven points of importance in the views, of the latter, but these add nothing of philosophic importance.

[2] Poussin, *Bouddhisme*, p. 198, n. 1. Bhāvaviveka is attacked by name in MKV., pp. 36, 190, 351; see also pp. 16, 25, and for this point the reality of *paratantra*, p. 76; *Bouddhisme* (1898), pp. 111, n. 3. For his polemic against Gauḍapāda or some predecessor, see Walleser, *Der ältere Vedānta*, pp. 16 ff., who calls him Bhava°; for his date cf. PP., pp. 3, 18.

CHAPTER XIV

THE IDEALISTIC NEGATIVISM OF THE VIJÑĀNAVĀDA

1. *The Doctrine of Knowledge*

THE Vijñānavāda formally, as in practice the Madhyamaka, recognizes the existence of three distinct forms of knowledge.[1] Absolute or perfect knowledge (*pariniṣpanna-lakṣaṇa*) admits only the final purification of thought which means the disappearance of consciousness, the complete destruction of the last thought element on which ensues Nirvāṇa. Nirvāṇa, the cessation of activity, and the ether are the sole realities to be admitted from the point of view of absolute truth, so that there is little real distinction between the view of the Vijñānavāda and the Madhyamaka on this score.

Below absolute truth is the realm of relative knowledge (*paratantralakṣaṇa*), which embraces the whole series of intellectual states into which the school resolves all the world of experience. But the extent of the reality of this knowledge is a matter of dispute;[2] in one view it is to be regarded as having absolute reality in the sense that it does exist and not as illusion, but disappears absolutely when the thought is purified and Nirvāṇa is attained. The other, and more prevalent view, seems to tend to a much lower estimate; the subject of knowledge, the object, and

[1] MSA. vi. 1; xi. 13 ff.; *Madhyāntavibhāga* in MKV., p. 445 (cf. p. 553), 274 f.; Mvy. 87; Wassilieff, *Bouddhisme*, pp. 292 ff.; Poussin, JA. 1903, ii. 380.

[2] BCA. ix. 12, 17, 18 assumes reality; but see MSA. vi. 1 where the two lower forms are sharply opposed to the higher; Dharmakīrti in *Upadeçasahasrī*, p. 308; SDS., p. 13; JBRAS. xviii. 94 f.; Wassilieff, *Bouddhisme*, pp. 309 ff., whose account gives many unintelligible distinctions of view, 289 f. (Dignāga as a realist).

knowledge itself should not be regarded as real in any sense; there is no distinction in actual truth, but merely an illusion. Thought, in itself absolutely pure (*vyavadāta*), by an inveterate error imagines itself to be infected or defiled (*kliṣṭa*), and thus conceives itself under the three forms of subject, object, and knowledge. The distinction between these views is obviously parallel to that between the orthodox interpretation of Buddhapālita of the Madhyamaka and the realistic preferences of Bhāvaviveka, who admits the the existence of phenomena as such.

Accepting, as they do, the sole existence of thought even in the modified sense of relative knowledge, it is not at first apparent what room there is in the system for a third class of knowledge, which can be called imaginary (*parikalpita*). But in deference to the demands of common sense the Vijñānavāda[1] admits that there is a clear distinction between the rope which is mistaken for a snake and the animal, the water of a mirage and real water, and the visions of a dream and ordinary reality. Things again are all internal, and there is no external being, but things do appear as if external (*bāhyavat*), and such imaginations fall within the third class of knowledge, as do also such beliefs as the conception of a permanent self. But a strict criterion between the relative and the imaginary is not available; in the case of sense perceptions, however, we can correct one by the other; the water of the mirage cannot be drunk or touched; the visions of a dream cannot be realized. But the Vijñānavāda, as little as the Madhyamaka, faces the problem of the fact that these imaginary experiences are caused, and have effects, so that in reality it is impossible to dismiss them as imaginary on the ground that they do not possess causal activity (*arthakriyākāritva*), though this activity is of a different kind from the normal. In both schools in fact the classification of knowledge is essentially based on metaphysical conclusions, and is not derived from any serious epistemological investigation. The fact is illustrated by the development in the Vijñānavāda of Dignāga, and probably also of Dharmakīrti, of a doctrine of logic,

[1] Or Yogācāra. The Chinese adopt a form equivalent to Yogācārya but also style it Vijñānamātra the Japanese Dharmalakṣaṇa; see Lévi, MSA. ii. 16, n. 1. On the older use of Yogācāra, magician, see Mhv. i. 120; Poussin, *Bouddhisme*, p. 356; Cf. *Yogāvacara*, Mil., pp. 43, 366.

which is not epistemological, but which for its own purpose treats the topic as if the existence of an external reality (*paramārthasat*) were admitted, and develops an interesting doctrine of inference on the basis of the metaphysical assumptions of the school.[1]

2. *Idealism and the Void*

The Vijñānavāda does not deny the doctrine of the void (*çūnyatā*) of the Madhyamaka, but it is unable to accept the view that illusion can exist by itself and in itself without any support; there must be, to explain illusion, a thought which suffers from illusion. Moreover, the conception of the void essentially connotes a receptacle without any content,[2] and this is afforded by the conception of void thought, devoid of any characteristic, and free from the distinction of subject, object, and knowledge. Moreover, this conception of reality has, it is urged, the full approval of the Buddha who was essentially an idealist, and, if this assertion can hardly be accepted in the light of the facts, at any rate the new school can fairly claim that it is continuation in a sense of the doctrine of the thought series which the Sautrāntika developed to replace the older and more vague speculations as to the nature of the substitute for the self.

External reality cannot possibly exist;[3] if it did it could not possibly be known, and it is obviously absurd to assert the existence of something of which it is certain that we can have no knowledge. We must recognize that we have in the world as it appears to us the result of mental construction; a perception involves an apparent datum,[4] but all that is known is essentially the network of mental construction which is imposed on this datum, and we cannot speak of the datum as anything external; without the mental construction it is simply nothing; it is,

[1] See below, ch. xviii. §§ 2, 3. [2] BSB. I. iv.

[3] See below, ch. xv, § 3; Wassilieff, *Bouddhisme*, pp. 307 f. The priority of Çūnyavāda to Vijñānavāda is logical and natural; it accords with all we know of the history of the schools unless the *Mahāyānaçraddhotpāda* is Açvaghoṣa's, and cannot be overthrown by arguments such as those of A. Guha, *Jīvātman in the Brahma-Sūtras*, pp. 39 ff.

[4] Cf. the distinction of consciousness as *khyāti-*, and *vastuprativikalpa*, Laṅk., pp. 21 f., 44; BSB. I. iv.

perhaps we may hold, the fact of the arising in consciousness as a result of past experience of a new content, which thus appears to be given, and not to be our own creation, but which on ultimate analysis is essentially the product of thought. There is no real external water, but our sense construction of smoothness produces this impression; similarly sense constructions of heat and movement produce our belief in external fire and wind. There is apparently an external chain of causation e. g. from seed to plant, but this is due only to our habit of projection of reality; we apply names and ideas (*nāmasaṁjñāvyavahāra*), and by this means we are the real sources of the apparent causal development conceived as without us.[1]

But we must not think that internal reality is any more absolutely real—at any rate on the orthodox view—than external reality. The apparent distinction of subject, object, and knowledge is not real. Thought cannot know itself any more than anything else, or there would be duality, and it would not be pure thought. The internal chain of causality, therefore, must not be regarded as anything real. It is merely the result of the infection of the purity of thought. This infection is the source of the illusion of subject, object, and knowledge, but its origin we cannot trace; there is no beginning in time to the process of illusion. The infection of our thought produces in us the holding of belief in eternity, in happiness, and induces us to action, good or bad, and these acts and thoughts leave within us the tendencies which produce again the same wrong views and acts, and continue for ever, unless enlightenment is attained, the process of illusion.[2]

We have here in effect the series of the Sautrāntikas, but there is developed a contrast between the originating or receptacle intelligence (*ālayavijñāna*), and the individual intellectual experiences of the process (*pravṛtti-vijñāna*), which clearly opens the way to a different conception of the final character of reality. On the strictly orthodox view[3] the receptacle thought may be held

[1] Cf. Lañk., p. 85; on our speech constructions, 87; MSA. vi.

[2] Ibid., pp. 100 ff., 44; MSA. xi. 38; xxi. 54; xi. 14 ff.

[3] Cf. MSA. i. 18; vi. 10; xi. 32, 44, 49; SDS., p .15; Mvy. 103; *Bhāmatī*, p. 353; NVT., pp. 144, 145; Wassilieff, *Bouddhisme*, pp. 287 ff.; *pravṛttivijñānataraṅga, anyonyahetuka udadhitaraṅga iva*, Lañk., pp. 45, 50, 126; TRD.,

to be nothing but a collective expression for the whole series of particular thoughts, or to put it in another light the receptacle intelligence at any moment consists of the actual particular intellectual action together with all the potencies latent in it, for, as with the Sautrāntikas, the intellectual moment is charged with impressions of the whole of the experience of the apparent individual from time immemorial. This view may be supported by the doctrine that the receptacle intelligence has no origination, duration, or destruction, which is an apt enough description of what is merely a collective expression, and does not denote any special concrete reality. The same impression may be derived from the comparison of the relation of the particular intellectual moments with the waves of the sea of the receptacle intellect. Intelligence appears under diverse aspects; as Citta it accumulates action, as mind it synthesizes, as Vijñāna it forms judgements, as sense it has consciousness of objects.[1] But this idea admits also of allowing a greater measure of reality and universality to the receptacle intellect;[2] we may treat it as parallel with the Vedantic absolute, and regard its infection and its development as parallel to that of the absolute under the influence of nescience. Or from another point of view we may hold that the flux of intellectual moments does not actually infect the receptacle intelligence, but is comparable to an image reflected in a mirror which remains untouched by it, or to a sound echoed by the rocks which suffer themselves no change. Thus the receptacle intelligence would be akin to the person (*puruṣa*) of the Sāṁkhya.

These tendencies, however, are opposed, it appears, to the fundamental conceptions of the school which embraces the conception of the void as the ultimate truth. It is essential to realize that all our determinations by name or conception are unreal; examine appearances and there is no substance to be found; the

p. 47; *Muséon*, v. (1904), 375 ff.; MA. vi. 46; Jacobi, JAOS. xxxi. 2; PGAB., p. 118.

[1] Laṅk., pp. 50 ff. (misrendered in Dasgupta, *Ind. Phil.* i. 146).

[2] Cf. Lévi, ii. 20, 16, n. 2, who makes it not the affirmation of self, a function of mind, but that which renders possible the activity of mind by giving it a centre of organization, the underlying reality. Cf. Suzuki's comparison (MB., p. 132) with the 'ego of transcendental apprehension', and Vasubandhu's *Viṅçakakārikā*; TDC., p. 65.

idea of matter or of extension will not bear examination; the atoms[1] of the Vaiçeṣika or the Sautrāntikas are absurd; they have six sides, since they face six contiguous atoms, and are therefore not truly indivisible; moreover, either contiguity or distance between the atoms is unthinkable. The relation of whole and part is absurd also, and any attempt to carry it out simply leads into difficulties; without parts there can be no whole, but it is impossible to describe any manner in which the whole can really be related to the parts, so that the entire conception must be laid aside. Nor must we think that even in negation we have truth; negations are equally appearances; the ultimate truth is one in which being and not being are one and the same (*bhāvābhāva-samānatā*).[2] The mind, indeed, ever tends to take things either as existing as this or the other (*ekatvānyatva*), as both or not both, as existing or not existing, or as eternal or transient, but all four modes of viewing things are incorrect. The true view is to regard things as void, and this can be done from various aspects. Thus we may remember that things are always interdependent, that they thus cannot have any nature of their own, and cannot be determined in terms of anything else, since, as they have no nature of their own, a reference to another nature does not serve as a determinant. Moreover, they can have no positive essence, since they spring up from a condition of natural non-existence. Or again, they are of an unknown type of non-existence (*apracarita-çūnyatā*), seeing that all the aggregates disappear in Nirvāṇa. Yet they appear phenomenally as connected, though void (*pracarita-çūnyatā*), since, while the aggregates have no real existence nor relations to others, they appear as if causally connected with other aggregates. Again, it is impossible to describe anything as having any definite character; their voidness is being inexpressible (*nirabhilāpya-çūnyatā*). There is no possibility of knowledge of things such as is brought by the effect of the obscuration of thought by defects which produce the illusion of experience. Further, things are void, since we assert their existence in time and place where they are not found (*itaretara-çūnyatā*). But in all

[1] BCA. ix. 87; *Viṅçaka*, 12–14; MKV., p. 93; cf. Ui, VP., pp. 72 f.
[2] MSA. xi. 41.

cases we find ourselves confronted with the emptiness of our conceptions.

What then is left in the universe, when the work of negation of reality and negation alike is completed? Nothing but a mere suchness or thusness (*tathatā*),[1] or voidness without origination or essence,[2] to which also the style is given of womb or source of the Tathāgata (*tathāgata-garbha*). We are, however, expressly warned by the *Laṅkāvatāra*[3] against the heresy of deeming that this conception is parallel to the Brahman or absolute of the Vedānta. On the contrary, the term expresses merely the nature of all phenomena as without essence of any kind, and as free from all characteristics. But the term Tathāgatagarbha is admitted to be a concession to meet the feeling of those who regard the idea of unsubstantiality as open to objection; the Vijñānavāda in effect, like the Buddha himself, is prepared to temper its teaching to some measure to the minds of those to be instructed.

In any case, however, the precise solution of the metaphysical question is not of prime importance for a doctrine of salvation, as the Mahāyāna is as emphatically as the Hīnayāna; the essential thing is to concentrate on the triple meditation which purifies the thought, and tears away the veil of illusion. It is essential to recognize that the self or the external world is a mere imagination; to realize instead the fundamental truth of thought without any characteristic whatever: and to abstain from any desire with regard to this transcendent reality.

The Nirvāṇa or release which is attained differs from that of the Hīnayāna because it rests on the realization of the nothingness and incomprehensibility of all phenomena, while the Çrāvakas are satisfied to know the momentary and painful character of all being. In this release all the impressions (*vāsanās*) which would normally manifest themselves in further thoughts and deeds are wiped out, and the mind ceases to act. This is not death, for there is no rebirth; it is not destruction, for destruction applies only to what

[1] Laṅk., p. 70; MSA. ix. 5, 22, 57; xi. 41; xviii. 87; xix. 44-6.

[2] Laṅk., p. 78.

[3] Laṅk., pp. 80 f. We see here the inruption of Vedānta influences; cf. JRAS. 1908, pp. 892 f.

is compound (saṁskṛta).[1] But how can this illusion cease? The Vijñānavāda, however, much as it denies it, seems to fall into the error charged against it by the Madhyamaka of allowing an unintelligible destruction of a real entity, namely the course of illusioned thought.

According to the *Laṅkāvatāra* the attainment of the highest knowledge may be accomplished by Bodhisattvas through the realization that things are nothing but mental creations; that there is no origination, existence or destruction of things; that external things can be said to exist or not exist only in the sense of a mirage, being produced by mental impressions from of old, and through the true apprehension of things in their ultimate nature. To aid in the attainment of this end a special series of meditations (*dhyāna*) is prescribed, which are obviously intended to take the place of the inferior meditations of the Hīnayāna. The first is that of the Çrāvakas and solitary Buddhas; it dwells on the doctrines of the non-existence of the soul and the transitory, miserable, and impure character of the world, ending in the suppression of ideation. This practice for beginners (*bālopacārika*) is followed by the searching investigation of things (*artha-pravicaya*), which reveals not only that there is no self, but that the doctrine of the self and other heretical views cannot be said really to have any existence, and that the world of appearance is truly unreal. In the third meditation it is realized that the thought that there is no self and no appearance is itself an outcome of delusion, and the mind then falls back on the conception of suchness (*tathatālambana*), while in the fourth meditation the mind achieves the complete and perfect appreciation of the nothingness and the incomprehensibility of all phenomena.

The Vijñānavāda, of course, did not satisfy the Madhyamaka, and two of the criticisms are of interest. It is impossible, it is argued,[2] to evade the heresies of existence and non-existence by the device of admitting the bare reality (*vastu-mātra*) of thought and its derivatives, the subject of defilement and purification which is relative or dependent (*paratantra*) reality—thus negating non-existence—and denying their possession of a peculiar nature

[1] Laṅk., p. 100. [2] MKV., pp. 274 f.

of their own, which is imaginary (*parikalpita*)—thus evading the heresy of existence. The theory in fact falls into both heresies, since it denies imaginary existence and affirms relative reality. Moreover, the Madhyamaka views all relative reality as being *qua* caused without any existence of its own.

A second point of criticism is the assumption of the power of consciousness to know itself (*svasaṁvitti, svasaṁvedanā*), which the Vijñānavādins assert, and which is obviously essential to their view. The direct objection is the contradiction in the idea of anything acting on itself, as shown by the case of the edge of a knife which does not cut itself or the finger tip which cannot touch itself.[1] Indirectly[2] the argument of the Vijñānavāda, derived from comparison with a lamp which lights up itself as well as the object, is refuted by the refutation of the general doctrine of origination (*utpāda*), where the case of the lamp is disposed of. There is no darkness either in the lamp itself nor in the place where it is; therefore there can be no question of the lamp illuminating either itself or anything else. Nor is it any use to argue that the light destroys the darkness by coming into being, for when there is light there is no darkness; on the other hand if the light destroys the darkness without coming into contact, then it should destroy all the darkness in the universe. Moreover, the senses cannot experience themselves; the eye cannot see itself and so forth.[3]

Nor is there any force in the contention[4] that self-consciousness is necessary to explain memory, since how else can we remember a thought? The answer is that, when an object has been perceived, there arises memory of it, and by association also of the perception of which it was the object. Equally impossible is it to strengthen the case by the power possessed in certain cases of magic to perceive the thought of another; by the use of certain unguents one can see a buried treasure, but another's consciousness is, like it, essentially something different from one's own consciousness. The further contention—that of Dignāga—that, if consciousness cannot know itself, it equally cannot know any object, and all

[1] Cf. Lañk., pp. 51, 59; MKV., pp. 62, 63, 114; BCAP. ix. 18.
[2] MK. vii. 9 ff.; BCA. ix. 18 ff. [3] MK. iii. 2. [4] BCA. ix. 24 ff.

experience is thus impossible, is denied; the Vijñānavāda by its effort to establish a relation between the true reality, void consciousness, and experience falls into hopeless difficulties; the Madhyamaka admits perception, inference, and authority as sources of experience,[1] but it asserts that on a critical examination the whole fabric of experience proves incapable of being sustained. Consciousness and its object cannot be identical, else there would be no subject and object; they cannot be different, since *ex hypothesi* there exists only consciousness; they cannot be both or neither, for these views are contradictory; in truth an unreal object is seen, an unreal consciousness sees. It is idle to argue that the unreal world of experience (*saṁsāra*) must have a foundation in the reality of void thought; the relation between unreal and real is unintelligible; the unreal cannot be stirred to activity by the real. It is equally wrong to talk of void consciousness, if there exist in it tendencies to create the distinction of subject and object.

The Vijñānavāda then makes an objection to the Madhyamaka position; granted that consciousness is unreal, how does the Madhyamaka arrive at the cessation of illusion and passion? the magician falls in love with the phantom of his creation. The answer is that the magician has not deprived himself of the tendency to regard things as existent; his knowledge of the unreality of his creation is inefficacious to destroy the natural emergence of passion. But, if one contemplates the void, one rids oneself first of the delusion of existence, and thereafter even of the delusion of non-existence and the end is reached.

[1] Cf. MKV., pp. 71 ff.

CHAPTER XV

THE DOCTRINE OF THE ABSOLUTE IN BUDDHISM AND THE VEDĀNTA.

1. *Suchness as the Absolute*

THE realistic implications of both the Vijñānavāda and the Madhyamaka must doubtless not be exaggerated; these schools have both specific doctrines which they fully accepted, and it is only as tendencies that we can see a movement to substitute for the negativism of the void or of empty thought, which is hardly more than the void, an absolute comparable to the absolute of the Vedānta. The further development of this tendency is seen in the *Mahāyānaçraddhotpāda* which tradition, as we have seen, ascribes to Açvaghoṣa, but which cannot be attributed to him with any confidence. It centres in the doctrine of suchness (*tathatā*), as the expression for the reality which must be held to remain when we discount al illusory appearances and leave the realm of relativity and contingency for that of absolute truth.[1]

It follows from the fact that we are not concerned with relative knowledge that any definition of suchness is utterly impossible; to apply to it empirical determinations is wholly misleading; to say that it is void is to ascribe to it the character which belongs to the phenomena of this world; to say that it exists is to suggest something individual like ourselves which, however, leads an eternal existence. It is necessary, then, to content ourselves either with silence or to choose the simple term suchness or suchness of being, an idea which in a simple form is known to the Hīnayāna. Suchness is above existence or non-existence or both or neither; similarly also it is neither unity nor plurality nor again both or neither.[2] It can, therefore, most easily be expressed by negations like the 'Not so, not so' of the Upaniṣads, and hence

[1] In addition to his translation, see Suzuki, BM. ch. v; vi.
[2] Trans. p. 59; cf. MK. i. 1; xxv. 17 f.

it is natural to treat it as the void. But we must not make the error of thinking this a real definition; the void is as void as anything positive.

Suchness in its ineffable absoluteness is thus beyond all comprehension and expression. Its real importance for us is that it comes into contact with empirical reality; by some mysterious act of self-determination, no better defined than as spontaneous, the absolute self affirms itself in the form of the receptacle intelligence (*ālaya-vijñāna*), which presents the two aspects of enlightenment and non-enlightenment. These, it must be remembered, have no separate and independent existence, but have being merely as relative to each other, and neither has any absolute existence, so that from the standpoint of absolute truth they can be identified. The origin of ignorance in the receptacle intelligence results in that which sees, that which represents, that which apprehends an objective world, and that which constantly particularizes, the entity which performs these functions being styled mind (*manas*). Five different aspects of its operations are distinguished. The first is activity intelligence (*karma-vijñāna*), when the unenlightened mind begins to be disturbed by the agency of ignorance; the second is intelligence as particular or evolving (*pravṛtti-vijñāna*), for, when the mind is disturbed, there arises the vision of an external world; the third is representation intelligence, when the mind reflects an external world as presented by the means of the senses; the fourth is particularization intelligence, which discriminates between things pure and infected; the fifth is succession intelligence: the mind directed by attention retains all experiences, securing the retribution of action, providing for the possibility of memory, and of the anticipation by imagination of the future. We see thus that from the absolute under the influence of ignorance we have the production of the self as a perceiver; of an external world, which exists for him and has no independent being as in the view of the Vijñānavāda; and of the constant round of births which mean misery. The unreal external world is the source of the origin of six phenomena on which misery depends. In the first place the mind, affected by the external world, becomes conscious of the distinction between what is agreeable and what is disagreeable. Secondly, it retains these feelings in a constant succession of changing states. Thirdly, from the retention and succession of feelings arises the desire of clinging. By clinging there is attachment to names and ideas which are ascribed to reality; from attachment to these concepts action is produced, and from action arises suffering. Every form of existence, the worlds of desire, of matter, and of non-matter, is merely a mental creation due to ignorance, precisely as in the Vijñānavāda.

We are, however, not condemned for ever to suffer from non-enlightenment, for suchness does not stand absolutely apart from the empiric world. The relation between it and ignorance is that of mutual perfuming (*vāsanā*) or impression. Ignorance affects suchness and produces those impressions (*smṛti*) which persist and maintain ignorance in being, creating an external world, and various modes of individuation, leading to action and misery. But suchness also affects ignorance; it thus induces in the mind of the individual in transmigration the hatred of the round of birth and death, and inspires in him the longing for release. Hence arises in the individual the conviction that he is really in possession of the pure nature of suchness, and that phenomena are merely the illusory manifestations of intelligence and have no absolute reality. The way is now open to practise with success the means of liberation, refraining absolutely from particularization, and from clinging to objects of desire. Ignorance can be overcome, because it is not absolutely distinct from enlightenment. The waves of the sea of consciousness which have been disturbed into motion by the wind of ignorance can be stilled, so that there remains only suchness in itself, unassociated with the mysterious disturbance which produces the manifestation of the individual and the world. It is freed from the coverings or obscuration of infections or ignorance (*kleçāvaraṇa, jñeyāvaraṇa*) and is immutable, calm, pure, and eternal.

The attainment of enlightenment and release is open to all beings, since there is always the perfuming of ignorance by suchness, but the intensity of ignorance with the principle of individuation accompanying it varies enormously, and thus accounts for the very diverse spiritual attainments of beings in the world. The inherent tendency of each mind to seek suchness is supported and promoted by the love and compassion of Bodhisattvas and Buddhas, who are higher embodiments of suchness; by hearing or seeing the Bodhisattvas man is enabled to acquire spiritual benefits, to win purity, to lay aside all hindrances, and to attain that clear insight which enables them to recognize the oneness of the universe and to see innumerable Buddhas and Bodhisattvas. There are stages in the degree of perfuming: adherents of the Hīnayāna or Çrāvakas, solitary Buddhas, and novice Bodhisattvas do not attain the state of non-particularization in unison with the essence of suchness, but Buddhas win this eminence. At this stage an end is put to the perfuming of ignorance, but the perfuming of suchness works on for ever and ever. Suchness is the effulgence of great wisdom, the illumination of the universe (*dharmadhātu*), true knowledge, the mind pure in its nature, eternal, calm, free, the womb of the Tathāgata, where the essence of Tathāgataship dwells, or the body of the law (*dharmakāya*). We have thus attained a more positive conception of suchness, but we are warned not to misunderstand the doctrine. The epithets of the idea are possible because there is in truth one reality only, so that there can be no question of particularizing or distinction which is utterly inapplicable to suchness; if it is said to be wisdom or knowledge, we must not suppose it has any object; if it is called universal illumination, we must not suppose there is anything to illumine.

Here we have, it is clear, something comparable with the absolute of the Vedānta, but at the same time there is much more reality in the new conception, and for all practical purposes a fundamentally novel mode of presenting the operation of the divine essence is revealed. We have in the conception of the activity of suchness as realized in the Bodhisattvas and Buddhas, unfolding itself in order to induce all beings to bring their store of merit to maturity, a much more effective version of the suggestion of the *Kaṭha Upaniṣad*[1] that the attainment of deliverance is due to the grace

[1] ii. 20; Çvet. Up. iii. 20; Taitt. Ār. x. 10. 1; Oldenberg, LUAB., pp. 245, 273 ff.; Suzuki's trs., pp. 62, 70.

of the Lord; the absolute itself is ever co-operating with the individual to secure him attainment of itself both directly and through the means of others.

2. *Cosmic and Individual Consciousness*

In the form[1] in which it has deeply influenced Chinese and Japanese thought the doctrine of the Yogācāra or Vijñānavāda has a formal view of consciousness in its development which is far more positive than negative. We may regard the receptacle consciousness as the foundation both of the external and the internal world; it is the essence or energy that lies behind inanimate nature, the life that strives upwards in the vegetable world; in this aspect it is the form or essence of the material world. The next higher stage is that in which it attains sensation and perception, and distinguishes objects, a power possessed by animals and men; thus one phase of the underlying unity becomes aware of another, one current of another current in the stream of being. The power of sensation and perception develops; by retention, comparison, and association of impressions there arises thought and ideation, found only in the higher animals and man, while finally the highest order of sentient beings develops self-consciousness or reflection.

This may be regarded as the cosmic evolution of consciousness; in the individual the process is traced from the receptacle consciousness in the following mode. The receptacle consciousness gives rise to the corresponding receptacle consciousness of the individual, as well as to the sense organs and sense objects. Then develops—from the influence of past impressions—the infected or defiled mind (*kliṣṭa-manas*), which distinguishes subject and object; fecundated by the receptacle consciousness, it becomes aware of a world as external, and confers on it mental determinations of form and shape. Then develops mind or normal consciousness (*mano-vijñāna*), which discriminates between the various phenomena,

[1] Cf. McGovern, *Intr. to Mahāyāna Buddhism*, pp. 144 ff., Suzuki, MB. ch. vi.; *Muséon*, v. (1904), 370 ff. In this aspect the Vijñānavāda is parallel to the Viçiṣṭādvaita school of Vedānta, while when the evolution is regarded as illusory it is parallel to the Vivartavāda.

and it, fecundated by the receptacle consciousness, develops the conception of like and dislike, associating it with other matters as cause and effect, &c. Then come the five forms of consciousness corresponding to the sense organs, visual, oral, nasal, taste, and touch consciousness, which, fecundated by the receptacle consciousness, give the presentation of the world of experience. The interaction of the whole body of these factors is necessary for the knowledge of the world; without, for instance, sight consciousness there could be no vision of colour, but mind is necessary for the discrimination of phenomena; without the infected mind one could not discriminate form or size, and without the receptacle consciousness neither the individual nor the world would exist. Or, in the terminology of causation, mind is the cause proper (*hetu*), infected mind and the receptacle consciousness the conditions (*pratyaya*), and the experienced world the fruit. The ordinary mind sees in the infected mind the final reality; Bodhisattvas recognize beneath it the receptacle consciousness as its *prius*.

3. *Nirvāṇa as the Absolute*

With the development of the positive side of the Mahāyāna there appears inevitably a certain change in the sense attributed to Nirvāṇa.[1] In the *Vijñānamātraçāstra* four forms of Nirvāṇa are distinguished. The first aspect is that in which Nirvāṇa is equivalent to the body of the law (*dharmakāya*); it is thus possible to view it in two aspects; in the one it is the absolute wholly simple, above all determinations of any empirical kind; in the other it is the reality which underlies the whole of existence, and in this sense, as a commentator on the Çastra says, it is present in every man in whatever stage of mental development. The second form is Nirvāṇa with residue (*upādhi-çeṣa*) which denotes the state achieved in life by the man who achieves complete enlightenment, but who still continues to work out his accumulated action. On death the result is Nirvāṇa without residue (*anupādhi-çeṣa*).[2] The fourth form of Nirvāṇa is that without

[1] See Suzuki, MB. ch. xiii.
[2] MSA. iii. 4; MKV., p. 519 (xxv. 1).

basis or stay (*apratiṣṭhita*),[1] which is the state superior to that of the Çrāvakas and the solitary Buddhas; in it the adept rises superior to the ideas of transmigration (*saṁsāra*) and Nirvāṇa itself. He lays aside the idea of contenting himself with the Nirvāṇa of the Çrāvaka and determines to deliver his fellow creatures from all misery and bring them to final emancipation and supreme bliss.

There are in fact in the Mahāyāna two strains of thought regarding Nirvāṇa. The negativism of Nāgārjuna asserts that it is not created, not liable to destruction, not eternal, not passing away, not acquired, not wanting, and leaves it therefore in the same condition of negativism as anything else, so that it can be asserted to be the same as Saṁsāra, since both are purely negative in character, and two negations can be identified. But the doctrine can be given a positive aspect, and this is clearly seen in the *Vimalakīrti Sūtra*,[2] in which insight is said to grow amid the defilement of passion and sin, even as the lotus grows in the watery mire, as the seed springs up in muddy soil, not in the air. Passion is intelligence; Nirvāṇa is Saṁsāra; the two are vitally connected, and the attainment of Nirvāṇa must be in and through life, not in annihilation or abstention from its activities. Hence in Asañga's *Mahāyānasaṁparigrahaçāstra* we have the character of a Buddha including superiority to attachment and defilement and yet connected with the passions of mankind, since depraved souls are to be rescued by the compassion of the Buddha. It is wrong, Vasubandhu explains, to see either the transitoriness of existence alone or the eternity of Nirvāṇa; from the standpoint of suchness the implications of both are essentially connected.

The advantage of this metaphysical conception of existence and release as inseparably connected is that it affords a moderately sound foundation on which to base the importance both of intuition and compassion in the process of attainment of the end. Intuition destroys egoistic thought, compassion encourages altruism; intuition destroys the attachments to self inherent in ordinary minds, compassion uproots the intellectual attachment of the Çrāvakas and solitary Buddhas which lead to seeking annihilation

[1] Lévi, MSA. ii. *21, 27, n. 4.
[2] Cf. Ç., pp. 325 f. (as courtesans); *Ratnolkadhāraṇī*, Ç., pp. 330 ff.

in Nirvāṇa ; by virtue of intuition Nirvāṇa in its transcendental sense is not rejected, by virtue of compassion existence with its round is not rejected ; by virtue of insight the truth of Buddhism is attained, by virtue of compassion other beings are made ripe for its attainment also. It is not difficult hence to rise to a more complete conception of Nirvāṇa as the absolute and to insist on the importance of compassion as bringing about the realization of that absolute which is the true Nirvāṇa.

4. *The Pre-eminence of the Mahāyāna*

It is now possible to understand the claims of pre-èminence over the Hīnayāna insisted upon for the Mahāyāna by both Asaṅga and and Vasubandhu. In the *Mahāyānasaṁparigrahaçāstra* Asaṅga enumerates seven points in which his school surpasses the Çrāvakas.[1] The Mahāyāna is comprehensive ; whatever has been taught by Buddhas, not by Çākyamuni in one life alone is accepted ; nay more, as we have seen, whatever is well said is to be deemed the word of a Buddha. Secondly, the Mahāyāna aims at general salvation, not at individual release, thus excelling in love for all created things. Thirdly, the Mahāyāna is intellectually wider in range than the Hīnayāna ; the latter denies the reality of the self, the former goes so far as to deny all phenomenal reality whatever. Fourthly, the Mahāyāna inculcates spiritual energy ; to seek swift release for oneself is not its aim as it is that of the Çrāvaka. Fifthly, the Mahāyāna is skilled in the manifold means (*upāya*)[2] to lead men to salvation ; it is unwearied in their varied application. Moreover, it leads to a far higher ideal ; the adept aims to become, not a mere saint, but a Buddha in his complete perfection. Lastly, when an adept becomes a Buddha, he has the infinite power of manifesting himself throughout the universe in a body of bliss.

A different presentation of the important aspects of Mahāyānism is given in another treatise which is specially concerned with the aspect of the Mahāyāna represented by Asānga and his brother.

[1] See Suzuki, MB. ch. ii.

[2] The *Upāyakauçalya Sūtra* is cited in Ç., pp. 66, 165, 167, 168 on committing even sin to save beings.

Ten points here are given. The first is the conception of the receptacle consciousness and its relation to the mind as defiled by ignorance. The second is the threefold classification of knowledge and degrees of reality. Thirdly, comes the idealistic conception of the world, underlying which is the further recognition of even this as the product of ignorance and illusion. Fourthly, the school inculcates the practice of the six perfections of generosity, not clinging to worldly goods; of non-violation of moral precepts; of not feeling dejected in the face of evils (*kṣānti*); of not being indolent in well doing (*vīrya*); of practising meditation and concentration (*samādhi*); and of intuition (*prajñā*), recognizing only the existence of an ideal world. Fifthly, the school has the scheme of ten stages of spiritual progression. Sixthly, it practises a morality which is spiritual, not merely physical or literal; the Çrāvaka follows the letter, not the spirit, and for a selfish end; the Bodhisattva will violate the letter to save the souls of others. Seventhly, the Bodhisattva aims at conformity with the essence of suchness and the body of the law.[1] Eighthly, his insight is free from non-particularism (*anānārtha*); he is not deceived either by Saṁsāra or Nirvāṇa, but reaches the absolute, as the abode of non-particularization. Ninthly, he realizes that Nirvāṇa which is without stay; that is, he does not end his existence, but takes part in the life of the world, without, however, even being defiled by that life. Lastly, the school has the sublime doctrine of the body of the law as well as of the other two bodies of the Buddha.

5. *Vedānta and Mahāyāna*

The appearance of a tendency to recognize an absolute in the *Mahāyānaçraddhotpāda* has been naturally enough attributed, on the theory that the author of that treatise is Açvaghoṣa, to the Brahmanical training of that accomplished poet. In any case the parallel between Vedāntic absolutism and Mahāyāna tenets is striking and undeniable. In the Vijñānavāda we have definitely the conception of void intellect as the final reality, and, though the Vedāntic absolute is being, thought, and bliss, we are aware

[1] A different account seems to be given in *Muséon*, v. (1904) 372 where Samādhi is the excellence.

that thought here has no object and is therefore, if intelligible in any sense, nothing essentially different from the void intellect of the Vijñānavāda. The bliss of such a void intellect is too mysterious a matter to inquire into, and its existence is clearly on a par with the existence of the void intellect of the Vijñānavāda.

The similarity of result, however, does not necessarily mean borrowing on either side, for parallel developments of different initial conceptions, one of absolute reality, one of absolute nothingness, might lead to results not dissimilar, and it is, of course, true that there is a vital difference between the two doctrines. The truth of convention or appearance (*vaiyavahārika*) of Çaṅkara is certainly false from the point of view of absolute truth, but it rests on a reality, for illusion (*māyā*) is, and the magician who causes it is a Lord, while Nāgārjuna's truth of obscurity is utterly unreal, like the horn of a hare or the son of a barren woman.[1]

It is, however, of importance that the later supporters of the doctrine of duality, adherents of the Sāṁkhya as well as of Viçiṣṭādvaita Vedānta, do not hesitate to pronounce judgement against the monist Vedānta by accusing it of being nothing but Vijñānavāda Buddhism concealed; in this Puranic evidence concurs with Vijñānabhikṣu, and the earlier testimony of Yamunācārya, spiritual grandfather of Rāmānuja, so that the accusation was evidently current shortly after Çaṅkara had established the orthodoxy of the Māyāvāda.[2] On the other hand, it is obvious that the Buddhists themselves were aware of the approximation of the Vijñānavāda in some of its aspects to the Vedānta; we have in the *Laṅkāvatāra*[3] a direct challenge of the similarity of the doctrine of the Tathāgatagarbha and the Vedānta self, though the Buddha repudiates the charge of plagiarism by insisting that his teaching is merely *ad populum*. Again in the *Çuklavidarçanābhūmi*[4] it is shown that a famous Buddha's utterance: 'This threefold world is only thought', is equivalent to the doctrine of the Upaniṣads: 'Verily all this universe is Brahman.' Similarly,

[1] See Poussin, JRAS, 1910, pp. 129 ff.; Jacobi, JAOS. xxxiii. 51 ff.; Sukhtankar, VOJ. xxii. 136 ff.

[2] *Sāṁkhyapravacanabhāṣya*, i. 22; *Padma Purāṇa*, Bodl. Cat. i. 14; *Siddhitraya*, p. 19; *Çrībhāṣya*, ii. 27.

[3] pp. 80 f. [4] JRAS. 1908, p. 889; *Chāndogya Upaniṣad*, iii. 14.

a verse in the *Pitāputrīyasaṁhitā* (elsewhere attributed to Vārṣagaṇya's *Ṣaṣṭitantra*):[1] 'The real nature of things does not fall within sight, and what is visible is absolutely void and illusion,' is identical in sense with the doctrine of the *Bṛhadāraṇyaka Upaniṣad.*

There is, however, clear evidence of a direct influence of Buddhist conceptions on Gauḍapāda whose Kārikās certainly are of importance in the development of the Vedānta, and who passes for the spiritual grandfather of Çañkara.[2] The origin of plurality is explained by the simile of the firebrand, whose point waved in a circle produces the appearance of fiery lines without the addition of anything to the brand itself; so, too, the conclusion is, the many phenomena of the world are merely vibrations of the one consciousness, and this consciousness, we find, is without distinction of subject, object or knowledge, and thus is hardly other than the Vijñānavāda absolute. The simile is Buddhist; the *Lankāvatāra*[3] and the *Abhidharmakoçavyākhyā*, Vijñānavāda and Sautrāntika sources, apply it to show the nothingness of things; cloth is not real because the grasping of it depends on the grasping of its parts as in the case of the firebrand circle. The whole content is also Buddhist in tone; birth and destruction are hotly denied; the cause cannot be identical with or different from the effect since neither being nor not-being nor being and not-being can exist, and so causation is impossible. In absolute truth there is no destruction or birth, no bound, no accomplishing release, no seeking release, and no release. From a magic seed is born a magic sprout and there is no permanence, just as from void things void things ever arise without abiding substance. Things come into being neither by themselves, nor by another, nor by both, nor by neither.[4] These and numerous other phrases are conclusive of

[1] Garbe, *Sāṁkhya-Philosophie*, p. 76.

[2] Walleser, *Der ältere Vedānta* (Heidelberg, 1910), pp. 24 ff.; cf. JRAS. 1910, pp. 1361 ff. Walleser (pp. 16 ff.) gives substantial grounds for placing Gauḍapāda before Bhāvaviveka (before A. D. 600) and Çāntirakṣita (c. A. D. 730), and renders the alleged relationship implausible. He knows the Vijñānavāda; JAOS xxxiii. 53 f.

[3] p. 95; AKV. (Paris MS.) f. 267a. Cf. Maitr. Up. vi. 24; Wassilieff, (*Bouddhisme*, p. 284) gives it as illustrating the illusion of simultaneity of consciousness from swiftness of motion.

[4] ii. 32; iv. 59; 7; 22.

close relationship, and if Gauḍapāda[1] and his co[mmentator,] whose identity with Çaṅkara need not be assumed[2]—de[nies that the] Buddha taught as finally real that knowledge without [—] which has no distinction of knower, known and knowledg[e, the] fact goes flatly in the face of all Buddhist evidence. Gauḍapā[da] in fact borrows without wishing to admit his debt in full. Bu[t] in a sense he had, of course, the right as an Aupaniṣada in his Kārikās, whatever his earlier faith, to borrow; the Mahāyāna in its turn had doubtless drawn from the stream of Aupaniṣada tradition in its conception of the final reality of the world.

The attitude of Çaṅkara is interesting, as he expounds with much clearness the Vijñānavāda position, in opposition to the realistic doctrines of the Sarvāstivādins, whether Vaibhāṣikas or Sautrāntikas, and explains fully his own objections to the Vijñānavāda.[3] The Vijñānavāda maintains the sole existence of the threefold process of knowledge, which may be analysed as apparent subject, object, and consciousness or knowledge. The existence of external things is denied on the score of impossibility; they must either be atoms or aggregates of atoms; if the former they are incomprehensible on the score of minuteness; if aggregates, they must either be different from the atoms, which is a contradiction in terms, or they must be non-different, in which case they cannot produce impressions of gross non-atomic bodies. Moreover, our cognitions constantly differ in content; this is impossible unless they take the form of the objects, and, if this is so, it is needless to assume external things. Further, we are always conscious simultaneously of the act and the object of knowledge which proves identity, since else we could at one time know the object, at another know consciousness. Again, we have the fact of dream consciousness

[1] iv. 99.

[2] Cf. Deussen, *Sechzig Upanishads*, p. 478, n. 1.

[3] On BS. ii. 2, 28 ff. For Nyāya criticism cf. Jacobi, JAOS. xxxi. 9 ff.; Keith, JRAS. 1914, p. 1090; ILA., pp. 22 f., 99 f., 208 ff.; NM., pp. 536 f., 548 f.; for Mīmāṅsā, Keith, KM. pp. 46 ff. For a formal examination from a Kantian standpoint see Walleser, *Der ältere Vedānta*, pp. 40 ff. For Rāmānuja's critique, see *Çrībhāṣya*, ii. 2. 27. Of the original sense of the Sūtra it is difficult to be certain; cf. JAOS. xxxi. 13 ff.; V. S. Ghate, *Le Vedānta*, pp. 44 f. For Sāṅkhya criticism see Aniruddha on SS. i. 42 f.; in v. 77–9 it is shown that on either Madhyamaka or Vijñānavāda principles liberation is inconceivable; in v. 91–3 the existence of genus is defended.

existence from non-existence, while at the same time it holds that all mental complexes are derived from the four psychical aggregates and material complexes from the atoms. The Madhyamaka doctrine fares even worse, being dismissed contemptuously on the ground that its tenet of vacuity is contradicted by every means of knowledge.[1]

[1] On BS. ii. 2. 32. Rāmānuja (ii. 2. 30) points out that nothingness is merely a form of existence, and that its proof involves the existence of the proof, and contradicts the result.

exte...
s without such ...
plained by the presence in ou...
f ideas, the stream of ideas and impr...
for ever, and excluding any need of external re...
The Vedānta reply is that the analysis given is a...
our perception of external reality we have the consciousness a...
the object as two distinct and irreducible psychological elements. This is in effect admitted by the Vijñānavāda which admits that objects appear as if external (*bāhyavat*), an expression which is explicable only because those who use it at the bottom of their hearts recognize the existence of that which is external. It is useless to urge that the expression is justified, because external things are impossible: possibility must be judged on the basis of the operation of the means of correct knowledge, and not made to depend on *a priori* ratiocination. Possible is whatever is apprehended by perception or other means of cognition, and external things are essentially so apprehended, a fact which outweighs the sophistical dilemma of difference or non-difference from atoms. Examination of perception reveals that the idea is the means of knowing the external object which dictates its shape; the distinction of consciousness and external reality can be made clear, if we consider the perception and recollection of a jar, where there is change in consciousness with permanence of object, or the successive consciousness of two different objects, when consciousness remains in principle the same, but its distinctive attributes differ.

More fundamental still is the onslaught on the momentary character of ideas; this doctrine, if logically followed out, is fatal to the distinction of ideas, to the differentiation of classes and individuals, to the conception of the leaving of impressions on the mind, to the doctrine of the confusion owing to nescience of existence and non-existence, and consequently to the doctrine of bondage and release, for all these matters depend on the possibility of comparison of ideas, which is inconceivable unless there is a permanent knowing subject and not merely momentary ideas. It is idle to seek to evade this result by holding that the idea knows itself, as a lamp illuminates itself. But this is false;

CHAPTER XVI

THE BUDDHIST TRĪKĀYA

1. *The Dharmakāya, Body of the Law*

THE doctrine of the three bodies of a Buddha[1] is specifically a possession of the Mahāyāna, but it is not without precursors in the earlier history of Buddhism, and it is the special distinction of the Mahāyāna to have converted a doctrine merely theological into an ontological and cosmogonical speculation. In various aspects the theory is found both in the Madhyamaka, the Vijñānavāda, and the *Mahāyānaçraddhotpāda*; it is modified slightly to meet the metaphysical aspects of each theory, but these changes are slight, nor is it always possible to say precisely what view in detail was held by the schools.

We find already in the Hīnayāna the conception of the distinction between the mere physical body of the Buddha which passes away, and the body of the law, which is the doctrine taught by him, to be realized by each man for himself. Later we find the idea that the material body of the Buddha is his body, while the law is the soul.[2] The law, however, which is the true nature of the Buddha, is true knowledge or the insight or intuition (*prajñā*) which is attained by a Buddha. The body of the law, therefore, can be equated with enlightenment (*bodhi*),[3] or with release (*nirvāṇa*). But for the Madhyamaka release, enlightenment, and the body of the law are ultimately no more or less than the highest and only true reality, the void, which lies underneath every phenomenal thing. For the Vijñānavāda in the same way

[1] Poussin, JRAS. 1906, pp. 943 ff.; Kern, *Muséon*, vii. (1906), 46 ff.; Wassilieff, *Bouddhisme*, p. 127; Rockhill, *Buddha*, pp. 200 ff. See also Poussin, *Muséon*, 1913, pp. 257 ff.

[2] *Divyāvadāna*, pp. 19 f. See DN. iii. 84; Geiger, PD., p. 78.

[3] PP., pp. 94, 462; BCAP. ix. 38.

the body of the law as highest reality is the void intelligence, whose infection (*saṁkleça*) results in the process of birth and death, while its purification brings about Nirvāṇa or its restoration to its primitive transparence.

At the same time the body of the law must be considered, not merely abstractly, but also in its relation to the world of phenomena. The schools are agreed that the only truth is Nirvāṇa or Buddhahood or cessation or purification of thought; that such purification is impossible, if infection or defilement is real; and that every individual being is only illusion; hence it follows that the body of the law is the true reality of everything. Or, as it is defined in a verse [1] possibly by Nāgārjuna, it is neither one nor multiple, it supports the great blessing of salvation for oneself and for others, it neither exists nor does not exist, it is homogeneous like the ether, its nature is unmanifested, it is undefiled, unchanging, blessed, unique in its kind, diffused, transcendant, and to be known by every one in himself. It is neither one, since it pervades everything, nor multiple, since it remains identical with itself. This appertains to every Buddha, but at the same time each Buddha is asserted to have a Dharmakāya of his own, and receives a special denomination in this aspect; Amitābha, for instance, is named thus as Dharmakāya, but Amitāyus as Sambhogakāya, body of enjoyment. In the case of Mañjuçrī,[2] who is essentially an embodiment of wisdom, the term body of knowledge (*jñānakāya*) appears in lieu of body of the law.

The Dharmakāya has an equivalent in suchness (*tathatā*) or suchness of being, a term which in some aspects stresses the primitive non-differentiation of reality, and has, therefore, so far, analogies with the matter of the Sāṁkhya. It also may be equated with the womb of the Tathāgata (*tathāgata-garbha*), which is primarily intuition or true knowledge, and, derivatively, the source of every individual being.[3] Further, though it cannot be identified with, it underlies the store of phenomena (*dharma-dhātu*,

[1] JRAS. 1906, p. 955, n. 2, from the Chinese of Fa-T'ien (A.D. 982) and comm. on *Nāmasaṁgīti*.
[2] On the supposed Chinese origin of this person, see Eliot, HB. ii. 19.
[3] Laṅk. p. 80.

-*rāçi*), the collection of unconscious mental elements, which are liable to be perceived as sound, or matter, or happiness.[1]

2. *The Sambhogakāya, Body of Bliss*

The conception of a body of bliss, the state in which a Buddha enjoys his merits as a Bodhisattva, is not known to the Pali Canon, although it is apparently in error attributed to the Sautrāntikas,[2] and it can hardly be doubted that those who worshipped the relics and symbols of the Buddha conceived of him rather as a living deity than a dead saint, powerless to aid, whose cult was merely one of commemoration, not of prayer and adoration. In the view, further, that a Tathāgata can live, if he please, a cosmic age, there is present in germ the conception of such a body as is accepted by the Mahāyāna. Each Buddha in his heaven is conceived as possessing a body of ineffable brilliance, and the Bodhisattvas who are his officers are also clad in glory, though the term body of bliss is not assigned to their forms; Avalokita in special has a peculiarly splendid body of glory; in the pores of his skin there are worlds with hosts of meditating or praising saints, a conception reminiscent of the famous apparition of Kṛṣṇa to Arjuna in a shape in which is lodged the whole universe.[3] It is manifested in the assembly of Bodhisattvas for their delight; it is visible and manifested, though it is made of, or by, mind; its manifestation is above the three worlds of desire, matter, and non-matter, and is inexplicable (*acintya*), and it constantly emits the sublime sound of the good law, while it bears the thirty-two characteristic marks of the Buddha.

The relation of this body of bliss to the body of the law is explained by Candrakīrti[4] who holds that equipment of knowledge (*jñāna-sambhāra*), leads to the attainment of the body consisting of the law, whose characteristic is no birth, while equipment of merit (*puṇya-sambhāra*) results in a body of bliss, marvellous, inexplicable, and multiform, a reference perhaps to its power to appear

[1] Nāgārjuna's *Sramatoddeça*; JRAS. 1906, p. 954, n. 3.

[2] Wassilieff, *Bouddhisme*, p. 286 (cited to this effect in JRAS. 1906, p. 958, n. 3) says the contrary.

[3] *Kāraṇḍavyūha* in Burnouf, *Intr.*, p. 224; *Bhagavadgītā*, xi.

[4] MA. iii. 12.

under many forms or imaginary bodies. As merit is essentially the lot of Bodhisattvas, it is natural that they should have similar bodies. But a real difficulty arises as to the body of bliss of a Buddha who has attained enlightenment, and the body of the law, for Candrakīrti appears to hold that none the less his body of bliss endures. This also agrees with the general picture of relations in the literature ; Amitābha has attained enlightenment ; yet there exists in Sukhāvatī his immaterial, yet visible, image, and so with Çākyamuni himself according to the *Saddharmapuṇḍarīka.* It is possible to explain the apparent discrepancy on strictly Mahāyāna principles ; granted that his body of bliss becomes nothing for a Buddha, still his store of merit is available for others, and so presents to Bodhisattvas and to men respectively a body of bliss or magic body for their edification. Or perhaps we need not press the belief that on enlightenment the Buddha ceases interest in mundane things ; he is freed from Nirvāṇa and from transmigration,[1] that is, he can be active and conscious, while yet his activity does not defile him, since he is above becoming. Though he has by wisdom attained Nirvāṇa, yet through compassion he may continue in his body of bliss for ever in the world of becoming. A further refinement of the doctrine conceives apparently of the bodies of bliss of the Buddhas uniting to form one marvellous appearance in the abode of the gods, Akaniṣṭhas, which takes the place of the innumerable paradises of the older view.[2]

Ontologically the Vijñānavāda has a simple place for the conception of body of bliss. In accord with the Tāntrika conception of the body of bliss as an emanation from the body of the law,[3] it holds that from intelligence (*vijñāna*), pure, immaculate, and quiescent or void, that is, the body of the law, springs mind, which, when infected or defiled (*kliṣṭa*), originates the whole complex of thought which constitutes the world. The body of bliss is parallel with the undefiled mind, or from another point of view the intellect, in so far as it is individualized as Buddha or Bodhisattva.

[1] Ç., p. 322. [2] Waddell, *Lamaism*, p. 85.
[3] Comm. on *Nāmasaṁgīti*, 79.

3. *The Nirmāṇakāya, Magic Body*

Even in the Hīnayāna we have from the lips of the Buddha himself an assertion of his power of leaving the assembly in which he preaches dubious as to his identity, and the *Kathāvatthu* records the docetic heresy of the Vetulyakas who held that the Buddha remained in the Tuṣita heaven, and merely a phantom appeared on earth. The idea is not known to the Mahāvastu, but it occurs repeatedly in the *Mahāyāna Sūtras*, with the substitution of some other abode of the real Buddha in lieu of the Tuṣita heaven, the Vulture peak in the *Saddharmapuṇḍarīka*, the Sukhāvatī paradise in the Vyūhas and Amitāyuḥ-sūtras. From time immemorial Çākyamuni or Amitābha or Vajrasattva has been emancipated, not first at Gayā, but he repeatedly appears in a magic form in the world, to lead an apparent life, teach the law, and be extinct.[1] A development of this conception is the five Mānuṣi-Buddhas corresponding to five Jinas or so-called Dhyāni-Buddhas in the mythology; the former are essentially artificial, the latter true Buddhas. Both Buddhas and Bodhisattvas may transform themselves thus, but the Bodhisattva Avalokiteçvara is *par excellence* the transformer of himself into the most varied shapes in his eagerness to succour men, and to fulfil his vow to secure the release of all beings. The shapes which may be assumed are not limited to Buddha appearances, though these are usual in the case of Buddhas, but any form may be chosen which serves the end aimed at.

Beside this conception, which is frequent and orthodox, there appears an analogous idea; on attaining enlightenment a Buddha is endowed with a body of bliss, and his old body disappears; but out of pity for the world he causes a magic body to survive so that men may see it and enclose its bones in a relic shrine, ignorant of the fact that the bones have no reality.[2]

Ontologically, the conception is fully employed in the *Mahāyānaçraddhotpāda*, where suchness as the absolute is conceived as the void and radiant intellect, which under the influence of

[1] *Saddharmapuṇḍarīka*; SBE. XXI. xxv. [2] Wassilieff, *Bouddhisme*, p. 127.

ignorance loses its clearness in some degree, and originates action intellect (*karma-vijñāna*), which evolves by thinking the bliss and enjoyment bodies. Further, by virtue of previous impressions (*vāsanā*), intellect develops into the state of discriminating particulars (*vastuprativikalpa*), in which it creates for itself the whole material world and the world of desire. Ordinary men, Çrāvakas, and solitary Buddhas thus generate inumerable magic bodies. The same power of creation is seen in the imagination which creates a real self, pleasant and unpleasant things, the great gods. Such people have no true idea of a Buddha; they have not mastered the truth of existence and non-existence; they believe in a human Buddha and his Nirvāṇa, which they desire for themselves. The Bodhisattvas on the contrary appreciate reality; they are aware of their substantial identity with the body of the law, but they have not realized it as they are still conscious of their identity. Though they are undefiled by the world, owing to their equipment of knowledge, they practise an equipment of merit which results in an unreal but purifying activity.

CHAPTER XVII

THE DOCTRINE OF SALVATION, BODHISATTVAS, AND BUDDHAS

1. *The Problem of Salvation*

THE metaphysics of the Mahāyāna in the incoherence of its systems shows clearly enough the secondary interest attaching to it in the eyes of the monks, whose main interest was concentrated on the attainment of release; the Mahāyāna no less than the Hīnayāna is concerned vitally with this practical end, and its philosophy is of value merely in so far as it helps men to attain their aim.

Now the knowledge of the ultimate truth, whatever the system, is not to be regarded as adequate to secure for man the release for which he hopes. It is true that both Vijñānavāda and Madhyamaka assert that release is possible, despite the formidable or insuperable difficulties which the metaphysics of either system presents to such an event. But both realize far too clearly the substantial existence of the world of phenomena to be under the impression that mere knowledge is always and in every case the mode of attaining enlightenment. There is a precise parallel between their view and that of the Vedānta; at a definite stage in the progress of the saint, there comes the period when the true knowledge is of decisive value in winning him release, but it is at the due stage only that such a result can be achieved. The Vedāntin must not neglect the duties of the world in which he lives, or ignore the devotion due to Brahmā; the Buddhist equally must not think that mere knowledge of the void[1] dispenses him from the practice of the noblest of virtues, that of charity. Granted that

[1] Or of the Brahman in the case of the Vedāntin. Compare the *Bhagavadgītā* doctrine of action; Poussin, JA. 1903, ii. 385 ff. See Ç., p 117, citing the *Ratnacūḍa Sūtra*.

it is true that in ultimate truth there is no distinction between virtue and vice, between infection of thought and purification, the vicious man so taught will pursue the way to destruction, while the good man will realize that all action is unreal, and will continue to do good, but with absolute detachment and freedom from desire of any kind.

The end, it is true, is the destruction of the illusion which veils the absolute void, or the void intellect, but it is impossible to deal with the illusion by the simple process of denying its reality. If there is no reality in consciousness, as the Madhyamaka asserts, nonetheless we must face the necessity of removing the illusion of reality, and the problem therefore is not seriously altered or simplified.[1] We must lay aside our knowledge that experience is false, because it is experience, and that all ideas on examination prove unreal because of the antinomies they contain, and pursue a knowledge (*darçana*), inferior indeed but indispensable, which will take account of the facts of experience, and find a path or vehicle or means to attain to the deliverance which is desired.

In a concrete form the problem may be posed as the method of reversing the chain of causation, and thus terminating the constant stream of lives. In the Hīnayāna the process, as we have seen, is simple enough in its operation. Each intellectual series or individual stands by himself as a causal sequence; there is no room in the conception for either the intervention of a deity, for freedom of will, or for human solidarity. It is the great achievement of the Mahāyāna that it has succeeded without too great violence to earlier ideas in finding a place both for human freedom and for solidarity among men and beings of higher order of merit. The method to attain such an end was presented by the floating character of the distinction between relative truth and imaginary knowledge; either was, from the point of view of absolute truth, without validity, and the boundary line between the two classes was difficult to draw, affording the Mahāyāna the opportunity to redefine the conception of truth and advance to the rank of relative reality matters once relegated to the position of mere imagination.

In accord with the Hīnayāna, the Mahāyāna holds that the mode

[1] BCA. ix. 4 ff.

of stopping the activity of the chain of causation demands essentially the co-operation of intuition (*prajñā*) and merit (*puṇya*). Intuition, viewed as the cause of release, involves study, reflection, meditation, and the diverse forms of applications of active attention (*smṛty-upasthāna*);[1] merit includes the inferior perfections of morality, generosity, and patience, and with this are connected the taking of refuge in the jewels, the Buddha, the law, and the order. Strictly speaking, merit is a means, but intuition as cause and merit are reciprocally means to each other, and their common aim is the attainment of intuition as fruition—that is, illumination (*bodhi*), the definite cessation of the activity of thought, or release.[2]

2. *The Equipment of Knowledge*

The essential cause of transmigration and bondage is the act accomplished with belief in the self; this delusion is the source of false views, of passion; it leads men to believe in the eternity or the destruction of the self, to love it or hate it. It is, then, essential to extirpate the delusion, to clear the mind of all the desires in which the self finds pleasure, and to realize the nothingness of all phenomena. But the task is a difficult one, for to achieve it directly involves an antinomy. The Vedāntin may desire release directly without injury, and may declare his identity with the absolute, because he is a believer in reality. But the Buddhist who seeks to be rid of the illusion of the self, or asserts boldly that he is void, is falling into the fatal error of holding as real, if not the self, at least the illusion of the self, and his action is in effect egoistic. The desire for non-existence (*vibhava-tṛṣṇa*) leads directly into the fatal heresy of belief in existence.[3] The Jinas have declared the vacuity as the remedy for all false views, but those who falsely attach themselves to vacuity they have declared beyond redemption. What does not exist cannot be the subject of a negation; to deny unreal appearances is really to

[1] See Mvy. 38; *Dharmasaṁgraha*, 44; Ç., ch. xiii, xiv for details.
[2] BCAP. ix. 1. The possibility of a sterile act is recognized in KV. xii. 2.
[3] *Udāna*, iii. 10; *Itivuttaka*, 49; AN. i. 83, ii. 11; MKV., p. 531; xxv. 10; BCAP. ix. 33; *Subhāṣitasaṁgraha*, JA. 1903, ii. 398; VP. i. 10; SN. v. 421; MN. i. 65; DN. ii. 308, iii. 216; DS., § 1314; SBB. ii. 340, n. 1; Beckh, *Buddhismus*, ii. 123. The sense is really clear.

affirm them. Employed untimely, the idea of vacuity is no better than poison; it is to practise negation, which is in essence affirmation and involves the heresy of the doctrine of destruction, an idea utterly repugnant to the schools, which agree that, if the illusion of the self really existed, it would be eternal.

The destruction of the idea of the self is, therefore, hardly to be achieved by direct means; it must in some degree come about by itself, as the result of far back causes, and as the outcome of following the methods laid down by ancient teachers. Meditation on the void is necessary, despite the danger of the method, for mere insistence on the void is even more evil than insistence on reality. Properly managed, like a magic rite duly accomplished, it attains its end, for, after causing the idea of existence to disappear, it ends with producing the disappearance of the idea of non-existence also. Just so a man who suffers from ophthalmia, if he learns that there are no real hairs floating before his eyes, first conceives the idea of the non-existence of the hairs, but, acting as if he saw none, finally comes to ignore even the illusion. Similarly, meditation on non-existence leads on to further advance culminating in the realization of the voidness of the void (*çūnyatā-çūnyatā*), and the mind freed from the ideas of existence and non-existence will rest for ever in the absence of any content or categories. The essential aim is to repudiate either affirmation or negation, or the combination of both or the denial of both; this is as ever the true middle way of the Buddhist.[1]

Nonetheless, it must be recognized that even the attainment of this way is not the absolute truth, for that is silence, unconsciousness, neither to be described in words nor to be comprehended by thought, which is burned in seeking to penetrate it.[2] The absolute is beyond speech, beyond knowledge, even that of the completely equipped Buddha, but it reveals itself to the Ārya, a conception closely parallel to the doctrine of the revelation of the absolute in the Vedānta.[3]

It is, however, fully realized in the Mahāyāna that, despite all

[1] BCA. ix. 32, 35; BCAP. ix. 2; Mvy. 37; *Dharmasaṁgraha*, 41; MKV., p. 1; cf. BCA. ix 78.

[2] MKV., p. 57; BCA. ix. 2. [3] BCAP. ix. 2; MKV., p. 373 (with n. 2).

elaboration of meditation, the attainment of the end is far more difficult than is suggested in the Hīnayāna, where realization of the truth is presented as something comparatively simple, often to be achieved even in the present life. To attain a state of trance is possible, but there is constant need for effort, since consciousness is active, and even in unconscious ecstasy (*asaṁjñi-samāpatti*) it is apt to come into activity despite the utmost efforts of concentration on vacuity.[1] Even if one as a god attains the heaven of unconsciousness, there comes a time of awakening, just as, though infinitely more rapidly, the monk who attains trance must pass out of it. In face of this fact it is necessary to remember the other side of the picture of life. Our actions, until final enlightenment is reached, are ever active, compelling us to new births; if, then, it is so hard to attain full enlightenment, and if no action of our intelligence can directly effect it, as we have seen, it is all the more incumbent on us to practise morality, to aim at the production of the perfection of virtue, thus assuring ourselves of progressive happiness in the course of our lives, and rendering more and more favourable the change of release, if indeed we actually demand release, for the Mahāyāna is conscious that the demand of the average man is not for a mysterious and ineffable condition, but for the delights of happier lives to come. The pursuit of virtue thus enters into a new career of usefulness.

3. *The Equipment of Merit*

Merit lies in the abstention from evil, and the performance of good. True, both good and evil are ultimately unreal, like release and transmigration themselves,[2] but this consideration has no validity for practice, since practice itself is unreal in the same sense; granted evil be unreal, still the doer fetters himself in unreal chains and prolongs the misery of conscious existence unreal as it is. Good action is also unreal, but to practise it ends in aiding enlightenment. Experience shows, then, that to deal with illusion we must accept illusion and combat it by itself, not

[1] BCA. ix. 49. For this state cf. Mvy. 68, 104; *Dharmasaṁgraha*, 82; MKV., p. 48. The Andhakas assert consciousness even of gods in it, KV. iii. 11 f.

[2] See BCA. ix. 8 ff.: thought is an illusion, but one difficult to be rid of; it has produced the false Vijñānavāda belief (ix. 15 ff.); ix. 78.

by the mere occasional introduction of recognition of its illusory nature.

What is good, and what evil? The Mahāyāna, as little as the Hīnayāna, develops any theory of the nature of good or evil; good results, it is true, in a pleasant future existence, evil in misery, but there is no attempt to work out the goodness or badness of acts on the basis of their results; on the contrary, it is no doubt rather[1] the truth that an action brings pleasure because it is good, not is good because it brings pleasure, and we have the formal doctrine that an act performed for the sake of pleasure in this life is unmeritorious. But in general the view of Buddhism is that of popular morality; a standard of morals is assumed as recognized, and the Buddhist would be a fool indeed if he could not recognize what even a Cāṇḍāla understands.[2] But in detail the subject is difficult; we have seen the conflict of schools on the question of the position of volition in sin, and it is necessary that merit should be relative to the end which is release. But, fortunately, the Mahāyāna need not rely on reason to decide what is necessary, for the Buddha is an authority whose words will give the necessary guidance to practice, or at any rate suggest the requisite principles.[3]

It is necessary, then, to avoid the sins forbidden by the Buddha, to escape from desire, hatred, dullness, and to attain calm (*çamatha*); to be patient in suffering, recognizing the brevity of such human suffering, and valuing the opportunity afforded to show strength of character and recognition of the non-existence of the self. It is well to reflect on the misery of existence, the horrors of decomposition, the terrors of hell. True, these things are at best only relative reality, or even perhaps wholly imaginary —the product of a mere nightmare,[4] but such reflections will stay the wicked from evil and anguish, and strengthen even the adept whose final success is hindered by imaginary terrors. They are means, ineffective in absolute reality, but for all practical ends fully accomplishing their purpose.

But these means are essentially negative, and the Mahāyāna has

[1] Poussin, JA. 1903, ii. 405; AKV. (Paris MS.), f. 236 *b*.
[2] BC. vii. 19; cf. *Çlokavārttika*, p. 209. [3] Cf. ch. ii, § 1. [4] MKV., p. 50.

room for positive action. It is clear that neither intuition of vacuity nor charity or compassion (*karuṇā*) alone is sufficient to lead to the abandonment of existence (*sattva-tyāga*); without compassion vacuity is hard to comprehend; without intuition compassion may be carried too far by the force of passion. We have as emphatic an assertion as in the Hīnayāna that intuition alone is not enough.[1] It is obvious that there is difficulty in demanding action from those aware of the vacuity of existence; the insensibility, the wooden immobility,[2] of the monk of the Hīnayāna seems especially appropriate to the adept of the Mahāyāna, but this logical conclusion is not drawn. Instead, the resources of reason are used to establish the propriety of compassion and its efficacy; doubtless it was not by reasoning that the importance of compassion was arrived at; that was demanded by the needs of the heart, and the service rendered by reason was the adaptation of the conception to the system as a whole. Buddhist philosophy, like philosophy generally, exists not to create fundamental beliefs but to defend and explain them in systematic development. Nor pyschologically is it difficult to understand the combination of beliefs in the minds of Mahāyānists; to believe in the self is certainly a hindrance to love of one's neighbour; to recognize the illusory character of all phenomena is no bad motive for compassion for all creatures

4. *The Virtue of Generosity or Compassion*

While insight by intense application of effort aims to eradicate the idea of being and the conception of the self, whose manifestations are directly attacked by the practice of calm of spirit (*çamatha*), generosity as a perfection (*pāramitā*) suppresses, by the abandonment of self-interest which it assumes, the manifestation of action and will; action thus serves effectively to destroy action.

The giver must not give for any personal advantage; he must practise what he is to realize in theory, the absence of difference between himself and others: what distinction is there between my pain and another's? If one should be relieved, so should

[1] Ç., pp. 165, 270; *Pañcakrama*, vi. 7; the doctrine is specially Tantric; JA. 1903, ii. 412, n. 1; *Subhāṣitasaṁgraha*, *Muséon*, v (1904), 250.

[2] Hardy, *Eastern Monachism*, p. 312; BCA. v. 50 ff.

that of another. He who loves himself must not love himself; to guard himself he must refrain from guarding himself. He must treat his neighbour precisely as himself.[1] We may support the idea by analogies; the pain which affects a limb is not that of the hand, yet the hand moves to relieve the injured member.[2] But a religious motive may have underlain the conception, and it is expressed frankly in Çāntideva;[3] every sin committed by us is committed against the saints who suffer from it, and our only method to recompense these blessed benefactors is to show kindness to others.

But, whatever the origin of the sentiment, it can be recognized only if accommodated to the system, and, if this forbids egoism, it equally forbids altruism, and sees no merit in the simple pity of the human heart for distress.[4] Altruism implies existence and is therefore fatal; there is no perfection, compassion, morality, patience (*kṣānti*), energy, concentration (*samādhi*), unless it be permeated by the essential intuition of nothingness; otherwise these virtues are blind and unavailing.[5] The gift, therefore, to be useful must be accompanied by the threefold purity—recognition of the non-existence of the gift itself, of the giver, and of the recipient; it must be born of compassion, indeed, but also of vacuity.[6] There is obvious difficulty in such a prescription; if there is no object to receive the gift, how can there be any giving? The answer[7] is that the recipient is imagined (*parikalpita*) by an error which is admitted in view of an end to be obtained (*kārya-moha*). The true end, of course, is Buddhahood, exempt from all form of imagination, all obscuration; but this is impossible without abstention from all phenomena on the part of the mind. This can be realized only by a long course of perfection of intuition, and the origin of the course lies in compassion, which at first accepts the relative reality of the existence of a suffering being, then dwells on the suffering alone, without accepting the existence of a sufferer, and finally has no

[1] BCA. viii. 90 ff.; Ç., p. 357.

[2] BCA. viii. 91.

[3] BCA. vi. 119, 122, 124; cf. ii. 51, 54, 64 ff.

[4] BCA. iii. 22; v. 87.

[5] PP. in BCAP. ix. 2.

[6] BCAP. ix. 4; Ç., p. 271. So of love (*maitrī*), Ç., p. 212.

[7] BCA. ix. 76 with comm. Voidness means much more than freedom from lust, hate, and delusion (Ç. trs., p. 247, n. 2).

object whatever. There are, we must admit, the two realms of truth, absolute and relative; the Buddha as intuition is well aware that there is no reality in the world, but, when moved by compassion, his love for the world is that of a father for his sick child. In the Buddha there is no idea of existence, but his pity is overflowing for beings troubled by the misery of life. There is an object for compassion, in the shape of the empirical individual composed of the aggregates (*skandhas*), even if that individual has no absolute reality.

But what is the end to be obtained which justifies the imagination of an individual? If there is no reality, how can any end be pursued? Is it not wrong to seek an illusion, since ignorance is essentially what must be laid aside to attain release? The answer is that there are two kinds of illusion: that which leads to implication in transmigration is evil, but that which holds out as our end the pursuit of the supreme truth with a view to save mankind is a noble belief to be commended and cherished. This element of seeking to assuage the sufferings of others robs the pursuit of enlightenment of its apparent egoism; the supreme end is to realize the vacuity of all things; but to attain this end it is necessary to accept the illusion of the end: the absolute truth must be approached through the realm of relativity.

The practical effect of the doctrine is to encourage the ideal of compassion for all beings; the taking of the vow not to attain Buddhahood[1] until all creatures have been delivered is the logical outcome of the spirit of this reasoning; the true Bodhisattva cannot be delivered until all creatures are delivered, and egoism is thus entirely annihilated. Such general compassion demands great energy in giving, for which even study should be sacrificed.[2] But generosity has its own reward; the Çrāvaka claims that his meditation is the more rapid way of gaining release, but in truth the Mahāyānist attains enlightenment (*bodhi*) and Buddhahood more rapidly by his practice of generosity;[3] when he takes the resolve to become a Buddha for the good of others, all his thoughts are dominated by the thought of enlightenment (*bodhi-citta*), all in

[1] For its terms cf. cit. in Ç., pp. 14, 228; *Sukhāvatīvyūha*, §§ 8 ff.
[2] BCA. v 101.
[3] BCA. vii. 29.

him becomes meritorious, and the car of the Mahāyāna bears him inevitably to the enlightenment which he does not desire for himself but seeks to attain solely for others. From physical suffering he is exempt, since he sins not; from moral suffering because he has knowledge; while others strive vainly for unsatisfying ends, he has pure delight in his own action of compassion.[1]

Compassion is a perfection of peculiar merit; while the rule is that the perfections should be practised in order of merit, an inferior being postponed to a superior, there is an exception for compassion, which is always permissible.[2] But what is more important, compassion excuses sin; it may be that its power is sufficient to turn desire, which else had secured torment in hell, into virtue rewarded by rebirth in the heaven of Brahmā; but even if it has not this power, yet a Bodhisattva will for the sake of compassion face the tortures of hell with alacrity.[3] The way is thus opened for the rehabilitation in some measure of desire; there is admitted a noble pride, which consists in combating pride and claiming the performance of distressing duties; the Bodhisattva may enjoy the pleasures of life, but by his power of intuition still secure rebirth in Brahmā's heaven; the virtue of charity covers a multitude of sins, while hatred is utterly condemned; there are means to counteract the errors of desire, which are hardly avoidable in the action of compassion.[4]

Compassion, however, must not lead to folly in generosity; Çāntideva has no illusions as to the folly of the man who hands over his body to the wild beast for food when he could confer on others the precious gift of knowledge of the true faith. Excessive giving is reprobated; there must be borne in mind the good of beings in general; neither egoism nor indiscriminate action is wise. Charity is one thing in the novice, another in him who has entered effectively into the path of salvation. The Mahāyāna may exaggerate the virtues of generosity, as is natural in a com-

[1] BCAP. ix. 76; BCA. i. 18 f.; vii. 27 f.; 63. On Bodhicitta, see JRAS. 1908, p. 891, correcting Suzuki, MB., pp. 52, 299 ff.; possessed of it, a man is Buddhagarbha, an embryo Buddha; Ç., p. 103.

[2] BCA. v. 83; Ç., p. 11.

[3] BCA. vi. 120; Ç., p. 167; cf. BCA. v. 42, 84.

[4] Ç., p. 165; on good *māna* see BCA. vii. 49, 54; cf. *Mahāvastu*, ii. 279; NP., p. 87. On hate see Ç., p. 165.

munity which lived on the exercise of that virtue by their patrons, but the relative sobriety of the doctrine is noteworthy.[1]

5. *Devotion and the Transfer of Merit*

So far the doctrine of the Mahāyāna does not essentially depart from views which the Hīnayāna allows, however different the emphasis. But the principle, that illusion may be encouraged if it serves to dispel illusion, opens up the way to the development of new ideas, or rather the acceptance by Buddhist philosophy of ideas too popular to be banished by a sane creed, which seeks to save mankind. Popular religion believed that devotion to a god, be it Kṛṣṇa, Viṣṇu, or Çiva, would aid in securing heaven or even liberation; it believed in the divine grace which the *Kaṭha Upaniṣad* and the Vedānta recognize as means of salvation. The Hīnayāna could find no room for either conception; the Buddha is a dead man, not a living and gracious god; each man must accept the result of his own actions, must work out his own salvation. The Mahāyāna departs from the rigour of either dogma; it is useful and therefore legitimate for man to believe in Bodhisattvas and Buddhas[2] who are eager to save and who can transfer merit; it is useful for Bodhisattvas in their career to have the belief that their intention to save others is actually capable of fulfilment. The doctrines therefore are legitimate, but the question remains whether or not they are valid merely on the basis of imaginary (*parikalpita*) reality, or whether they can be deemed relatively real—that is, as real as the doctrines of momentariness and causation. As a religion the Mahāyāna accepted without hesitation the reality of devotion and transfer of merit; the philosophy of the school, as might be expected, follows in its footsteps with hesitation, and realization of the real incompatibility of the new faith with the old doctrines. True, it is possible to revise these doctrines, for we have now the maxim that whatever is well said is a saying of the Buddha, but it is difficult to pour new wine into old bottles, and we must bear in mind the strength of the

[1] Ç., pp. 19 ff.; cf. p. 281; BCA. viii. 105.

[2] 'Those who worship the Bodhisattvas and read the Mahāyāna Sūtras are called the Mahāyānists'; I-Tsing (trans. Takakusu), p. 14.

tradition, which the Mahāyāna texts repeat: 'the Tathāgata alone is the witness; the Tathāgata alone knows; I know not.'[1]

Hence we find a curious medley of aspects presented in the Mahāyāna. The doctrine of the act is asserted in full force, and refined: the injuries suffered by a Bodhisattva are no longer penalties of past crime; they are opportunities earned for him by his merits to display his perfections of virtue[2] and goodness. But the matter may be carried farther; we owe it to the law itself that we are able to attain salvation, for even if it is our own past action which has won for us our voyage in the ship of humanity across the ocean of misery, under the rule of the law, still without the law this fate could not be ours. To the law, therefore, to the Buddha who taught the law, and to the order in which it is visibly embodied, we owe respect and devotion, and in paying homage to the three jewels and to the relics and shrines of the Buddha we strengthen our intention of following in the footsteps of the master, just as we strengthen our meditations by every exercise of our powers.[3]

This is in accord with even the Hīnayāna, but the Mahāyāna recognizes in the Bodhisattvas, who are alive, the qualities which permit of true devotion. It is, indeed, asserted that these holy beings can do us no good that we have not merited, though they are styled as 'loving without cause' and 'givers of fruits not asked'; but the essential fact is that we can profit ourselves by acts towards them which are openly and avowedly acts of pious worship and devotion. We owe them homage and adoration; we confess to them our sins: the misery we have caused to men is misery to the Bodhisattvas, the compassionate ones, and we admit our wrongdoing that the saints whom we have injured may pardon it.[4] We rejoice in the merits acquired by the Bodhisattvas; we supplicate the Buddhas to light the lamp of the law, and beg them to delay their entry into Nirvāṇa in order that they may continue to save creatures. We apply also our merit for the

[1] Ç., p. 55.
[2] BCA. vi. 106. Cf. KV. xvi. 3: no one can give happiness or misery to another.
[3] BCA. vi. 112 ff.; vii. 14; ix. 37; BCAP. ii. 49.
[4] BCA. vi. 119, 122, 124. Cf. Ç., pp. 160 ff.

benefit of others; we cannot in any other way serve the Bodhisattvas, who have no need of our devotion for themselves, but rejoice in the work of salvation. The culminating act of this devotional service or Bhadracaryā[1] is an action, the surrender of oneself to the Bodhisattvas and Buddhas (*ātmabhāvaniryātanā*),[2] a rite interesting because it is mentioned by the orthodox Buddhaghosa. The formula in Sanskrit is decisive of the spirit of the action: 'I hand myself over to the Jinas, and to their sons, all in all. Accept me, ye sublime beings. With devotion (*bhakti*) I become your slave.' We have in this the fullest acceptance of theism; the Bodhisattvas and their spiritual fathers, the Buddhas or Jinas, conquerors, are regarded as powerful to save, endowed with the power of forgiving sins. But we must not be deceived into believing that we are on the ground of relative truth; there is nothing to prove that we are in anything more than the region of imagination.

It is less certain if the transfer of merit (*puṇya-pariṇāmanā*) is to be deemed purely imaginary, or if it belongs to the realm of relative truth. For the transfer may be regarded as nothing more than the carrying to the logical extremity of the perfection of generosity; it is certainly no true gift that is given for one's own advantage, and it is a logical result to conclude that the giver should will that the fruit of his giving, which accrues as the result of his unselfish gift, should pass to the recipient of the gift also.[3] But a strongly religious aspect is introduced by the doctrine that by the transfer of merit one can best please the merciful Bodhisattvas and Buddhas; the sincerity of this belief in Çāntideva is unmistakable, and it is clear that the borderland between imaginary and apparent truth is reached in his view. The importance of the idea is capital; it is carried even to the grotesque;

[1] See the *Bhadracarīpraṇidhānagāthā* (Leipzig, 1912); Ç., p. 290, emphasizes the features as confession of sin (*pāpadeçanā*); delight in merit (*puṇyānumodanā*); and solicitation of the Buddhas (*buddhādhyeṣaṇā*); BCA. ii. 24 ff.; iii. 1 ff.; v. 98 f.; x; *Dharmasaṁgraha*, 14; *Adikarmapradīpa* (in Poussin, pp. 106, 226 ff.); *Svayambhū Purāṇa*, pp. 117 f.; MKV., p. 292, n. 4 (*triskandhaka*).

[2] BCA. ii. 8; Sumañg. i. 231 ff.

[3] Cf. the Vedānta doctrine of indifference to the fruit of deeds (*ihāmutraphalabhogavirāga*). For the Hīnayāna denial of the Hetuvādin precursor of Pariṇāmanā see KV. xvi 3; on the term cf. *Mahāyānaçraddh.*, p. 146; JRAS. 1908, p. 887. Cf. Ç., pp. 28 f., 170, 213, 296.

nothing whatever—save enlightenment itself which reconciles altruism and egoism—should be sought for the self; even food which the layman enjoys, which the adept of the Hīnayāna takes as nourishment, should be consumed merely to gratifiy the eighty-four thousand animalculae which live in the human organism. True, it is Buddhas alone who can be certain that they can transfer merit with success, but that does not prevent us from seeking to transfer ours, even if we err in our aim. The excellence of the cause excuses failures in performance.[1]

6. *The Doctrine of the Act and the Causal Series*

How far is it possible to reconcile the new doctrine with the metaphysical views of the Mahāyāna schools? The question is difficult, and not the less so because it is one which these schools themselves do not clearly pose or perhaps realize; in this, as always, Buddhist philosophy is content with partial enunciations and makes no effort to systematize its conceptions and reduce them to a coherent whole, even within the limits possible.

From the point of view of the Vijñānavāda there seems no chance of permitting either divine intervention or the transfer of merit; it denies the external world; it admits only the existence of thought series, self-determining, and the whole apparatus of salvation cannot be accorded any real basis. The case is not so simple with the Madhyamaka, which accepts the double form of the chain of causation, internal and external, though it denies either any absolute reality. It is true that, though the intervention of external objects thus becomes possible and in a sense real, as real as the intellectual elements, strictly speaking the material universe ought to provide its material forms for the carrying into effect of the fruition of earlier actions; the eye should give vision for enjoyment or misery to a being who has merited such recompense, just as the embryo is formed in the womb to receive such and such a consciousness.[2] Such a scheme,

[1] BCAP. vi. 50. As to eating cf. Mil., pp. 367, 378; BCA. v. 85; Ç., p. 127.
[2] Poussin, JA. 1903, ii. 442 ff. His view that the Pali Abhidhamma recognizes this doctrine is clearly invalid in view of KV. xvii. 3, for xvi. 3 is limited in application, dealing only with a form of transfer doctrine, not

it is plain, excludes rigidly the freedom of the will, or any solidarity between men or super-men; there exist, we admit, numerous series, some alive, some without life, each causally determined, but without true interaction of any sort or kind.

But it does not seem that the Mahāyāna was content to rest in this position, though there is no formal abandonment of it.[1] We find, however, the chain of causation styled incomprehensible (*acintya*); compassion produces the knowledge of the true reality, despite the utter disparity of cause and effect; consciousness perceives an external object simultaneously.[2] Moreover, the problem of release is insoluble also; it appears that the thought of enlightenment contends with the sins of man,[3] and that ultimately an innate tendency of the mind, without any effort being required, causes the balance to incline to the desired result. Is it not, then, possible that the mind whose resolves can mould nature should be able to affect other minds by the power of its will or desire? The formal application of one's merit in the formula of truth (*satya-vacana*) avails to reanimate the dead; can it not equally create a good thought in the mind of another? Avalokita, we know, has consecrated his name for the comfort of all who invoke it,[4] and, as Çāntideva tells us, 'the Omniscient alone knoweth the incomprehensible path of action, in that he doth lead to release men even when they have abandoned thought of enlightenment.'[5] There is room here for solidarity as well as liberty, but the Mahāyāna is too immeshed in its own negations to lead us to any effective development.

7. *The Career of the Bodhisattva*

On the basis of these confused reasonings and practices is built the imposing edifice of the career of the Bodhisattva, whose being

generally with action as uncaused by anything extraneous to itself, so that it does not affect the denial of action from action in xvii. 3. Truth to tell, the problem is not clearly envisaged. Cf. p. 173.

[1] Poussin, JA. 1903, ii. 394, n. 2, 447 ff.

[2] BCAP. ix. 4; BCA. ix. 100. In the Nyāya Īçvara is incomprehensible, BCA. ix. 127, and so is the Buddha's law and the happiness of his life; Ç., pp. 260, 213.

[3] BCA. iv. 11; cit. in *Bhāmatī*, p. 25; JBRAS. xviii. 343.

[4] BCA. viii. 118.

[5] BCA. iv. 27.

is enlightenment because he aims at that end in the form of Buddhahood. The Bodhisattva is indeed the characteristic feature of the Mahāyāna, the ideal which distinguishes it from the Hīnayāna with its conception of the Arhant intent on his own salvation in the attainment of Nirvāṇa. The path of the Bodhisattva appears, indeed, sometimes as the only true way of salvation; the ideal of the Hīnayāna is essentially merely a stage on the route which is mistaken by the Çrāvakas for the reality, even as travellers are cheered on their way by the sight of a magic city created by the clever leader of the caravan; we are all sons of the Buddha, and Buddhas to be, but we may long fail to realize the high glory to which we are called, and think even the reward of Nirvāṇa far too great for our humble merits. The supreme meditation of the Hīnayāna is deemed but a preliminary exercise (*bālopacārika*) by the Vijñānavāda of the *Lañkāvatāra*. The Hīnayāna indeed commits the fundamental error of not realizing the difficulty of realizing the truth, for he does not understand the truth; he accepts the non-existence of the self, he strives to eliminate desire. But he believes in the aggregates as real, he accepts misery as real, and he does not know that in thought there is the food which nourishes desire for ever. To destroy thought is essential, and that is far from easy even for those who know that all is void; it is impossible for the Çrāvaka; all his efforts in earth can procure him merely a few minutes of unconsciousness, or if he die in trance—no easy matter—rebirth in the world of the unconscious gods, which again is a mere transitory state, one into which the Buddha has never deigned to enter. There is absurdity also in the idea that the desire of Nirvāṇa is anything else save egoistic; the Çrāvaka goes a very little way in his conception of the true dangers of egoism which his own career too closely illustrates.[1]

The true ideal is a very different one, that of the search for enlightenment undertaken for the sake of others without any touch of egoism, and prolonged for three incalculable (*asaṁkhyeya*)[2] periods, during which the Bodhisattva develops the perfections of virtue, above all generosity and charity, for the benefit of

[1] BCA. viii. 145.

[2] See Poussin, *Bouddhisme*, p. 294, n. 1.

others. The idea is not wholly strange to the Hīnayāna; we have the Buddha's own authority for the advent of Maitreya, but it is in the latest phase alone, the *Jātakas* and the *Abhidharmakoça*, that, the idea becomes distinct. The legend of Pūrṇa,[1] in outline canonical, however, reveals the spirit of the new faith; suddenly converted, the monk demands a summary of the doctrine that he may straightway teach others the doctrine of salvation, and his chosen field of work is the barbarous people of Çroṇāparantaka, where he is assured of suffering. The later version of the legend accords to him some of the distinctive marks of the Buddha himself, proof of his extraordinary merit. With this legend accord the birth-tales of the Buddha, destined to exhibit the superhuman generosity and compassion which mark him out, a trace perhaps of a real characteristic of a master of whom, despite the Canon, we know personally so little that seems real. But in the Hīnayāna these elements are indeed of secondary importance, and do not alter the essential fact that the ideal set before us is the Arhant and Nirvāṇa.

The Bodhisattva, on the other hand, has chosen a very different lot; of himself, or rather at the suggestion of the Buddhas, for such a resolve is too sublime for human conception unaided, he has taken the vow, which Çākyamuni and all the Buddhas have taken before him, to become a Buddha—for the Buddhas alone can save beings—and to accumulate for salvation the vast store of merits of the career of a Buddha to be. This involves the utter renunciation of the temptation to enter Nirvāṇa, and the resolution to remain in transmigration for incalculable ages, and to sacrifice himself entirely to others. This is the undertaking of the thought of enlightenment, and the solemn vow is preceded by calm deliberation on the deeds to be done and the sufferings to be endured, followed by the paying of homage to the Buddhas and Bodhisattvas.[2] The formula in one version[3] runs: 'I, N.N., in the presence of my master, N. N., and of all the Buddhas, produce

[1] SN. iv. 60; MN. iii. 267; *Divyāvadāna*, pp. 24 ff, For the same ideas in Mahāyāna cf. BCA. viii. 125-9, 134-6, 173, 174; *Saddharmapuṇḍarīka*, x. 25.

[2] BCA. ii. 7; iii. 6-21.

[3] *Bodhisattvaprātimokṣa* in Poussin, *op. cit.*, p. 303. Cf. *Bodhicitta* of Vasubandhu, in Suzuki, MB., pp. 307 ff.

the thought of enlightenment. I apply to the acquisition of the quality of the perfect Buddha the merit of my confession, of my taking refuge in the three jewels, Buddha, the law and the order, and of my production of the thought of enlightenment. May I in this universe of creatures, at a time when no Buddha appears, be the refuge, the shelter, the safety, the island of creatures; may I make them cross the ocean of existences. I adopt as mother, father, brothers, sons, sisters, all creatures. Henceforth for the happiness of creatures I will practise with all my power generosity, morality, patience, energy, meditation, knowledge, skill in the means of salvation. I am a Buddha to be. May my master accept me as a Buddha to be.' A formal acceptance by the master completes the rite.

The monk then enters on the first part of his long journey to Buddhahood, during which he is only a beginner (*ādikarmika*), capable of sin and of suffering in hell, for great as is his undertaking the more heinous his departures from virtue. But his progress is sure; his prayers render it certain. He studies misery, destroying pride and begetting charity and love for the compassionate Buddhas. He practises patience; injuries done to us are either penalties for ancient evil or opportunities for our exercise of virtue. He eradicates the belief in self by meditation and study, largely also by charity, humility, and self-sacrifice. He learns the hard lesson of treating one's neighbour as oneself,[1] of regarding all beings as if they were Buddhas. It is his aim to serve every creature on earth so long as any of them is not delivered from the round of existence.

After a long period of preliminary effort[2] the Bodhisattva attains a stage at which with utter sincerity and full appreciation he can repeat definitely the vow with which he started on his course, and thus he enters on the first of the ten stages into which an elaborate and unsatisfactory scholasticism[3] divides the progress of the

[1] BCA. viii.

[2] Divided into two stages, *gotra-bhūmi*, in which the aspirant forms himself, or is formed by birth, to take the vow; *adhimukticaryā-bhūmi*, the preliminary preparation for entering on the stages.

[3] The classical authority is the *Daçabhūmaka*; see also the *Mahāvastu*, i. 63-193; *Dharmasaṁgraha*, 64. A *Daçabhūmikleçacchedikā* is alleged to have been trans. in A.D. 70; Poussin, *Bouddhisme*, p. 309, n.

Bodhisattva, inventing distinctions without substantial difference. There is now no possibility of failure, no chance of an inferior birth, his passions are consumed in the fire of his charity, he enjoys a series of glorious births, universal monarch, the god Brahmā, king of the highest heavens, where he propagates the reign of justice. From the seventh stage his knowledge and his meditative power accord with his merits; thereafter he figures as a prince in the heaven of some Buddha, descending in magic incarnations to earth to accomplish his work of conversion. In the tenth stage, the cloud of the law (*dharma-meghā*) he attains the position of Lord of the Law, he becomes a Buddha, and creates a body endowed with all the magic signs to play the part on earth of Çākyamuni and countless other Buddhas.

Intuition of vacuity and compassion are the two great concerns of the Bodhisattva; two whole incalculable ages must pass ere he attains in the eighth stage the knowledge of the wholly empty character of all phenomena. Aware as he his from the outset of the vacuity of things, he acts as if they were real and as if their misery were real; his occupation is active [1] and energetic exhibition of compassion to all suffering creatures, and, as we have seen, this compassion leads assuredly if indirectly to the attainment of that complete insight which ensures Buddhahood.

It would be easy, but fruitless, to insist on the incoherence and confusion of the doctrine of the stages of progress, but there are some fundamental features of the stages which are worth mention; the process as it appears to Asañga [2] is one in which the adept rises from the mere self to appreciate that absolute in which the ideas of self and other are wholly lost, with the loss of the distinction of self and object. The appreciation is in experience very different from the mere knowledge of the fact of vacuity, which is attained in the first or Joyous (*muditā*) stage; he realizes the emptiness of self, and of other things (*dharma*) also; he appreciates their common nature as merely ideal (*dharmatā*). In the second or Pure (*vimalā*) stage there is freedom from sin; thought freed from the infections or defilement engages in meditation (*dhyāna*)

[1] BCA. vii. 65.
[2] See Lévi, ii.* 21 f, and cf. Suzuki, MB. ch. xii from a variety of texts.

and mystic union (*samādhi*). The third stage of Illumination (*prabhākarī*) permits the aspirant to enter the world of desire without running risk of corruption, and to engage in his work of preparing creatures for salvation. He aims at winning intuition (*prajñā*), and in the fourth stage, that of Brightness (*arciṣmatī*), he practises the thirty-seven wings of enlightenment (*bodhipakṣa*)[1] and through them he is able to conquer the defilements and ignorance, and to transfer the benefit of his already enormous merits for the benefit of creatures. The fifth stage, Hard to win (*durjayā*), is one in which wisdom attains higher development; all is appreciated as reducing itself to the four noble truths. The next stage, Right in front (*abhimukhī*), advances to the appreciation of the chain of causality (*pratītyasamutpāda*) alone; it is right in face of Nirvāṇa as of transmigration. All is pure; there is neither good nor evil; all personal feeling is utterly eliminated. The seventh stage, Going far (*dūraṁgamā*), completes the work of the other six; there is now gained the fruit of previous study, while further study is unnecessary, but the passivity of thought is affected by the impressions of earlier mental activity.

The eighth stage, the Immovable (*acalā*), marks a definite advance; the aspirant now knows where and when he will become a Buddha, and the usual formal prophecy (*vyākaraṇa*) of his advent in that capacity is now made by a Buddha on his behalf. His powers of aiding mortals now perfect themselves; his means are never lacking nor ineffective. He attains complete impassivity, and need not apply himself to develop the thought of enlightenment, which itself develops without his collaboration as the result of the past. The idea of production utterly disappears for him; the ideal world sinks into final rest. In the ninth stage of Good Thought (*sādhumatī*), possessed of complete wisdom, he brings to pass the preparation of creatures for Nirvāṇa. In the tenth stage, Cloud of the Law (*dharmameghā*), he receives from all the Buddhas consecration for Buddhahood; his body of the law is now complete, and he can exhibit those magic transformations which mark the end of the career of a Bodhisattva.

This is not very intelligible, and there are some fundamental

[1] *Dharmasaṁgraha*, 43; Kern, *Ind. Buddh.*, p. 67; DN. ii. 120; SBB. iii. 128 f.

issues worthy of attention. Has the monk any real choice? Is the only way to salvation the road of the Bodhisattva, so that the desire to acquire enlightenment and the vow undertaken are inevitably connected? If this query were to be answered in the affirmative,[1] the merit of the Bodhisattva would sensibly be reduced, and there is, as we have seen, Mahāyāna evidence in favour of this view. But the more orthodox doctrine of the school seems otherwise; Hiuen-Tsang evidently did not accept the view that all men were destined to be Buddhas, and we hear of Arhants in the heaven of Amitābha, so that the choice of Bodhisattvahood seems a genuine act of free will. But is the career of the Bodhisattva so full of real self-sacrifice as the terms used of it suggest?

The query is hard to answer. Bodhisattvas indeed are encouraged to endure sufferings for the sake of the salvation of mortals, but are their sufferings real? In some cases certainly not;[2] when great deities like Vajrapāṇi, Mañjughoṣa, Padmapāṇi, descend to hell, they turn the fierce flames and biting cold of the lower regions into abodes of paradise, or bring away with them, purified from sin, the hosts of the damned. On the other hand, there is developed the conception[3] of the Bodhisattva who seeks to take upon himself all the sins of the world, content to bear the punishment for them because he has undertaken the vow to save all the creatures of the world. What is the import of the doctrine, whose Christian savour has attracted misconception? It is clear that it is largely due to the need for some mode of terminating the eternal punishment of sin; sin not merely produces a fruit of suffering, but begets a sinful disposition,[4] in which no merit can arise to win the possibility of release from punishment; the merits of others, therefore, are necessary for their redemption, while the sins cannot fail of fruition and so must be imputed to the saint. The doctrine is indeed an extreme development of the

[1] *Saddharmapuṇḍarīka*, iv. But see MA., p. 280; Watters, i. 164.

[2] BCA. x. 11 ff.; cf. viii. 107; Ç., p. 360.

[3] *Vajradhvaja Sūtra*, Ç., p. 280; BCA. x. 36; vii. 49 f. See Kumārila's retort on the absurdity of a Kṣatriya's teaching Brahmins, *Tantravārttika*, p. 116.

[4] *Vipāka-* and *Niṣyanda-phala*. KV. xiii. 2 condemns this as an Uttarāpathaka heresy.

belief in the power of thought to affect other lives, as well as creating a powerful impression for good in one's own, and the Indian belief in the magic power of speech may have rendered it more easy of acceptance. But the whole is utterly ideal; there is no real acceptance by the Bodhisattva of punishment for the sins of others, no real taking upon himself of their sin as morally evil, and a crushing burden on the soul. Even for his own earlier sins the Bodhisattva pays merely a nominal penalty,[1] and, having once entered upon the stages, his virtue is supreme and neither physical nor moral evil can assail him.

It is true, however, that in practice there was some tendency to impose on the Bodhisattva the endurance of physical suffering, extending even to cremation among Chinese monks, as in the case of a Buddha of the *Saddharmapuṇḍarīka*, and we hear even in Çāntideva of the possibility of the gift of one's flesh, an idea familiar from the Jātakas; it is possible, since by losing any belief in self the painful sensation is not felt by the Bodhisattva as his. But I-Tsing denies that such rites are for novices, and most Buddhists are content at most with the minor sacrifice known in Tibet and Cambodia, which leaves the corpses of the devout for animals to devour.[2] But these ideas are normally suppressed by the good sense of Buddhism; Çāntideva insists on the care which the Buddha takes of his own body, of his keeping his robe, of his judgement in deciding when self-sacrifice of any sort is just and in the interest of creatures as a whole; to do him justice, but for tradition his exposition would probably have been free from exaggeration and folly.[3]

The true gift of the Bodhisattva is not his flesh, but the gift of the law, and the Mahāyāna[4] recognizes the missionary activity of such beings while history records their influence on Chinese, Scythians, Turks, Tibetans, and many other races. Other works of the Bodhisattvas are study of the law, the composition of treatises upon it, the copying of manuscripts, a busy intellectual

[1] MA., p. 39.

[2] J. J. M. de Groot, *Code du Mahāyāna en Chine*, p. 230; BCA. vi. 25 f.; MA., p. 29; Takakusu, ch. xxxviii, xxxix[1]; Ç., p. 158. Contrast MV. vi. 23.

[3] BCA. v. 86 f.; BSB. I. ix; Ç., pp. 34 ff.

[4] As also the Hīnayāna; MV. i. 5. 12.

existence from non-existence, while at the same time it holds that all mental complexes are derived from the four psychical aggregates and material complexes from the atoms. The Madhyamaka doctrine fares even worse, being dismissed contemptuously on the ground that its tenet of vacuity is contradicted by every means of knowledge.[1]

[1] On BS. ii. 2. 32. Rāmānuja (ii. 2. 30) points out that nothingness is merely a form of existence, and that its proof involves the existence of the proof, and contradicts the result.

nothing can act on itself, the lamp cannot manifest itself save with the concurrence of the eye; the idea must be known by the self. Nor is there any regress *ad infinitum* here: the self is self revealed, not the object of an idea, and is not an idea.

The argument from the nature of dreams or illusions is effectively refuted by insisting, first, that dreams and illusions are shown to be different from waking consciousness because their objects are negated by that consciousness, while waking consciousness has objects which are not negated by any other state. Secondly, dream consciousness is founded on remembrance as opposed to immediate consciousness and the distinction between the two is felt by all to be based on the absence and presence of the object respectively. To argue that waking consciousness is false, because it resembles dream consciousness, is as absurd as to argue that water is hot, because it shares attributes with fire or *vice versa.*[1]

The attempt to deduce the external world from mental impressions is also refuted. It involves an idle *regressus ad infinitum* in order to avoid the normal admission that impressions are derived from external things. Moreover, it is impossible for any impression to be left when there is no permanent substratum like a self on which the impression is to be recorded. If the receptacle intellect (*ālayavijñāna*) is put forward as the substratum, then the Buddhist either contradicts the doctrine of momentariness and supplies a quasi-self, or, if he maintains momentariness of this intellect also, his position is impossible; remembrance, recognition, and so on require some permanent reality. Recognition of 'this' as similar to 'that' cannot be made without the presence of a self which can remember and compare; recognition of a thing as the same attests also the permanence of the object, and is illustrated completely by the recognition of the permanence of the self on which no one is mistaken.[2] The Vijñānavāda, therefore, is no more tenable than the view of the realists which fails utterly to account for the existence of the aggregates making up the self, which advances a theory of causation absurd on account of the parallel theory of momentariness, and which asserts the origin of

[1] On BS. ii. 2. 29. [2] On BS. ii. 2. 30, 31.

without external things, whence we deduce that all consciousness exists without such things; the variety of our experience is explained by the presence in our consciousness of the impressions of ideas, the stream of ideas and impressions continuing unbroken for ever, and excluding any need of external reality.

The Vedānta reply is that the analysis given is artificial; in our perception of external reality we have the consciousness and the object as two distinct and irreducible psychological elements. This is in effect admitted by the Vijñānavāda which admits that objects appear as if external (*bāhyavat*), an expression which is explicable only because those who use it at the bottom of their hearts recognize the existence of that which is external. It is useless to urge that the expression is justified, because external things are impossible: possibility must be judged on the basis of the operation of the means of correct knowledge, and not made to depend on *a priori* ratiocination. Possible is whatever is apprehended by perception or other means of cognition, and external things are essentially so apprehended, a fact which outweighs the sophistical dilemma of difference or non-difference from atoms. Examination of perception reveals that the idea is the means of knowing the external object which dictates its shape; the distinction of consciousness and external reality can be made clear, if we consider the perception and recollection of a jar, where there is change in consciousness with permanence of object, or the successive consciousness of two different objects, when consciousness remains in principle the same, but its distinctive attributes differ.

More fundamental still is the onslaught on the momentary character of ideas; this doctrine, if logically followed out, is fatal to the distinction of ideas, to the differentiation of classes and individuals, to the conception of the leaving of impressions on the mind, to the doctrine of the confusion owing to nescience of existence and non-existence, and consequently to the doctrine of bondage and release, for all these matters depend on the possibility of comparison of ideas, which is inconceivable unless there is a permanent knowing subject and not merely momentary ideas. It is idle to seek to evade this result by holding that the idea knows itself, as a lamp illuminates itself. But this is false;

close relationship, and if Gauḍapāda[1] and his commentator—whose identity with Çañkara need not be assumed[2]—deny that the Buddha taught as finally real that knowledge without duality which has no distinction of knower, known and knowledge, the fact goes flatly in the face of all Buddhist evidence. Gauḍapāda in fact borrows without wishing to admit his debt in full. But in a sense he had, of course, the right as an Aupaniṣada in his Kārikās, whatever his earlier faith, to borrow; the Mahāyāna in its turn had doubtless drawn from the stream of Aupaniṣada tradition in its conception of the final reality of the world.

The attitude of Çañkara is interesting, as he expounds with much clearness the Vijñānavāda position, in opposition to the realistic doctrines of the Sarvāstivādins, whether Vaibhāṣikas or Sautrāntikas, and explains fully his own objections to the Vijñānavāda.[3] The Vijñānavāda maintains the sole existence of the threefold process of knowledge, which may be analysed as apparent subject, object, and consciousness or knowledge. The existence of external things is denied on the score of impossibility; they must either be atoms or aggregates of atoms; if the former they are incomprehensible on the score of minuteness; if aggregates, they must either be different from the atoms, which is a contradiction in terms, or they must be non-different, in which case they cannot produce impressions of gross non-atomic bodies. Moreover, our cognitions constantly differ in content; this is impossible unless they take the form of the objects, and, if this is so, it is needless to assume external things. Further, we are always conscious simultaneously of the act and the object of knowledge which proves identity, since else we could at one time know the object, at another know consciousness. Again, we have the fact of dream consciousness

[1] iv. 99.

[2] Cf. Deussen, *Sechzig Upanishads*, p. 478, n. 1.

[3] On BS. ii. 2, 28 ff. For Nyāya criticism cf. Jacobi, JAOS. xxxi. 9 ff.; Keith, JRAS. 1914, p. 1090; ILA., pp. 22 f., 99 f., 208 ff.; NM., pp. 536 f., 548 f.; for Mīmāṅsā, Keith, KM. pp. 46 ff. For a formal examination from a Kantian standpoint see Walleser, *Der ältere Vedānta*, pp. 40 ff. For Rāmānuja's critique, see *Çrībhāṣya*, ii. 2. 27. Of the original sense of the Sūtra it is difficult to be certain; cf. JAOS. xxxi. 13 ff.; V. S. Ghate, *Le Vedānta*, pp. 44 f. For Sāṅkhya criticism see Aniruddha on SS. i. 42 f.; in v. 77–9 it is shown that on either Madhyamaka or Vijñānavāda principles liberation is inconceivable; in v. 91–3 the existence of genus is defended.

activity which is not suggestive of renunciation or unhappiness. For the layman who is a Bodhisattva there is always the duty of aiding the monks, of providing for their needs and building them monasteries. The Mahāyāna in fact provides for monks and laity alike a vista of helpful and cheerful activity, imbued with the desire to aid others as the only possible means indirectly of aiding oneself.

8. *Defects of the New Ideal*

It was natural[1] enough that the Hīnayāna should deny the authenticity of Mahāyāna scriptures, should proclaim the doctrine of the void and of the ten stages new inventions without the authority of the master, should inveigh against the blasphemy of multiplying Buddhas and urging each person to become one, and should insist on the supreme importance of Nirvāṇa and the ideal of the Arhant, who is infinitely superior, as legend shows, to any Bodhisattva, even Maitreya himself, who now dwells in the Tuṣita heaven awaiting his descent. They could censure also the strict régime of the new faith which forbade all use of meat,[2] and not merely that of meat killed expressly for the monks, the foolish mutilations sometimes practised, the idolatry and temple worship of the Buddhas and Bodhisattvas, and the abandonment of monastic discipline. Some of their complaints were justified, if some were not, and the new doctrine undoubtedly presented points of serious weakness. It was doubtless well to realize the difficulty of contending with desire, and to be discontented with the narrow ideal of the Arhant. But there was also dangerous laxity in the concessions made to the spirit of accommodation to life. The doctrine of benefiting others leads to permission to sin if thus the happiness of others can be attained, and it is a vital point that it is left to the judgement of the Bodhisattva to decide for himself whether sin will bring happiness to others; there is no strict code, enacted by authority, to fetter his judgement.[3] The sin may bring him pleasure, but that is no reason why he should not

[1] Poussin, *Bouddhisme*, pp. 315 ff.; Wassilieff, *Bouddhisme*, pp. 262 ff.
[2] Ç., pp. 132, 174; BCA. v. 97.
[3] BCA. v. 84; Ç., p. 167.

commit it if he has the excuse of conferring benefits on others. Marriage thus can always be justified, for it brings pleasure to the other party to the union; any vow, however strict, may be broken for a greater gain, the breaker being the sole judge. There is no disgust with life, no turning away from the world required; indeed one who for incalculable periods will remain in existence after existence could not possibly carry out his plan, if he did not love in his own way the world. A Bodhisattva, then, can enjoy to the full all forms of pleasure of sense, and if he sins in the pursuit, even then he has succour available. The thought of enlightenment will, renewed, secure him immunity from penalty, and beyond this there is available a simple daily rite which removes sin; by confession morning, midday, and evening, by homage to the Buddhas, and the expression of universal love, the Bodhisattva secures his purity, extinguishing at each time the sins committed in the preceding period. He is surrounded in his everyday life by influences interested for his good; his minor transgressions he casts aside by confession to his fellow monks, from ten to one in number according to the nature of his fault, while the grave crimes, such as those of schism, parricide, slaying an Arhant or Buddha, breaking of relics, are pardoned without the necessity of auricular confession by the thirty-five Buddhas of confession.[1] Small wonder if the Mahāyānist can regard his vehicle as drawn by antelopes in comparison with the crawling ox-cart of the Hīnayāna,[2] with its uncertainty of a successful journey, with dim hope of the remission of sins, without Buddhas to comfort or aid, with strict celibacy and monastic observances, and without the inspiration of benefiting creatures. We have here a very different aspect of the ideal of the Bodhisattva from that which regards him as accepting misery for the sake of the world, and doubtless one more psychologically true. The Mahāyāna claimed adherence generally not as adding to the burdens of men, but as supplying them with an ideal more human, more attractive, than that of the narrow selfish aims of the Arhant.

One must not, of course, exaggerate the laxity of the system; in many regards the monastic ideal of the Mahāyāna was strict,

[1] Ç., pp. 169 ff. [2] Ç., p. 7.

stricter than the Hīnayāna in its insistence on refraining from the use of meat, and the permission given to the Bodhisattva to sin in the cause of compassion is rather a glorification of the merits of compassion[1] than an invitation to violate the moral law. But the risk of laxity was present, and the danger was made essentially real by the relaxation of the monastic system under whose aegis the Hīnayāna had developed the teaching of the Buddha. The old difficulty regarding the possibility of the layman becoming an Arhant has totally disappeared; the married man is peculiarly suited for the task of a Bodhisattva, for Çakyamuni lived in the world and is his prototype; only he who has a wife is capable of the supreme act of generosity recorded of saints, the gift of wife and children to others, and only a wife can take the typical vow of marital faith, to live with her husband from existence to existence.[2] In lieu, then, of the rigours of monasticism as the sole path to salvation, we find the attainment of Buddhahood available to the man in family life; religion penetrates into the family life; each family of believers is one of Buddhas to be, with its relics and images, a domestic ritual, and rules laid down by sages for the conduct of domestic life.[3]

The roots of monasticism were thus threatened; the Hīnayāna had permitted, perhaps illogically,[4] the withdrawal at pleasure of the monk from his vows, but this sensible provision becomes transformed into the absurdity by which the monastic vows are formally taken and a few days after the monk admits his inability to keep them and asks acceptance instead as a Buddha to be, forthwith returning to the world. In Nepal, as once in Kashmir, the final step was taken; the idea of monasticism was utterly overthrown and a married community, a caste in itself, filled the convents once devoted to celibate monks or nuns.[5] The discipline

[1] See also BCA. vii. 67 ff. on control of passion.

[2] Possibly this is referred to in KV. xxiii. 1 (Andhakas and Vetulyakas).

[3] Cf. Ç., pp. 78 ff. On the evils resulting cf. *Rāṣṭrapālaparipṛcchā*, pp. ix f., 28 ff.

[4] VP. iii. 27; Mil., p. 246; Minayeff, *Recherches*, pp. 271 ff.; Köppen, *Rel. des Buddha*, i. 338; Hardy, *Eastern Monachism*, p. 46; De Groot, *Code du Mahāyāna*, p. 211. The advantages of a temporary acceptance of Buddhist vows in gaining Amitābha's heaven are stated in Ç., p. 175.

[5] Hodgson, *Essays*, pp. 52, 139; S. Lévi, *Le Népal*, ii. 30; for Kashmir, *Rājataraṅgiṇī*, iii. 12.

had broken to pieces, and yet it must be said that the result was not incompatible with the doctrines of the Mahāyāna.[1]

9. *The Buddhas*

In the Mahāyāna the humanity of the Buddha, enfeebled already in the Hīnayāna, definitely disappears. The Buddha of the *Saddharmapuṇḍarīka* and generally of the texts has attained enlightenment at a period unknown to us, presumably at the beginning of the cosmic age, but he claims to have taught the law for numberless periods of tens of millions of cosmic periods. He possesses the true body of enjoyment of a Buddha, revealed to the Bodhisattvas who in countless numbers hearken to his teaching, and the *Saddharmapuṇḍarīka* exhausts its fertility, as well as the patience of its readers, in its account of the marvels[2] which accompany his teaching. To mortal men, on the other hand, there is normally visible only a transformation body, such as that of the historical Çākyamuni, created for the purpose of edification of the multitude. In point of fact the Buddha's true body dwells in a heaven of supreme bliss, waiting until the true Nirvāṇa, when it will, in accordance with his vow, enter into a Stūpa, a celestial parallel to the relic chambers made by men on earth. There he will enjoy the pleasure of repose after his toil of enlightenment, to rise from time to time at the request of a colleague.[3]

The idea of colleagues is a sufficient sign of divergence between the Hīnayāna and the new view. That school contended that two Buddhas could not coexist in the same universe, perhaps not even in different systems;[4] only six earlier Buddhas appear in the Nikāyas; even at the close of the Pali Canon no more than twenty-four prior Buddhas had been enumerated.[5] But speculations on

[1] In I-Tsing (trs., p. 15) we find already the doctrine of the void as a source of neglect of morality. The *Tathāgataguhyaka* (NBL., pp. 261–4) and *Subhāṣitasaṁgraha* (ed. Bendall), p. 41, advocate sin as a mode of attaining the end.

[2] The miraculous tongue of the Buddha is compared by Kern (p. xxxi) with *Bhagavadgītā*, xi. 30.

[3] Kern, p. 227.

[4] AṄ. i. 27; KV. xxi. 6, against the Mahāsaṅghikas.

[5] The Bharhut sculptures know only six. For cosmic speculations see DN. ii. 2 ff.

cosmic ages are already known to the Canon; the plurality of worlds was accepted, and it was no difficult step to draw the conclusion that Buddhas might coexist, as well as to carry back to infinity the line of Buddhas. Hence we attain the result achieved already in the *Mahāvastu* and the *Lalitavistara*, which regards Buddhas as coexisting in countless numbers in time and space.[1] The advantages of such a view are obvious; space is given for the development of a complete pantheon and for the gratification of varied tastes in divinity.

The process is somewhat unkind to Çākyamuni. Some at least regard him with less than complete favour; his paradise is only just above the regions of the sensual gods, of men, animals, and hell beings; his universe is composed of evil as well as good. There is, however, a deity who reigns over a paradise of bliss, Sukhāvatī, peopled with the elect and the saints, who, miraculously conceived, grow in the hearts of lotuses, nourished by the echo of the divine teaching, and emerge grown to manhood, when the rays of the Buddha have brought the flowers to opening. The lord of this realm is Amitābha or Amitāyus, sovereign of the land of the setting sun, himself a relic of sun worship; to meditate on the sun is the mode of attaining the revelation of the realm of Amitābha. It is interesting once more to find the sun motive entering into Buddhist mythology. But Amitābha has attained his position by special endeavours; long ages ago as the monk Dharmākara he took the vow in the presence of the then reigning Buddha, Lokeçvararāja, to become one day a Buddha, and to rule a realm peopled by saints and without suffering. The results of this vow, matured by ages of charity and meditation, were the appearance of Dharmākara as Amitābha, of his paradise, and of the potency which brings there the elect to birth. The spiritual merit of Amitābha is sufficient, transferred to others, to secure that even the most evil, by merely uttering the name of Amitābha, perhaps but in blasphemy, are reborn in paradise; the gravest punishment inflicted, even on those whose crimes would normally be rewarded by immediate precipitation into hell, is but delay in the opening of the lotus wombs, in which they grow until they have been

[1] BCA. vii. 18.

duly reformed by the sound of the divine instruction. But such extravagance of view, familiar in Brahmanic religion, does not go unreproved; others hold that those who commit great sins are excluded, or demand piety and good works, or at least the appropriation by faith of the original vow of the god.[1]

Unlike a Brahmanical god, Amitābha claims no speciality of origin; there are other Buddhas and future Buddhas who by their merits and their devotion are able to save the faithful; Maitreya is recognized already as a Bodhisattva in the Hīnayāna, but ranks in importance far below Avalokiteçvara,[2] the lord of compassion *par excellence*, whose name is variously interpreted to mean 'he who gazes down upon the world', or 'he on whom men gaze', or 'the lord of the dead'. His vow is not to become a Buddha until he has introduced all men into Nirvāṇa. Prominent also are the Buddha Padmottara, and the Bodhisattva Mañjuçrī, while Buddhism, which denies that a Bodhisattva can be a woman,[3] recognizes the feminine element in the deities styled helpers, Tārās, whose name suggests a stellar origin.[4] Moreover, each Buddha has normally two Bodhisattvas of the first rank as his coadjutors, who visit the earth and hell, solace the dying, conduct souls to paradise, and assume such forms as will most effectively promote the conversion of sinners.

In this way Buddhism has secured for itself the prestige of a true religion, which can offer its devotees all that can be desired by the heart. Yet for the philosophy of Buddhism it remains true that these Buddhas and their heavens have no absolute reality, and the doctrine of the handing over ot merit is not absolutely real. But all that is not absolute reality is recognized by the Vijñānavāda to be an intellectual projection, and nothing hinders the extension of such a projection to the creation even of Amitābha's paradise.

It was inevitable, in view of the strong theological influences

[1] See texts in SBE. xlix; ERE. i. 98 ff.; Grünwedel, *Buddh. Kunst*, pp. 169 ff.; Foucher, *Iconographie bouddhique*; Keith, *Indian Mythology*, ch. vii.

[2] ERE. ii. 256 ff.; *Saddharmapuṇḍarīka*, xxiv.

[3] *Saddharmapuṇḍarīka*, xi. 51. Contrast the Chinese Kuanyin, a feminine Avalokiteçvara. Cf. Mañjuçrī in Nepal; Haraprasād, *Nepalese MSS.*, p. lxvii.

[4] De Blonay, *La déesse bouddhique Tārā*, Paris, 1895; Waddell, JRAS. 1894, pp. 68 ff.; Hirananda, MASI. xi.

operating on Buddhism, that the effort should not be made to create a primordial Buddha, to be the source whence other Buddhas could emanate. In the *Kāraṇḍavyūha* metrical version is found the person of Ādi Buddha, the first lord, self-created, from whose meditation the world comes into being, precisely as in the Brāhmaṇas and Upaniṣads the world proceeds from Brahmā. Avalokiteçvara, the hero of the text, shares in the process; he comes forth from the spirit of the Ādi Buddha, and from his eyes he creates the sun and moon, from his forehead Maheçvara, from his shoulders Brahmā, from his heart Nārāyaṇa, and from his teeth Sarasvatī, goddess of speech. The conception was already prevalent in the fourth century A.D., for it is condemned by Asañga,[1] who points out that it needs accumulation both of knowledge and work to bring a Buddha into being, as well as the existence of another Buddha to inaugurate his career. There is no absolute beginning possible for even a Buddha. It has been conjectured[2] that this doctrine of a primaeval Buddha was held by the Lokottaravādins, since in the *Mahāvastu* the Buddha of remote antiquity, near whom the historical Çākyamuni took the vow to become a Tathāgata, is called also Çākyamuni; but it would be dangerous to lay any stress on this argument. What is certain is that the doctrine, rejected by Asañga, and certainly incompatible with the principles of the schools, is an accepted tenet of the Aiçvarika sect of Nepal, doubtless theists, who have adopted a smattering of Buddhism.[3]

Another allusion in Asañga[4] reveals the existence in Buddhism of Tantric rites, in which the union of the Buddha or Bodhisattva with the personification of wisdom, Prajñāpāramitā, is reproduced on earth as one simple and effective mode of realizing the true identity of the individual with the Buddha; for the doctrine of the absolute lends itself to the Vedāntic identification of the self and the supreme reality, and permits and even encourages the

[1] ix. 77. [2] Kern, *Ind. Buddh.*, p. 66, n. 2.

[3] Cf. the *Svayambhū Purāṇa* (ed. BI. 1894–1900; by Poussin, Gand, 1893); NBL., pp. 249 ff.; Hodgson, *Essays*, pp. 115 ff.; Lévi, *Le Népal*, i. 208 ff.; Poussin, ERE. i. 95 ff.; Waddell, *Lamaism*, pp. 126 ff,; Eliot, *Hinduism and Buddhism*, ii. 117 ff.

[4] MSA. ix. 46.

violation of all morality by denying any real distinction between right and wrong; where all is illusion, woman is the most attractive form of that illusion. It would, however, be unjust to ascribe such doctrines as essential parts of the Mahāyāna, though tradition ascribes to Nāgārjuna the Tantric *Pañcakrama*, to Āryadeva the *Cittaviçuddhiprakaraṇa*, and makes Asaṅga an authority; we need see no more here than the eternal desire to father on ancients new doctrines badly needing some person of repute to vouch for them.[1]

[1] Poussin, *Bouddhisme* (1898), ch. v; *Bouddhisme* (1909), pp. 343 ff.; *Tathāgatayuhyaka*, NBL., pp. 261 ff.

PART IV

BUDDHIST LOGIC

CHAPTER XVIII

THE ORIGIN AND DEVELOPMENT OF BUDDHIST LOGIC

1. *Logic in the Hīnayāna*

Of logical theory the earlier Canon has not a trace; the Buddha is a reasoner whose interlocutors are not his match; his weapons against them, beside his authority, are analogy, simile, parable, and an occasional trace of induction by simple enumeration of cases; definition and division are prominent by their absence. We hear of men skilled in logic or sophistry and reasoning, but there is nothing to show that they had a science of any sort. Exception must, however, be made for Sañjaya of the Belaṭṭha clan; he seems as an agnostic to have been the first to formulate the four possibilities of existence, non-existence, both, and neither, and Buddha in the indeterminates makes lavish use of this device. But of conscious consideration of this principle we have nothing, nor was anything to be expected from a teacher whose aim was to steer a middle path between affirmation and negation, and was therefore by no means likely to develop a logic of non-contradiction.

The later texts were doubtless contemporaneous with the beginnings of logical study; the *Milindapañha* may allude to logicians, though the reference is but vague; it records the traditional mode of discussion, distinction and counter-distinction being drawn and errors unravelled, but in method it differs not at all from the Canon.[1] A difference appears in the late *Abhidhamma Piṭaka*. In the *Kathāvatthu* we find the technical terms, Upanaya, for minor premiss in an argument, Niggamana for the conclusion

[1] Keith, ILA., pp. 13 f.; Mil., pp. 28 ff.

Pariññā for the proposition, and we may suppose a contemporary logic, but nothing of it is said.[1] The method, followed however, is interesting; it runs: *Q.* Is A B? *A.* Yes. *Q.* Is C D? *A.* No. *Q.* But if A be B, then C is D. That B can be affirmed of A, but not D of C, is false. Hence your first answer is refuted. In the inverse (*paṭiloma*) method we have: If D be denied of C, then B should have been denied of A. (But you affirmed B of A.) Therefore that B can be affirmed of A but not D of C is wrong. There are further developments, but of the same type; the logical clearness is not at all adequate.[2] In the *Yamaka* again the distribution of terms is known and the process of conversion is elaborately illustrated, but without trace of appreciation of logical theory. The *Paṭisambhidāmagga*[3] deals with analytical insight into words and things, grammatical analysis, and insight into those processes, but it is quite valueless as logical theory. But, what is far more important, the Abhidhamma has not, despite the intention of the work to contain definitions of conceptions, any theory or effective practice of definition. The *Nettipakaraṇa* shows some advance in this regard, but it is only in Buddhaghosa that we find the fourfold style of definition as essential mark, property, resulting phenomenon, and proximate antecedent.[4] Thus mind is defined as following the sense impression, as having the essential mark of cognizing sights, sounds, &c., as the property of receiving the same, the resulting phenomenon of truth, and as its proximate antecedent the vanishing of the sense impression. Buddhaghosa shows also some understanding of the principles of identity, contradiction, and excluded middle.

In northern India Buddhism must have grown up amid an eager logical activity, but we have scanty available records; the forms of reasoning employed by Maitreya, Asañga, and Vasubandhu are recorded on Chinese authority, but it would be premature to draw any definite conclusion from them as to their logical

[1] *Points of Controversy*, pp. xlviii f., 377 f.; *Vibhañga*, pp. 293 ff.
[2] e. g. KV. i. 6. 55, 'past is existent' is converted to 'all existent is past'.
[3] cf. Geiger, PD., p. 62.
[4] That Buddhist logic knew in Asoka's time the terms and forms of syllogism (Dasgupta, *Ind. Phil.* i. 157) is a misreading of Aung's statement in *Points of Controversy*, p. l. On definition cf. *Compendium*, pp. 2, 7.

competence. With Maitreya, at any rate, argument does not seem to have advanced beyond the simple procedure from example, e.g. sound is non-eternal, because it is a product, like a pot, but not like ether.[1]

2. *Dignāga*

The date of the great Buddhist logician Dignāga is still uncertain, though there are grounds on which he may be assigned to not later than A.D. 400, and in any event a much later date is out of the question. His services to logic are difficult to estimate precisely, because a vital question is involved of his relative priority or posteriority to the Vaiçeṣika authority, Praçastapāda, in whom appear very important changes in the logical doctrines hitherto professed in the Nyāya and Vaiçeṣika schools. Reasons for the probable priority of Dignāga have been advanced elsewhere;[2] the suggestion that these innovations of Praçastapāda are in fact to be found in Kaṇāda is clearly erroneous;[3] the logic of Kaṇāda is unquestionably primitive, and would have been very different had it been inspired by the much more mature ideas which appear quite openly in Praçastapāda. There remains, however, the possibility of derivation of both advances in Buddhism and in the Nyāya-Vaiçeṣika from a school not yet known to us.

As a philosopher Dignāga appears a champion of Vijñānavāda idealism, but his work on logic is interesting, because it is inspired by other than epistemological and metaphysical considerations; from his logical works, so far as known from Dharmakīrti, it would be impossible to learn precisely his conception of reality.[4] But we know that in perception he distinguished sharply between the element of sensation and imagination; each idea requires both sensation and the activity of the imagination to give any result;

[1] ILA., p. 108. The name is usually a pious fraud for Asañga; Lévi, MSA. ii. 7 f.

[2] ILA., pp. 93 ff.; Ui, VP., p. 17, n. 3. He is said to have been a pupil of Vasubandhu.

[3] Dasgupta, *Ind. Phil.* i. 351. That Kaṇāda is pre-Buddhistic (i. 280) is quite impossible.

[4] His Vijñānavāda position appears clearly in his *Ālambanaparīkṣā* (preserved in Tibetan); Poussin, JRAS. 1903, ii. 383, n. 2. On logic we have in Tibetan his *Pramāṇasamuccaya*; *Hetucakrahamaru*; *Trikālaparīkṣā*; and his or Çañkarasvāmin's *Nyāyapraveça* (Ui, VP., p. 68, n. 2); see MSIL., pp. 82 ff.

the mere percept is inexpressible and a momentary experience, which imagination presents as a series of moments (*kṣaṇa-saṁtāna*), and therefore capable of expression. This view is already attacked by Praçastapāda, without naming its author, whose identity with Dignāga is affirmed by Vācaspati Miçra.

Still more important was Dignāga's doctrine of inference; it seems to have rested on the assurance that knowledge did not express real relations of external character; the relation of ground and conclusion (*anumānānumeya-bhāva*) rests upon the relation of inherence and essence, quality and subject (*dharmadharmi-bhāva*), which is imposed by thought (*buddhyārūḍha*). The doctrine harmonizes entirely with his doctrine of perception, for the product there is a creation of imagination (*kalpanā, utprekṣā*), and all that is left undecided is the nature of the contact in simple perception with some reality; nothing hinders[1] to accept this reality as merely a mental creation, a projection of the basic consciousness (*ālaya-vijñāna*), but for logic the point is unimportant. The power of the mind to impose laws on phenomena affords us the possibility of those general prepositions (*vyāpti*) on which all reasoning rests, and enables Dignāga to develop a true syllogism: Sound is non-eternal, because it is produced; all the produced are non-eternals, like a pot; no non-produced are non-eternals, like ether. The examples serve to illustrate, but the general law is one of the intellect.

Dignāga also defined the essential conditions of the middle term or cause (*hetu*); it must be present in the subject or minor term, e.g. smoke on the mountain; it must be comprehended in the major or predicate, e.g. where there is smoke, there must always be fire; the middle must not exist in things heterogeneous to the major term, e.g. smoke is entirely absent where there is no fire. The doctrine, like that of universal connexion, is criticized by Nyāya writers of the orthodox school, like Uddyotakara. On

[1] Cf. BSB. I. iv; AKV. (Paris MS., f. 267ª) in Poussin, JRAS. 1910, p. 136, n. The something (*vastu-mātra*) at the basis is the Vijñāna or Ālayavijñāna; JRAS. 1906, p. 953. All determinations as substance, attribute, action, universality, and particularity (Vaiçeṣika categories) are in a sense false as conceptual and mediate (*savikalpaka*); *Hetuvidyānyāyadvāraçāstra* in Ui, VP., p. 67.

defects in this relation are based the fallacies of the middle, and Dignāga recognizes also fallacies of the thesis and the example, which the later logicians reject, but which influenced Praçastapāda. The logical advance in rejecting these fallacies is obvious.

To Dignāga further belongs the credit of establishing the distinction between the actual process of reasoning for the ascertainment of truth and the reasoning for another, which takes the form of communication by the syllogism of three members.[1] He based this distinction on the rejection of the authority of the teacher's utterance as such (*çabda*).[2] If we are asked to accept authority, we ask: Is the person who uttered the saying credible, or is the fact itself credible? If the former, then our belief in his sayings is inference from his credibility; if the fact is credible then it is a case of perception. The only value, therefore, to be assigned to syllogism is indirect; the word has value, therefore, only as a conclusion or consequence of the fact; real fact gives a true conclusion. Thus the sources of knowledge are reduced to two, perception and inference. Comparison, a separate source of knowledge in the Nyāya theory, he also rejected; when we recognize a thing by similarity to something else, the operation is essentially perception.

We must, however, remember that, despite the elaboration of logical doctrine and the stress laid on attaining correct results, we are not to suppose that we are actually in touch with reality; the one point of contact with something not certainly and immediately mental is inexpressible;[3] what we deal with, as far as we can express ourselves, is mental concepts, which present a regular system of discourse, but whose relation to reality lies outside the province of Dignāga's logic.[4]

[1] Cf. Ui, VP., p. 82, n. 2; Keith, ILA., pp. 85 ff., 122 ff.

[2] NV., p. 260; NVT., p. 286. On the Āpta, cf. NB., p. 117; BC. ix. 66; MKV., p 268; see AKV. (MS. Burn., f. 470ᵃ), JA. 1902, ii. 264, n. 2. Dignāga accepts, of course, Buddha's authority; see Kumārila's refutation, *Tantravārttika*, pp. 169 ff.; JRAS. 1902, pp. 369 ff.

[3] This is regular Vijñānavāda doctrine; BSB. I. iv; the ultimate and only real is void thought.

[4] It is possible that Maitreyanātha, author of the *Abhisamayālaṁkāra*, preceded Dignāga in rejecting comparison (*Upamāna*), as certainly did Asaṅga; Nāgārjuna mentions all four, as equally invalid; cf. MKV., p. 75; Ui, VP., p. 86 (*Vigrahavyāvartanī*).

3. *Dharmakīrti's Doctrine of Perception and Knowledge.*

The misfortune which has reduced us to mere translations of Dignāga's works has been escaped by Dharmakīrti,[1] who falls in the seventh century A.D., and whose *Nyāyabindu* with the commentary of Dharmottara (ninth century A.D.) still remains the premier source for our knowledge of the details of Buddhist logical development. In this case again there is some doubt as to the philosophical tenets which lay at the base of the author's contentions, for, while he appears in another text as a definite adherent of the Vijñānavada, it is held by the author of the *Nyāyabinduṭīkāṭippaṇī*,[2] a commentary on Dharmottara's commentary, that the *Nyāyabindu* is written from the Sautrāntika point of view—that is, recognizing the reality of an external world, known to us by inference only from the content of our experience. The point is hardly soluble with our evidence; the similarity of the views of Dignāga and Dharmakīrti, as we have them, is very close, and, assuming that Dignāga wrote as an idealist,[3] the issue resolves itself into the question whether Dharmakīrti has so modified the view of Dignāga as to allow of reference to an external reality which Dignāga would have declined to accept. But it is obvious that it would be extremely difficult to decide this point without express intimation of the author's definite views; it is not enough to make a man a realist in metaphysics, because in a logical treatise he speaks of an element as fact (*artha*), external (*bāhya*), or having a distinct character (*svalakṣaṇa*). His metaphysical views, he is entitled to ask, shall be gathered from treatises in which he has set them out, not inferred from logical doctrines which do not formally discuss the metaphysical nature of the given element in presentation. As regards, however, the question of knowledge, there is no point in urging the question; it is perfectly clear that

[1] ILA., pp. 28, 48, 71, 84, 97, 101 ff., 127, 136 ff. Cf. TRD., pp. 32 ff.; NK., pp. 189 ff.; NM., pp. 93 ff.

[2] ed. Petrograd, 1909. It cites views of Vinītadeva and Çāntabhadra (seventh century A.D.). Cf. MSIL., pp. 119 f.

[3] The solution of the difficulty, pointed out by Poussin (JA. 1903, ii. 308, n. 2), is probably the fact that, as Wassilieff (*Bouddhisme*, p. 290) states, Dignāga accepted the reality of sense knowledge, i. e. of the *paratantra*, and did not treat it as illusory.

the Sautrāntikas accepted the existence of ideas only as known to us, whence we infer an external reality; if, then, we accept the suggestion that Dharmakīrti was an adherent of that school in the ordinary sense of the term, we cannot suppose that he held the doctrine that ideas copy reality. In fact, whether Dharmakīrti was a Sautrāntika or a Vijñānavādin, his position might be expressed in the same terms; equally in either case all knowledge is of ideas; logical analysis must accept this fact; whether the source of the sensation is external or results from the action of consciousness, the sensation as such is unknowable and momentary. This is the essence of the doctrine of Dharmakīrti; the sensation (*kṣaṇa*) cannot be grasped (*kṣaṇasya jñānena prāpayitum açakyatvāt*);[1] it becomes an object of knowledge only in so far as imagination gives it the necessary characteristics for knowledge. This is done by the action of the intellect in clothing the momentary impression with the result of past and the presage of future experience; it is the intellect which concerts the sensation into a knowable object, a moment series. Take away the work of the imagination (*niçcaya*,[2] *kalpanā*, *adhyavasāya*), and you have nothing knowable left; you have merely the bare fact of sensation. The parallelism with the Kantian conception of the synthesis of apprehension is quite clear, however less effectively brought out. There is, however, the vital difference that in the view of Dharmakīrti, as of Dignāga, the addition of the intellectual element deprives perception of the truth of sensation (*abhrānta*); that is, he fails to realize the inconsistency of introducing the idea of error; truth being obviously an ideal conception, it is absurd to attribute error to it because it is not something different from itself. The expression of the idea of mere sensation by Dharmakīrti is doubtless faulty,[3] but it is not necessary to deny him credit for following Dignāga in recognizing it. The particular sensation is unique, and it is developed by the imagination (*vikalpa*)[4] into the knowledge of the object; when we are told that the sensation of blue is thus transformed into the perception 'This is blue', we must understand the doctrine in the light of

[1] NBT., p. 16. [2] NBT., p. 30; TRD., pp. 33, 41.
[3] NBT., p. 16; NB., p. 103. [4] NBT., pp. 4, 14.

common sense.[1] It is clear that the sensation as such cannot be described as blue; it is an immediate feltness, which results in our perception that the object is blue, and the sensation therefore can properly be called one of blue *ex posteriori.* It is not really because we have an awareness of blue that we speak of having perceived a blue object; it is because we have a perception of blue that we describe our ineffable sensation as an awareness of blue. This is seen by the avoidance of the term cause and result for the relation and the preference for determinant and determined (*vyavasthāpana, vyavasthāpya*).[2] The momentary sensation is absolutely real (*paramārthasat*),[3] and is grasped in sensation alone; inference cannot reach the moment; it deals only with generalities (*sāmānya-lakṣaṇa*).

The idea of the process of knowledge in perception thus suggested is that of an object as endowed by the activity of the imagination with a definite ideal character, which is represented to us in the idea of the object; there is therefore sameness between the object and our idea, and we have not the absurdity of an idea copying something non-ideal. It is the experience or realization of the sameness which results in the assertion 'This is blue'. The ground of this state, if inquired into, can be answered on the Vijñānavāda basis, as Dharmakīrti does in his *Pramāṇa-viniçcaya* preserved in Tibetan; consciousness develops itself into the ultimately unreal complex of the object, subject, and consciousness of the object by the subject.[4] In this may lie the apparent outwardness of the presentation.

The idea of truth or correctness in relation to knowledge is clearly not possible of statement as accordance with the object, which is known only in idea, and with this accords admirably the fact that the criterion adopted is not correspondence, but one applicable to both perception and inference,[5] namely, verification

[1] Cf. Stcherbatskoi in Dasgupta, *Ind. Phil.* i. 409, n. 1. For a Sāṁkhya critique of the Buddhist doctrine of perception, see Aniruddha on SS. i. 89; for a Madhyamaka critique, see MKV., pp. 73 ff., where it is shown that it is illegitimate and too narrow.

[2] NBT., pp. 19 f.

[3] NBT., p. 17; NB., p. 103.

[4] See cit. in SDS., p. 13; Poussin, JRAS. 1910, p. 132.

[5] Cf. TRD., pp. 33, 41; NB., p. 103; NBT., pp. 6 ff.; NBTT. pp. 16 ff.

by experience on acting upon the knowledge. If we have a perception, or arrive at some proposition by inference, then we put it to the test of fact, and, if that agrees with our perception or inference, we have assurance that our knowledge is right. We have the presentation or idea; we are prompted to act upon it; we realize the object in accordance with our endeavour based on the presentation or percept. Only in this way can we be assured of the correctness of our knowledge; otherwise we have knowledge which may be true or false. That we have illusory percepts, e.g. when through derangement we see as yellow the white conch shell or have dreams, we know by experience; if we act on the faith of the presentations we do not attain what we should. True, we cannot possibly realize the precise object which gave the presentation, since all is momentary; but the imagination supplies the belief in the absence of difference between the aspect of the series which is gone and that which is realized in the present.[1] Of course we must not think that right knowledge is the direct cause of our realization of anything, for that is effected through the desire, which itself is a product arising from memory of past experiences evoked by the presentation. The pragmatic nature of truth is thus strongly asserted, but it must be remembered that we are merely dealing with empirical matters, not with ultimate reality.

4. *Dharmakīrti's Theory of Inference*

Inferential knowledge is essentially of generality; it cannot reach to the immediateness of presentation; the mountain inferred as fiery is not the presentation of the fire on the mountain at a definite point of time. Its validity must be verified, if desired, by the usual process of action; we must, for instance, go to the mountain and see the fire, which we have inferred from the smoke cloud. An advance is made on Dignāga in the process of examination of the conditions of a correct middle term; the middle must be present in those things only in which the thing to be inferred exists, and absent in all those things in which it is not found; the rule must be observed fully in either case, or the

[1] NBTT., p. 11: *abhedādhyavasāyāt*, NBT., p. 5; cf. TRD., p. 40.

inference will be doubtful. Cases where there is the necessary invariable connexion are limited to three only, in Dharmakīrti's view, namely, identity of nature or essence (*tādātmya*), effect of a cause, and non-perception or non-existence. It has been ingeniously, but quite legitimately, pointed out[1] that this gives a classification of judgement on the basis of positive and negative, with the division of the affirmative judgements into analytical, relation of identity, or causal, relation of effect to cause. Reasoning, therefore, which is defined as knowledge of the inferable derived through the middle term, is of three main types: 'This is a tree, because it is a pine,' relation of identity, the species allowing the inference of the genus; 'Here there is fire, because there is smoke,' the cause fire is inferred from the effect smoke; and 'Here is no smoke, because it is not perceived,' as smoke would, if existent, be perceived. This third variety, based on non-perception or non-existence, is divided into eleven classes, of a somewhat needlessly varied character. The ground of the inference, it will be observed, is thus always a general proposition, which rests on mental activity, and falls under one of three categories.[2]

Inference for the sake of another, or syllogism, is defined as the verbal declaration of the middle term—that is, when the reason is set out in words in order to produce a conviction in others.[3] Inference is properly a form of knowledge, and words are, therefore, only inference in a secondary sense, namely, as producing knowledge, the name of the cause being derived from the effect. Such a form of inference is two-fold, either direct or homogeneous (*sādharmyavat*) or indirect or heterogeneous (*vaidharmyavat*): either 'Sound is non-eternal, because it is a product; all products are non-eternal, like a pot', or 'Sound is non-eternal, because it is a product; no non-eternal thing is a product, like ether'. This, however, is a needlessly full form of the syllogism; Dharmakīrti is content with the simple form 'The hill is fiery, because it is

[1] Stcherbatskoi, *Muséon*, v (1904), p. 144, n. 6.
[2] NBV., p. 31; NB., pp. 104 ff.; TRD., pp. 41 ff, where four classes of non-perception are enumerated: perception of the contrary, of contrary effect; non-perception of cause, of identity.
[3] NB., pp. 108 ff.; NBT., pp. 46 ff.

smoky', the express formulation of the general proposition being unnecessary, since it is contained in the reason 'because it is smoky'. The omission of the example he defends[1] against Dignāga by insisting that the term 'smoke' includes the case cited in the example and also the negative example; but he concedes that it has the value of giving particularity to what is pointed out in a general way by the middle term; the complete enunciation of the reasoning with the concrete example is more effective.

Fallacies[2] are classed by Dharmakīrti according to the old division of fallacies of the thesis, i.e. the minor term combined with the major, e.g. the fiery hill, as insisted upon by Dignāga; of the middle; and of the example, divided according to the homogeneous and the heterogeneous example. His classification of fallacies of the middle, the only important class, is on the basis that a fallacy arises if a characteristic of the middle is unproved (*asiddha*), e.g. 'Sound is eternal, because it is visible,' visibility being admitted by neither party to the supposed argument; uncertain (*anaikāntika*), e.g. 'Sound is non-eternal, because it is knowable,' where 'knowable' is too wide since it covers both eternal and non-eternal things; and as contradictory (*viruddha*), e.g. 'Sound is eternal, because it is a product,' the middle contradicting the major. He differs from Dignāga in rejecting two of the forms of fallacy allowed by the former, the first[3] being reduced very sensibly to a mere form of contradiction, while the latter[4] is laid aside on the interesting ground that it does not rise from true reasoning but is based on the scriptures of the two disputants, and scripture alone is no authority for Dharmakīrti.

5. *Controversies with the Nyaya*

Dharmakīrti's three-fold basis of inference, and the insistence, which accompanies it, that inference could not rest on any mere observation either of positive or negative instances, being in essence an ideal construction, caused naturally much concern to

[1] NB., pp. 115 f.; MSIL., p. 114, n. 2. [2] NB., pp. 111 ff.; NBT., pp. 65 ff.
[3] NB., p. 113; NBT., p. 78; Pathak, JBRAS. xix. 51.
[4] NB. p. 115; NBT., p. 84; JBRAS. xix. 49.

the Nyāya-Vaiçeṣika school, which was not prepared to accept this rejection of experience. The criticisms of Vācaspati Miçra[1] are of interest. He argues that in the case of identity of essence there is no true inference at all, inference being inconsistent with identity. The case of cause and effect is equally unsound; it is assumed that the cause immediately precedes the effect, e. g. fire precedes smoke, but there is no way of showing that in each case the smoke is not really caused by fire, but by some invisible power. Moreover, even if the argument of the Buddhists were accepted, then all we could infer is not the present, but the antecedent existence of fire. But still more serious is the fact that the Buddhist rule excludes perfectly genuine cases of effective inference: the sunrise of one day may be inferred from that of preceding days. The mode of obtaining a universal is observation of positive and negative instances, and searching for vitiating conditions (*upādhi*) which prevent a true universal being established, e. g. where there is smoke, there is always fire, but, where fire, there smoke, only if green wood be burned. If on observation no such condition appears, an inference is valid. We learn that the Buddhists had devised an ingenious five-condition (*pañcakāraṇī*)[2] method in order to determine causal connexion, viz. the perception neither of cause nor of effect; the perception of the cause; the perception of the effect in immediate succession; the disappearance of the cause; and the disappearance in immediate succession of the effect. But it was argued that this method also did not succeed in establishing effectively the relation of cause and effect, and that therefore it was better to rely on the simple fact of invariable relation without limiting it to the causal category.

In his commentary on the *Bṛhadāraṇyakabhāṣya* Sureçvarācārya,[3] the pupil of Çaṅkarācārya, also attacks Dharmakīrti. He admits that the positive and negative examples in the syllogism are not probative, but holds them useful to remove doubts, when knowledge is obtained. But the three principles of Dharmakīrti are

[1] NVT., pp. 105 ff.; cf. NM., pp. 113 ff.

[2] SDS., p. 6; see Seal, *Positive Sciences of the Ancient Hindus*, pp. 258 ff.; NK., p. 206.

[3] See Pathak, JBRAS. xviii. 91 ff.; xix. 54 ff.; Ānandāçrama ed., pp. 1515 ff. For the Vaiçeṣika criticism see Çrīdhara, NK., pp. 207 ff.

idle lumber. If we assume that fire is inferred from heat, that being its special nature, on the basis of identity, we see that heat may also give rise to the inference of fire, as the effect of fire as cause, so that we have two different principles operating equally effectively, which is absurd. Again, heat is not merely the special nature of fire, but is found also elsewhere, e. g. in the sun, so that we could infer the sun equally with fire. Similarly, from touch we could infer not merely earth, but also water, fire, and wind. If, however, it be contended that we Buddhists do not accept anything as the peculiar nature of anything else, if it is found in more than one thing, the answer is that you do assert the possibility of arguing from the Çiñçapā being a tree, although the nature of a tree is shared by others, e. g. the Dhāva. Moreover, if you assert a Çiñçapā is a tree because of invariable concomitance of characteristics, you contradict your doctrine of momentariness as the peculiar nature of things. Again, what is common to many things, like momentariness, cannot be the peculiar nature of any one. Smoke is seen coming not only from fire but also from smoke, so that fire cannot be made its sole cause. Just so, also, touch has more sources than one, and it is impossible to conclude, because it is found in the wind, that it is not also the specific nature of earth, for that is asserted effectively by popular knowledge. Further, if one thinks to establish by invariable concomitance the peculiar nature or cause of anything, it will be found that invariable connexion does not follow from peculiar nature alone—that is, that there may be invariability, e. g. of the sequence of constellations when there can be no idea of peculiar nature, or of cause.

In the *Sarvadarçanasaṅgraha* [1] we find the Buddhist reply to the Nyāya critique. To the Nyāya reliance on the observation of concurrence positive and negative, it is objected that it is impossible to feel assurance that there will not emerge some discrepancy in the past or future. The rather obvious retort that the Buddhist position itself is no more secure is countered by the argument that doubt is only permissible when it does not land us in practical absurdities; in this case the idea that an effect could exist

[1] p. 6.

without a cause would land us in hopeless difficulties by paralysing action. The argument establishes the validity of inference from effect to cause, and inference from identity is established by the fact that to deny it is absurd; if the Çiñçapā should cease to be a tree, it would lose its own nature. Moreover, such an inference is real; it is impossible where there is absolute sameness, or absolute divergence, but applies in every case of species and genus.

As against the contention of the materialist Cārvākas the Buddhists defend the validity of inference. If inference is denied as a valid means of proof, the contention runs, it must be by some form of argument, since a mere assertion is utterly worthless as proof. But, if argument is used, analysis shows that the opponent in effect admits unconsciously the three forms of inference used by the Buddhists. By arguing on the basis of validity of perception as a means of proof against the apparent means of proof which is inference, he really argues on the basis of the community of nature between the two, which is the Buddhist form of inference from identity of nature. By being conscious of the dissent of his adversaries he shows that he recognizes inference from cause, since he knows the dissent expressed in words. By denying the existence of any object on the ground of it not being perceived, he admits the form of inference from non-perception.

A further refinement of logical doctrine is contained in the *Antarvyāptisamarthana* of Ratnākara Çānti in the tenth century.[1] It is necessitated by considerations affecting the proof of the momentariness of things. Normally an inference gives us in the example the concomitance of the middle and the major in some object; for instance, fire on the mountain is proved from the presence of smoke there with the aid of the example of the kitchen where smoke and fire co-exist. But this is impossible in the case of momentariness *ex vi termini*. Moreover, the conclusion in the normal case takes the form of the presence of the invariable relation in some subject, e. g. the relation of

[1] See *Six Buddhist Nyāya Tracts in Sanskrit* (BI. 1910), pp. 103 ff., v. ff.; MSIL., pp. 140 f.

smoke and fire in the mountain, and the inference to establish momentariness cannot be given such a form. The new doctrine insists that it is possible to prove the relation within (*antar*), that is simply between the thing to be proved and the thing by which it is to be proved, without the intervention of something external (*bahis*) in which the relation is to exist.

Somewhat earlier, perhaps, is a tract on *Apohasiddhi* by Ratnakīrti, which deals with the significance of words, and promulgates the Buddhist doctrine that the word has both a positive signification and a negative, in that it differentiates the thing referred to from others; these two sides of its activity are simultaneous and not successive; the tract is interesting because it refutes in succession the views of Kumārila, Trilocana, Nyāyabhūṣaṇa, Vācaspati Miçra, and Dharmottara.[1]

An interesting link between Buddhism and the Nyāya and Vaiçeṣika schools is provided in the conception of the perception of Yogins, which forms in Dharmakīrti[2] the fourth of the forms of perception, the other three being sense perception in the narrow sense, mental perception which really forms one with sense perception, and self-consciousness which is regarded as essentially accompanying every psychical occurrence, an idea which Dharmottara illustrates, but not very lucidly, seeming, in part at least, to confound self-consciousness with the presence of feeling as emotion simultaneously with perception, e. g. of colour. There was an obvious difficulty for Buddhism with its doctrine of momentariness in allowing for self-consciousness, which none of the schools effectively faced; the later Nyāya doctrine frankly made the element of self-consciousness a secondary product supervening on consciousness. Self-consciousness is perception, since it reveals the self (*ātmanaḥ sākātkṣāri*), is devoid of imagination (*nirvikalpaka*), and free from error (*abhrānta*). The perception of Yogins is also without error, for it deals with matters such as the four noble truths which ar

[1] *Ibid.*, pp. 1 ff., iii. Cf. Stcherbatskoi, *Muséon*, v (1904), pp. 165 ff.; ILA., p. 106; MSIL., p. 140; NM., pp. 303 ff.

[2] NB., p. 103; NBT., pp. 14 f.; *Nyāyasāra*, pp. 3 f., 82 ff.; TRD., pp. 39 f. (using NBT.); NM., pp. 103 ff.; Gañgeça, *Tattvacintāmaṇi*, i. 795; ILA., pp. 73, 76, 258 f.

over and above the ordinary means of proof; it is without imagination, consisting of clear insight, which supervenes on intense concentration on the matters. This is interesting as a rationalized statement of the intuition (*paññā*) of the Pali Canon. It has a parallel in the perception of seers (*ārṣa*) which figures in the Vaiçeṣika,[1] and in the doctrine of the *Nyāyasāra* of Bhāsarvajña, which recognizes an indeterminate (*nirvikalpaka*) intuition on the part of Yogins engaged in meditation (*samādhi*).

Uddyotakara[2] discusses in an interesting way the doctrine apparently ascribed to Vasubandhu, which defines perception as cognition proceeding from just that object (*tato 'rthāt*), the terms after cognition being asserted to be without meaning. They cannot serve to discriminate perception from inference, on the score that perception is derived from the object only, while inference involves other factors, for the definition is perfectly compatible with inference. Nor can it serve to distinguish perception of colour, &c., from perception of an object as such, e.g. a jar, for the perception of colour and of a jar are two perfectly distinct perceptions, and it is quite erroneous to assume that there is no such thing as a jar, but merely perception of colour, &c. Nor is it of any avail to exclude wrong cognition, for it is not the case, as assumed by the Buddhists, that false perception arises from something which is not the object, e.g. that the incorrect apprehension of silver in a shell is produced by something which is not-shell. Further, the Buddhists' view is open to the fatal objection that it makes the object the cause of cognition; now a cause must precede the effect; the object perceived thus exists before the perception, and, as momentary, has ceased to be before it is perceived, and this is plainly absurd, since perception is only of what is immediately present. It is hopeless to argue that the disappearance of the object and the emergence of perception are simultaneous, in the face of the impossibility of establishing any such effect; moreover, in any case, the object is admitted to have disappeared, and therefore to

[1] *Vaiçeṣika Sūtra*, ix. 1. 13; *Praçastapādabhāṣya*, p. 187; NK., pp. 189 ff.; ILA., pp. 81 ff.

[2] NV., pp. 42 ff.; NVT., p. 100; MKV., p. 71.

be past at the very moment when it is being perceived as present, which is fatal to the Buddhist view.

The question of falsity touched on here is further confuted by the Nyāya[1] in connexion with the doctrines of Asatkhyāti and Ātmakhyāti, under which they discuss the explanations of incorrect cognition offered by the Madhyamaka and the Yogācāra schools respectively. The former view holds that wrong cognition is a manifestation or making known of something which is unreal, non-existence (*asat*); to see silver in a shell is to assert the existence of something unreal. The obvious objection to this view is that it asserts that a non-existing thing can produce an effect, but this is met by the Madhyamaka contention that it is not necessary that the non-existing thing should have any such potency; it is enough to assume that cognition has the power of presenting the thing apprehended as existent or non-existent. The Nyāya answer insists instead that the false cognition proceeds from a real object which is misapprehended, understood otherwise than is correct (*anyathā-khyāti*).

In the case of the Vijñānavāda, incorrect cognition is explained by the fact that what is merely idea is referred erroneously to the external world, ignoring the fact that there is no real difference between the self, the object of knowledge, and knowledge. The Nyāya criticism[2] is that, if the premisses of the Buddhist were correct, the cognition which arises would take the form not of 'this is silver' but 'I am silver', and this is obviously not the case. Moreover, the view is open to all the objections always available against the doctrine of the non-existence of external reality. Finally, even on its own merits the doctrine is not preferable to the Nyāya doctrine of Anyathākhyāti, since in fact, even on the Buddhist view, error lies in cognizing a thing as something which it is not, and this is precisely the Nyāya doctrine.

[1] NVT., pp. 53 f.; *Vivaraṇaprameyasaṁgraha*, trs., pp. 85 ff.; cf. *Bhāmatī*, pp. 12 ff.; NM., pp. 545 f.

[2] So Aniruddha, SS. i. 42.

ENGLISH INDEX

SANSKRIT INDEX